INTENSIVE READING

题源报刊精品阅读 30篇（精读）

主编 朱伟

北京理工大学出版社
BEIJING INSTITUTE OF TECHNOLOGY PRESS

版权专有　侵权必究

图书在版编目(CIP)数据

题源报刊精品阅读 30 篇：精读 / 朱伟主编. — 北京：北京理工大学出版社，2019.8
ISBN 978 - 7 - 5682 - 7373 - 2

Ⅰ. ①题… Ⅱ. ①朱… Ⅲ. ①英语 - 阅读教学 - 研究生 - 入学考试 - 自学参考资料 Ⅳ. ①H319.37

中国版本图书馆 CIP 数据核字 (2019) 第 169017 号

出版发行 / 北京理工大学出版社有限责任公司
社　　址 / 北京市海淀区中关村南大街 5 号
邮　　编 / 100081
电　　话 / (010)68914775(总编室)
　　　　　(010)82562903(教材售后服务热线)
　　　　　(010)68948351(其他图书服务热线)
网　　址 / http://www.bitpress.com.cn
经　　销 / 全国各地新华书店
印　　刷 / 三河市鑫鑫科达彩色印刷包装有限公司
开　　本 / 787 毫米 × 1092 毫米　1/16
印　　张 / 20.75
字　　数 / 518 千字
版　　次 / 2019 年 8 月第 1 版　2019 年 8 月第 1 次印刷
定　　价 / 52.80 元

责任编辑 / 武丽娟
文案编辑 / 武丽娟
责任校对 / 刘亚男
责任印制 / 李志强

图书出现印装质量问题，请拨打售后服务热线，本社负责调换

主编的话
CHIEF COMPILER'S WORDS

无论参加何种英文考试,在基本功夯实阶段,大家只需做两件事:背单词和大量阅读相关真题题源文章。这是我从录制"恋练有词"课程开始就坚持的理念。很多考生会迫不及待地去做真题,但是我要告诉大家,请不要受他人复习节奏的影响,做真题无须过早开始。你要相信,学习英语和学习武术是一个道理,师父总是先让你老老实实扎一年马步,然后才教你各种招数。所以,各位同学,一开始就做真题的效果并不会太理想,必须先从结合文章记忆单词开始。

那么单词应该怎么记呢?比如参加研究生英语考试的同学在看到单词 value 时会觉得过于简单,甚至会认为,一本考研英语词汇书里出现这么简单的词是在骗钱。但是,考试还会考查它的形近词,例如,devalue 表示"低估", overvalue 表示"高估",这些你都知道吗?考研英语主要考查这两个词的前缀 de- 和 over-。其次,知道一个词的含义还不够,与其有关的短语也需要了解和掌握,如 place a high value on sth. 表示什么意思呢?一旦考试中出现对 value 动词含义的考查,很多同学会不知其意。例如,Yet, being friendly is a virtue that many Americans value highly and expect from both neighbors and strangers. 这句话中的 value 和 expect 是两个并列的动词,很多考生根本没有接触过 value sth. highly 这样的用法,更不用说把它活学活用到写作中去了。可见,只记忆单词 value 的名词含义是无法获得语感的。与学习其他语言一样,学习英语也是有规律可循的。英语并不难学,考生不要心存畏惧,只要遵循正确的学习方法,慢慢就能培养出语感,找到适合自己的学习方法和途径。

大量阅读题源文章和背单词同样重要,首先给大家推荐一个免费的英文泛读素材库,即FT中文网,这是英国《金融时报》的中文版网站。网站内的很多文章可以进行中英文双语切换,是比较稀缺的优质资源。伟哥对大家的要求是:每天坚持阅读里面的一到两篇文章,至于读什么无所谓,可以根据你个人的喜好进行选择。当然,有些同学会质疑:"我参加的考试很少考到FT的文章啊。"对于这一问题,我的回答是:少一些功利主义的追求,多一些不为什么的坚持(Less interests, more interest),这样你会有意想不到的收获。是的,FT确实不是考研英语真题的主要来源,因为根据统计分析,考研英语真题阅读部分的文章主要会从《经济学人》《卫报》《美国新闻和世界报道》《时代》《新闻周刊》《大西洋月刊》《新科学家》《科学》《哈佛商业评论》等出版物中选取，但遗憾的是，这些报纸杂志在国内很少有官方实时更新的中英文双语素材库。

为了增强国内同学对英语文章的整体泛读和精读能力，我们从近10年来最为流行的13种考研英语阅读题源中选取了近1 000篇文章，并从中精选出100篇符合考研学生阅读水平和要求的优质文章，组织编写了《题源报刊精品阅读100篇（泛读）》；精选出30篇符合考研英语阅读理解命题规律和大纲要求的优质文章，组织编写了《题源报刊精品阅读30篇（精读）》。这两本书所收录的100余篇文章，涵盖环境、生物、经济、文学、医学、语言、家庭、传媒、教育、交通、人才、农业、历史、健康、法律、能源、体育、心理、信息、大气等数十个话题，是一套市面上相对完整的原版题源报刊阅读辅导书。《题源报刊精品阅读100篇（泛读）》旨在帮助考生训练快速阅读的技巧，提高考生的阅读速度和抓住文章主旨的能力；而《题源报刊精品阅读30篇（精读）》除了要帮助考生训练快速阅读的技巧和能力之外，还根据每篇文章内容提供5道符合考研英语命题规律和特点的试题，并配以原文剖析、答案和讲解，不仅能锻炼大家从宏观上梳理文章的能力，还能完善细节理解的技巧。

考生可在备考的第一阶段先做泛读，再做精读，好好地把这两本书吃透，以应对未来考试中可能出现的各种体裁和话题的文章。

此外，通过经常阅读考研英语题源文章，大家也会慢慢熟悉西方人的行文结构及逻辑论述的展开方式，这对于今后从事与英文有关的工作的考生而言有巨大的实际意义。

优秀没有偶然，请大家从现在开始，破除对人世间最具欺骗性的两个字——"捷径"的幻想，脚踏实地，亲身体会自己实实在在的进步。伟哥也将与编写团队一起，专门开设基于这一系列图书内容的在线直播课，带着大家好好梳理，共同学习。各位读者朋友们，让我们一起加油！

主编　朱伟

前 言
PREFACE

在全国硕士研究生招生考试的英语试卷中,阅读理解部分的分值占比最大,因此"攻克"阅读理解成了考生获得高分的重要一步。近几年来,考研英语阅读理解的命题思路有所调整,考试难度有所下降,更多地考查考生利用题干信息进行定位的能力,原文定位点前后的内容相对于前几年也变得更为简单。

针对考研英语阅读理解近年来出现的命题趋势和选材特点,本书精选30篇英美题源报刊文章,在保留文章"原汁原味"的基础上,配以参考译文、原文剖析、长难句解析和生词解析。此外,根据每篇文章的不同特点,以及考研英语阅读部分的命题规律和大纲要求,本书精心选取5道原创单选试题,配有详细的答案解析,并在最后一章提供15篇模拟阅读文章及相关试题,可作为考生"练手"和培养做题技巧的上乘之选。

一、本书特点

1. 文章选材精准,内容百里挑一

本书所有文章均选自考研英语阅读理解近10年来选材最频繁的13本英美报纸杂志,从上千篇文章中精心挑选,选材内容涵盖人文科学、社会科学和自然科学三大领域,具体包含环境、生物、经济、文学、医学、语言、家庭、传媒、教育、交通、人才、农业、历史、健康、法律、能源、体育、心理、信息、大气等方面。本书在文章长度、段落数、词汇难度、长难句数量以及重要考点方面进行了相应调整,力图真实"拷贝"考研英语阅读理解的历年真题特点。

2. 结构编排得当,贴近考生需要

本书内容编排得当。首先对考研英语阅读理解的题型和命题趋势进行了整体分析,分析其选材范围、选项特点以及做题思路;然后将精选的30篇文章,按不同的领域划分为经济贸易类、政治文化类和科技研究类;最后,在每一篇文章中,都提供了对段落内容、设题角度以及具体字词和长难句的分析。这样,考生不仅能宏观掌握整个考研英语阅读理解的脉络与重难点,还能在实战训练中具体掌握做题的思路与技巧。

3. 语篇分析详细,设题点睛准确

本书的特点之一就是对每篇文章中每个段落的结构和内容进行了详细分析,并针对段落特征给出了可能的设题思路,对段落中出现的转折关系、比较关系、因果关系、"否定+解释"关系、"观点+例证"关系、正反对比关系等处都进行了详细的标注和解释。考生可通过阅读本书,或配合《考研英语历年真题深度精解(技巧版)》《考研英语(一)历年真题深度精解(试卷版)》和《考研英语(二)历年真题深度精解(试卷版)》,进一步体会命

题人设置阅读理解考点的风格和偏好。

4. 选项设置科学，贴近真题标准

本书中，作者对选项的设置力求科学准确，其中有相当一部分考题在错误选项"迷惑性"的设计上贴近甚至超越了真题，因此读者需要仔细阅读试题解析部分，抓住设题思路，不断提高自己的鉴别能力。本书中，文章的难易程度并不相同，作者并非一味选择难度较高的文章，而是根据历年真题难度存在波动性的特点进行设置。此外，不同的难度系数和主题范围使本书同时适合参加考研英语（一）和考研英语（二）的考生备考。

5. 完善备考功能，提供自测机会

与上一版不同的是，这一版"30篇"增加了"题源报刊精选文章模拟自测"一章，更好地完善和加强了本书辅助考生备考的功能。所选取的15篇模拟文章也源于经典的国外题源报纸杂志，所涉题材广泛，并配有仿真单选题。该章位于全书最后，方便读者在阅读完前几章内容、积累了相关阅读技巧和经验后自测使用。

二、用法指导

考生在使用历年真题进行备考的过程中，会出现两个"空窗期"：一是暑假综合复习前的半个月到一个月的时间段，即考生以过去10年考研真题为素材、以做题技巧为目标的基础阶段训练完成之后；二是从9月到12月中旬，即考生以最近10年考研真题为素材、以实战演练为目标的强化阶段训练结束后到考前半个月。这是因为如果考生以一种紧凑的方式安排复习，那么过去10年的真题应在暑假之前完成，最近10年的真题应在12月中旬前消化完毕。因此在以上提到的这两个时间段内，考生手上可能并没有可以用来训练的权威资料。为弥补这一空缺，并进一步提高英语阅读能力、掌握解题技巧以及熟悉命题规律，考生可通过阅读英文原版报纸或杂志来继续自己的备考工作，而这两个"空窗期"也是我们建议考生使用本系列书的最佳阶段。

不仅如此，对于准备考研的考生来讲，在3月份到6月份结束了考研英语阅读理解的泛读训练之后，可以在暑假开始之前利用"30篇"中的5~10篇文章进行阶段性自我测试，主要目的是考查自己在经过一段时间的外文泛读训练后，面对"实战型"的模拟题是否已具有适应性。这个阶段的重点不在于选出正确选项，而是要求考生能将精力更多地用于体会这5~10篇文章中的"原文剖析"和"设题点睛"上。而在进入12月最后阶段的复习时，考生可以在反复练习并研究真题的基础上，通过"30篇"最后章节的模拟训练来提高自己的做题能力。在这一阶段反复练习真题和"30篇"中的模拟题之后，考生会在实战时做到胸有成竹，对题干中的关键点定位准确，有效提炼长难句主干，在阅读时发掘重要考点，以及有效排除错误选项。

无论你是处于备考初期、中期还是冲刺阶段，本书都可成为你的良师益友，助你一臂之力。最后，衷心祝愿大家都能金榜题名！

由于时间仓促，本书难免存在疏漏与不足之处，恳请广大读者指正。

编者

目 录 CONTENTS

第一章 考研英语真题题源分析
  第一节　考研英语真题题源介绍 …………………………………………………… 2
  第二节　考研英语真题题源回顾 …………………………………………………… 3

第二章 考研英语阅读理解命题解读
  第一节　考研英语阅读理解重难点 ………………………………………………… 8
  第二节　考研英语阅读理解命题规律 ……………………………………………… 20
  第三节　考研英语阅读理解选项特征 ……………………………………………… 27

第三章 题源报刊精选文章试题精讲
  第一节　经济贸易类 ………………………………………………………………… 32
    Text 1 ……………………………………………………………………………… 32
    Text 2 ……………………………………………………………………………… 42
    Text 3 ……………………………………………………………………………… 51
    Text 4 ……………………………………………………………………………… 59
    Text 5 ……………………………………………………………………………… 69
    Text 6 ……………………………………………………………………………… 78
    Text 7 ……………………………………………………………………………… 86
    Text 8 ……………………………………………………………………………… 96
  第二节　政治文化类 ………………………………………………………………… 104
    Text 9 ……………………………………………………………………………… 104
    Text 10 …………………………………………………………………………… 114
    Text 11 …………………………………………………………………………… 122
    Text 12 …………………………………………………………………………… 131

Text 13	140
Text 14	149
Text 15	158
Text 16	165
Text 17	174
Text 18	182
Text 19	191

第三节 科技研究类

Text 20	200
Text 21	208
Text 22	216
Text 23	225
Text 24	234
Text 25	243
Text 26	252
Text 27	261
Text 28	270
Text 29	279
Text 30	287

第四章 题源报刊精选文章模拟自测

Text 1	297
Text 2	298
Text 3	300
Text 4	302
Text 5	303
Text 6	305
Text 7	307
Text 8	308
Text 9	310
Text 10	312
Text 11	313
Text 12	315
Text 13	317
Text 14	319
Text 15	321

第一章 考研英语真题题源分析

CHAPTER ONE

第一节　考研英语真题题源介绍

　　历年考研英语阅读理解所选文章大多是从以下几本英美权威报纸杂志所发表的文章中改编而来的,如《新闻周刊》(Newsweek)、《今日美国》(USA Today)、《纽约时报》(The New York Times)、《华盛顿邮报》(The Washington Post)、《卫报》(The Guardian)、《美国新闻与世界报道》(U.S. News and World Report)、《经济学人》(The Economist)、《时代》(Time)、《自然》(Nature)等。

　　各大英美报刊的报道各有侧重点,其内容选材也各有不同。《时代》是美国影响最大的三大时事性周刊之一,有世界"史库"之称,该刊的宗旨是要使读者充分了解世界大事,设有经济、教育、法律、批评、宗教、医药、艺术、人物、书评和读者来信等多个栏目。《新闻周刊》的语言较《时代》易懂,除了重点报道国内外大事以外,还设有其他栏目,如紧密结合国际形势,对各国政治及外交人士进行的采访等。《纽约时报》在全世界发行,有相当大的影响力,其新闻报道经常被世界上其他报纸和新闻社直接引用作为新闻来源。《华盛顿邮报》是美国华盛顿最大、最老的报纸,擅长报道美国国内的政治动态,还因为多次获得普利策奖而在新闻界备受瞩目。《今日美国》是美国唯一的彩色版全国性日报,内容覆盖美国新闻、市场、金融、气象、娱乐、体育等方面,该报注重使用简洁明快的报道文体,偏爱使用短句、短词来浓缩文章。《卫报》是英国全国性综合日报,与《泰晤士报》(The Times)、《每日电讯报》(The Daily Telegraph)并称为"英国三大报",发展到今日,《卫报》成为了"严肃、可信、独立新闻"的代名词,在英国,人们也把《卫报》戏称为"愤青报纸"。《经济学人》是一份包含新闻、政治、经济观点和深度分析的英国周刊,该杂志的文章往往机智、幽默、有力度、严肃又不失诙谐,并且注重用最小的篇幅告诉读者最多的信息,杂志主要关注政治和商业方面的新闻,但是每期也有一两篇针对科技和艺术的报道,以及一些书评。英国著名杂志《自然》是世界上最早的国际性科技期刊,也是一份在学术界享有盛誉的综合性国际学术期刊,很多最重要、最前沿的研究结果都是以短讯的形式发表在《自然》上的。

　　考生在准备考研的过程中,应多阅读上述英美报纸杂志上的文章,尤其是与人文科学、社会科学和自然科学这三大领域有关的文章,重点关注其中的议论、评论、报道和分析文章等。这样做有助于考生掌握最新讯息,积累背景知识。

　　从体裁上看,考研英语阅读理解真题所选取的文章大多为说明文或者议论文,对这两类文章,考生应该采用不同的阅读方式。阅读说明文,重点是弄清楚文章所说明的对象、所采用的事实和数据;而阅读议论文,重点是掌握作者的态度、论点和论据。考生在阅读英美报刊时,可以带着做题的心理去审视这些文章,看完文章后自己进行归类总结,比如思考这篇文章属于什么类型和题材,所包含的要素(what,when,where,why,who)是哪些等。在考前阅读此类英美报刊原文,对考生培养英语语感、掌握英美文章的逻辑结构以及英美国家的社会及政治热点都有很大的帮助。

第二节 考研英语真题题源回顾

随着社会的快速发展,考研英语阅读理解部分的取材也具有很强的时效性,大多是近两年内甚至是当年的文章。以 2016 年为例,考研英语(一)阅读理解的四篇文章中只有 Text 2 是出自 2014 年 11 月刊登在《卫报》(*The Guardian*)上的一篇文章,其余三篇分别出自 2015 年 4 月的《基督教科学箴言报》(*The Christian Science Monitor*)、2015 年 6 月的《经济学人》(*The Economist*)和 2015 年 3 月的《大西洋月刊》(*The Atlantic*)。

为了让考生对考研英语真题中的阅读理解部分有一个较为直观的把握,本书特意整理了近几年来考研英语阅读理解 Part A 中的文章来源和主题,以及出题较为集中的题源,详见表 1 和表 2:

表 1　2010—2019 年考研英语阅读理解 Part A 真题题源汇总

年份	考试科目	篇目	篇目	主题	题源
2019	英语(一)	Part A	Text 1	耐心是企业的美德	*The Christian Science Monitor*
			Text 2	大学"分数宽恕"政策的兴起	*The Atlantic*
			Text 3	人工智能可以具有价值甚至意识	*The Christian Science Monitor*
			Text 4	高等法院:网上购物者可能被迫支付销售税	*US News*
	英语(二)	Part A	Text 1	当内疚成为一种好事	*The Atlantic*
			Text 2	利用森林对抗气候变化	*Bloomberg*
			Text 3	没有外国工人,美国农场将失去竞争力	*Bloomberg*
			Text 4	假装杜绝使用吸管可以解决塑料污染	*HuffPost*
2018	英语(一)	Part A	Text 1	机器人与中产阶级	*Bloomberg*
			Text 2	网络分享中的审辩式思维	*The Christian Science Monitor*
			Text 3	医疗领域的数字霸权问题	*The Guardian*
			Text 4	美国邮局的转型之路	*The Washington Post*
	英语(二)	Part A	Text 1	实践教育观	*The Christian Science Monitor*
			Text 2	可再生能源已达临界点	*The Christian Science Monitor*
			Text 3	科技巨头对用户数据的攫取	*The Guardian*
			Text 4	管理自己的精力	*BBC*

年份	考试科目	篇目		主题	题源
2017	英语（一）	Part A	Text 1	美国航空安检和"预查计划"	The Washington Post
			Text 2	在夏威夷莫纳克亚山上安装望远镜受抵制	Scientific American
			Text 3	GDP 的局限性	The Independent
			Text 4	关于美国一起州长腐败案的讨论	The Christian Science Monitor
	英语（二）	Part A	Text 1	公园跑活动的成功给伦敦奥运会带来的启示	The Guardian
			Text 2	电子产品和亲子关系	Scientific American
			Text 3	推迟一年上大学的好处	The Huffington Post
			Text 4	美国联邦经费过多地用于解决野外火灾问题	The Christian Science Monitor
2016	英语（一）	Part A	Text 1	法律对模特身材的规定	The Christian Science Monitor
			Text 2	英国乡村的规划	The Guardian
			Text 3	企业的社会责任	The Economist
			Text 4	纸质出版物的未来	The Atlantic
	英语（二）	Part A	Text 1	学生早接触计算机知识的好处	The Atlantic
			Text 2	美国对小草原榛鸡的保护	Science
			Text 3	有效阅读	The Guardian
			Text 4	美国年轻一代的成功之路	The Atlantic
2015	英语（一）	Part A	Text 1	欧洲皇室的存废	The Guardian
			Text 2	手机信息安全	The Washington Post
			Text 3	学术杂志对论文数据的审核	Nature
			Text 4	新闻从业人员的道德准则缺失	The Guardian
	英语（二）	Part A	Text 1	男女在家庭和工作中压力的异同	Time
			Text 2	第一代大学生的问题	Inside Higher Education
			Text 3	办公室用语的变化	The Atlantic
			Text 4	美国的就业变化	The Huffington Post
2014	英语（一）	Part A	Text 1	英国财政大臣针对失业者的改革计划	The Guardian
			Text 2	美国法律服务价格昂贵的原因	The Economist
			Text 3	作者对自然科学界新科研奖项的分析与评价	Nature
			Text 4	美国艺术与科学院报告的缺陷	The Wall Street Journal
	英语（二）	Part A	Text 1	如何快乐花钱	The Economist
			Text 2	人们对自己评价过高的原因	The Guardian
			Text 3	人机竞争	Big Think
			Text 4	英国住房危机	The Guardian

续表

年份	考试科目	篇目		主题	题源
2013	英语(一)	Part A	Text 1	对快速时尚业的批判	Business Week
			Text 2	广告商追踪用户上网行为引发的争议	The Economist
			Text 3	人类的未来充满光明	New Scientist
			Text 4	最高法院对亚利桑那州移民法的最后判决	The Wall Street Journal
	英语(二)	Part A	Text 1	科技变革对社会的影响	The New York Times
			Text 2	美国移民问题	The Washington Post
			Text 3	大脑的快速反应	The New York Times
			Text 4	欧洲性别歧视问题	Project Syndicate
2012	英语(一)	Part A	Text 1	同辈压力能否起到积极作用	Time
			Text 2	安特吉公司违背承诺及其后果	Boston.com
			Text 3	科学发现的取信过程	The Scientist
			Text 4	工会阻碍公共部门改革	The Economist
	英语(二)	Part A	Text 1	家庭作业新政策的弊端	Los Angeles Times
			Text 2	粉色成为女孩子专用色的由来	The Guardian
			Text 3	基因专利的法律纠纷	The Economist
			Text 4	经济大萧条的利与弊	The Atlantic
2011	英语(一)	Part A	Text 1	古典音乐现场演出的危机	Commentary
			Text 2	高级经理"裸辞"现象	Businessweek
			Text 3	营销中的新媒体	McKinsey Quarterly
			Text 4	明星父母对大众生育观的影响	Newsweek
	英语(二)	Part A	Text 1	如何留住公司的外部董事	The Economist
			Text 2	美国报业"一息尚存"	The Economist
			Text 3	简约即美	The New York Times
			Text 4	欧盟统一货币体系与欧洲经济的未来	The Economist
2010	英语(一)	Part A	Text 1	报纸文艺评论辉煌不再	Commentary
			Text 2	商业方法专利的数量将被削减	Businessweek
			Text 3	社会潮流的形成	Harvard Business Review
			Text 4	会计准则制定者面临的压力	The Economist
	英语(二)	Part A	Text 1	世界艺术品市场疲软	The Economist
			Text 2	夫妻交流困难的原因	The Washington Post
			Text 3	某些消费习惯是商业行为的产物	The New York Times
			Text 4	美国陪审团制度的发展	——

表2 2010—2019年考研英语阅读理解Part A 选材集中的题源

题源	选材篇数	对应真题
The Economist	共11篇	2016年英语（一）Text 3；2014年英语（一）Text 2 2014年英语（二）Text 1；2013年英语（一）Text 2 2012年英语（一）Text 4；2012年英语（二）Text 3 2011年英语（二）Text 1；2011年英语（二）Text 2 2011年英语（二）Text 4；2010年英语（一）Text 4 2010年英语（二）Text 1
The Guardian	共11篇	2018年英语（一）Text 3；2018年英语（二）Text 3 2017年英语（二）Text 1；2016年英语（一）Text 2 2016年英语（二）Text 3；2015年英语（一）Text 1 2015年英语（一）Text 4；2014年英语（一）Text 1 2014年英语（二）Text 2；2014年英语（二）Text 4 2012年英语（二）Text 2
The Christian Science Monitor	共8篇	2019年英语（一）Text 1；2019年英语（一）Text 3 2018年英语（一）Text 1；2018年英语（二）Text 1 2018年英语（二）Text 2；2017年英语（一）Text 4 2017年英语（二）Text 4；2016年英语（一）Text 1
The Atlantic	共7篇	2019年英语（一）Text 2；2019年英语（二）Text 1 2016年英语（一）Text 4；2016年英语（二）Text 1 2016年英语（二）Text 4；2015年英语（二）Text 3 2012年英语（二）Text 4
The Washington Post	共5篇	2018年英语（一）Text 4；2017年英语（一）Text 1 2015年英语（二）Text 2；2013年英语（二）Text 2 2010年英语（二）Text 2
The New York Times	共4篇	2013年英语（二）Text 1；2013年英语（二）Text 3 2011年英语（二）Text 3；2010年英语（二）Text 3
Nature	共2篇	2015年英语（一）Text 3；2014年英语（一）Text 3
Time	共2篇	2015年英语（二）Text 1；2012年英语（一）Text 1
US NEWS	共1篇	2019年英语（一）Text 4
Bloomberg	共2篇	2019年英语（二）Text 2；2019年英语（二）Text 3
Huff Post	共1篇	2019年英语（二）Text 4

第二章 考研英语阅读理解命题解读

第一节　考研英语阅读理解重难点

一、推测生词语意

考生会在历年真题文章中发现大量背景常识类词汇，如果没有比较好的知识储备，会很难理解文章大意，即使强行拆分词汇，将其顺译成中文，意思也往往会让考生感到莫名其妙、一头雾水。如 2011 年考研英语（一）Text 3（主题是"营销中的新媒体"）中出现了大量与 media 有关的短语（如 paid media、earned media、owned media），考生看见 media 的第一反应是"媒体"，如果将 paid media 翻译成"买媒体"，将 earned media 翻译成"挣钱媒体"显然都是不合适的。查阅资料后可知，对 paid media 的正确译法是"付费媒介"，earned media 指"赢得媒介"。但即便知道这两个短语的专门含义，考生还是无法将其与日常生活中的事物联系起来，在理解原文时势必会受到较大影响，很可能就算做完了题目，但对文章的中心论点还是不甚了解。涉及文章背景的问题，我们将在后面的讲解中给出具体的应对方法。

考生在记忆单词的时候，最关注的往往是这个词的第一个或第二个意思，但在研究生英语考试中经常对一词多义或熟词僻义进行考查。例如，绝大多数考生只知道 minute 表示"分钟"，却不知道该词还可以作形容词，表示"微小的"；只知道 project 是名词，有"项目"的意思，却不知道其动词形式还有"投射出，展示出"的意思。实际上，即便某个单词不存在一词多义的特点，但在不同的语境下，也会表示完全不同的意思。例如，考生对 fail 这个词的第一反应是"失败"，那请思考一下，以下几句中的 fail 分别表示什么意思？

①My friends failed me when I was in trouble.
②After I saw the touching movie, words failed me.
③My history teacher failed me in the final examination.

分析：如果将以上三个句子中的 fail 都译为"失败"，整句话的意思会让人感到晦涩生硬。实际上，句①中的 fail 应理解为"使失望，背叛，放弃"；句②整个句子应理解为"电影太感人，我都感动得说不出话了"，其中的 fail 用了比喻义，表示"说不出话来"；句③中的 fail 翻得"接地气"一点就是"挂科"。就算考生对 fail 这个词的本义记忆得再好，也背不完 fail 的这些引申义。因此从这点上看，考研英语阅读理解对考生结合上下文理解词义的能力提出了比较高的要求。

考生遇到生词时，一般会依靠这个词所在的单句以及相邻的上下句来猜测其大概含义。根据对历年真题的分析，我们将能够帮助考生猜测词义的有效结构整理如下：

1. 单句内及上下句间的并列或递进关系

例　Science has long had an uneasy relationship with other aspects of culture. Think of Galileo's 17th century trial for his rebelling belief before the Catholic Church or poet William Blake's harsh remarks against the mechanistic worldview of Isaac Newton. The <u>schism</u> between science and the humanities has, if anything, deepened in this century. [1998年考研英语 Text 3]

Q: The word "schism" in the context probably means _____.	问：文中的"schism"很可能表示_____。
A. confrontation	A. 对峙
B. dissatisfaction	B. 不满
C. separation	C. 分离
D. contempt	D. 蔑视

【解题思路】C。schism 所在单句的主干是 The schism between science and the humanities has deepened in this century(20 世纪科学与人文学科之间的 schism 加深了)。由单词 deepen(加深)判断，本句和上一句之间的语意存在递进关系。因此可推断上一句的内容也涉及科学和人文学科之间的 schism。本段首句为主题句，大意是科学和文化中其他方面的关系一直很紧张；第二句举了两个例子，一个是 17 世纪伽利略与天主教的对抗，另一个是诗人威廉·布莱克对牛顿的攻击。这两个例子都说明科学和其他人文学科(如宗教和文学)之间具有冲突性或对抗性的特点。由于第三句的语意对前两句进行承接和递进，因此 schism 所表现出来的感情色彩与 rebelling 和 harsh 类似，暗示"科学"和"人文学科"之间偏负面的关系，选项 B(不满)和选项 D(蔑视)所表现出的是一方对另一方的消极看法，而不是双方之间的对抗关系，因此排除。选项 A(对峙)无法与谓语动词 deepen 呼应，因此选项 C(分离)正确。

2. 单句内及上下句间的转折或否定关系

例　No two comets ever look <u>identical</u>, but they have basic features in common, one of the most obvious of which is a coma. [2002年托福考试真题]

Q: The word "identical" is closest in meaning to which of the following?	问：单词"identical"与以下哪项的意思最接近？
A. Equally fast.	A. 同样快的。
B. Exactly alike.	B. 完全一样的。
C. Near each other.	C. 距离近的。
D. Invisible.	D. 看不见的。

【解题思路】B。本句话 but 转折之后的大意是它们的基本特性是相同的，则转折前应该是说两者有些许不同，转折前的大意是没有两颗看起来是 identical 的彗星，将 identical 一词翻译成"相同"符合转折前后大意相反的要求，所以选项 B 是正确答案。

3. 生词前后的定语或定语从句

例　"Scientific" <u>creationism</u>, which is being pushed by some for "equal time" in the classrooms whenever the scientific accounts of evolution are given, is based on religion, not science. Virtually all scientists and the majority of nonfundamentalist religious leaders have come to regard "scientific" creationism as bad science and bad religion. [1996年考研英语 Text 5]

Q: "Creationism" in the passage refers to _____.	问：文中的"creationism"指_____。
A. evolution in its true sense as to the origin of the universe	A. 关于宇宙起源真正意义上的进化
B. a notion of the creation of religion	B. 有关宗教起源的学说
C. the scientific explanation of the earth formation	C. 地球形成的科学解释
D. the deceptive theory about the origin of the universe	D. 关于宇宙起源的虚假理论

【解题思路】D。首句出现对 creationism 的解释，该句主干为"Scientific" creationism is based on religion, not science，其大意是"科学的"创世说基于宗教而不是科学。其中的"科学"一词加上了双引号，说明该学说并非是科学的，对应该段最后一句所说的几乎所有科学家和大多数非原教旨主义的宗教领袖都将"科学的"创世说看作拙劣的科学和拙劣的宗教，因此选项 D 正确。或可通过排除其他三项的方法选定正确选项。选项 A 错在创世说并非进化论，选项 B 错在创世说并非关于宗教的起源，选项 C 错在创世说并非科学解释。

4. 生词前后的状语或状语从句

例　Today, river discharges are increasingly controlled by human intervention, creating a need for international river-basin agreements. The filling of the Ataturk and other dams in Turkey has drastically reduced flows in the Euphrates, with potentially serious consequences for Syria and Iraq. [2012年托福考试真题]

Q: The word "drastically" in the passage is closest in meaning to _____.	问：文中"drastically"的意思最接近于_____。
A. obviously	A. 明显地
B. unfortunately	B. 不幸地
C. rapidly	C. 快速地
D. severely	D. 严重地

【解题思路】D。生词所在句的大意是土耳其水坝的注水(filling) drastically 减少了幼发拉底河的水流量。drastically 是对 reduce 的修饰，而本句中还有一个 with 结构作伴随状语，对主句所产生的后果进行说明，大意是可对幼发拉底河下游的叙利亚和伊拉克造成潜在的严重后果，因此只有选项 D 的 severely 可以对应 serious consequences，该项正确。

5. 生词后的解释类信息(举例、插入语，以及破折号和冒号后的内容)

例　Supporting evidence comes from research showing that aggressive people often distort other people's motives. For example, they assume that other people mean them harm when they do not. [2011年托福考试真题]

Q: The word "distort" in the passage is closest in meaning to _____.	问：文中"distort"的意思最接近于_____。
A. mistrust	A. 不信任
B. misinterpret	B. 误解
C. criticize	C. 批评
D. resent	D. 憎恨

【解题思路】B。distort 所在句的大意是源自研究的支撑性证据显示，具有攻击性的人经常会 distort 他人的动机。根据本句内容无法理解 distort 的意思，下一句为明确的例子，用来支持本句，该例子的意思是这些人认为别人会对其造成伤害，而其实别人并不会，说明这些人误解了别人的意图。所以选项 B 是正确答案。

6. 生词的词根或词缀

例　A folk culture is small, isolated, cohesive, conservative, nearly self-sufficient group that is <u>homogeneous</u> in custom and race, with a strong family or clan structure and highly developed rituals.［2012 年 GRE 考试真题］

Q: The word "homogeneous" is closest in meaning to which of the following?	问："homogeneous"的意思最接近以下哪项？
A. Uniform.	A. 统一的。
B. General.	B. 一般的。
C. Primitive.	C. 原始的。
D. Traditional.	D. 传统的。

【解题思路】A。homogeneous 的前缀为 homo-，表示"同一，相似"，因此可以直接判断选项 A 正确。如果考生不了解 homo- 这一前缀的意思，也可将四个选项代入原文判断，该句可分别翻译为"血缘社会是小型的、孤立的、紧密的、保守的、近乎自给自足的群体，群体在习俗和种族上是统一的/一般的/原始的/传统的，具有强大的家庭或部族结构以及高度发展的仪式。"其他三项都无法修饰"种族"，因此都可排除。本句中的 folk culture 相当于 folk society，是个人类学概念，应理解为"（封闭式小型）血缘社会"。

二、长难句的要点

考研英语阅读理解 Part A 中的另一个难点就是长难句，真题中出现的长难句往往结构复杂，在主句的基础上还会有各种结构及从句，使一个句子不仅冗长，而且难以理解。在面对长难句时考生往往不得其法，归结起来，还是在对长难句核心信息的提取上"修炼"不足。

应对长难句最基本的思路就是化繁为简，这里的"化"就是指对句中的核心信息进行提取。一个长难句的核心信息，主要包括两方面的内容：一是语法主干；二是逻辑关系。

1. 语法主干

长难句的语法主干指的是其主谓宾成分，以及当主语或宾语为抽象名词时，能够对其作进一步解释说明的成分（如定语或状语）。具体来说，长难句的语法主干可分为以下八

种情况:
　　①主句的主语、谓语、宾语、表语为主要内容;
　　②主句的主语从句、宾语从句、表语从句(充当主、宾、表语)为主要内容;
　　③主句中对主语和宾语进行明确解释的定语、状语(包括定语从句、状语从句)为主要内容;
　　④长难句的并列结构:若前后大意不同,均需保留;若前后大意差不多,可合并理解;
　　⑤长难句的插入语为次要内容(双逗号或双破折号之间的内容);
　　⑥长难句中的举例为次要内容;
　　⑦长难句中破折号或冒号后的解释性内容,只需理解其意思明确的部分;
　　⑧从句中若没有重要的逻辑关系,可省略不看。
　2. 逻辑关系
　　长难句中往往存在一些特殊的逻辑关系,其所在部分是句子的重要内容。常见的重要逻辑关系有以下五大类,当长难句中出现了以下这五大类逻辑关系时,逻辑关系所在的句内部分是考生需要留意并重点理解的。
　(1)转折关系
　　①强转折关系特征词:but,however,yet,nevertheless;
　　②弱转折关系特征词:though,although,even,even if,even when,despite,in spite of。
　　强转折关系所在部分为句内重要信息,弱转折关系所在部分可忽略不看。
　(2)否定关系
　　①显性否定关系特征词(明确的否定词):no,not,never,none,without,few,little,hardly,rarely;
　　②隐性否定关系特征词(含有否定意味的词):ignore,lack,absent,fail,oppose,miss,fade,different;
　　③含有否定关系的结构:
　　　A rather than B(是A而不是B,重点看A);
　　　A. Rather, B(rather表示"更确切地说",是B而不是A,重点看B);
　　　A instead of B(A替代了B,是A而不是B,重点看A);
　　　A. Instead, B(instead表示"反而",是B而不是A,重点看B);
　　　More A than B(A比B多,是A而不是B,重点看A);
　　　Less A than B(A比B少,是B而不是A,重点看B)。
　(3)比较关系
　　①显性比较关系:
　　　同级比较特征词:and,or,as well;
　　　比较级特征词:more/less,-er;
　　　最高级特征词:most/least,-est;
　　②隐性比较关系:
　　　同级比较特征词:similar to,equal to,same as,as well as;
　　　比较级特征词:increase=more,decrease=less(数量变化);
　　　　　　　　　improve/develop=better,degenerate/destroy=worse(程度变化);

最高级特征词:favorite,top,peak,outstanding,unique,dominate,max,min。

(4)因果关系

①因果关系特征词:because(of),so,reason,result,cause,consequence,since,for,as,hence,therefore,accordingly,thus;

②引出结果:
- 表示"导致":cause,lead to,result in,contribute to,give rise to,and,make;
- 表示"为……负责":be blamed for,be responsible for;
- 表示"意味":show,mean,present,reflect,suggest,imply,demonstrate;

③引出原因:
- 表示"归结":thanks to,due to,attribute to,owe to;
- 表示"源自":come from,arise from,originate from,stem from,derive from,result from;
- 表示"基于":base on,depend on,resort to,on the assumption of (that)。

(5)条件关系

条件关系特征词:if,unless,only if,as long as,without,so long as。

以上是长难句中经常出现的五类逻辑关系,考生需要牢记并有意识地在阅读的过程中加以辨别,因为长难句内部的重点逻辑关系、段落内带有重要逻辑关系的单句往往会成为考点,理清长难句的句内逻辑关系对于做题也有很大帮助。

下面,我们就利用提取长难句核心信息的阅读技巧来分析历年真题中曾考查过的长难句。

例 A string of accidents, including the partial collapse of a cooling tower in 2007 and the discovery of an underground pipe system leakage, raised serious questions about both Vermont Yankee's safety and Entergy's management—especially after the company made misleading statements about the pipe. [2012年考研英语(一)Text 2]

【原文剖析】该句的语法主干是 A string of accidents raised serious questions about both Vermont Yankee's safety and Entergy's management(一系列的意外事件使得人们对佛蒙特州扬基核电站的安全和安特吉公司的管理能力提出了质疑)。including the partial collapse of a cooling tower in 2007 and the discovery of an underground pipe system leakage 在语法上属于插入成分,其功能是对 accidents 进行举例说明,不重要,可忽略;especially after the company made misleading statements about the pipe 是破折号之后的内容,用于对主干中人们提出质疑的原因做进一步说明;经过以上分析,可总结出该句想要表达的重点是人们不信任核电站的安全和公司的管理。

Q: According to paragraph 4, Entergy seems to have problems with its _____.	问:根据第四段,安特吉公司似乎在其_____上出现了问题。
A. managerial practices	A. 管理方式
B. technical innovativeness	B. 技术创新性
C. financial goals	C. 经济目标
D. business vision	D. 企业愿景

【解题思路】A。本题的定位点就是上述长难句,通过提取长难句的主干信息,可知选项 A 是对原文内容的高度概括,因此是正确答案。

三、段落结构

虽然考研英语阅读理解 Part A 给考生留了每篇 15 到 20 分钟的做题时间(用于理解题干、定位原文和排除选项),但有的考生仍觉得时间不够用,题目做不完。除去生词、长难句等干扰因素外,很重要的一个原因是考生无法有效区分并提取一篇文章中的重点段落和段落中的重点信息,在阅读和理解上浪费了时间。

1. 段落主题句的辨别

段落主题句(topic sentence)是可以概括段落大意的单句,主题句的确定对考生迅速确定段落结构和大意有很大帮助。从设题上讲,旨在考查例子功能和细节理解的常见真题总是和段落主题句有很大关系,如果考生在快速阅读时就确认了段落的主题句,则可大大提高做题效率。

段落主题句在内容上往往具有以下特点:
①主题句一般是肯定的判断句;
②主题句一般是高度抽象和概括的句子;
③整个段落的内容一般都会围绕主题句展开。

段落主题句在位置和逻辑上往往具有以下特点:
①是位于段落开头或结尾处的强转折句;
②是位于段落开头或结尾处的人物观点句;
③是位于段落开头的设问句及设问句之后的回答(答语往往是主题句);
④是位于段落转折或否定之后的原因解释句。

2. 段落结构的辨别

考研英语阅读理解 Part A 所选文章中常见的段落结构可分为:总分结构、分总结构、无主题句结构。

(1)主题句+支撑信息——总分结构

这种段落主题句的位置一般并不确定,可以出现在段落首句,也可以出现在铺垫信息之后,还可以被置于段落开头的错误观点之后,通过反驳前文观点的方式给出。

① 段落首句为主题句。

例 This success, coupled with later research showing that memory itself is not genetically determined, led Ericsson to conclude that the act of memorizing is more of a cognitive exercise than an intuitive one. In other words, whatever inborn differences two people may exhibit in their abilities to memorize, those differences are swamped by how well each person "encodes" the information. And the best way to learn how to encode information meaningfully, Ericsson determined, was a process known as deliberate practice. Deliberate practice entails more than simply repeating a task. Rather, it involves setting specific goals, obtaining immediate feedback and concentrating as much on technique as on outcome. [2007年考研英语 Text 1]

【原文剖析】段落首句的语意主干为 This success led Ericsson to conclude that the act of memorizing is more of a cognitive exercise than an intuitive one(这个实验的成功让埃里克森总结出记忆行为更多靠认知训练而不是本能产生)。第二句开头处的 in other words 说明此句与第一句的观点相同,同属道理论证。从第三句开始,通过对 deliberate practice (刻意训练)的进一步解释,再次论证 cognitive exercise(认知训练,等同于 deliberate practice)更加重要。在理解整段语意后可知本段的主题句就是段落首句。

Q:According to Ericsson, good memory _____.	问:根据埃里克森的看法,好的记忆 _____。
A. depends on meaningful processing of information	A. 依靠对信息的有意义的加工
B. results from intuitive rather than cognitive exercises	B. 源于直觉而非认知训练
C. is determined by genetic rather than psychological factors	C. 由基因而非心理因素决定
D. requires immediate feedback and a high degree of concentration	D. 要求迅速反馈和注意力高度集中

【解题思路】A。通过顺序原则可将本题定位到以上段落。根据本段首句,埃里克森明确认为记忆能力的高低主要取决于认知训练(cognitive exercise)而不是天分(intuitive one),是确定的观点句,第二句对首句观点作进一步解释,因此首句是本段主题句。第二句谈到换句话说,不管两个人在记忆能力方面表现出来的先天差异有多大,这种差异都会被每个人解码信息能力的强弱所掩盖。选项 B 与观点句内容矛盾,因此排除。选项 C 中的"基因"等同于选项 B 谈到的"直觉",因此也可排除。选项 D 中的"迅速反馈"和"高度集中"与第二句中的关键信息"解码信息能力"无法呼应,可排除。因此只有选项 A 正确,其中"对信息的有意义的加工"是对第二句谈到的"解码信息能力"的同义替换。

②段落一开始给出错误观点,后文对其进行驳斥后给出主题句。

段落一开始给出错误观点的结构往往具有明确特征:一般而言,首句是对过去观点或是大众观点的描述,继而证明这种观点是错误的(真理往往掌握在少数人手中,或过去的想法并未与时俱进);首句之后会通过转折或者否定的方式对错误观点进行驳斥,考生要注意的是这一句往往只对错误观点进行否定,作者的真正观点很可能隐藏在否定或者转折句之后。

例 In the idealized version of how science is done, facts about the world are waiting to be observed and collected by objective researchers who use the scientific method to carry out their work. But in the everyday practice of science, discovery frequently follows an ambiguous and complicated route. We aim to be objective, but we cannot escape the context of our unique life experience. Prior knowledge and interests influence what we experience, what we think our experiences mean, and the subsequent actions we take. Opportunities for misinterpretation, error, and self-deception abound. [2012年考研英语(一)Text 3]

【原文剖析】本段首句给出了错误观点:科学研究的理想形式是用科学的方法进行研

究的客观研究者观察并且收集关于这个世界的事实。第二句随即用 but 进行转折,并给出新的观点,即现实中的科学发现过程是含糊且复杂的。第三句到第五句针对第二句中的 ambiguous and complicated route 进行解释说明。

Q: According to the first paragraph, the process of discovery is characterized by its _____.	问:根据第一段,发现的过程具有_____的特征。
A. uncertainty and complexity	A. 不确定性和复杂性
B. misconception and deceptiveness	B. 误解性和欺骗性
C. logicality and objectivity	C. 逻辑性和客观性
D. systematicness and regularity	D. 系统性和常规性

【解题思路】A。本题询问科学发现过程的特点,可直接定位至以上段落中的第二句,也就是该段的主题句。选项 A 中的 uncertainty and complexity 是对该主题句中 ambiguous and complicated 的同义替换,因此是正确答案。

(2) 支撑信息 + 主题句——分总结构

这种段落一般先通过引用、举例、对比等方式给出事实或背景,然后引出主题句。这种结构存在两种具体情况:第一种是在段落的开始处给出例证,例证结束之后立刻给出观点句;第二种是在开篇首段给出例子,接着从第二段开始表达观点。

例 It's no surprise that Jennifer Senior's insightful, provocative magazine cover story, "I Love My Children, I Hate My Life," is arousing much chatter—nothing gets people talking like the suggestion that child rearing is anything less than a completely fulfilling, life-enriching experience. Rather than concluding that children make parents either happy or miserable, Senior suggests we need to redefine happiness:instead of thinking of it as something that can be measured by moment-to-moment joy, we should consider being happy as a past-tense condition. Even though the day-to-day experience of raising kids can be soul-crushingly hard, Senior writes that "the very things that in the moment dampen our moods can later be sources of intense gratification and delight." [2011 年考研英语(一)Text 4]

【原文剖析】段落首句给出了一个具体事例,谈到詹妮弗·西尼尔的一篇文章引起了人们的讨论。第二句中转折逻辑词 rather than 以及冒号后的内容(尤其是 we should consider being happy as a past-tense condition)进一步阐述了詹妮弗·西尼尔对于如何抚养孩子的观念,即不能以即时的愉悦为衡量标准。第三句对以上观点做进一步说明,指出正是这些让人沮丧的事情能成为日后强烈满足感和快乐的源泉。可明显看出,本段首句提供例子和背景,第二句对首句进行总结并为第三句的观点作铺垫,本段的观点出现在第三句,该句自然而然也就成为本段的主题句。

Q: Jennifer Senior suggests in her article that raising a child can bring _____.	问:詹妮弗·西尼尔在其文章中指出养育子女可以带来_____。
A. temporary delight	A. 暂时的快乐
B. enjoyment in progress	B. 当下的愉悦
C. happiness in retrospect	C. 回顾过去时的幸福感
D. lasting reward	D. 长久的回报

【解题思路】C。根据题干中的Jennifer Senior和raising a child可直接定位至本段。对第三句进行分析后发现该句与选项C所表达的意思对应，该项中的happiness in retrospect与该句中的later be sources of intense gratification and delight属于同义替换。

(3) 段落并不存在主题句

并非每个段落都有主题句，有些段落中并不设主题句。这种情况往往发生在文章的首段中，往往整段都是对某一事例的描述或介绍，目的是通过特定事实引出下文的观点性内容。当这种段落结构出现时，命题人往往会针对首段谈到的例子设置例子功能题。随着考研英语阅读理解Part A中文章段落数量的增加，所选文章的中间部分偶尔也会出现这种情况的段落，即整段都由数字、时间、专有名词等细节组成，用于支持上一段的观点或引出下一段内容，但这种在文章中间部分出现的细节段落被考到的概率较低。

例 Rosenberg, the recipient of a Pulitzer Prize, offers a host of examples of the social cure in action：In South Carolina, a state-sponsored antismoking program called Rage Against the Haze sets out to make cigarettes uncool. In South Africa, an HIV-prevention initiative known as loveLife recruits young people to promote safe sex among their peers. [2012年考研英语(一)Text 1]

【原文剖析】这是该篇文章的第二段，列举了用于证明"社会治疗"有效的两个例子，分别是美国南卡罗来纳州反吸烟运动和南非的预防艾滋病运动。这两个例子起到了两个作用，一是支撑第一段中罗森伯格对于社会治疗具有积极作用的观点；二是引出作者的观点，后文将通过分析这两个运动的结果来表达作者对社会治疗有效性的质疑。第二段本身因为不存在重要观点或主题句，因此不会成为设置考点的关键内容。

四、背景知识

考研英语阅读理解Part A的四篇文章大多选自英美报纸或杂志，改编后的长度一般为400~500词。考生只要具备基本的常识和较为扎实的语言功底，都可以理解文章的大部分内容，但是文章中偶尔也会出现较为生僻的专业观点，或出现对某一问题的解释很少甚至不给任何背景信息的情况。在面对以上情况时，考生首先会在心里打退堂鼓，认为自己无法理解原文，虽然通过仔细阅读，考生也可以利用文中的蛛丝马迹找出正确答案，但在考场上极度紧张的氛围下，"这篇文章讲的东西我知道"和"这篇文章在讲什么"的两种心理对考生的影响不言而喻。但考生需要牢记的是，命题人在设置考题时往往会绕开或间接绕开超出考生知识或理解范围的内容，最终保证考生可以在不借助相关专业知识的情况下找出正确选项。

考生可以通过对2013年考研英语(一)阅读理解Part A中有关"对快速时尚业的批判"文章(Text 1)进行分析，揣摩并掌握如何在文章背景信息不足的情况下解题。

例 In the 2006 film version of The Devil Wears Prada, Miranda Priestly, played by Meryl Streep, scolds her unattractive assistant for imagining that high fashion doesn't affect her. Priestly explains how the deep blue color of the assistant's sweater descended over the years from fashion shows to department stores and to the bargain bin in which the poor girl doubtless found her garment. [2013年考研英语(一)Text 1]

【原文剖析】本篇文章的首段提到了几年前一部非常有名的电影——《穿普拉达的女王》(The Devil Wears Prada)。这部电影主要讲述了一个在顶级时尚杂志掌门人手下工作的质朴女实习生如何从对时尚一窍不通的临时助理变身为掌门人最为器重的白领"女神"的故事。文章首段描述了这部电影一开始的片段，看过这部电影的考生就算没有理解甚至阅读前两句内容，也能凭借对电影情节的回忆，明白首段中的米兰达应该对助理低下的时尚审美能力感到不屑。因此，考生可以直接选出该题的正确答案选项B。

但是，如果考生没有这样的背景知识，也未必不能选出正确答案。命题人在命制考研英语阅读试题时始终要遵循的一个基本原则就是——正确选项出自对应的原文内容。那么本题也可以依靠原文信息得出最佳答案。

Q: Priestly criticizes her assistant for her _____.	问：普里斯特利因其助理的_____而批评她。
A. poor bargaining skill	A. 糟糕的谈判技巧
B. insensitivity to fashion	B. 较差的时尚敏感性
C. obsession with high fashion	C. 对高级时装的迷恋
D. lack of imagination	D. 想象力的缺乏

【解题思路】B。考生首先需要做的是根据题干要求定位原文。根据以下理由可以判定答案位于首段：首先，题干中的criticize对应原文首段的scold；其次，首段首句带有明确观点(其实就是正确答案的出处)，第二句为长难句，最有可能进一步解释首句；最后，第二段开始已经没有涉及普里斯特利的内容了。仔细观察可注意到选项B和选项C的意思正好相反。考研英语阅读理解Part A的选项设置所遵循的常见规律之一就是反义选项中有一个是正确答案(考查作者观点态度的题目除外)。原文首句中high fashion does not affect her的意思是"时尚对她没有影响"，与选项B的情感方向和大意一致，因此选项B是正确答案。

从表面上看，在第一句描述不充分的情况下，第二句成为解题关键合情合理，但第二句难就难在作者用很少的信息描述了一个比较抽象的时尚演变过程，即普里斯特利告知助手她所穿的普通深蓝色针织衫近年来是如何从时尚表演的舞台降格到普通百货店中，并最终沦落到廉价折扣店处理品的，而这个可怜的姑娘就是在那里淘到了这件衣服。理解这一句的意思对选出正确答案看似没有帮助。因为这段话的背景是电影中的助理认为自己即使没有时尚观念也能好好工作、好好生活，但是普里斯特利利用她那件普通深蓝色针织衫的出处来嘲笑她，指出她就活在一个被时尚包围的世界中，她那件毛衣的经典深蓝色就是一个经久不衰的时尚色彩，而她却对此毫不知情。如果第二句能把"而她却对这种传统的时尚色彩一无所知"的隐含内容加入进去的话，相信对考生解题会有很大帮助。问题是，作者和改写文章的命题人都没有这么做，因此第二句也就成了鸡肋信息，对解题基本无用。

由此可总结出，对文章背景了解越多的考生，其心理优势越明显，但是就算对背景了解不多的考生，也可以通过命题人给出的其他信息来解题。因此背景知识的多寡不会是左右考生正确率的重要因素。

接下来我们再以2013年考研英语(一)阅读理解Part A的Text 4为例，体会文中隐藏的两点背景知识。

首先,这篇文章所讨论事件的前因后果在开篇没有给出清晰的介绍,本文涉及2010年4月23日亚利桑那州的女州长布鲁尔颁布的亚利桑那州移民法案。简而言之,该法案的核心就是将中央权力地方化。法案一经出台就受到了奥巴马政府以及社会上一些相关利益部门的攻击,并逐渐演化为中央政府与地方政府之间的司法"对抗"。在文章的前两段中关于以上背景只进行了只言片语的描述,如"最高法院以5∶3的投票否决了移民法案中的三条核心内容""但是同时以8∶0的比例支持了其中一条非常有争议的条款——允许州政府的警察盘查身份可疑的移民者"。因此考生在存在文化差异且没有充分了解事情发生的背景的情况下,即便看懂了文字,也会在心里打一个大大的"问号"。

其次,文章中的特定名词也让许多考生费解,如文章中涉及了以下三方:Justice 不同于一般意义上的法官,这里指美国最高法院(Supreme Court)中的九名大法官,审议州及州以上级别的案件。Congress 指美国国会。考生需要对美国三权分立的司法体系和政党组成有一定了解。美国国会由人民直接选举产生,总统由选团制度间接选举产生,而最高法院的法官由总统提名、经国会参议院批准产生,总统的行政班子(即内阁)也由参议院批准产生。总统不向国会负责,国会无权解散政府,总统也无权解散国会。总统向宪法负责,统揽美国的行政大权,集国家元首、政府首脑、军队统帅及执政党领袖于一身,可以随时罢免行政班子成员,而不需要参议院通过;行政班子成员必须执行总统的决定,通过向国会提出咨文,指导立法,还可以否决国会通过的法案,停止国会的会期,但期满后国会将自行复会。国会是唯一的联邦级立法机关,由两院通过的法律必须由总统签字批准才能生效,但经总统否决的法案经两院再次通过后可自动生效。Administration 指在美国权力最大的中央政府,本文指以奥巴马为领导的美国政府及其内阁。

当考生对这些名词不了解时,心中的疑惑随即产生——这场纷争究竟是在哪几方之间发生的?Congress 在其中扮演了什么角色?Justice 又是谁?谁支持谁?谁抵制谁?接下来,我们就看看在没有这些背景知识的情况下,如何根据原文正确解题:

例 In *Arizona v. United States*, the majority overturned three of the four contested provisions of Arizona's controversial plan to have state and local police enforce federal immigration law. The Constitutional principles that Washington alone has the power to "establish a uniform Rule of Naturalization" and that federal laws precede state laws are noncontroversial. Arizona had attempted to fashion state policies that ran parallel to the existing federal ones. [2013年考研英语(一)Text 4]

Q: Three provisions of Arizona's plan were overturned because they _____.	问:亚利桑那州计划的三个条款之所以被推翻,是因为它们_____。
A. deprived the federal police of Constitutional powers	A. 剥夺了联邦警察的宪法权力
B. disturbed the power balance between different states	B. 扰乱了不同州政府间的权力平衡
C. overstepped the authority of federal immigration law	C. 僭越了联邦移民法的权限
D. contradicted both the federal and state policies	D. 与联邦和州政策冲突

【解题思路】C。题干中出现了比较明确的定位词,虽然考生可能无法准确理解 three provisions 是什么意思,但仍可定位至本段首句。考生首先要判断出题干中 they 所指的是亚利桑那州的计划,或直接看作该州政府,四个选项的第一个动词都偏贬义("剥夺""扰乱""僭越""冲突"),其宾语分别为"联邦警察""不同州政府""联邦移民法""联邦和州政策"。因此查找该段中有关亚利桑那州政府的负面信息即可。

从考点设置上来说,本段最容易出现考点的应该是第二句,因为它是一个带有并列关系的长难句,且描述了 Constitutional(宪法)给出的观点(principles),从语意上看也非常重要。考生也许不能理解本句中宾语从句前半句里 Washington(华盛顿,或者叫华府,代表奥巴马政府)及 Naturalization(移民,归化)两词的含义,但是由于并列前后所描述的内容应一致,根据之后的内容 federal laws precede state laws are noncontroversial(联邦法高于州一级的法案这点是毋庸置疑的)可推断出与其并列的前半句也应体现中央高于地方的观点。换句话说,州一级的法案被推翻的原因自然是因为州一级政府做了只有联邦政府(Washington)能做的事,也就是选项 C 的内容。

考生在处理本题时,需要明确本文中的 federal 实际等同于 Washington,是和 state 相对的一方,其实也可以从上一段最后一句 between the federal government and the states 中看出两者的对立性。总之,考生只要能够充分理解并有效利用文章给出的信息,还是可以在背景知识不足的情况下顺利选出正确答案的。

第二节 考研英语阅读理解命题规律

无论是哪一个等级的英语能力考试,都存在一些普遍的命题规律。一提到命题规律,考生的脑海里往往会浮现出诸如"转折之后是考点""每段首尾句很重要"这样的做题"心法"。这些流传已久的做题"心法"从应试的效果上看并没有错,因为通过对历年真题文章出题点的分析和统计,我们确实可以发现种种常见的命题规律。那么问题是,在大家都知道这些命题规律,且在考生努力程度相似、接受的培训强度相似、练习的模拟试题相似的条件下,为什么分数却呈现如此大的差异呢?实际上,原因无外乎以下几种:

- 英语基本功不同
- 对常见命题点的敏感程度不同
- 对命题规律的理解程度不同

不论是阅读理解的哪一道题,在命制过程中出题人所借助的原文内容往往都会存在某种特殊结构,而这类结构也可被看作一种"命题规律"。由于考研英语阅读理解 Part A 所给出的做题时间比其他英语能力水平考试阅读部分所给出的时间更为宽裕,所以考生完全有时间利用这一命题规律对文章中的特殊结构进行分析,而不只靠定位原文来解答题目。常被命题人利用的文章特殊结构包括以下几种:

一、人物观点的引用

人物观点在任何英语能力水平考试的阅读部分都是极易被考查到的内容。考研英语的阅读文章中所出现的人物观点一般分为两大类:第一类是作者观点,通常以 I 或者是 We 一类的词开头,这种情况比较少见,因为作者往往不太喜欢在文中直接表明自己的看法,这样会显得不够"以理服人";第二类是对他人观点(第三者观点)的引用,一般会呈现"人物 + 人物背景 + 人物观点"的行文结构,人物观点部分的内容有时用引号直接引出,有时用间接引语阐明。段落内类似这样的人物观点往往会和段落主旨呼应,也就是说,人物观点极可能就是段落要表达的观点或者批判的观点,被考查的概率很大。命题人可以直接针对此人观点设置题目或选项,考生也可以通过此观点排除错误选项。

例 Advertisers are horrified. Human nature being what it is, most people stick with default settings. Few switch DNT on now, but if tracking is off it will stay off. Bob Liodice, the chief executive of the Association of National Advertisers, says consumers will be worse off if the industry cannot collect information about their preferences. People will not get fewer ads, he says. "They'll get less meaningful, less targeted ads." [2013 年考研英语(一) Text 2]

Q: Bob Liodice holds that setting DNT as a default _____.	问:鲍勃·里奥迪斯认为将 DNT 设为系统预置_____。
A. may cut the number of junk ads	A. 可能减少垃圾广告的数量
B. fails to affect the ad industry	B. 没能影响广告业
C. will not benefit consumers	C. 将不会使消费者受益
D. goes against human nature	D. 与人性相背离

【解题思路】C。根据题干内容可看出本题考查鲍勃·里奥迪斯的观点,通过人名可直接定位至本段。根据题干中的 DNT 和选项内容可知,本题实际询问鲍勃·里奥迪斯对于将 DNT 设置为默认状态所产生的影响。原文中鲍勃说了两句话,一句是不带引号的间接引语,即 consumers will be worse off if the industry cannot collect information about their preferences(如果广告界无法收集有关消费者喜好的信息,消费者的境况会变得更加糟糕),另一句是带有引号的直接引语,即 They'll get less meaningful, less targeted ads(消费者会收到更多对他们没有什么意义和针对性的广告)。这两句话的核心观点是一致的,与选项 C 可直接对应。类似这种直接对文章中的人物观点进行考查的题目比较常见,考生需要认真理解原文定位句中人物所给出的观点,一般情况下,如果根据题干容易定位到原文,则正确选项对原文同义替换的难度就会加大。

二、观点加例证

"观点加例证"的结构也可理解为"总分"结构。一般结构严谨的议论文和说明文大多会在主体论述部分采用总分结构,即在开始处给出观点,之后采用道理论证或者举例论证的方法对观点加以说明或阐述。举例论证的部分其实很好分辨,只要段内出现了时间、数字或专有名词("人名 + 观点"的情况除外),基本上都是作者在进行举例论证。

例 Immigrants are quickly fitting into this common culture, which may not be altogether elevating but is hardly poisonous. Writing for the National Immigration Forum, Gregory Rodriguez reports that today's immigration is neither at unprecedented levels nor resistant to assimilation. In 1998 immigrants were 9.8 percent of population; in 1900, 13.6 percent. In the 10 years prior to 1990, 3.1 immigrants arrived for every 1,000 residents; in the 10 years prior to 1890, 9.2 for every 1,000. Now, consider three indices of assimilation—language, home ownership and intermarriage. [2006年考研英语 Text 1]

Q: The text suggests that immigrants now in the U.S. _____.	问：本文指出如今美国移民_____。

A. are resistant to homogenization　　　　A. 抗拒同化

B. exert a great influence on American culture　　B. 对美国文化有很大影响

C. are hardly a threat to the common culture　　C. 对共同的文化几乎不构成威胁

D. constitute the majority of the population　　D. 构成了人口的大多数

【解题思路】C。根据题干中的 immigrants now in the U.S. 可以直接定位至本段。本段的结构非常清晰，首句即整段的主题句，大意是移民正在快速融入美国的文化之中，也许这并不会为美国带来好处，但是也没坏处。第二句给出格雷戈里·罗德里格斯的观点，表示移民既没有达到史无前例的规模，也没有对同化产生抵触，对首句进行论证。作者从第三句开始大量引用数据，利用细节信息支持首句观点。选项 C 所表示的意思与本段主题句一致，因此是正确选项。通过观察可以看出，单纯通过题干中的关键词并不能直接定位到段落首句。如果不阅读本段首句，依靠对第二句至最后一句的理解，外加排除错误选项，也能选出正确答案，但主题句的功能在于可以更快、更准确地帮助考生确认或验证答案。

三、因果关系

　　因果关系是一个非常重要的逻辑关系，在日常生活和科学研究中，经常需要对问题产生的根源以及现象背后的本质进行挖掘和探讨，这就是一个知果索因的过程，因此考生也需要对文章中出现的因果关系保持敏感。考研英语阅读的题目和原文中存在的因果关系相对明显，存在以下两种情况：首先，当题干中带有明确的原因类词汇（如 why, because）时，回指原文的难度变小，无外乎要求考生在原文中寻找 for, as, reason 等词，尽管有时原文的因果逻辑不会那么明显，比如用 and, but 或者 make 表示因果关系，但相对而言，文中的因果逻辑关系还是容易直接找出来的；其次，目前考研英语阅读理解 Part A 一般不会针对原文中的因果关系直接设置题干，而会将因果关系的细节内容设置成选项，题干反而用 According to paragraph XX, which of the following statements is true 表示，无形中增大了定位难度。

　　例 The defining term of intelligence in humans still seems to be the IQ score, even though IQ tests are not given as often as they used to be. The test comes primarily in two forms: the Stanford-Binet Intelligence Scale and the Wechsler Intelligence Scales (both come in adult and children's version). Generally costing several hundred dollars, they are usually given only by psychologists, although variations of them populate bookstores and the World

Wide Web. Superhigh scores like vos Savant's are no longer possible, because scoring is now based on a statistical population distribution among age peers, rather than simply dividing the mental age by the chronological age and multiplying by 100. Other standardized tests, such as the Scholastic Assessment Test (SAT) and the Graduate Record Exam (GRE), capture the main aspects of IQ tests. [2007年考研英语 Text 2]

Q: People nowadays can no longer achieve IQ scores as high as vos Savant's because _____.	问:如今人们不再能获得与沃斯·莎凡特一样高的 IQ 分数,是因为 _____。
A. the scores are obtained through different computational procedures	A. 分数是通过不同计算方法获得的
B. creativity rather than analytical skills is emphasized now	B. 现在强调的是创造性而非分析技巧
C. vos Savant's case is an extreme one that will not repeat	C. 沃斯·莎凡特的情况是一个不会重演的极端事例
D. the defining characteristic of IQ tests has changed	D. IQ 测试的定义性特征已经发生改变

【解题思路】A。根据题干中的 because 可明显看出本题考查因果关系。通过题干中的 no longer achieve IQ scores as high as vos Savant's 可以很快定位至本段第四句,该句的后半部分以 because 开头,是个很明显的原因状语从句(because scoring is now based on a statistical population distribution among age peers, rather than simply dividing the mental age by the chronological age and multiplying by 100),该句的难点在于 rather than 要肯定的内容实际是之前的部分,即原文中的 scoring is now based on a statistical population distribution among age peers(现在评分是以同龄群体的统计人口分布为基础的),说明目前的记分方式出现了变化,因此这是题干所考查的原因所在。本题的另一个难点在于正确选项对原文做了比较复杂的同义替换,干扰项中也存在与原文类似的成分,如选项 B 中的 rather than。如果考生将定位句进行简化,可得出 scoring is now based on A rather than B 的结构,表示 IQ 测试的评分现在基于 A 而非 B,言下之意就是 IQ 测试的评分方式出现了变化,因此可直接得到选项 A 这一正确答案。

四、转折关系

毋庸置疑的是,无论是在阅读、完形填空还是听力的题目中,转折关系都是很关键的语意逻辑点。提到转折关系,绝大多数考生首先想到的就是 but, yet, however 这三个连词,但是考生还需要从以下几个方面对转折关系有新的认识:
①转折关系偶尔还可以表示因果关系,这在考研英语真题中比较少见;
②转折关系并非一定是考点,需要结合题干进行判断;
③转折关系的出现并不一定意味着作者推翻了之前的观点,但是转折之后往往会出现重要的解释性文字。

例 The tourist streams are not entirely separate. The sightseers who come by bus—

and often take in Warwick Castle and Blenheim Palace on the side—don't usually see the plays, and some of them are even surprised to find a theatre in Stratford. However, the playgoers do manage a little sight-seeing along with their playgoing. It is the playgoers, the RSC contends, who bring in much of the town's revenue because they spend the night (some of them four or five nights) pouring cash into the hotels and restaurants. The sightseers can take in everything and get out of town by nightfall. [2006年考研英语 Text 2]

Q: It can be inferred from paragraph 3 that _____.	问：从第三段中可知_____。
A. the sightseers cannot visit the Castle and the Palace separately	A. 观光游客不能分别游览城堡和皇宫
B. the playgoers spend more money than the sightseers	B. 看戏的游客比观光的游客花费得更多
C. the sightseers do more shopping than the playgoers	C. 观光游客比看戏的游客买的东西更多
D. the playgoers go to no other places in town than the theater	D. 看戏的游客只去小镇的剧场

【解题思路】B。根据题干中的 inferred 可看出本题是个推论题，考生需要在对本段进行整体理解的基础上选出答案。本段第三句出现转折，因此是重要内容，从选项中也可看出本题考查转折前后的内容。转折前一句的大意是观光客一般不去剧院消费，第三句转折指出而去剧院的游客一般还会观光消费一下。结合两句的意思可看出，选项 B 的推断正确。同样，考生还可以注意转折句之后的第四句是个带有原因状语从句的长难句，指出看戏游客的消费项目是吃饭和住宿，对转折句进行了补充和解释，和本段最后一句(而观光客在天黑前就会结束游览并离开)形成了对比。

五、比较和对比关系

1. 句子之间或段落之间的并列关系

例　Two paradoxes exist throughout this credibility process. First, scientific work tends to focus on some aspect of prevailing knowledge that is viewed as incomplete or incorrect. Little reward accompanies duplication and confirmation of what is already known and believed. The goal is *new-search*, not *re-search*. Not surprisingly, newly published discovery claims and credible discoveries that appear to be important and convincing will always be open to challenge and potential modification or refutation by future researchers. Second, novelty itself frequently provokes disbelief. Nobel Laureate and physiologist Albert Szent-Gyorgyi once described discovery as "seeing what everybody has seen and thinking what nobody has thought." But thinking what nobody else has thought and telling others what they have missed may not change their views. Sometimes years are required for truly novel discovery claims to be accepted and appreciated. [2012年考研英语(一)Text 3]

Q: Albert Szent-Gyorgyi would most likely agree that _____.	问:艾尔伯特·圣乔其最有可能同意以下哪项?
A. scientific claims will survive challenges B. discoveries today inspire future research C. efforts to make discoveries are justified D. scientific work calls for a critical mind	A. 科学声明将经受住挑战 B. 目前的发现能启发未来的研究 C. 为发现所做的努力被证明是值得的 D. 科学研究需要批判性思维

【解题思路】D。本段首句明确提示段落中会出现两个比较大的并列关系,因此命题人针对其中一个内容设置选项的概率极大。题干中的人名 Albert Szent-Gyorgyi 明确提示定位点在并列的第二个部分中,这部分出现的人物观点也就是正确选项的内容。原文中此人明确指出 seeing what everybody has seen and thinking what nobody has thought(见世人所见,思无人所思)的观点,言下之意就是要用合理的、反思性的眼光看待同一个问题,这种眼光所体现的也就是"批判性思维"的特点,与选项 D 中的 critical mind 相符。

2. 句子之间或段落之间的递进关系

例 The researchers studied the behaviour of female brown capuchin monkeys. They look cute. They are good-natured, co-operative creatures, and they share their food readily. Above all, like their female human counterparts, they tend to pay much closer attention to the value of "goods and services" than males. [2005 年考研英语 Text 1]

Q: Female capuchin monkeys were chosen for the research most probably because they are _____.	问:研究选用雌性卷尾猴最可能是因为其_____。
A. more inclined to weigh what they get B. attentive to researchers' instructions C. nice in both appearance and temperament D. more generous than their male companions	A. 更倾向于衡量它们所得之物 B. 留意研究人员的指导 C. 无论是外表和性格都很好 D. 与雄性相比更大方

【解题思路】A。根据题干可知本题考查原因。本段第四句开头的 above all(尤其是,最重要的是)往往用于引出递进或强调的内容,因此所在句被考查的概率极高,原文大意是它们往往比雄性猴子更加注意商品和服务的价值,与选项 A 的内容属于同义替换,因此该项正确。

3. 句子之间或段落之间的正反对比关系

例 Up until a few decades ago, our visions of the future were largely—though by no means uniformly—glowingly positive. Science and technology would cure all the ills of humanity, leading to lives of fulfillment and opportunity for all.

Now utopia has grown unfashionable, as we have gained a deeper appreciation of the range of threats facing us, from asteroid strike to epidemic flu and to climate change. You might even be tempted to assume that humanity has little future to look forward to. [2013 年考研英语(一)Text 3]

Q: Our vision of the future used to be inspired by _____.	问：我们对未来的展望过去常被_____所启发。
A. our desire for lives of fulfillment B. our faith in science and technology C. our awareness of potential risks D. our belief in equal opportunity	A. 我们对圆满人生的渴望 B. 我们对科技的信心 C. 我们对潜在风险的意识 D. 我们对平等机会的信仰

【解题思路】B。仔细阅读题干后可发现，本题实际考查过去我们对未来的看法一般受什么因素的影响。文章前两段分别从过去和现在两个角度阐述了我们对未来的看法。首段首句为该段的主题句，主干是 our visions of the future were positive（我们对未来的展望是积极的）。第二段首句也是该段的主题句，主干是 Now utopia has grown unfashionable（如今乌托邦式的展望已经过时了），言外之意就是现在人们不看好未来了。由于题干询问过去的情况，因此应该在第一段中寻找，第一段第二句是对首句观点的支撑，说明之所以认为未来光明的原因在于我们有强大的科学技术，与选项 B 中的 faith in science and technology 对应，因此该项正确。命题人根据原文前两段的对比和首段"主题句＋支撑句"的结构综合设计出了本题，考查了考生的综合阅读能力。

六、特殊符号

考研英语阅读理解 Part A 原文中出现的某些标点符号往往会成为考查的对象，常见的特殊标点符号有冒号、破折号以及括号等，其常见用法及考点设置思路如下：

①冒号之后的内容一般用于解释前文，则考点往往出现在冒号之后；

②破折号的情况分为两种：一种是双破折号中间的插入语，这种情况下考查的重点往往不是插入语，而是破折号两边的内容；另一种是单破折号引出的内容，这种破折号的功能和冒号类似，用于对前文进行解释说明，考查的重点往往在破折号之后；

③括号内的内容往往用于解释前文，是容易出现因果关系考点的部分。

例　There's no doubt that our peer groups exert enormous influence on our behavior. An emerging body of research shows that positive health habits—as well as negative ones—spread through networks of friends via social communication. This is a subtle form of peer pressure: we unconsciously imitate the behavior we see every day. [2012 年考研英语（一）Text 1]

Q: Paragraph 5 shows that our imitation of behaviors _____.	问：第五段表明我们对行为的模仿_____。
A. is harmful to our networks of friends B. will mislead behavioral studies C. occurs without our realizing it D. can produce negative health habits	A. 对我们的朋友网有害 B. 将误导行为学研究 C. 在我们没有意识到的情况下发生 D. 能产生不良的健康习惯

【解题思路】C。根据题干要求定位至本段，该段共有三句话。首句是观点句，指出同龄群体对我们的行为会产生影响；第二句是带有双破折号的长句，用于支撑首句观点，表

示研究表明正面的和负面的健康习惯都可通过社交网络在朋友之间传播；第三句对第二句进行总结，冒号后的解释性内容表示人们会无意识地模仿每天看到的行为，选项 C 是对该句的同义替换，因此是正确答案。

七、特殊问句

考研英语阅读理解 Part A 文章中的问句一般分为三类：疑问句、反问句和设问句。设问句采用自问自答的形式，在考研英语阅读理解的文章中出现的次数相对较多，设问之后的回答往往给出观点，因此常作为重要考点。

例 Also unclear is why Microsoft has gone it alone. After all, it has an ad business too, which it says will comply with DNT requests, though it is still working out how. If it is trying to upset Google, which relies almost wholly on advertising, it has chosen an indirect method: There is no guarantee that DNT by default will become the norm. DNT does not seem an obviously huge selling point for Windows 8—though the firm has compared some of its other products favourably with Google's on that count before. Brendon Lynch, Microsoft's chief privacy officer, blogged: "We believe consumers should have more control." Could it really be that simple? [2013 年考研英语（一）Text 2]

Q：The author's attitude towards what Brendon Lynch said in his blog is one of _____.	问：对布伦登·林奇在其博客里所说的话，作者持_____的态度。
A. indulgence	A. 宽容
B. understanding	B. 理解
C. appreciation	C. 欣赏
D. skepticism	D. 怀疑

【解题思路】D。本题考查作者观点，询问作者对布伦登·林奇观点的看法。全文最后一句很明显是一个反问句，该句用"真的（really）有那么简单吗"的疑问语气表达与字面意义相反的意思，即该反问句的言下之意是作者并不相信或认可布伦登·林奇的观点。所以选项 D 是正确答案。

第三节 考研英语阅读理解选项特征

一、错误选项的设置规律

考研英语阅读理解题目中的错误选项往往也基于原文，但并不忠实于原文。常见错误选项的设置规律可总结为以下四种：

① 无中生有；
② 答非所问；
③ 部分杜撰；
④ 过度推断。

二、正确选项的设置规律

考研英语阅读理解题目中正确选项的设置也存在一定的规律，常见正确选项的设置规律可总结为以下四种。

1. 表述不绝对的选项正确的概率大

这一规律分为以下两种情况：

① 在考查观点态度的题目中，正确选项一般客观且感情不过于强烈（如 supportive 要比 enthusiasm 更可能成为正确项）；

② 其他题型中，正确选项一般会提到 may，some，can，possible 等表示"比较"或"相对"的词汇；出现 must，all，only 等词汇的选项往往为干扰项。

例 It is not yet clear how advertisers will respond. Getting a DNT signal does not oblige anyone to stop tracking, although some companies have promised to do so. Unable to tell whether someone really objects to behavioral ads or whether they are sticking with Microsoft's default, some may ignore a DNT signal and press on anyway. [2013 年考研英语（一）Text 2]

Q: Which of the following is true according to paragraph 6?	问：根据第六段内容，以下哪项正确？
A. Advertisers are willing to implement DNT. B. DNT may not serve its intended purpose. C. DNT is losing its popularity among consumers. D. Advertisers are obliged to offer behavioral ads.	A. 广告商愿意执行 DNT 要求。 B. DNT 也许达不到它预期的目的。 C. DNT 正越来越不受消费者的欢迎。 D. 广告商有义务提供行为广告。

【解题思路】B。 该段首句的大意是还不确定广告商会如何回应，第二句 although 引导的让步状语从句忽略不看，主句的大意是 DNT 信号无法要求广告商停止追踪用户，后句对其进行解释说明。第三句是一个长难句，其核心大意是由于广告商无法确定用户是因为反感行为广告而自己开启 DNT 还是浏览器默认开启 DNT，一些广告商会忽略 DNT 信号而继续追踪用户，综上可知，DNT 设置并没有起到应有的作用，用户还是会受到广告商的追踪。因此选项 B 与对原文的推断相符，此外，选项 B 中带有 may，拥有潜在正确项的特点。

2. 外形相似的两个选项中存在正确选项的概率大

"外形相似"是指两个选项中存在相同的词或短语，或从不同角度分析相同的问题。特别是当两个选项一开始就出现重复时，其中隐藏正确选项的可能性较大。

例 Stratford-on-Avon, as we all know, has only one industry—William Shakespeare—but there are two distinctly separate and increasingly hostile branches. There is the Royal Shakespeare Company (RSC), which presents superb productions of the plays at the Shakespeare Memorial Theatre on the Avon. And there are the townsfolk who largely live off the tourists who come, not to see the plays, but to look at Anne Hathaway's Cottage, Shakespeare's birthplace and the other sights.

The worthy residents of Stratford doubt that the theatre adds a penny to their revenue. They frankly dislike the RSC's actors, them with their long hair and beards and sandals and noisiness. It's all deliciously ironic when you consider that Shakespeare, who earns their living, was himself an actor (with a beard) and did his share of noise-making. [2006年考研英语 Text 2]

Q: From the first two paragraphs, we learn that _____.	问：从前两段中可知_____。
A. the townsfolk deny the RSC's contribution to the town's revenue	A. 镇上的人否认 RSC 公司对小镇经济有贡献
B. the actors of the RSC imitate Shakespeare on and off stage	B. RSC 公司的演员在台上和台下都模仿莎士比亚
C. the two branches of the RSC are not on good terms	C. RSC 公司的两个分支关系不好
D. the townsfolk earn little from tourism	D. 镇上的人从旅游业中赚取的收益很少

【解题思路】A。此题所对应的原文内容较多，涉及两段。首段主要介绍了小镇上有关莎士比亚的两个产业，接着第二段第一句指出小镇居民怀疑 RSC 公司没有给小镇增加收入 (doubt that the theatre adds a penny to their revenue)，选项 A 是对第二段第一句的同义替换。从考点设置来看，第二段首句给出了明确的观点并含有隐性的否定逻辑 (doubt)，本身成为设题点的可能性就非常大。选项 A 和选项 D 都以核心词 the townsfolk 开头，属于相似选项，根据以上原则，其中出现正确答案的可能性较大。

3. 内容相反的两个选项中存在正确选项的概率大

例 Two of the three objecting Justices—Samuel Alito and Clarence Thomas—agreed with this Constitutional logic but disagreed about which Arizona rules conflicted with the federal statute. The only major objection came from Justice Antonin Scalia, who offered an even more robust defense of state privileges going back to the Alien and Sedition Acts. [2013年考研英语(一) Text 4]

Q: It can be inferred from paragraph 5 that the Alien and Sedition Acts _____.	问：从第五段中可推断出《关于处置外侨和煽动叛乱的法令》_____。
A. violated the Constitution	A. 违背了宪法要求
B. undermined the states' interests	B. 损害了州的利益
C. supported the federal statue	C. 支持了联邦法律
D. stood in favor of the states	D. 支持了州的主张

【解题思路】D。根据题干关键词 Alien and Sedition Acts 可定位至以上段落的第二句。考生应该并不十分了解 Alien and Sedition Acts，因此需要利用本段其他信息猜测其内容。going back to the Alien and Sedition Acts 是现在分词短语作后置定语，对 state privileges（州特权）进行说明，由此推断这部分内容表示早在 the Alien and Sedition Acts 的法案中就已经确定了州政府拥有的特权，因此只有选项 D 正确。选项 A 和选项 B 均体现负面意义（violated, undermined），选项 C 和选项 D 体现正面意义（supported, stood in favor of），原文体现正面的语意，因此选项 C 和选项 D 中有一项是正确的。

4. 正确选项的核心逻辑与所对应的原文内容保持高度一致

例 More apparent reasonableness followed. There will now be a seven-day wait for the jobseeker's allowance. "Those first few days should be spent looking for work, not looking to sign on," he claimed. "We're doing these things because we know they help people stay off benefits and help those on benefits get into work faster." Help? Really? On first hearing, this was the socially concerned chancellor, trying to change lives for the better, complete with "reforms" to an obviously indulgent system that demands too little effort from the newly unemployed to find work, and subsidizes laziness. What motivated him, we were to understand, was his zeal for "fundamental fairness"—protecting the taxpayer, controlling spending and ensuring that only the most deserving claimants received their benefits. [2014 年考研英语（一）Text 1]

Q: What prompted the chancellor to develop his scheme?	问：促使这位财政大臣制定这项计划的根源是什么？
A. A desire to secure a better life for all.	A. 为全民谋求更好生活的愿望。
B. An eagerness to protect the unemployed.	B. 保护失业者的急切心理。
C. An urge to be generous to the claimants.	C. 对申请人慷慨的冲动。
D. A passion to ensure fairness for taxpayers.	D. 确保对纳税人公平的热情。

【解题思路】D。本题考查的是财政大臣制定这一计划的原因，因此可定位至本段最后一句中的 what motivated him was his zeal for "fundamental fairness"。破折号后的内容是对引号中"基本公平"的解释。选项 D 中的 ensure fairness for taxpayers 是对文中 fundamental fairness 和 protecting the taxpayer 的同义替换。passion 是文中 zeal 的同义词，因此选项 D 为正确答案，该项中出现的 fairness 和 taxpayers 与原文一样。按照正确选项的核心逻辑与所对应的原文内容保持高度一致的原则，也要优先考虑选项 D 是否为正确答案。

第三章 题源报刊精选文章试题精讲

CHAPTER THREE

第一节 经济贸易类

Text 1

Like banks, insurers need a cushion of capital to ensure that they can meet customers' claims in the event of unexpectedly big payouts or poor investment performance. As at banks, these cushions have at times proved woefully thin. In theory, all that changes on January 1st—in the European Union, at least—when a new set of regulations known as Solvency 2 comes into force. After more than ten years of negotiation, all European insurers will have to follow uniform rules on capital that are designed to make the firms more robust and allow investors and customers to assess their strength much more easily.

Not everyone is thrilled at this prospect. Mention "upcoming regulatory changes" to an insurance executive and a tirade inevitably follows about ambiguities and inconsistencies within the new rules, discrepancies in enforcement and the mountains of paperwork involved. Some firms have had to bolster capital in anticipation: Delta Lloyd, a Dutch insurer, announced in November that it would raise 1 billion ($1.1 billion). The rules favor diversified firms, so those that offer just one form of insurance are under pressure to merge. That impetus contributed to several deals involving specialist insurers in 2015, including Fairfax's purchase of Brit in February and XL's takeover of Catlin in May. Anxious bosses have trimmed the industry's own debts to relatively low levels.

Some of the disgruntlement is legitimate. Regulators themselves seem to agree that the current risk weightings unduly penalize investments in long-term debt tied to infrastructure; some government bonds, in contrast, may be considered too safe. European firms with big international operations say it is not clear to what extent Solvency 2 applies to their non-European subsidiaries. Transitional rules designed to make life easier for German life insurers in particular will shield them from some elements of the new rules for up to 16 years.

Then there is the question of how many insurers will be allowed to substitute internal models for the standardised formulae used to calculate capital requirements. Some big firms, including 19 in Britain, have persuaded their national regulator that their own calculations are at least as good as the prescribed ones. More firms will apply in 2016, in the hope of trimming the amount of capital required and thus increasing profits.

To some extent that undermines the logic of a uniform system, by making insurers using internal models and those using the standard one hard to compare, says Jim Bichard of PwC, an accounting firm: "The solvency ratios will be all over the place and there's a high risk of misinterpretation." It also raises the concern that some of the national regulators charged with applying the new rules will be more lenient than others. The British and Dutch ones, for example, are thought to be more exacting than their Italian counterpart.

Yet whatever Solvency 2's failings, the new regime will still provide a continent wide benchmark for the first time. "It will confirm who is strong and who is weak," says David Prowse of Fitch, a rating agency. The strong will presumably start to put their excess capital to work, making acquisitions or returning cash to shareholders. The weak, meanwhile, will have to boost their capital, trim their liabilities by offering stingier policies, sell capital-intensive parts of the business or fall into the arms of one of their brawnier counterparts.

(*The Economist*, 2015.12)

1. The enforcement of Solvency 2 will _____.
   A. strengthen investors and customers' abilities
   B. avoid the unexpected big payouts for banks
   C. ensure the rights for clients and investors
   D. make the bank's investment performance robust

2. The example of Fairfax's purchase of Brit is mentioned to show that _____.
   A. insurance companies are thrilled at the rules
   B. diversified business is essential for the survival of insurance company
   C. bosses are anxious for a relatively low debt level
   D. new rules are full of ambiguities and inconsistencies

3. According to paragraph 3, what contributes to the legitimacy of the disgruntlement?
   A. An obvious unfairness in the enforcement of Solvency 2.
   B. The benefit designed exclusively for government bonds.
   C. The risk faced by long-term debt tied to infrastructure.
   D. The easy accessibility offered by transitional rules.

4. It can be learned from paragraph 4 and 5 that _____.
   A. big firms are immune to the standardised calculation
   B. the internal model of calculation is as good as the standardised one
   C. leniency is a priority element in carrying out the rules
   D. the system is sapped for its inconsistency and inequality

5. According to the author, Solvency 2 will act as _____.
   A. a benchmark to inspire the industry all over the continent
   B. a gauge in judging the company's capacity
   C. an agency to supervise the acquisitions
   D. a policy to enhance the liability of the weak firms

语篇分析与试题精解

Para. 1 ①Like banks, insurers need a cushion of capital to ensure that they can meet customers' claims in the event of unexpectedly big payouts or poor investment performance. ②As at banks, these cushions have at times proved woefully thin. ③In theory, all that changes on January 1st—in the European Union, at least—when a new set of regulations known as Solvency 2 comes into force. ④After more than ten years of negotiation, all European insurers will have to follow uniform rules on capital that are designed to make the firms more robust and allow investors and customers to assess their strength much more easily.

参考译文 ①和银行一样，保险公司需要资本缓冲，从而在面临意外巨额理赔或投资不利的情况下，仍能满足客户的索赔需求。②然而，与银行类似，这种资本缓冲不足的情况时有发生。③理论上，从1月1日起，《欧盟偿付能力Ⅱ》(Solvency 2) 新规的生效至少会在欧盟内部改变这一局面。④经过历时十多年的谈判，欧洲所有的保险公司都必须遵循统一的资本规定，这些规定用于提升保险公司的稳健性，并使投资者和客户更容易地评估这些公司的实力。

原文剖析 本段前两句分别陈述理论情况和现实问题，即保险公司同银行一样需要资本缓冲，但这种资本缓冲不足的情况时常发生。后两句针对现实问题引出解决方案，指出《欧盟偿付能力Ⅱ》新规的设计初衷和作用。

设题点睛 本段采用了"提出问题 + 解决问题"的行文结构，第四句为长难句且含有观点性内容，为重点句，可用来设置考点。

生词解析

cushion n. 起缓冲作用的事物
in the event of 如果，万一……发生
at times 有时，偶尔，不时
solvency n. 偿付能力
robust adj. 强健的；健康的
claim n. （尤指向公司、政府等）索赔
payout n. （通常指大笔的）付款
woefully adv. 不幸地；使人痛苦地
come into force （政府法令、法律、协议等）开始生效

长难句解析

After more than ten years of negotiation, all European insurers will have to follow uniform
　　　　　　时间状语　　　　　　　　　　　主语　　　　　　　谓语　　　　　宾语
rules on capital that are designed to make the firms more robust and allow investors and
　　　后置定语　　　　　　　　　　定语从句
customers to assess their strength much more easily.

本句是主从复合句。本句主干为 all European insurers will have to follow uniform rules…，宾语后的 on 介词短语作后置定语，说明 rules 的内容，其后 that 引导的定语从句的先行词是 uniform rules，该定语从句中包含两个并列的谓宾成分，第一个不定式作目的状语，第二个不定式作宾语补足语。

1 The enforcement of Solvency 2 will _____.　　《欧盟偿付能力Ⅱ》的实施将_____。

A. strengthen investors and customers' abilities　　A. 加强投资者和客户的能力

B. avoid the unexpected big payouts for banks
C. ensure the rights for clients and investors
D. make the bank's investment performance robust

B. 为银行避免意外的大额支付
C. 确保客户和投资者的权利
D. 使银行的投资表现强健

【解题思路】C。推理引申题。根据题干关键词(Solvency 2)定位到文章第一段的第三句和第四句。本题实际考查 Solvency 2 的作用。第四句中的定语从句部分对 Solvency 2 的规定进行补充说明,指出"这些规定用于提升保险公司的稳健性,并使投资者和客户更容易地评估这些公司的实力",be designed to 这一短语表示"目的是;被设计用于做",引出某事物存在的作用或目的,其中谈到的使投资者和客户更容易地评估公司实力(allow investors and customers to assess their strength much more easily)对应选项 C 的内容,该项提到的"权利"(rights)中包括对公司实力的评估,因此该项正确。

【排他分析】首段最后一句的意思是使投资者和客户更容易地评估前面所提到的保险公司的实力,选项 A 中 strengthen 的宾语是原文的主语,因此该项与原文不符,可以排除。本段前两句描述的是客观事实,指出保险业在面对巨额理赔时需要资本缓冲,但《欧盟偿付能力Ⅱ》的实施并非可以避免这一客观事实,只是减轻所造成的影响,因此排除选项 B。选项 D 中的 robust 对应本段最后一句,该部分提到"这些规定用于提升保险公司的稳健性"(make the firms more robust),并未提到该项中的"银行的投资表现",因此排除。

Para. 2 ①Not everyone is thrilled at this prospect. ②Mention "upcoming regulatory changes" to an insurance executive and a tirade inevitably follows about ambiguities and inconsistencies within the new rules, discrepancies in enforcement and the mountains of paperwork involved. ③Some firms have had to bolster capital in anticipation: Delta Lloyd, a Dutch insurer, announced in November that it would raise 1 billion ($1.1 billion). ④The rules favor diversified firms, so those that offer just one form of insurance are under pressure to merge. ⑤That impetus contributed to several deals involving specialist insurers in 2015, including Fairfax's purchase of Brit in February and XL's takeover of Catlin in May. ⑥Anxious bosses have trimmed the industry's own debts to relatively low levels.

参考译文 ①并非所有人都看好这一新规。②如果跟保险公司的高管提及此事,对方往往会做一番激烈的长篇演说,对新规中模棱两可和前后矛盾的地方进行抨击,诟病该法规在执行过程中的差异性以及与此相关的大量文书工作。③一些公司不得不预先增资:荷兰保险公司德尔塔·劳埃德集团十一月宣布将募资 10 亿欧元(11 亿美元)。④新规对多样化经营的公司有所倾斜,因此那些保险品种较为单一的公司则面临兼并的压力。⑤在这种刺激下,多家专业保险公司在 2015 年进行了兼并重组,其中包括费尔法克斯金融公司二月对英国生命保险公司的收购,以及信利集团公司五月接手凯林集团。⑥压力之下,保险公司的老总们已将企业的负债降到了相对较低的水平。

原文剖析 本段首句为总起句和观点句。第二句通过对情景进行描述体现保险公司的高管对新规的抨击态度,暗示新规存在问题,指出部分保险公司并不愿意执行。第三句进行举例论证,指出针对以上问题,一些公司采取预先增资的应对方案。第四句转而指出新规因为偏好多样化经营的公司,使专业性公司面临兼并重组的风险增加,第五句再次进行举例论证。最后一句指出保险行业应对新规的另一个做法(降低企业负债率)。

设题点睛 本段连续出现两次"观点+例证"的总分结构,其中的观点性内容较为重要,可用来设置正确选项。

生词解析

thrill *vt.* 使……感到兴奋或激动　　　　tirade *n.* (批评或指责性的)长篇激烈演说
discrepancy *n.* 不符;矛盾;相差　　　　in anticipation 预先
impetus *n.* 刺激;促进;推动力　　　　trim *vt.* 修剪;剪掉

长难句解析

Mention "upcoming regulatory changes" to an insurance executive and a tirade inevitably
　谓语1　　　　　宾语　　　　　　　　状语　　　　　　　　主语

follows about ambiguities and inconsistencies within the new rules, discrepancies in enforcement
谓语2　　　　　　　　　　　后置定语

and the mountains of paperwork involved.

本句是并列复合句。本句的主干为 mention "upcoming regulatory changes" and a tirade follows,由 and 连接的两个句子组成,由于第一个分句是祈使句,因此本句中的连词 and 可表示两个并列的命令或请求,也可以表示顺承,等同于 then,相当于两个相继出现的动作。about 引出的较长的介宾短语作后置定语,实际修饰的是 tirade,体现其内容。

2 The example of Fairfax's purchase of Brit　　以费尔法克斯金融公司收购英国生命
　　is mentioned to show that _____.　　　　保险公司为例是为了说明 _____。

A. insurance companies are thrilled at the　　A. 保险公司对新规感到兴奋
　　rules
B. diversified business is essential for the　　B. 多样化业务对于保险公司的生
　　survival of insurance company　　　　　　存而言至关重要
C. bosses are anxious for a relatively low　　C. 老板们急于达到较低的负债水平
　　debt level
D. new rules are full of ambiguities and　　D. 新规中充满模棱两可和前后矛
　　inconsistencies　　　　　　　　　　　　盾之处

【解题思路】**B**。推理引申题。根据题干关键词(Fairfax's purchase of Brit)定位到第二段第五句。本句的主干部分指出"在这种刺激下,多家专业保险公司在 2015 年进行了兼并重组",之后用题干所述的例子进行证明。但在各项中并没有找到有关"兼并重组"的内容,因此需要在前文中寻找答案。本句所说的"刺激"(impetus)回应第四句"因此那些保险品种较为单一的公司则面临兼并的压力"中的"压力"一词,因此第五句所谈到的兼并根源为第四句中的"压力",即第四句谈到的"新规对多样化经营的公司有所倾斜",可理解为新规对多样化业务的保险公司要求不那么苛刻,因此多样化经营对保险公司而言很重要,否则就会面临重组的风险,选项 B 的推断正确。

【排他分析】选项 A 中的 thrilled 对应本段首句，原句为否定句，因此与该项的意思直接相反，可排除。选项 C 对应本段最后一句，原文指出焦虑的保险公司（Anxious bosses）为应对兼并压力采取降低企业负债率的方法，纯属"保命"的无奈之举，而该项中 be anxious for 这一短语所表达的意思是急切想要达成某个目标，且并非题干所问例子要说明的内容，因此排除。选项 D 中的 ambiguities and inconsistencies 对应本段第二句，虽然原文确实提到部分保险公司认为新规存在"模棱两可和前后矛盾的地方"，但"充满"（full of）之意无从看出，且原句并非是题干所问的兼并事例想要表明的观点，因此排除。

Para. 3 ① Some of the disgruntlement is legitimate. ②Regulators themselves seem to agree that the current risk weightings unduly penalize investments in long-term debt tied to infrastructure; some government bonds, in contrast, may be considered too safe. ③European firms with big international operations say it is not clear to what extent Solvency 2 applies to their non-European subsidiaries. ④Transitional rules designed to make life easier for German life insurers in particular will shield them from some elements of the new rules for up to 16 years.

参考译文 ①有一些不满情绪是合乎情理的。②监管者们自己似乎也认同，当前的风险权重对与基础设施有关的长期债务投资规定得有点过严；相比之下，一些政府债券或许被认为过于安全了。③旗下有较大跨国业务的欧洲公司表示，尚不清楚《欧盟偿付能力Ⅱ》对于其欧洲之外子公司的适用程度。④过渡期法则尤其会让德国的人寿保险企业好过些，因为这些企业可在未来长达16年的时间里，免受部分新法规的约束。

原文剖析 本段首句为观点句，对上一段部分保险公司的怨言表示理解，从第二句开始对这种不满的合理性进行了解释，包括相对于政府债务而言，新规对于长期债务投资的风控太过严格，对欧盟企业位于欧洲外部的子公司的适用性并不明确，某些保险公司可因过渡期法则免于一定约束等内容。首句与后三句构成了总分关系。

设题点睛 本段为明确的总分结构，但是由于首句观点较为抽象，并无实质性信息，因此之后的解释从逻辑上看是更为重要的考点内容。

生词解析

disgruntlement *n.* 不满（disgruntle 的变形）　　legitimate *adj.* 合理的；正当的；合法的
risk weighting 风险权重；风险权数　　unduly *adv.* 过度地；不适当地
transitional *adj.* 过渡期的；变迁的　　shield from 庇护使免遭

长难句解析

Regulators themselves seem to agree that the current risk weightings unduly penalize investments
　　主语1　　　　复合谓语1　　　　　　宾语从句
in long-term debt tied to infrastructure; some government bonds, in contrast, may be
　　　　　　　　　　　　　　　　　　　主语2　　　　　　　　复合谓语2
considered too safe.
　　补语

本句为并列复合句。本句主干为 Regulators seem to agree that...; some government bonds may be considered…，全句由分号前后的两个完整的句子构成，前一句为主谓宾结构，宾语为一个从句，该从句中的 in long-term debt 和 tied to infrastructure 作后置定语分别修饰 investments 和 long-term debt。第二句中的形容词 safe 作主语 some government bonds 的补语。

3 According to paragraph 3, what contributes to the legitimacy of the disgruntlement?

A. An obvious unfairness in the enforcement of Solvency 2.
B. The benefit designed exclusively for government bonds.
C. The risk faced by long-term debt tied to infrastructure.
D. The easy accessibility offered by transitional rules.

从第三段可知，以下哪项使得这种不满情绪合理？

A.《欧盟偿付能力Ⅱ》的实施明显存在不公平的地方。
B. 专为政府债券设计的福利。
C. 与基础设施有关的长期债务所面临的风险。
D. 过渡期法则提供的便利。

【解题思路】A。推理引申题。根据题干要求定位到文章第三段首句，本题实际考查原因。本段首句是观点句，后两句做出具体解释。第二句利用对比结构指出对政府债券的安全性评估太高，而对基础设施长期债务投资的风控太严格（current risk weightings unduly penalize investments in long-term debt tied to infrastructure）。第三句指出新规不一定能监管到欧洲之外的子公司（not clear to what extent Solvency 2 applies to their non-European subsidiaries），并且德国的人寿保险公司可以在接下来的 16 年里因过渡期法则可躲避一些新规条款的限制（shield them from some elements of the new rules）。以上三点可证明该新规的实施本身存在不公平性，与选项 A 的内容一致。

【排他分析】选项 B 和选项 C 的内容对应本段第二句，该句用对比的方式指出新规对政府债券的安全性评价过高，与后两句一起表达新规存在的不公平性，回应首句观点，而不是单纯地表示新规低估基础设施的长期投资，而看重政府债券的安全性，因此排除这两项。选项 D 中的 transitional rules 对应本段最后一句，但原文并没有指出其 easy accessibility（易获得性），因此可以直接排除。

Para. 4 ①Then there is the question of how many insurers will be allowed to substitute internal models for the standardised formulae used to calculate capital requirements. ②Some big firms, including 19 in Britain, have persuaded their national regulator that their own calculations are at least as good as the prescribed ones. ③More firms will apply in 2016, in the hope of trimming the amount of capital required and thus increasing profits.

参考译文 ①接下来的问题是，在资本的计算要求方面，新规允许多少保险公司用内部模式替换标准化公式？②包括19家英国公司在内的大型保险企业已经说服其国家监管部门，表示它们自己的算法起码和规定的一样可行。③2016年，将会有更多公司申请使用内部模式进行计算，希望以此减少所要求的资本额，从而增加盈利。

原文剖析 本段前两句提出新规面临的一个新的问题,即在计算资本时有保险公司用内部计算模式替换新规的标准公式,暗示以后还会有更多企业这么做。第三句指出企业这样做的目的是增加盈利。该段以几家英国大公司成功劝说监管部门允许其使用内部计算模式为例,再次暗示新规在实施过程中存在的不公平性。

设题点睛 本段虽然提出了一个新的问题,但主要用于叙述事实,并未体现观点,因此不适合用来设置考题。

生词解析

substitute A for B 用 A 替代 B　　　　formula *n.* 公式;配方
prescribed *adj.* 规定的　　　　　　　in the hope of 怀着……的希望

长难句解析

Some big firms , including 19 in Britain , have persuaded their national regulator that their
　　主语　　　　　　插入语　　　　　　谓语　　　　　　　宾语　　　　　宾语从句
own calculations are at least as good as the prescribed ones.

本句是主从复合句。本句主干为 Some big firms have persuaded their national regulator that…,including 可看作介词短语作插入语,补充说明主语内容,谓语部分采用了 persuade sb. that 的结构,其中 sb. 为直接宾语,that 从句作间接宾语,从句内的表语采用了"as + *adj.* +as"结构。

Para. 5 ①To some extent that undermines the logic of a uniform system, by making insurers using internal models and those using the standard one hard to compare, says Jim Bichard of PwC, an accounting firm: "The solvency ratios will be all over the place and there's a high risk of misinterpretation." ②It also raises the concern that some of the national regulators charged with applying the new rules will be more lenient than others. ③ The British and Dutch ones, for example, are thought to be more exacting than their Italian counterpart.

参考译文 ①这样做在一定程度上弱化了这个统一系统的逻辑性,因为很难将使用内部模式和使用标准化公式的保险企业进行比较,普华永道会计师事务所的吉姆·比沙德(Jim Bichard)认为:"偿债能力比率将比比皆是,且误释的风险较高"。②还有人顾虑,一些国家负责实施新规的监管机构会比其他国家的相关机构更宽松一些。③例如,英国和荷兰的监管机构就被认为比意大利的监管机构更为严苛。

原文剖析 本段首句承接上段,以会计师事务所专业人士之口指出以偿债能力比率和误释两个标准判断,上一段提到的公司计算标准的不一致性将影响新规的规范性。第二句提出第三个问题,即不同国家的监管机构的严苛程度不同。第三句进而举例说明,两句话构成总分结构。与首句一起再次说明新规在实施过程中可能出现不公平现象。

设题点睛 本段给出两个新的问题,但所要暗示的内容一致,两者呈现并列关系,都可以用来设置正确选项。

生词解析

undermine *vt.* 破坏,渐渐破坏　　　　all over the place 各处,到处;乱七八糟
lenient *adj.* 宽大的;仁慈的　　　　　exacting *adj.* 要求严格的;苛刻的

长难句解析

To some extent that undermines the logic of a uniform system, by making insurers using
　状语1　　　主语1　　　谓语1　　　　　宾语　　　　　　　　　状语2
internal models and those using the standard one hard to compare, says Jim Bichard of PwC,
　　　　　　　　　　　　　　　　　　　　　　　　　　　　　　　　　　　　插入语
an accounting firm: "The solvency ratios will be all over the place and there's a high risk of
　同位语　　　　　　　主语2　　　　系动词　　表语　　　　　　　there be 句型
misinterpretation."

本句为并列复合句。本句主干为 that undermines the logic of…: "The solvency ratios will be all over the place and there's a high risk of…",本句实际由冒号前后两个完整的句子构成,前一句是间接引语,后一句是直接引语。前一句中的主语 that 回指前文,其实也是 by 所引出的方式状语的内容,该方式状语的主干为 by making… and… hard to compare,形容词 hard 作 making 宾语的补语,using 引导的成分作后置定语分别修饰 insurers 和 those,不应将该结构理解为 by making… using…。

4 It can be learned from paragraph 4 and 5 that _____.　　从第四段和第五段可以推测出_____。

A. big firms are immune to the standardised calculation　　A. 大公司不受标准化计算公式的影响

B. the internal model of calculation is as good as the standardised one　　B. 内部计算模式与标准化计算公式一样好

C. leniency is a priority element in carrying out the rules　　C. 宽容是实施新规过程中的首要因素

D. the system is sapped for its inconsistency and inequality　　D. 该体系因其不一致性和不平等性而遭到削弱

【解题思路】D。推理引申题。根据题干要求定位到文章第四段和第五段。在没有更加准确的定位点的情况下,优先考查这两段中的观点性内容以及特殊的逻辑结构。第四段第二句指出有的大型保险公司已经说服国家监管部门让它们使用自己的算法而非规定的算法。第五段首句谈到这样做会导致"偿债能力比率将比比皆是,且误释的风险较高",该段后两句又指出"一些国家负责实施新规的监管机构会比其他国家的相关机构更宽松一些",以上观点句共同体现新规实施的不一致性和不平等性。因此选项 D 正确。

【排他分析】选项 A 对应第四段第二句,原文确实指出英国目前有 19 家大公司可以使用其原有的内部计算模式,但并不等同于所有大公司都有此特权,因此排除该项。选项 B 同样对应第四段第二句,该项所谈到的是这 19 家保险公司劝说其所在国监管部门的理由,不一定是事实,因此排除。选项 C 中的 leniency 对应第五段第二句,但原文并未提及与 priority element 有关的内容,因此排除。

Para. 6 ① Yet whatever Solvency 2's failings, the new regime will still provide a continent wide benchmark for the first time. ② "It will confirm who is strong and who is weak," says David

参考译文 ①然而,尽管《欧盟偿付能力Ⅱ》存在种种瑕疵,这一新体系将成为首个在全欧洲推行的单一标准。②"哪家强哪家弱,一测便知。"

Prowse of Fitch, a rating agency. ③The strong will presumably start to put their excess capital to work, making acquisitions or returning cash to shareholders. ④The weak, meanwhile, will have to boost their capital, trim their liabilities by offering stingier policies, sell capital-intensive parts of the business or fall into the arms of one of their brawnier counterparts.

惠誉评级公司的大卫·鲍罗斯(David Prowse)如是说。③实力较强的公司将很可能开始利用其多余资本开展收购活动或给股东返现。④而实力较弱的公司则需要继续融资，采用更紧缩的政策来削减债务，还要出售资本较集中的业务，否则它会被实力更强的同行们收购。

原文剖析 本段首句以 Yet 开始，转折前文观点，指出新规也有好处（提供统一标准）。第二句借专业人士之口进一步解释这一好处使新规具有区别公司强弱的作用，回应首段谈到的新规的设计初衷（使投资者和客户更容易评估这些公司的实力）。最后两句承接第二句的观点，通过比较指出实力不同的公司针对新规的不同应对策略。

设题点睛 本段提出与前文截然不同的观点，采用总分结构，在提出新规作用的同时分析不同公司的应对方式，属于重要的考点内容。

生词解析

failing n. 缺点，过失；弱点
benchmark n. 基准；参照
liabilities n. [复数]【会计学】债务，欠款
brawny adj. 强壮的；肌肉结实的
regime n. 体制；社会制度
presumably adv. 很可能；大概；据推测
stingy adj. 吝啬的，小气的

5 According to the author, Solvency 2 will act as _____.

A. a benchmark to inspire the industry all over the continent
B. a gauge in judging the company's capacity
C. an agency to supervise the acquisitions
D. a policy to enhance the liability of the weak firms

根据作者的观点，《欧盟偿付能力Ⅱ》将充当 _____。

A. 激励整个欧洲保险行业的标准
B. 判断公司能力的标准
C. 监管并购活动的部门
D. 提升弱小企业责任感的政策

【解题思路】B。观点态度题。根据顺序原则定位到文章最后一段。本段前两句给出了全新的观点，即"这一新体系将成为首个在全欧洲推行的单一标准"(provide a continent wide benchmark)，且具有测试公司强弱的作用(It will confirm who is strong and who is weak)，与选项 B 的内容直接对应。该项中的 gauge 是首句中 benchmark 的同义替换，judging company's capacity 对应原文中的 confirm who is strong and who is weak。

【排他分析】选项 A 中的 benchmark 对应本段首句，但是原文并没有体现该法规可 inspire（鼓舞）整个欧洲保险业的这一作用，因此排除。选项 C 中的 acquisitions 对应本段第三句，句中指出较为强大的公司会用多余的资金进行并购(making acquisitions)，但并没有提到是否由《欧盟偿付能力Ⅱ》来监管，因此排除。选项 D 中的 liability 对应本段最后一句，liability 的单数形式指"责任"，复数形式表示"债务"，原文使用了该词的复数形式，因此与该项所指的"责任"并无关系，因此排除。

Text 2

Sometimes it takes a group of economists to confirm reality. Last year, a team of German academics released a study on the effects of major financial crises on politics, examining 800 elections over 140 years in 20 advanced economies. They found that after such crises, right-wing populist parties and politicians typically increase their vote share by about 30%. (The same isn't true in the wake of more mild recessions.) If that sounds familiar, it's because we are living through a season of the very same: persistent economic malaise since the 2008 crisis—punctuated by scandal after scandal—has laid bare the ways in which elites collude to create a system that mostly benefits elites.

Since 2010, there have been major scandals at banks on nearly every continent for every reason. Meanwhile, the Panama Papers leak earlier this year confirmed what many already assumed: that world leaders, celebrities and billionaires are adept at shielding their wealth from fair taxation. No wonder surveys show that the trust gap between the 1% and the 99% has never been greater.

In all of these cases, elites enabled by a fundamentally flawed global finance culture fly over the nation-state system. That voters in countries around the world want to punish leaders at the polls for all of this isn't surprising. But the effects on civil society are more corrosive than one election return. If nothing changes, the building blocks of developed countries are at risk.

Take the trouble at Deutsche Bank, which recently saw its share price plunge after the threat of a $14 billion fine for dicey derivatives trades. The case is a reminder of how Europe managed its debt crisis in the interest of banks, rather than citizens. "Sick banks, some still owned by governments, are all over Europe," says Stanford professor Anat Admati, co-author of *The Bankers' New Clothes: What's Wrong With Banking and What to Do About It*. "They refuse to let them die but rather do backdoor bailouts (claiming they are in the interest of preserving E.U. unity, rather than bank solvency) that perpetuate the situation."

Cases like this foster the message that institutions and rich individuals can float above the system—and that has serious ramifications. Italy, for example, has the largest "unofficial economy" (read: level of tax evasion) in Europe. Studies show that the black market in Italy makes up around 27% of the nation's total economy. Citizens of country like this tend to lose faith in the system and stop doing their civic duty, like paying taxes, filing for business permits, obeying the rule of law in general. This only widens the gap between haves and have-nots.

In this sense, Trump may be a canary in the coal mine for the U.S. This election cycle has brought the public-approval rating of government to new lows. The GOP nominee has gone from obscuring how little he pays in tax to arguing that it qualifies him to fix the system. If his argument works, it is likely to make things worse, not better.

People will never love paying taxes. But when they stop trusting the system altogether, the foundations of a country begin to crumble.

(*Time*, 2016.10)

1. The study released by the team of German academics reveals that _____.
   A. right-wing politicians always get more support in the financial crisis
   B. most voters are in favor of elites during more mild recessions
   C. political scandal is a major cause for the past economic recessions
   D. elites may be the culprit rather than savior of the financial crisis

2. It can be learned from paragraph 2 and 3 that _____.
   A. the flawed financial culture is more serious in developed countries
   B. leaders will be punished for their feeble governance in civil societies
   C. the corruptive finance culture will threaten the foundation of advanced economy
   D. rich people seldom shield their wealth from cruel taxation

3. Anat Admati believes the backdoor bailouts will _____.
   A. worsen rather than solve the current crisis
   B. cure the sickness of the banks all over Europe
   C. strive to protect the unity for European banking industry
   D. keep the European citizens away from the financial crisis

4. The example of Italy (Para. 5) is cited to _____.
   A. show the Italians' fury against the institutions and rich individuals
   B. highlight the importance of the political system and civic duty
   C. stress the serious influence brought by the "unofficial economy"
   D. illustrate the severe consequences caused by the flawed finance culture

5. Trump is described as "a canary in the coal mine" because _____.
   A. he is deemed to save the US political system
   B. he may be used to judge the rightness of the system
   C. he pays little in tax comparing to other nominees
   D. his argument may weaken the confidence of US government

语篇分析与试题精解

Para. 1 ① Sometimes it takes a group of economists to confirm reality. ② Last year, a team of German academics released a study on the effects of major financial crises on politics,

参考译文 ①有时候，认清现实需要一些经济学家的共同努力。②去年，德国的一个学术小组在研究了140多年里在20个发达经济体举行的800

examining 800 elections over 140 years in 20 advanced economies. ③They found that after such crises, right-wing populist parties and politicians typically increase their vote share by about 30%. (The same isn't true in the wake of more mild recessions.) ④If that sounds familiar, it's because we are living through a season of the very same: persistent economic malaise since the 2008 crisis—punctuated by scandal after scandal—has laid bare the ways in which elites collude to create a system that mostly benefits elites.

场选举之后,发布了一个重大金融危机对于政治之影响的研究结果。③他们发现在类似的金融危机爆发后,右翼民粹党派和政客的选票一般会增加30%左右。(如果是较温和的经济衰退,则不会发生这样的情况。)④这个结论并不陌生,因为这与我们目前的处境十分类似:2008年金融危机以来,持续性的经济萎靡以及接踵而来的丑闻暴露了精英们沆瀣一气,一手搭建了这个能使他们利益最大化的体系。

原文剖析 本段首句为引入句,表达了作者的观点。第二句和第三句采用了"研究+结论"的结构,支撑了首句的抽象观点,结论指出金融危机会让右翼民粹党派和政客得到更多选票支持。第四句用2008年金融危机之后的情况分析该研究结果产生的原因,即精英们创造了能使自己利益最大化的体系,此处的精英与前一句谈到的右翼民粹党派和政客应该是同一批人。

设题点睛 本段第三句为研究结果,被第四句的例子解释和支撑,且第四句为长难句,可用来设置正确选项。

生词解析

right-wing *adj.* 右翼的;右派的
in the wake of 随着,紧跟
malaise *n.* (发病前或初病时的)身体不适
scandal *n.* 丑闻;流言蜚语
elite *n.* 精英;精华;中坚分子

populist *adj.* 平民党的;人民党的
recession *n.* (商业活动等的)衰退(现象)
punctuate *vt.* 不时打断
lay bare 揭发,暴露;公开
collude *vi.* 勾结;串通;共谋

长难句解析

If that sounds familiar,   it's   because we are living through a season of the very same：
  条件状语从句   主语1+系动词   表语从句

persistent economic malaise since the 2008 crisis—punctuated by scandal after scandal—
        主语2   后置定语1   后置定语2

has laid bare the ways in which elites collude to create a system that mostly benefits elites.
  谓语   宾语   定语从句

本句可看作并列复合句。由冒号前后的两个完整的句子构成。前半句为带有if条件句的主从复合句,其表语从句由because引导。后半句的主干为persistent economic malaise has laid bare the ways,破折号之间的部分作后置定语,修饰主语,将主语与谓语和宾语隔开,宾语采用了the ways in which的结构,in which作定语从句修饰先行词the ways。

1. **The study released by the team of German academics reveals that _____ .**

   A. right-wing politicians always get more support in the financial crisis
   B. most voters are in favor of elites during more mild recessions
   C. political scandal is a major cause for the past economic recessions
   D. elites may be the culprit rather than savior of the financial crisis

由德国学者团队所公布的研究揭示了_____。

A. 右翼政客总能在金融危机中获得更多支持
B. 在更为温和的经济衰退中,大多数选民支持精英
C. 政治丑闻是造成过去经济衰退的一个主要原因
D. 精英们可能是金融危机的罪魁祸首,而非救星

【解题思路】D。推理引申题。根据题干关键词(the team of German academics)定位到首段。本题实际考查该研究的发现,因此可定位至第三句和第四句。第三句指出研究所发现的现象,即"金融危机爆发后,右翼民粹党派和政客的选票一般会增加30%左右",暗示右翼党派和政客反而会因较大的金融危机获利,第四句进一步分析出现这种结果的原因在于"精英们沆瀣一气,一手搭建了这个能使他们利益最大化的体系"。由此看出,第四句是对现象的根本性分析,可推断金融危机产生的根源之一就是精英所构建的这个体系,与选项 D 的含义一致。

【排他分析】选项 A 中的 right-wing politicians 对应首段第三句,但该项中的 always 与原文括号中的"如果是较温和的经济衰退,则不会发生这样的情况"矛盾,因此排除,同理可证选项 B 错误。选项 C 中的 scandal 出现在第四句两个破折号之间,原文并列指出"持续性的经济萎靡"和"接踵而来的丑闻"揭露了这个精英共谋的体系,由此看出这两项属于表象而非原因,可理解为经济危机和丑闻是由该精英体系导致的,该项本末倒置,可以排除。

Para. 2 ①Since 2010, there have been major scandals at banks on nearly every continent for every reason. ②Meanwhile, the <u>Panama Papers leak earlier this year confirmed what many already assumed: that world leaders, celebrities and billionaires are adept at shielding their wealth from fair taxation</u>. ③No wonder surveys show that the trust gap between the 1% and the 99% has never been greater.

参考译文 ①2010 年以来,世界各地的银行业均爆出了各种丑闻。②与此同时,今年早些时候的《巴拿马文件》所泄露的内容证实了很多人的猜测,即国家领导人、名人和富豪们在避税方面技艺娴熟。③难怪多项调查显示目前 1% 的富人和 99% 的一般人之间的信任鸿沟从未如此巨大。

原文剖析 本段呼应上一段最后一句的分析。前两句分别以银行业丑闻和《巴拿马文件》泄密事件为例,引出第三句的结论,即穷人和富人之间出现了巨大的信任鸿沟。本段谈到的《巴拿马文件》泄露事件发生在 2016 年,当时一家名为莫萨克·冯赛卡(Mossack Fonseca)的法律服务公司泄露了 1 100 多万份机密文件,这些文件披露了该公司如何协助

其客户洗钱、避开制裁以及逃避税赋等非法行为。

设题点睛 本段举例支持上段观点,因此不适合单独设置考题。

生词解析

leak *n.* 泄露;泄露出来的事实　　　　billionaire *n.* 亿万富翁
be adept at 擅长做某事　　　　　　　shield *vt.* 庇护;包庇;掩盖

长难句解析

Meanwhile, the Panama Papers leak earlier this year confirmed what many already assumed:
　　　　　　主语　　　　　后置定语　　　　　　　谓语　　　　　宾语从句1
that world leaders, celebrities and billionaires are adept at shielding their wealth from fair taxation.
　　　　　　　　　　　　　　　　　　　　宾语从句2

本句是主从复合句。本句主干为 the Panama Papers leak confirmed...,谓语 confirmed 实际带有两个宾语从句,冒号后的 that 从句也是其宾语,表示"证实"的具体内容。

Para. 3 ①In all of these cases, elites enabled by a fundamentally flawed global finance culture fly over the nation-state system. ②That voters in countries around the world want to punish leaders at the polls for all of this isn't surprising. ③But the effects on civil society are more corrosive than one election return. ④If nothing changes, the building blocks of developed countries are at risk.

参考译文 ①所有这些案例中,由于全球金融文化存在根本性的瑕疵,使得精英们在国家体制中风生水起。②因此,世界各国的选民们想要因此在选举时惩罚领导人的做法就毫不意外了。③但是,这对公民社会的腐蚀性作用比一份选举结果报告要大得多。④如果继续维持现状,将会撼动发达国家的基石。

原文剖析 本段首句回应首段观点,再次说明是精英所创造的具有瑕疵的体系导致了经济危机的发生。第二句回应第二段中谈到的信任鸿沟,指出选民会通过投票的方式体现对领导人的不信任。第三句和第四句评价首句谈到的有瑕疵的金融体系对公民社会的严重破坏作用(具有腐蚀性、撼动发达国家根基)。

设题点睛 本段最后两句转折进一步指出这种精英建立的金融系统带来的危害性不仅使人民不信任领导者,还会对国家和民族造成更为严重的危害,该观点第一次出现,因此是重要的设题内容。

生词解析

fundamentally *adv.* 根本地,从根本上　　flawed *adj.* 有缺陷的;有瑕疵的
nation-state *n.* 单一民族的独立国家　　　corrosive *adj.* 腐蚀的;侵蚀性的
election return 选举结果报告　　　　　　be at risk 处于风险之中

2 It can be learned from paragraph 2 and 3 that _____.

　A. the flawed financial culture is more serious in developed countries
　B. leaders will be punished for their feeble governance in civil societies
　C. the corruptive finance culture will threaten

从第二段和第三段中可得知_____。

　A. 有缺陷的金融文化在发达国家更为严重
　B. 在公民社会中,领导人将因其软弱的执政能力而受到惩罚
　C. 腐败的金融文化将威胁发达

the foundation of advanced economy	国家的根基
D. rich people seldom shield their wealth from cruel taxation	D. 富人们很少躲避严苛的税收

【解题思路】C。事实细节题。根据题干要求定位到第二段和第三段,在没有准确定位点的情况下,优先考查段落主旨句或者特殊逻辑结构。第三段第三句转折指出"这对公民社会的腐蚀性作用比一份选举结果报告要大得多(more corrosive than one election return)","这"回指首句提到的"存在根本性瑕疵"的全球金融文化,第四句继而指出如果再不做出改变,发达国家的基石将会受到影响(the building blocks of developed countries are at risk)。选项 C 中的 corruptive finance culture 和 threaten the foundation of advanced economy 分别对应第三段第三句和第四句的关键语意,因此是正确答案。

【排他分析】选项 A 中的 flawed financial culture 对应第三段首句,但该句并没有直接指出此类的问题在哪类国家更严重,developed countries 出现在段尾,该项是对两个细节的随意拼凑,因此排除。选项 B 中的 feeble governance 在文中并未出现,第三段第二句谈到领导人受民众投票惩罚的原因并非是领导人的管理问题,因此排除。选项 D 直接对应第二段第二句的内容,该项与原文中的 are adept at shielding their wealth 和 fair taxation 均矛盾,因此排除。

Para. 4 ①Take the trouble at Deutsche Bank, which recently saw its share price plunge after the threat of a $14 billion fine for dicey derivatives trades. ②The case is a reminder of how Europe managed its debt crisis in the interest of banks, rather than citizens. ③"Sick banks, some still owned by governments, are all over Europe," says Stanford professor Anat Admati, co-author of *The Bankers' New Clothes: What's Wrong With Banking and What to Do About It*. ④"They refuse to let them die but rather do backdoor bailouts (claiming they are in the interest of preserving E.U. unity, rather than bank solvency) that perpetuate the situation."

参考译文 ①譬如,德意志银行因不确定的金融衍生品交易面临140亿美元罚款,之后其股价暴跌。②这次事件提醒人们,欧洲在处理其债务危机时,是从银行的利益,而非公民的利益出发。③斯坦福大学教授、《银行家的新装:银行业的问题和对策》一书的作者之一阿纳特·阿达马提(Anat Admati)指出:"有问题的银行在欧洲比比皆是,有的仍归政府所有。"④"政府宁可秘密救助这些银行(这种救助会使银行业的问题一直存在),也不会眼睁睁看着它们倒闭,宣称它们这样做是为了维持欧盟一体化,而非银行的偿付能力。"

原文剖析 首句表明本段以举例为主,目的是对上一段的观点进行论证,指出金融行业的腐败以及政府对银行利益而非公众利益的保护。后两句利用人物言论继续支持这一观点。

设题点睛 本段后两句用直接引语的方式明确指出目前政府和金融行业的问题所在,属于重要内容,可用来设置正确选项。

生词解析
plunge *vi.* 下降;急降;突降
derivatives *n.* [复数]金融衍生工具
dicey *adj.* 不确定的;危险的;投机的
in the interest of 为了……的利益

sick *adj.* 不活跃的；不兴旺的，衰落的　　backdoor *adj.* 秘密的
bailout *n.* （尤指政府对陷于财政困难的企业，特别是大公司的）紧急救济（尤指财政援助）

长难句解析

"They refuse to let them die but rather do backdoor bailouts (claiming they are in the
主语　谓语1　　　宾语1　　　　　　　谓语2　　宾语2　　　　　伴随状语
interest of preserving E. U. unity, rather than bank solvency) that perpetuate the situation."
　　　　　　　　　　　　　　　　　　　　　　　　　定语从句

本句是并列复合句。本句由连词 but 连接的两个句子构成（but 在此处不是介词，因其介词词性表示"除……以外"），but 后省略了主语 they，括号中 claiming 的动作发出者为 they，因此可看作伴随状语。括号后的 that 从句作定语，其先行词应是括号前的 backdoor bailouts。

3 Anat Admati believes the backdoor bailouts will _____.　　阿纳特·阿达马提认为这种秘密资助会_____。

A. worsen rather than solve the current crisis　　A. 加重而非解决目前的危机
B. cure the sickness of the banks all over Europe　　B. 纠正欧洲各地银行的问题
C. strive to protect the unity for European banking industry　　C. 努力保护欧洲银行业的一体化
D. keep the European citizens away from the financial crisis　　D. 让欧洲人民远离金融危机

【解题思路】A。推理引申题。根据题干关键词（Anat Admati 和 backdoor bailouts）可定位到第四段的第三句和第四句，这两句都是对此人观点的引用，指出欧洲政府宁可秘密资助，也不会眼睁睁看着这些出问题的银行倒闭。此人的观点与前文之间不存在转折，因此是对前两句语意的顺承，为了进一步支持第二句"欧洲在处理其债务危机时，是从银行的利益，而非公民的利益出发"的观点，这种只为精英谋福利的做法与第三段谈到的腐败的金融文化本质上一致，根据作者在第三段最后的表述，这种情况会撼动整个国家的基石，因此只能让情况变得更为糟糕，与选项 A 的意思一致。

【排他分析】选项 B 与正确答案选项 A 的意思相反，因此与原文语意相反，可排除。选项 C 中的 unity 出现在第四段第四句的括号中，原文指的是"维持欧盟一体化"，而非维持"欧洲银行业的一体化"，且这种说法是政府提出的，并非题干所问的阿纳特·阿达马提的观点，因此排除。第四段作者的观点与题干所问的阿纳特·阿达马提的观点一致，与政府为自己行为的辩解相反，两者的看法应该对应第二句所表达的"从银行的利益，而非公民的利益出发"，与选项 D 的表述相反，故选项 D 排除。

Para. 5 ①Cases like this foster the message that institutions and rich individuals can float above the system—and that has serious ramifications. ②Italy, for example, has the largest "unofficial economy" (read: level of tax evasion) in Europe. ③Studies show that the black market in Italy

参考译文　①类似事件会进一步让人们感觉机构和富人可以凌驾于体系之上，这会造成严重后果。②譬如，意大利拥有欧洲规模最大的"非官方经济"（参阅该国的逃税程度）。③研究显示，意大利的黑市经

makes up around 27% of the nation's total economy. ④Citizens of country like this tend to lose faith in the system and stop doing their civic duty, like paying taxes, filing for business permits, obeying the rule of law in general. ⑤This only widens the gap between haves and have-nots.

济约占其国民经济的27%。④在意大利这种国家生活的公民很容易会对体系丧失信心，并拒绝履行包括纳税、办理经商许可和守法在内的公民职责。⑤这种情况无疑会扩大贫富差距。

原文剖析 本段开始处的 Cases like this 回指上一段内容，继续指出欧洲国家政府包庇金融腐败文化的做法会产生的严重后果。第二句到第四句以意大利为例对首句进行例证，说明具体的严重后果，如黑市贸易横行、公民对体系丧失信心和拒绝履行公民职责。第五句总结本段内容，指出一系列效应的最终结果是扩大了贫富差距。

设题点睛 本段采用了"总分总"结构，最后两句是本段的观点句，可用来设置正确选项。

生词解析
foster vt. 助长，促进
ramification n. 后果；衍生物
civic adj. 市民的；公民的
float vi. 不受约束，不卷入；无牵无挂
lose faith in 不再信任；对……失去信心
haves and have-nots 富人和穷人；

4 **The example of Italy (Para. 5) is cited to _____.**

A. show the Italians' fury against the institutions and rich individuals
B. highlight the importance of the political system and civic duty
C. stress the serious influence brought by the "unofficial economy"
D. illustrate the severe consequences caused by the flawed finance culture

作者引用意大利的例子（第五段）是为了_____。

A. 表明意大利人对机构和富人的愤怒
B. 强调政治体系和公民义务的重要性
C. 强调"非官方经济"带来的严重影响
D. 体现这一有缺陷的金融文化导致的恶果

【解题思路】D。例子功能题。根据题干要求定位到文章第五段。本段从第二句开始介绍意大利的情况，说明意大利经济所遇到的问题，明显是为了证明首句观点，即"机构和富人可以凌驾于体系之上，这会造成严重后果"，float above the system 与第三段第一句中的 fly over the nation-state system 意思相同，由于第三段首句还指出这种情况是由"全球金融文化存在根本性瑕疵"导致的，因此第五段首句也是金融文化缺陷所导致的恶果，与选项 D 的意思一致，该项中的 severe consequences 对应第五段句首处的 serious ramifications，且从例子的具体内容中也可看出并非是正面的影响。

【排他分析】虽然第五段第四句谈到了意大利人对这种腐败体系的反应（拒绝履行公民职责），但这种反应无法体现选项 A 所概括的 fury（愤怒），因此该项属于过度推断，可排除。选项 B 中的 civic duty 对应本段第四句，该句旨在表现意大利人民对政府或体系的失望之情和应对方式，并非用来强调公民职责的重要性。选项 C 中的"unofficial economy"出现在本段第二句，该句提到的"非官方经济"是首句所说"机构和富人凌驾于系统之上"的严重后果之一，"非官方经济"本身并非是本段讨论的主题，因此该项属于片面观点，可排除。

Para. 6 ①In this sense, Trump may be a canary in the coal mine for the U.S. ②This election cycle has brought the public-approval rating of government to new lows. ③The GOP nominee has gone from obscuring how little he pays in tax to arguing that it qualifies him to fix the system. ④If his argument works, it is likely to make things worse, not better.

参考译文 ①从这个意义上看,特朗普对于美国而言,就像矿井中的金丝雀一样,可起到预警作用。②在这次的选举中,公众对政府的正面评价创历史新低。③这位共和党候选人在回应其纳税太少时含糊其词,甚至辩称,这使他有能力修复该体系。④如果他的说法起了作用,那么事态只会更糟,而不会变得更好。

原文剖析 首句承接上段,将话题引回美国,说明美国现在也面临着相似的问题,并给出作者观点(特朗普有警示作用)。第二句到第四句解释首句观点,表示以特朗普为首的精英政客用蹩脚的谎言使政府的公信力更低。第一句中的 canary in the coal mine 直译为"矿井中的金丝雀",为比喻手法,17世纪在采矿设备相对简陋的条件下,英国矿井工人们每次下井都会带上一只金丝雀作为"瓦斯检测指标",以便在危险状况下紧急撤离,"煤矿中的金丝雀"现在表示"某人/某物是危险将至的预警标志"。

设题点睛 本段首句为抽象观点,之后内容与首句构成总分关系,可用来设置题干或正确选项。

生词解析

canary n. 金丝雀
nominee n. 被提名者;被任命者
fix vt. 修理,校正;修补
GOP abbr. Grand Old Party 老大党(共和党)
obscure vt. 掩盖,遮盖,隐藏

长难句解析

The GOP nominee has gone from obscuring how little he pays in tax to arguing
　主语　　　　　　谓语　　　状语　　　　　宾语从句1　　　　　状语

that it qualifies him to fix the system.
　　　宾语从句2

本句是主从复合句。本句主干为 The GOP nominee has gone from... to...,from 和 to 都是介词,后接名词性内容,共同作表示范围的状语。go from... to... 可看作固定用法,表示语意递进。其中,how 和 that 引导的从句分别作 obscuring 和 arguing 的宾语。

Para. 7 ①People will never love paying taxes. ②But when they stop trusting the system altogether, the foundations of a country begin to crumble.

参考译文 ①没有人喜欢纳税。②然而,当人民都不再信任体制时,一个国家的根基便开始崩塌。

原文剖析 本段明显是作者观点的总结。首句和第二句形成语意上的转折关系,再次强调当国家体系失去公信力时,国家根基将被动摇这一严重后果,体现了作者的担忧和警告。

设题点睛 本段内容是对前文观点的重复和总结,不适合单独设置考题。

生词解析

crumble *vi.* 崩溃；破碎，粉碎

5 Trump is described as "a canary in the coal mine" because ＿＿＿＿.

A. he is deemed to save the US political system

B. he may be used to judge the rightness of the system

C. he pays little in tax comparing to other nominees

D. his argument may weaken the confidence of US government

特朗普被称为"矿井中的金丝雀"是因为＿＿＿＿。

A. 他被认为是美国政治体系的大救星

B. 他可用来判断美国体系的合理性

C. 相对于其他候选人，他几乎不纳税

D. 他的言论可能让美国政府丧失信心

【解题思路】B。语意理解题。根据题干中的"a canary in the coal mine"可定位至文章第六段首句。本题实际考查作者采用该比喻手法的目的。这个成语来源于过去人们利用金丝雀来判断矿井空气是否安全的普遍做法，因此"矿井中的金丝雀"表示具有警示作用的人或物。如果并不了解这个典故的出处，还可以从后文中推断得出。本段第三句指出特朗普在面对个人缴税太少的质疑时，先是含糊其辞，最后甚至辩称由于做到了合理避税，因此其有资格修正整个体系，也就是说特朗普逃税而不被惩罚的事实说明美国政治体系或税收体系存在漏洞，起到了警示作用，因此选项 B 的表述正确。

【排他分析】第六段最后一句明确指出"如果他的说法起了作用，那么事态只会更糟，而不会变得更好"，和选项 A 的内容相反，因此排除。选项 C 对应第六段第二句，但原文并没有拿特朗普与其他候选人进行对比，因此直接排除。选项 D 对应第六段最后一句，原文表示如果让特朗普修正这个体系，那"事态只会更糟"，回应前文，这是因为特朗普代表社会精英，他们所创建的体系只为其利益服务，前文指出这种体系会弱化公众对政府的信任，但与美国政府对自身的信心无关，因此排除该项。

Text 3

Uber's initial public offering, due after *The Economist* went to press, will be one of the largest in tech history. The hoopla cannot drown out uncertainty about the firm's future. They have been virtuosic losers of money. Lyft made an operating loss of nearly ＄1bn in 2018; Uber, about ＄3bn. The flow of red ink mainly represents subsidies from investors to riders: cash that allows average Joes to feel as though they have a personal car at their beck and call.

The mania for tech platforms that match cars with riders rests on the idea that they can turn car-hire into critical urban-transport infrastructure. Perhaps ride-hailing could spare millions of people the cost of owning cars that mostly sit idle, and allow vehicles and roads to be used more efficiently. But increased scale has yet to turn losses to profits. To remain viable, Uber and its peers must make more money per trip. They could increase fares. But cheap rides have been crucial to building their user bases. However dominant one or another becomes, competing transport options remain, from personal cars to public transport to travellers' own two feet. Higher fares will make those alternatives more attractive.

Perhaps instead the firms could cut their per-ride costs. Payments to drivers are the juiciest target, and indeed Uber is keen to develop a fleet of driverless taxis (as are other firms, including Waymo and Tesla). Yet even these may struggle to turn a profit. A recent analysis concludes that driving your own vehicle costs about $0.72 per mile, whereas the lowest break-even fare an operator of driverless taxis could expect to charge is $1.31 per mile. While on duty, taxis rack up costs for items such as petrol, whether or not a fare-paying passenger is in the car. Furthermore, driverless cars would need some minding by human safety monitors, whose salaries must be covered by fares.

Until they turn profits, ride-hailing firms will be vulnerable to a loss of investors' patience. But drivers of private vehicles also receive plenty of implicit support. Drivers impose environmental hazards on others at no financial cost to themselves, from the health effects of local air pollution to the climate change resulting from carbon emissions. And then there is congestion. The right to use scarce road space is valuable. When it is given away, drivers overuse available roads, and clog them. The waste is colossal.

Removing the subsidy to drivers means pricing road space by levying tolls that increase with traffic. That would deter driving, and reduce congestion and other social costs of automobile use. Such charges are rarely popular with drivers. But governments' enthusiasm for new, untolled roads has dimmed. And they do not help much with traffic. Gilles Duranton of the University of Pennsylvania and Matthew Turner of Brown University posit a "fundamental law of road congestion": unless road space is priced appropriately, new capacity reduces the cost of driving, thereby inducing more of it, leading, eventually, to renewed congestion.

(*The Economist*, 2019.5)

1. According to paragraph 1, Ubers' service is _____ for the ordinary people.
    A. luxurious
    B. considerate
    C. pleasurable
    D. unaffordable

2. We may infer from paragraph 2 that _____.
    A. ride-hailing does make an efficient use of roads
    B. raising ticket price is not a proper way for Uber
    C. Uber has become an important means of transportation
    D. Uber aroused a price war in the transportation industry

3. The word "juiciest" (Para. 3) most probably means _____.

   A. most superior

   B. most profitable

   C. most appropriate

   D. most tempting

4. A recent analysis is cited to _____.

   A. illustrate the higher cost of driveless taxis

   B. stress the serious influence brought by monitors

   C. highlight the importance of attracting passengers

   D. show the infeasibility of relying on driverless taxis

5. According to the "fundamental law of road congestion" (Para. 5), the government is called on to _____.

   A. set a proper price for road space

   B. build new roads for more private cars

   C. take steps to ease the traffic pressure

   D. alleviate the impact of private cars on the air

语篇分析与试题精解

Para. 1 ①Uber's initial public offering, due after *The Economist* went to press, will be one of the largest in tech history. ②The hoopla cannot drown out uncertainty about the firm's future. ③They have been virtuosic losers of money. ④Lyft made an operating loss of nearly $1bn in 2018; Uber, about $3bn. ⑤The flow of red ink mainly represents subsidies from investors to riders: cash that allows average Joes to feel as though they have a personal car at their beck and call.

参考译文 ①《经济学人》付印之后,优步的首次公开募股将成为科技史上规模最大的募股行动之一。②大吹大擂掩盖不了公司未来的不确定性。③在金钱上,他们一直是输家。④2018年,来福车运营亏损近10亿美元;优步亏损约30亿美元。⑤赤字的流动主要来自投资者对乘客的补贴:让普通乘客觉得他们有让一辆私人汽车随时听候差遣的现金。

原文剖析 本段首句指出优步的首次公开募股将成为科技史上规模最大的募股行动之一。第二、三句转折指出其实他们一直都在亏损,第四、五句分别指出亏损的具体数目及去向。

设题点睛 本段前几句包含转折之意,可用于设置正确选项,最后一句为观点态度句,可设置题目。

生词解析

initial public offering 首次公开发行股票　　go to press 付印;出版
hoopla *n*. 大吹大擂;喧闹　　drown out 淹没,压过
red ink 赤字　　average Joe 普通人
at one' beck and call 有求必应

长难句解析

The flow of red ink mainly represents subsidies from investors to riders; cash that
主语　　后置定语1　　　　谓语　　　宾语　　　　后置定语2　　　　同位语
allows average Joes to feel as though they have a personal car at their beck and call.
　　　　　　　　　　　　　　　定语从句

本句是主从复合句。本句主干为 The flow represents subsidies, of 介词短语作主语 the flow 的后置定语, mainly 为程度副词, 修饰谓语 represents, from 介词短语作宾语 subsidies 的后置定语, cash 作 subsidies 的同位语, that 引导的是定语从句。

1 According to paragraph 1, Ubers' service is _____ for the ordinary people.

根据第一段,优步的服务对普通人来说是_____。

A. luxurious
B. considerable
C. pleasurable
D. unaffordable

A. 奢侈的
B. 相当大的
C. 令人愉快的
D. 负担不起的

【解题思路】C。推理判断题。根据题干关键词定位到第一段, 题干中的 the ordinary people 与文中的 average Joes 为同义替换, 那么本题就精确定位到第一段最后一句。该句指出, 赤字的流动主要来自投资者对乘客的补贴; 让普通人觉得他们有让一辆私人汽车随时听候差遣的现金。有一辆私人汽车随时听候差遣的体验感是令人愉悦的, 选项 C 属于合理推断, 故为正确答案。

【排他分析】文章提到的 cash 是投资者对乘客的补贴, 因此这并不是奢侈的, 也不是负担不起的, 选项 A 和选项 D 错误。选项 B 容易与 considerate 混淆, considerable 意为"相当大的", 显然与题干不符, 故排除。

Para. 2 ①The mania for tech platforms that match cars with riders rests on the idea that they can turn car-hire into critical urban-transport infrastructure. ②Perhaps ride-hailing could spare millions of people the cost of owning cars that mostly sit idle, and allow vehicles and roads to be used more efficiently. ③But increased scale has yet to turn losses to profits. ④To remain viable, Uber and its peers must make more money per trip. ⑤They could increase fares. ⑥But cheap rides have been crucial to building their user bases. ⑦However dominant one or another becomes, competing transport options remain, from personal cars to public transport to travellers' own two feet. ⑧Higher fares will make those alternatives more attractive.

参考译文 ①对将汽车与乘客相匹配的科技平台的狂热, 建立在这样一个理念之上: 它们可以把租车变成至关重要的城市交通基础设施。②或许网约车可以让数百万人省下大部分闲置车辆的购置成本, 让车辆和道路得到更有效的利用。③但规模的扩大尚未将亏损转化为利润。④为了维持生存, 优步以及其同行们每单必须赚更多的钱。⑤他们可以提高票价。⑥但便宜的交通工具对于打好用户基础至关重要。⑦无论哪种交通方式占据主导地位, 相互竞争的交通方式依然存在, 从私家车到公共交通, 再到旅行者自己的双脚。⑧更高的票价将使这些可替代的选择更具吸引力。

原文剖析 本段首句指出网约车的理念,第二句指出网约车可能带来的益处,第三、四句转折指出事实并非如此,为了生存,优步以及其同行们必须采取措施。接着分析了提高票价不应成为解决之道。

设题点睛 本段第三句有 but 转折,可设置正确选项,后面几句包含作者的观点态度以及因果关系,可设置题目。

生词解析

mania *n.* 狂热;热衷
viable *adj.* 能存活的;能独立生存的
spare *vt.* 留出;拨出;抽出
alternative *n.* 供替代的选择

长难句解析

However dominant one or another becomes, competing transport options remain,
　　　　让步状语从句　　　　　　　　　　　主语　　　　　谓语
from personal cars to public transport to travellers' own two feet.
　　　　　　　　　　后置定语

本句是主从复合句。主句主干为 competing transport options remain,句首的 however 表示让步,该从句的词序为 however + 形容词或副词 + 主语 + 谓语,这样用的 however 具有连词的功能,用以引导让步状语从句,from personal cars to... 为介词短语作 transport options 的后置定语。

2	We may infer from paragraph 2 that _____.	我们可以从第二段推出_____。
	A. ride-hailing does make an efficient use of roads	A. 网约车确实有效利用了道路
	B. raising ticket price is not a proper way for Uber	B. 对优步来说,提高票价不是正确的方式
	C. Uber has become an important means of transportation	C. 优步已经成为一种重要的交通工具
	D. Uber aroused a price war in the transportation industry	D. 优步在运输业引发了一场价格战

【解题思路】B。推理判断题。根据题干关键词直接定位到第二段。根据第五、六句,他们可以提高票价,但便宜的交通工具对于打好用户基础至关重要,可见作者对于提高票价是持不赞成的态度的,再结合最后一句,更高的票价将使这些可替代的选择更具吸引力。those alternatives 指的就是 competing transport options,由此可知,higher fares 对于优步来说不是解决之道,选项 B 符合此意,故为正确答案。

【排他分析】第二句提到,或许网约车可以让车辆和道路得到更有效的利用,而不是网约车确实有效利用了道路,选项 A 曲解文意,因此排除。文章只提到了规模的扩大,但并未提及优步已经成为一种重要的交通工具,选项 C 无中生有,因此排除。选项 D 根据文中的个别词汇 increase fares、cheap rides、competing 等主观臆断而来,故排除。

Para. 3 ①Perhaps instead the firms could cut their per-ride costs. ②Payments to drivers are the juiciest target, and indeed Uber is keen to develop a fleet of driverless taxis (as are other firms, including Waymo and Tesla). ③Yet even these may struggle to turn a profit. ④A recent analysis concludes that driving your own vehicle costs about ＄0.72 per mile, whereas the lowest break-even fare an operator of driverless taxis could expect to charge is ＄1.31 per mile. ⑤While on duty, taxis rack up costs for items such as petrol, whether or not a fare-paying passenger is in the car. ⑥Furthermore, driverless cars would need some minding by human safety monitors, whose salaries must be covered by fares.

参考译文 ①相反，这些公司或许可以降低每单的成本。②付给司机的钱是最赚钱的目标，而且优步确实热衷于发展无人驾驶出租车车队（就像其他公司一样，包括慧摩和特斯拉）。③然而，即使是这些公司也可能难以盈利。④最近的一项分析得出的结论是，自己开车每英里的成本约为0.72美元，而无人驾驶出租车运营商预计的最低盈亏平衡点是每英里1.31美元。⑤在值班期间，无论是否有乘客，出租车都会增加汽油等物品的成本。⑥此外，无人驾驶汽车需要人类安全监察员的关注，这些监察员的工资必须由车费支付。

原文剖析 本段承接上文，首句指出与上文相反的观点。接着引用最近的一项分析结果指出发展无人驾驶出租车车队也不是个好方法。

设题点睛 本段采用了"观点+例证"的结构，其中的观点性内容较为重要，可用来设置正确选项。

生词解析
be keen to 热衷于；渴望
on duty 值班；上班
break-even *adj.* 收支平衡的
rack up 大量获得（利润）

长难句解析

<u>A recent analysis</u> <u>concludes</u> <u>that driving your own vehicle costs about ＄0.72 per mile</u>,
　　　主语　　　　　谓语　　　　　　　　　宾语从句

<u>whereas</u> <u>the lowest break-even fare</u> <u>an operator of driverless taxis could expect to</u>
　状语从句　　　　　　　　　　　　　　　　定语从句

charge is ＄1.31 per mile.
状语从句

本句是主从复合句。主句主干为 A recent analysis concludes that…，that 引导的是宾语从句，whereas 引导的是状语从句，该从句中又包含一个省略了引导词的定语从句。

3 The word "juiciest" (Para. 3) most probably means _____.

A. most superior
B. most profitable
C. most appropriate
D. most tempting

单词"juiciest"（第三段）最有可能的意思是_____。

A. 最优秀的
B. 最有利可图的
C. 最合适的
D. 最诱人的

【解题思路】B。语意理解题。根据题干关键词直接定位到第三段。单词所在句指出，付给司机的钱是_____的目标，而且优步确实热衷于发展无人驾驶出租车车队（就像其他公司一样，包括慧摩和特斯拉）。结合第三句"然而，即使是这些公司也可能难以盈利"可知，发展无人驾驶出租车车队是为了获益更多，单词所在句与"而且优步……"为并列递进的关系，可知单词所在句的句意与获益有关，付给司机的钱是目标的话，发展无人驾驶出租车车队自然是最盈利的，因此选项B符合此处语境，故为正确答案。

【排他分析】由以上分析可知，其余三个选项均不符合单词所在句的语境，故均排除。

4 A recent analysis is cited to _____.　　一项最近的分析被引用来_____。

A. illustrate the higher cost of driveless taxis　　A. 说明无人驾驶出租车的成本更高
B. stress the serious influence brought by monitors　　B. 强调监察员带来的严重影响
C. highlight the importance of attracting passengers　　C. 强调吸引乘客的重要性
D. show the infeasibility of relying on driverless taxis　　D. 表明依赖无人驾驶出租车不可行

【解题思路】D。推理判断题。根据题干关键词（A recent analysis）可直接定位到第三段。根据该分析的具体内容，自己开车每英里的成本约为0.72美元，而无人驾驶出租车运营商预计的最低盈亏平衡点是每英里1.31美元。无人驾驶汽车将需要人类安全监察员的关注，这些监察员的工资必须由车费支付。无人驾驶汽车的成本是更高的，印证了上句，即使是这些公司（发展无人驾驶出租车车队）也可能难以盈利，所以依赖无人驾驶出租车获利也不可行，选项D为正确答案。

【排他分析】选项A是通过该分析可得出的直接结论，并未指出该分析的进一步所指，故排除。文章提到监察员的工资必须由车费支付，意在强调无人驾驶车的成本高，且选项中的serious influence程度过于严重，故排除选项B。选项C根据"在值班期间，无论是否有乘客，出租车都会增加汽油等物品的成本"臆断而来，可排除。

Para. 4 ①Until they turn profits, ride-hailing firms will be vulnerable to a loss of investors' patience. ②But drivers of private vehicles also receive plenty of implicit support. ③Drivers impose environmental hazards on others at no financial cost to themselves, from the health effects of local air pollution to the climate change resulting from carbon emissions. ④And then there is congestion. ⑤The right to use scarce road space is valuable. ⑥When it is given away, drivers overuse available roads, and clog them. ⑦The waste is colossal.

参考译文 ①在实现盈利之前，叫车公司很容易使投资者失去耐心。②但私家车司机也得到了很多隐性支持。③从当地空气污染对健康的影响，到碳排放导致的气候变化，司机们将环境危害强加于他人，而自己却没有付出任何经济代价。④还有交通堵塞。⑤使用稀少道路空间的权利是宝贵的。⑥当它被分发出去时，司机们会过度使用可用的道路，并堵塞道路。⑦其带来的浪费是巨大的。

原文剖析 本段指出私家车对空气、气候以及交通的影响,过度使用可用的道路并堵塞道路带来的浪费是巨大的。

设题点睛 本段讲了私家车带来的几方面影响,可对其影响的几方面进行总结并考查。

生词解析

be vulnerable to 易受……的伤害
impose sth. on 把……强加给……
congestion n. (交通)拥塞;塞车
clog vt. 阻塞;障碍

implicit adj. 含蓄的,不直接言明的
hazard n. 危险,风险
scarce adj. 稀有的;不足的
colossal adj. 巨大的;庞大的

Para. 5 ①Removing the subsidy to drivers means pricing road space by levying tolls that increase with traffic. ②That would deter driving, and reduce congestion and other social costs of automobile use. ③Such charges are rarely popular with drivers. ④But governments' enthusiasm for new, untolled roads has dimmed. ⑤And they do not help much with traffic. ⑥Gilles Duranton of the University of Pennsylvania and Matthew Turner of Brown University posit a "fundamental law of road congestion": unless road space is priced appropriately, new capacity reduces the cost of driving, thereby inducing more of it, leading, eventually, to renewed congestion.

参考译文 ①取消对司机的补贴意味着通过征收通行费来为道路空间定价,通行费会随着交通流量的增加而增加。②这将阻止驾驶,并减少开车导致的拥堵和其他社会成本。③这样的收费很少受到司机的欢迎。④但是,政府对新建不收费公路的热情已经消退。⑤而且它们对交通也没有多大帮助。⑥宾夕法尼亚大学的吉尔斯·杜兰特和布朗大学的马修·特纳提出了一个"道路拥堵基本定律":除非道路空间的价格合适,否则新容量会降低驾驶成本,从而导致更高的驾驶成本,最终导致新的拥堵。

原文剖析 本段前几句指出取消对司机的补贴会带来负面影响,接着指出新建不收费公路不可行,最后阐述了宾夕法尼亚大学的吉尔斯·杜兰特和布朗大学的马修·特纳提出的一个"道路拥堵的基本定律"。

设题点睛 本段中有一个转折句,可用于设置正确选项,最后一句带引号的内容可设置考点。

生词解析

levy vt. 征收(税等)
untolled adj. 不收费的
posit vt. 假设;认定

deter vt. 制止,阻止
dim vi. 减弱,变暗淡

长难句解析

Gilles Duranton of the University of Pennsylvania and Matthew Turner of Brown
　　　主语1　　　　　后置定语1　　　　　　主语2　　　后置定语2
University posit a "fundamental law of road congestion": unless road space is priced
　　　谓语1　　宾语1　　　　后置定语3　　　　　　条件状语
appropriately, new capacity reduces the cost of driving, thereby inducing more of it,
　　　　　　　主语3　　谓语2　宾语2　　　　　　结果状语1

leading, eventually, to renewed congestion.

　　　　　结果状语2

本句是主从复合句。主句主干为 Gilles Duranton and Matthew Turner posit a "fundamental law of road congestion", of 介词短语作相应的主语或宾语的后置定语。冒号后面是对主句宾语的解释说明。unless 引导条件状语从句,inducing… 和 leading… 是动名词短语作结果状语。

5 According to the "fundamental law of road congestion" (Para. 5), the government is called on to _____.

根据"道路拥堵基本定律"(第五段),政府被呼吁_____。

A. set a proper price for road space
B. build new roads for more private cars
C. take steps to ease the traffic pressure
D. alleviate the impact of private cars on the air

A. 为道路空间设定合适的价格
B. 为更多的私家车修建新的道路
C. 采取措施缓解交通压力
D. 缓解私家车对空气的影响

【解题思路】A。推理判断题。根据题干关键词定位到最后一段。这个定律指出,除非道路空间的价格合适,否则新容量会降低驾驶成本,从而导致更高的驾驶成本,最终导致新的拥堵。由此可知该定律强调政府应设定合理的道路空间价格,因此选项 A 为正确答案。

【排他分析】原文指出,但是,政府对新建不收费公路的热情已经消退,选项 B 与文意相悖,故排除。选项 C 利用 reduce congestion 作干扰,该选项与题干关系不大,可排除。选项 D 中对空气的影响是上文的内容,可直接排除。

Text 4

Over the past decade, quinoa, one of the few crops that thrive on Bolivia's high plains, 13,000 ft. above sea level, has become a pinnacle product for foodies, health nuts and fair-trade fanatics. The gluten-free staple—in Bolivia it is produced solely by small-scale farmers and 90% is organic—often adorns plates from celebrity chefs like Giada De Laurentiis and Bobby Flay and has inspired entire cookbooks devoted to salads, soups and stuffings touting its nutritional goodness. It's an unaccustomed role for such a humble crop, which poorer Bolivians often grew and ate instead of buying rice. "It was always comida para los indios (food for Indians)," says Benjamin Huarachi, a member of the board of Bolivia's largest quinoa growers' association, Anapqui, almost laughing. "Today it's food for the world's richest."

It's also food for thought about the complications that arise when rich nations try to support farmers in the developing world. The colorful tall tufts, which yield one of the healthiest foods on the planet, have <u>become Huarachi's golden goose</u>. As global food prices have risen, the price of quinoa has tripled in the past five years, to $1 per lb., a boon to growers in the poorest region of South America's poorest country. "Now we've got tractors for our fields and parabolic antennas for our homes," he says.

And trouble with the neighbors. In an economy dependent on volatile commodity exports, quinoa has made farmers richer, but it has also become an out-of-reach luxury for many Bolivians and fueled violent conflict. In February hundreds of farmers clashed over prime quinoa-growing territory, and dozens were injured. The high price of quinoa has cut domestic consumption dramatically, sparking concerns about malnutrition, with many farmers scrambling to export all their quinoa, even supplementing their diets with foods like pasta. The crop is also straining natural resources as land inhabited by grazing llamas is turned over to quinoa, causing erosion and a scarcity of llama-fertilized soil.

The litany of problems raises questions about whether the satisfying act of buying fair trade—which aims to help small farmers gain access to higher-end consumers abroad—can do more harm than good for the poor in developing countries. "When you transform a food into a commodity, there's inevitable breakdown in social relations and high environmental cost," says Tanya Kerssen, a food-policy analyst for the food-and development institute Food First, based in Oakland, Calif.

Quinoa, which has been cultivated in Bolivia since 3,000 B.C., took off in richer countries in the 1990s after NASA researchers recommended it as part of a potential space-colony diet and health-food addicts latched on. Bolivia, the world's No. 1 quinoa producer, now grows roughly half the global supply (Peru is a close second, Ecuador third), and the super-food is the country's fastest-growing export.

Rising incomes from quinoa farming have lifted the education and living standards of rural families in the quinoa heartland of Potosi, making it a strategic crop for Bolivia. The government says it's including quinoa in school breakfasts and offering $10 million in low-interest loans to farmers to make the food more affordable. Growers' associations say they're increasing the number of grazing llamas per acre to address erosion problems. And local producers haven't sold out to foreign agricultural conglomerates, which tend to strip farming communities of profits when their native crops go global, according to Aziz Elbehri, a senior economist at the U.N.'s Food and Agriculture Organization. Those efforts won't shield farmers from a sharp price drop if the quinoa fad fizzles. Says Kerssen: "Quinoa is now a free-market phenomenon. This is a boom, and there's definitely going to be a bust."

(*Time*, 2012.5)

1. According to the first paragraph, which of the following is true?
   A. Indians are too poor to enjoy quinoa in the past.
   B. Quinoa can only be planted on Bolivia's high plains.
   C. Only a small group of farmers have the right to grow quinoa.
   D. Quinoa has been recommended as a superior nourishment.

2. By saying "become Huarachi's golden goose" (Para. 2), the author implies that _____.
   A. quinoa has brought a fortune to local farmers
   B. quinoa is one of the healthiest foods on the planet

C. quinoa has stimulated a boom in global food prices

D. wealthy nations often support the poor farmers

3. According to paragraph 3, the planting of quinoa has caused _____.

   A. a serious reliance on volatile commodity exports

   B. a change in Bolivians' established way of life

   C. a luxury lifestyle for many Bolivians

   D. injuries and deaths of many greedy Bolivians

4. Which of the following would Tanya Kerssen most probably agree on?

   A. Quinoa can have a detrimental effect on Bolivian society.

   B. Breakdown in social relations is unavoidable in Bolivia.

   C. Food should never be treated as a commodity.

   D. Quinoa can help poor farmers gain access to higher-level consumers.

5. According to the last paragraph, it is suggested that Bolivian farmers _____.

   A. try to maintain the high price of quinoa

   B. hate the foreign agricultural conglomerates

   C. employ llamas to boost the crop yield

   D. may be the victim of the quinoa-craze

语篇分析与试题精解

Para. 1 ①Over the past decade, quinoa, one of the few crops that thrive on Bolivia's high plains, 13,000 ft. above sea level, has become a pinnacle product for foodies, health nuts and fair-trade fanatics. ②The gluten-free staple—in Bolivia it is produced solely by small-scale farmers and 90% is organic—often adorns plates from celebrity chefs like Giada De Laurentiis and Bobby Flay and has inspired entire cookbooks devoted to salads, soups and stuffings touting its nutritional goodness. ③It's an unaccustomed role for such a humble crop, which poorer Bolivians often grew and ate instead of buying rice. ④"It was always comida para los indios (food for Indians)," says Benjamin Huarachi, a member of the board of Bolivia's largest quinoa growers' association, Anapqui, almost laughing. ⑤"Today it's food for the world's richest."

参考译文 ①在玻利维亚海拔13 000英尺(≈3 962米)的高地平原上,能茁壮生长的作物为数不多,藜麦是其中一种。在过去的十年中,藜麦逐渐成了美食家、养生专家和公平贸易狂热分子所拥戴的高端食品。②玻利维亚只有小范围的农民种植该作物,且有机作物的比重高达90%。因此,这种无麸质的食材经常出现在诸如吉亚达·德·劳伦蒂斯(Giada De Laurentiis)和博比·福勒(Bobby Flay)等名厨的料理中。同时,该作物的风行也使各类推崇其营养价值的沙拉、汤羹及馅料的菜谱竞相出现。③这种不起眼的作物原本是玻利维亚的穷人因为吃不起大米而种植食用的,如今却摇身一变成了高端食品。④"以前这都是印第安人才吃的食物。"玻利维亚最大的藜麦种植协会理事会成员本杰明·胡安其(Benjamin Huarachi)笑着说。⑤"如今却成了世界各地富豪的盘中餐。"

原文剖析 本段首句提出观点：玻利维亚高原的藜麦在近十年来成为各类人士眼中的高端食品。第二句支持首句，继续介绍玻利维亚只有小部分地方可以种植这种有机比重占九成的食物，而且各种大厨都对藜麦的营养价值推崇有加。第三句通过对比给出事实：之前这种农作物其实是穷人吃的。第四句和第五句用人物观点给出例证：过去是贫穷的印第安人才吃的食物，现在却是有钱人的盘中餐。

设题点睛 本段第二句为长难句，一般会设置细节题。第四句和第五句为人物观点，同样也可用来设置细节题。

生词解析

quinoa n. 藜麦
nut n. 狂热的人
staple n. 主食
tout vt. 兜售
unaccustomed adj. 奇怪的

pinnacle n. 高峰
gluten-free 无麸质的
organic adj. 有机的
nutritional adj. 营养的

长难句解析

The gluten-free staple—in Bolivia it is produced solely by small-scale farmers and 90% is
　　　主语　　　　　　　　　　　　　　插入语
organic—often adorns plates from celebrity chefs like Giada De Laurentiis and Bobby
　　　　　状语　谓语1　宾语1　　　　　　　后置定语1
Flay and has inspired entire cookbooks devoted to salads, soups and stuffings touting
连词　　谓语2　　　　宾语2　　　　　　后置定语2
its nutritional goodness.

本句为主谓宾结构，主干为 the staple adorns plates and has inspired…。破折号中间为插入语，是 and 连接的两个并列句，其中状语 in Bolivia 前置。破折号后为并列的两个谓语和宾语，第一个后置定语修饰宾语 plates，第二个后置定语修饰 cookbooks，且第二个后置定语中还包含一个分词结构 touting… 作后置定语，对宾语2进行修饰。

1 According to the first paragraph, which of the following is true? 　　从第一段可知下面哪项正确？

A. Indians are too poor to enjoy quinoa in the past.
B. Quinoa can only be planted on Bolivia's high plains.
C. Only a small group of farmers have the right to grow quinoa.
D. Quinoa has been recommended as a superior nourishment.

A. 过去印第安人因太贫穷而吃不起藜麦。
B. 藜麦只能种植在玻利维亚的高地平原上。
C. 只有一小部分农民有权种植藜麦。
D. 藜麦被推荐为高级营养品。

【解题思路】D。事实细节题。根据题干要求定位到文章首段，在没有更详细的定位点的情况下，优先阅读段落中的重点结构。本段第二句主干为 The gluten-free staple often adorns plates and has inspired entire cookbooks touting its nutritional goodness（这

种无麸质的主食经常出现在名厨料理中,还使得推崇其营养价值的各类菜谱竞相出现),其中的 nutritional goodness 与选项 D 中的 superior nourishment 对应,而该项中的 recommended 对应原文的 touting,所以选项 D 为正确答案。

【排他分析】选项 A 对应本段第四句,原文中胡安其提到过去藜麦是印第安人的食物,而选项 A 的大意是印第安人过去太穷而吃不起藜麦,意思与原文相反,所以排除。选项 B 对应本段首句,原文虽然谈到在玻利维亚海拔 13 000 英尺的高地上,藜麦是为数不多能茁壮成长的农作物,但是并没有指出藜麦只能在玻利维亚的高原上生长,因此该项属于过度推断,可以排除。选项 C 对应本段第二句,原句提到藜麦只由小范围的农民种植(produced solely by small-scale farmers),应该和其生长条件有关,并不能由此断定只有一小部分农民有权种植藜麦,所以排除。

Para. 2 ①It's also food for thought about the complications that arise when rich nations try to support farmers in the developing world. ②The colorful tall tufts, which yield one of the healthiest foods on the planet, have become Huarachi's golden goose. ③As global food prices have risen, the price of quinoa has tripled in the past five years, to $1 per lb., a boon to growers in the poorest region of South America's poorest country. ④"Now we've got tractors for our fields and parabolic antennas for our homes," he says.

参考译文 ①藜麦的风行使发达国家鼓励发展中国家的农民大范围种植,这一现象也引发了人们对于由此产生的一系列问题的思考。②这种五颜六色的高秆、丛生的作物能够产出世界上最健康的食物之一,成了胡安其的摇钱树。③随着全球食品价格的节节攀升,藜麦的价格在过去五年里翻了三倍,达到了每磅 1 美金。对于南美洲最贫穷国家中最落后地区的农民来说,这个价格相当可观。④"如今我们的农田里配备了拖拉机,家里也安装了卫星天线。"胡安其说。

原文剖析 本段首句提出问题:富裕国家支持发展中国家农民种植藜麦这一现象值得人们思考。第二句开始描述现象,本句主干为 The colorful tall tufts have become Huarachi's golden goose(金鹅,言下之意就是摇钱树)。第三句和第四句对第二句做进一步解释:藜麦价格翻了三倍,对贫穷的农民来说有益处;藜麦为农民带来了拖拉机和卫星天线,暗指生活水平大幅提高。

设题点睛 本段第二句(观点)以及第三句和第四句(举例论证)构成重要的总分结构,一般会设置细节题或者篇章结构题。

生词解析
complication n. 混乱
boon n. 恩惠,利益
antennas n. 天线
tuft n. 一丛,一簇
parabolic adj. 抛物线的

2 By saying "become Huarachi's golden goose" (Para. 2), the author implies that _____.

A. quinoa has brought a fortune to local farmers

作者用"become Huarachi's golden goose"(第二段)这样的表达暗示_____。

A. 藜麦给当地农民带来了巨大的财富

B. quinoa is one of the healthiest foods on the planet
C. quinoa has stimulated a boom in global food prices
D. wealthy nations often support the poor farmers

B. 藜麦是世界上最健康的食物之一
C. 藜麦刺激了全球食品价格的增长
D. 富裕国家常常支持贫穷的农民

【解题思路】A。语意理解题。根据题干要求定位到第二段第二句,句中带有明显的比喻修辞(golden goose,金鹅,暗指摇钱树)。在处理语意理解题时,首先要通过本句进行理解(有时候中文和英文语意是相同的,如果无法理解,则根据上下文间的逻辑关系进行猜测)。本句和第三、四句构成明确的"观点+支撑"结构。即使考生对第四句中的 tractors 和 parabolic antennas 不理解,也可根据第三句中价格翻三倍及对贫穷农民是极好的意思进行推断。这两句应体现种植藜麦给当地人带来了财富的意思,选项 A 符合原文大意。

【排他分析】选项 B 对应本段中的第二句,其大意是这种五颜六色的植物能生产出全世界最健康的食物之一,本身与金鹅所代表的经济利益无法产生直接的因果关系,所以排除。选项 C 对应本段第三句,原文确实提到全球范围内食品价格暴涨,同时藜麦价格也翻了三倍,但是并没有体现藜麦的价格增长刺激了全球食品价格增长这一关系,自然也解释不了 golden goose 的意思,所以排除。选项 D 对应的是本段首句,首句中提到富裕国家支持发展中国家的农民种植藜麦,但这与 golden goose 之间同样没有直接联系,所以排除。

Para. 3 ①And trouble with the neighbors. ②In an economy dependent on volatile commodity exports, quinoa has made farmers richer, but it has also become an out-of-reach luxury for many Bolivians and fueled violent conflict. ③In February hundreds of farmers clashed over prime quinoa-growing territory, and dozens were injured. ④The high price of quinoa has cut domestic consumption dramatically, sparking concerns about malnutrition, with many farmers scrambling to export all their quinoa, even supplementing their diets with foods like pasta. ⑤The crop is also straining natural resources as land inhabited by grazing llamas is turned over to quinoa, causing erosion and a scarcity of llama-fertilized soil.

参考译文 ①藜麦的风行也导致了邻里不睦。②在一个依赖不稳定经济出口的经济体中,藜麦使农民更加富裕。但对于许多玻利维亚人来说,藜麦也成了不折不扣的奢侈品,并引发了激烈的冲突。③2月,上百名农民为争夺种植藜麦的最佳土地发生冲突,数十人受伤。④藜麦价格的增长导致该作物在国内的消耗骤减。农民们不惜改变自己的饮食习惯,改吃其他主食,如意大利面,反而争相把自己食用的藜麦出口到国外,这引起人们对于由此产生的营养不良问题的担忧。⑤该作物的种植还挤占了各类自然资源,如原本用于放牧羊驼的土地,如今也用来种植藜麦。地表因此受到侵蚀,原本因放牧而肥沃的土壤变得贫瘠。

原文剖析 本段首句提出观点:藜麦的种植会引发农民之间的矛盾。第二句和第三句对首句进行举例论证:藜麦的出口能带来财富,但是也会带来冲突,比如农民为了争夺最佳的藜麦种植地而发生冲突,导致多人受伤。第四句和第五句指出其他问题:迫使当地人改变饮食结构,同时传统的羊驼养殖业也因为藜麦种植地的扩张而受到影响,进一步带来水土流失和土壤肥力下降等后果。

设题点睛 本段最重要的结构是首句(观点)与第二、三句(事例)的总分结构,一般会设置例子功能题,同时第四句和第五句谈到的藜麦种植带来的其他问题可用来设置细节题。

生词解析

volatile *adj.* 不稳定的
scramble *vi.* 争夺
graze *vt.* 放牧
scarcity *n.* 不足,缺乏

malnutrition *n.* 营养失调
strain *vt.* 使(物资)耗尽,使紧张
llama *n.* 羊驼,美洲驼

3 According to paragraph 3, the planting of quinoa has caused _____.

A. a serious reliance on volatile commodity exports
B. a change in Bolivians' established way of life
C. a luxury lifestyle for many Bolivians
D. injuries and deaths of many greedy Bolivians

根据第三段,藜麦的种植导致_____。

A. 严重依赖不稳定的商品出口
B. 玻利维亚人改变已有的生活方式
C. 许多玻利维亚人形成了奢侈的生活方式
D. 许多贪婪的玻利维亚人伤亡

【解题思路】B。事实细节题。根据题干要求可定位到文章第三段,通过语篇分析可知第三段整段都用于描述藜麦种植可能带来的不利影响。本段第四句和第五句明确指出藜麦种植除了会引发居民之间的冲突之外,还会带来两个不利影响:改变当地人的饮食习惯,改变当地人的谋生方式(不养羊驼改种藜麦)。可以对应选项 B 所说的玻利维亚人的传统生活方式(established way of life)出现了变化。

【排他分析】选项 A 对应本段第二句,句中提到玻利维亚的经济依赖于价格波动大的商品出口,这是对事实的陈述,即使没有藜麦,玻利维亚也大幅度依赖出口,只不过藜麦的价格上涨使得种植户得到了更多的财富,所以选项 A 属于过度推断,可以排除。选项 C 对应本段第二句后半句中的转折,原文只是说藜麦本身成了一种奢侈品,并没有说藜麦的种植使得玻利维亚人过上了奢侈的生活,所以排除。选项 D 对应本段第三句,原文指出造成大量伤亡的原因在于当地人对藜麦种植地的争夺和冲突,并没有指出玻利维亚人是贪婪的,而且也没有提及有人在冲突中死亡,因此排除。

Para. 4 ① The litany of problems raises questions about whether the satisfying act of buying fair trade—which aims to help small farmers gain access to higher-end consumers abroad—can do more harm than good for the poor in developing countries. ② "When you transform a food into a commodity, there's

参考译文 ①一连串的问题引发了人们对于购买公平贸易行为的质疑——旨在帮助小农获取国外高端顾客销售渠道的购买公平贸易行为对发展中国家的穷人来说真的利大于弊吗? ②"当我们把一种食物转变为商品时,就不可避免地要面临社会关系破裂及

inevitable breakdown in social relations and high environmental cost," says Tanya Kerssen, a food-policy analyst for the food-and development institute Food First, based in Oakland, Calif.

高昂的环境成本问题。"总部位于加利福尼亚州奥克兰的"食为先"食物与发展研究所食品政策分析员塔尼娅·克森（Tanya Kerssen）如此表示。

原文剖析 本段首句对购买公平贸易行为（buying fair trade）提出质疑：帮助小农接触国外高端客户的贸易模式真的对贫穷的农民有利吗？言下之意是不利的。第二句给出人物观点：当食物转变为商品时，人际关系和环境都会受到损害。

设题点睛 本段第二句存在人物观点，一般会设置考点。

生词解析
litany n. 冗长枯燥的陈述　　　　　　gain access to 有接近……的权利

长难句解析
The litany of problems　raises　 questions about whether the satisfying act of buying fair
　　　主语　　　　　　　谓语　　宾语　　　　　　　　宾语从句
trade—which aims to help small farmers gain access to higher-end consumers abroad—
　　　　　　　　　　　　　　　　　插入语
can do more harm than good for the poor in developing countries.
　　　　　　　宾语从句

本句为主从复合句，主干为 problems raises questions…，about 引出的介词短语作宾语 questions 的后置定语，whether 引导的从句作该介词的宾语。两个破折号中间的非限制性定语从句是插入语，对 whether 宾语从句中的主语进行说明，whether 宾语从句的主干结构是 whether the act can do more harm than good。

4	Which of the following would Tanya Kerssen most probably agree on?	塔尼娅·克森最有可能同意以下哪种说法？
	A. Quinoa can have a detrimental effect on Bolivian society.	A. 藜麦可能对玻利维亚的社会产生不利影响。
	B. Breakdown in social relations is unavoidable in Bolivia.	B. 玻利维亚社会关系的破裂是不可避免的。
	C. Food should never be treated as a commodity.	C. 食物永远不应该被看作商品。
	D. Quinoa can help poor farmers gain access to higher-level consumers.	D. 藜麦可以帮助贫穷农民接触高端消费者。

【解题思路】A。事实细节题。根据题干人名定位到文章第四段。第二句为塔尼娅·克森的明确观点：当食物变成一种商品时，社会关系和环境都会受影响（breakdown），直接对应选项 A，选项 A 中的 detrimental effect 对应原文的 breakdown。

【排他分析】选项 B 同样对应第四段第二句人物观点中的 there's inevitable breakdown in social relations and high environmental cost，但是原文这句话的前提是当藜麦这种农产品变成商品的时候，选项 B 忽略了这个前提，因此不符合原文，所以排除。选项 C 同样对应第四段第二句话中的 transform a food into a commodity，原文并没有说不可以将食物变成商品，只是强调这样做会对社会关系和环境产生不利影响，选项 C 的意思过于绝对,所以排除。选项 D 对应第四段首句内容,虽然首句不是直接由 Tanya Kerssen 提出,但是阅读中只要人物没有对之前的内容进行质疑,也可将其视为人物观点,但选项 D 的大意是藜麦可以帮助贫穷农民接触高端消费者,而原文表示购买公平贸易行为旨在帮助农民接触高端消费者,两者意思并不一致,所以排除。

Para. 5 ① Quinoa, which has been cultivated in Bolivia since 3,000 B.C., took off in richer countries in the 1990s after NASA researchers recommended it as part of a potential space-colony diet and health-food addicts latched on. ② Bolivia, the world's No. 1 quinoa producer, now grows roughly half the global supply (Peru is a close second, Ecuador third), and the super-food is the country's fastest-growing export.

参考译文 ①早在公元前 3 000 年,玻利维亚就开始种植藜麦。20 世纪 90 年代,美国国家航空航天局(NASA)的研究人员将藜麦列入太空殖民计划的推荐食物之一,健康食物的拥趸就此认定藜麦是健康食品。自此,藜麦在发达国家流行开来。②玻利维亚是世界上最大的藜麦生产国,产量约占全球供应量的一半(秘鲁紧随其后,厄瓜多尔排名第三)。这一高端食品成为玻利维亚出口增长最快的商品。

原文剖析 本段首句指出藜麦种植的历史和受到发达国家欢迎的最初原因:因美国国家航空航天局推荐而开始被发达国家推崇。第二句介绍了玻利维亚目前是藜麦的最大生产国。

设题点睛 本段首句为带有原因内容的观点句,可能会设置考点。但是第二句为事实陈述,且内容简单,不易结合首句进行选项设置,因此本段不适合设置考题。

生词解析

take off 开始流行　　　　　　　　　　　　latch on 理解,明白;抓住

长难句解析

Quinoa, which has been cultivated in Bolivia since 3000 B.C., took off in richer countries
主语　　　　非限制性定语从句　　　　　　　谓语　　　　地点状语
in the 1990s after NASA researchers recommended it as part of a potential space-colony diet
时间状语　　　　　　时间状语从句
and health-food addicts latched on.

本句为主从复合句,主干结构为 Quinoa took off。which 引导的非限制性定语从句修饰主语 Quinoa,after 引导的时间状语从句的主干结构为 NASA researchers recommended it as… and health-food addicts latched on。

Para. 6 ①Rising incomes from quinoa farming have lifted the education and living standards of rural families in the quinoa heartland of Potosi, making it a strategic crop for Bolivia. ② The government says it's including quinoa in school breakfasts and offering $10 million in low-interest loans to farmers to make the food more affordable. ③Growers' associations say they're

参考译文 ①波托西是玻利维亚藜麦种植的重点地区,该地区通过种植藜麦增加了居民收入,进而提高了农村家庭的教育条件和生活水平,藜麦因此被列为玻利维亚的战略作物。②政府规定学校早餐中必须包含藜麦,并拨出一千万美金的低息贷款帮助农民,让他们吃得起这一食物。③种植协会表示,他们

67

increasing the number of grazing llamas per acre to address erosion problems. ④ And local producers haven't sold out to foreign agricultural conglomerates, which tend to strip farming communities of profits when their native crops go global, according to Aziz Elbehri, a senior economist at the U. N.'s Food and Agriculture Organization. ⑤ Those efforts won't shield farmers from a sharp price drop if the quinoa fad fizzles. ⑥Says Kerssen: "Quinoa is now a free-market phenomenon. This is a boom, and there's definitely going to be a bust."

正着力增加每亩耕地中的羊驼放养数量,以此解决土地侵蚀的问题。④国外大型农业集团欲借藜麦大量出口热销之机剥夺农民利润,而联合国粮农组织资深经济学家阿齐兹·艾尔伯瑞(Aziz Elbehri)研究发现,当地种植户并未将作物全部出售给此类集团。⑤一旦当前的藜麦热降温,以上举措并不能保护当地种植户免受价格下跌带来的影响。⑥克森说:"藜麦现象是自由市场的产物。现在是藜麦经济发展的繁荣期,但它也会走向萧条。"

原文剖析 本段首句承接上段,继续指出藜麦种植对当地社会的积极影响,即提升教育和生活质量。第二句到第四句提出各方在保护玻利维亚人以及藜麦市场等方面做出的各种努力:政府为玻利维亚农民提供低息贷款,让居民能吃得起藜麦,种植协会增加羊驼的数量来肥沃土壤,当地种植户也没有遭到国外农业集团盘剥。但是第五句否定指出这一系列行为也许都不能使农民免受藜麦价格崩盘带来的伤害,最后一句继续借用人物观点总结:藜麦现象是自由经济产物,有繁荣也会有萧条。

设题点睛 本段第五句和第六句为对之前四句内容的总结性观点,考查概率比较大。

生词解析

conglomerate *n.* 综合大型企业　　　　strip of 剥夺
shield *vt.* 保护　　　　　　　　　　　fizzle *vi.* 失败
bust *n.* 萧条

长难句解析

And local producers　haven't sold out to　foreign agricultural conglomerates,
连词　　主语　　　　　　谓语　　　　　　　宾语
which tend to strip farming communities of profits　when their native crops go global,
　　　　　定语从句　　　　　　　　　　　　　　　　　时间状语从句
according to Aziz Elbehri, a senior economist at the U. N.'s Food and Agriculture Organization.
　　　　状语　　　　　　　　　　同位语

本句主干结构为 local producers haven't sold out to…。句中 which 引导的非限制性定语从句指出宾语 foreign agricultural conglomerates 的意图。a senior economist at the U. N.'s Food and Agriculture Organization 作 Aziz Elbehri 的同位语,补充说明状语中此人的身份。

5 According to the last paragraph, it is suggested that Bolivian farmers _____.

A. try to maintain the high price of quinoa
B. hate the foreign agricultural conglomerates
C. employ llamas to boost the crop yield

最后一段暗示了玻利维亚的农民_____。

A. 尽力维持藜麦的高价位
B. 憎恨外国的农业企业集团
C. 利用美洲驼来增加藜麦产量

D. may be the victim of the quinoa-craze　　　　D. 可能是藜麦热的受害者

【解题思路】D。事实细节题。根据题干要求定位到文章最后一段。通过语篇分析确定本段最后两句的人物观点比较重要,大意是最终无论各方如何努力,藜麦的价格可能还是会大幅下滑,而农民不可避免地会受到影响。因此选项 D 是正确答案。

【排他分析】选项 A 中有关 price 的内容只在本段第五句中提到,但是原文没有明确指出要保持高价格,所以排除。选项 B 对应本段第四句,原文只是谈到种植户没有将所有的藜麦都卖给国外大型农业集团,并没说这是因为玻利维亚的种植户讨厌它们,选项 B 属于过度推断,所以排除。选项 C 对应本段第三句,原文指出增加羊驼数量解决土地侵蚀问题,这件事是由种植协会(growers' associations)来做的,而不是农民,所以排除。

Text 5

The rich are different, as F. Scott Fitzgerald famously wrote and so are their banking services. While most of us struggle to keep our balances high enough to avoid a slew of extra fees for everything from writing checks to making ATM withdrawals, wealthy individuals enjoy the special extras provided by banks, which increasingly seem more like high-end concierges than financial institutions. If you are rich, your bank will happily arrange everything from Broadway tickets to spa trips.

Oh, and you'll have an easier time getting a loan too. A recent report by the Goldman Sachs Global Markets Institute, the public-policy unit of the finance giant, found that while the rich have ample access to credit and banking services six years on from the financial crisis, low- and medium-income consumers do not. Instead, they pay more for everything from mortgages to credit cards, and generally, the majority of consumers have worse access to credit than they did before the crisis.

Banks are putting their future bets on wealth-management services catering to rich individuals rather than the masses. Banks would say this is because the cost of doing business with regular people has grown too high in the wake of Dodd-Frank regulation. It's true that in one sense, new regulations dictating how much risk banks can take and how much capital they have to maintain make it easier to provide services to the rich.

Regulation isn't entirely to blame. For starters, banks are increasingly looking to wealthy individuals to make up for the profits they aren't making by trading. Even without Dodd-Frank, it would have been difficult for banks to maintain their pre-crisis trading revenue in a market with the lowest volatility levels in decades. (Huge market shifts mean huge profits for banks on the right side of a trade.) The market calm is largely due to the Federal Reserve Bank's unprecedented $q trillion money dump, which is itself an effort to prop up an anemic recovery.

All of this leads to a self-perpetuating vicious cycle: the lack of access to banking services, loans and capital fuels America's growing wealth divide, which is particularly stark when it comes to race. A May study by the Center for Global Policy Solutions, a

Washington-based consultancy, and Duke University found that the median amount of liquid wealth (assets that can easily be turned into cash) held by African-American households was $200. For Latino households it was $340. Meanwhile, the median for white households was $23,000.

Policymakers and banks need to rethink who is a "good" borrower. One 10-year study by the University of North Carolina, Chapel Hill, for example, found that poor buyers putting less than 5% down can be better-than-average credit risks if vetted by metrics aside from how much cash they have on hand. If banks won't take the risk of lending to them, they may eventually find their own growth prospects in peril. After all, 1% can you only so far.

(*Time*, 2014.9)

1. Which of the following statements would F. Scott Fitzgerald agree to?
   A. Rich people can get Broadway tickets and spa trips easier.
   B. Wealthy individuals ignore the extra fees in the banking service.
   C. High-end concierges are welcomed by rich people.
   D. Banks are exclusively catering to the wealthy individuals.

2. The Dodd-Frank regulation has _____.
   A. pushed up the operational cost of the banking industry
   B. caused difficulties in maintaining the capital for the banks
   C. forced the banks to concentrate on certain services
   D. prompted the banks to cater to the masses' wealth-management

3. The bank could not maintain its pre-crisis revenue because _____.
   A. the market fluctuation is comparatively mild
   B. the financial industry is facing the anemic recovery
   C. the new regulation has taken effect in controlling the market volatility
   D. the Federal Reserve Bank interfered the market

4. The income comparison mentioned in paragraph 5 is used to _____.
   A. stress the importance of liquid wealth in America
   B. highlight the hardships faced by African-Americans
   C. illustrate the harsh reality of the income gap in America
   D. expose the increased wealth gap caused by ethnic inequality

5. The author's attitude toward the banks' current behavior is _____.
   A. contemptuous
   B. biased
   C. appreciated
   D. disapproving

语篇分析与试题精解

Para. 1 ①The rich are different, as F. Scott Fitzgerald famously wrote and so are their

参考译文 ①F·司格特·菲茨杰拉德写过一句名言:富人与众不同;他们享

banking services. ②While most of us struggle to keep our balances high enough to avoid a slew of extra fees for everything from writing checks to making ATM withdrawals, wealthy individuals enjoy the special extras provided by banks, which increasingly seem more like high-end concierges than financial institutions. ③If you are rich, your bank will happily arrange everything from Broadway tickets to spa trips.

受的银行服务也是如此。②当我们大部分人努力让银行账户上保持有足够多的余额,只为了避免在办理一些银行业务时(如开支票或在自动柜员机上取款等)再缴纳额外的手续费时,富人们却很享受银行的收费服务,银行对他们而言则更像一个高端的私人管家,而非金融机构。③只要你有钱,无论是百老汇的门票还是温泉旅行,你的银行都很乐意为你安排妥帖。

原文剖析 本段首句借用名人名言引出本文观点(富人们享受的银行服务与众不同)。后两句对比富人们和普通人对待银行服务的心理和行为,举例论证首句观点。

设题点睛 本段第一句为观点句,第二句为带有比较的长难句,适合设置正确选项。

生词解析

balance n. (收支)余额,余数
extra n. [常用于复数]另外收费的事物
concierge n. 管理人员;看门人

a slew of 大量的
high-end adj. 高端的;高档的

长难句解析

While most of us struggle to keep our balances high enough to avoid a slew of extra fees for
　　　　　　　　　　　　　　　　　状语从句
everything from writing checks to making ATM withdrawals, wealthy individuals enjoy
　　　　　　　　　　　　　　　　　　　　　　　　　　　　　　主语　　　　　谓语
the special extras provided by banks, which increasingly seem more like high-end concierges
　　宾语　　　　后置定语　　　　　　　　　非限制性定语从句
than financial institutions.

本句为主从复合句。本句主干为 wealthy individuals enjoy the special extras…,句子开始处为 while 引导的状语从句,其中的 while 为连词,所引导的从句含有对比、转折的意思,该从句较长,末尾处采用了 from… to… 的介词结构用于举例说明。本句末尾处的非限制性定语从句,对先行词 banks 进行说明。

1. Which of the following statements would F. Scott Fitzgerald agree to?

A. Rich people can get Broadway tickets and spa trips easier.
B. Wealthy individuals ignore the extra fees in the banking service.
C. High-end concierges are welcomed by rich people.

F·司格特·菲茨杰拉德可能会同意以下哪种说法?

A. 有钱人更容易获得百老汇门票和温泉旅行。
B. 有钱人无视银行服务需要缴纳的额外费用。
C. 高端的私人管家受到有钱人欢迎。

D. Banks are exclusively catering to the wealthy individuals.　　　　　　D. 银行只为迎合有钱人的需求。

【解题思路】D。推理引申题。根据题干关键词（F·Scott Fitzgerald）定位到第一段。首句谈到菲茨杰拉德的名言"富人与众不同"，作者随即用"他们享受的银行服务也是如此"表示同意菲茨杰拉德的观点，由于两人的观点相同，因此本题实际询问作者在本段中表达的观点。第二句和第三句具体说有钱人所享受的银行服务有何不同（富人在支付额外服务的费用后，银行可事无巨细地为他们安排一切大小活动），可由此看出本段作者意在表明银行会刻意设计某些迎合有钱人需要的服务，从而赚取费用，与选项D的意思一致。

【排他分析】选项A对应本段第三句中的细节事例，该事例只为了说明银行为富人提供服务的项目包罗万象、事无巨细，因此排除。选项B中的ignore含有"忽视，不在乎"之意，该项暗示富人并不在乎花钱，这与原文所述的富人们是为了享受服务而付费的观点并不完全相符，因此排除。选项C的错误理由同选项A，原文将银行与高端私人管家进行类比只为了说明银行为富人提供服务的项目包罗万象、事无巨细，因此排除。

Para. 2 ① Oh, and you'll have an easier time getting a loan too. ② A recent report by the Goldman Sachs Global Markets Institute, the public-policy unit of the finance giant, found that while the rich have ample access to credit and banking services six years on from the financial crisis, low- and medium-income consumers do not. ③ Instead, they pay more for everything from mortgages to credit cards, and generally, the majority of consumers have worse access to credit than they did before the crisis.

参考译文 ①对了，有钱人获得银行贷款也更容易。②金融巨头高盛公司下属的公共政策部门高盛全球市场研究所近期发布了一项报告，该报告发现，在经济危机爆发后的六年里，有钱人仍有很多机会获得信贷和银行服务，而中低收入的消费者却没有。③相反，中低收入的消费者还要为房贷或信用卡等银行服务支付更高的费用，而且通常情况下，与经济危机前相比，大部分消费者获得贷款的难度更大了。

原文剖析　本段首句承接上段观点，递进指出富人在获得银行贷款方面还要享受便利。后两句再次对比有钱人和普通人在经济危机后获得银行服务方面的不同境遇（有钱人仍可获得贷款，而普通消费者没有那么多机会且需要支付更高费用），用事实支持首句观点。

设题点睛　本段内容与上段呈并列结构，都在描述有钱人会获得银行优待的现象，由于观点重复，一般不会再设置考题。

生词解析

ample *adj.* 丰富的；足够的　　　　　　credit *n.* ［金融］贷款

Para. 3 ① Banks are putting their future bets on wealth-management services catering to rich individuals rather than the masses. ② Banks would say this is

参考译文 ①银行将其未来的发展押在了迎合富人而非大众需求的理财服务上。②银行会说，多德-

because the cost of doing business with regular people has grown too high in the wake of Dodd-Frank regulation. ③ It's true that in one sense, new regulations dictating how much risk banks can take and how much capital they have to maintain make it easier to provide services to the rich.

弗兰克条例实施之后,开展个人业务的成本实在是太高了。③从某种意义上说,情况确实如此,由于新条例规定了银行可承担风险的程度以及需要持有资金的数量,很容易使银行更倾向于为有钱人服务。

原文剖析 本段主要从银行的角度解释其迎合富人的理由。首句指出银行未来将着重发展富人需要的理财业务。第二句银行给出这样做的理由,即在多德-弗兰克条例的要求下,开展个人业务的成本太高。第三句是作者给出的客观分析,解释银行此举的原因在于新规的实施增加了银行的压力,使其倾向于做风险更小、利润更多的理财业务。

设题点睛 本段首句与之后的内容构成了"现象+解释"的结构,原因部分往往是重要内容,适合用来设置考点。

生词解析

put bets on 在……上下注
in the wake of 随着……而来;作为……的结果
cater to 迎合;为……服务
dictate *vt.* 发号施令地规定

长难句解析

It's true that in one sense, new regulations dictating how much risk banks can take and how
主系表　　　　　主语从句　　　　　　　　　后置定语
much capital they have to maintain make it easier to provide services to the rich.
　　　　　　　　　　　　主语从句

本句是主从复合句。本句主干为 it's true that…, it 作形式主语,真正的主语是之后的 that 从句,该从句的主干为 new regulations make it easier to provide services to the rich, regulations 后的 dictating 现在分词作后置定语,其后为两个由 how much 引导的并列的宾语从句,主语从句中的宾语 it 作形式宾语,真正的宾语为后面的不定式,使用了 make it *adj.* to do sth. 的结构。

2 The Dodd-Frank regulation has _____.

　A. pushed up the operational cost of the banking industry

　B. caused difficulties in maintaining the capital for the banks

　C. forced the banks to concentrate on certain services

　D. prompted the banks to cater to the masses' wealth-management

多德-弗兰克条例 _____。

　A. 提高了银行业的运营成本

　B. 为银行在维持资金方面制造了困难

　C. 逼迫银行专注于某类业务

　D. 促使银行迎合大众理财需求

【解题思路】C。推理引申题。根据题干关键词(Dodd-Frank regulation)定位到文章第三段,本题考查这一新规对银行产生的影响。该段首句谈到银行在未来将重点发展"迎合富人而非大众需求的理财服务",后两句从银行和作者的角度给出了这一做法的理由。第二句谈到银行抱怨多德-弗兰克条例的实施使普通的个人业务成本升高(the cost of doing business with regular people has grown too high),作者在第三句中表示银行的这种说法在某种意义上站得住脚,因为该新规的要求使银行的压力变大,促使银行选择风险更小、利润更大的富人理财业务(new regulations... make it easier to provide services to the rich),因此选项C正确。

【排他分析】选项A对应本段第二句,但原文明确指出新规使银行从事普通个人业务的成本太高了(the cost of doing business with regular people has grown),并非是"运营成本",因此排除。选项B对应本段第三句,该句体现新规对银行可承担的风险和需要准备的资金做出了规定,该项中的"制造困难"与原文所说的"规定(dictating)"的概念并不完全相同,且该项只涉及"资金"一个方面,以偏概全,因此排除。选项D对应本段首句,该句指出银行未来要重点发展的理财服务是"迎合富人而非大众需求"的,与该项矛盾,因此可快速排除。

Para. 4 ①Regulation isn't entirely to blame. ②For starters, banks are increasingly looking to wealthy individuals to make up for the profits they aren't making by trading. ③Even without Dodd-Frank, it would have been difficult for banks to maintain their pre-crisis trading revenue in a market with the lowest volatility levels in decades. ④(Huge market shifts mean huge profits for banks on the right side of a trade.) ⑤The market calm is largely due to the Federal Reserve Bank's unprecedented $9 trillion money dump, which is itself an effort to prop up an anemic recovery.

参考译文 ①这一切不能全部归咎于新法规。②首先,银行正越来越依赖富人来补偿其交易产生的利润空缺。③即便没有多德-弗兰克法案,银行也很难在一个数十年来波动性最小的市场中保持其在经济危机前的交易收入水平。④(市场变化越大,银行越处于交易的利好面,获得的利润也越高。)⑤市场之所以波澜不惊,主要是因为联邦储备银行拥有空前的万亿资金储备,用来给复苏乏力的经济提供支持。

原文剖析 本段与上一段内容并列,给出银行迎合富人的其他原因。首句为观点概括句,表示除新规这个外因之外,还有其他因素。第二句到第四句仔细解释了银行这么做的内部要求,指出即便没有该法规,银行也很难在波动性很小的市场中赚取足够利润来弥补交易中出现的利润缺失,括号中的内容解释市场波动性与银行利润的关系。最后一句进而补充说明目前市场波动性小的原因(联邦储备资金的支持)。

设题点睛 本段第二句为总结句,第三句和第四句解释第二句,体现出因果逻辑关系,可以用来设置考题。

生词解析
be to blame 该受责备,应承担责任
volatility *n.* 波动性
dump *n.* 堆集的储备物资
anemic *adj.* 无生气的;贫血的
for starters [口语] 首先,一开始
on the right side of 处于较好的一面
prop up 支撑;支持

长难句解析

Even without Dodd-Frank, it would have been difficult for banks to maintain their
　　状语1　　　　　　　形式主语　　系动词　　表语　状语2　　真正的主语

pre-crisis trading revenue in a market with the lowest volatility levels in decades.
                                          状语3

本句是简单句。本句的主干为 it would have been difficult for banks to...，主干部分使用了 it is *adj*. for sb. to do sth. 的句型，it 为形式主语，不定式为真正的主语，谓语部分使用了 would have done 的虚拟语气，表示对过去的假设。句首处的 even without 相当于一个让步状语从句，因此后面的主句用虚拟语气。

3 The bank could not maintain its pre-crisis revenue because _____.	银行无法维持其经济危机前的收入水平，因为_____。
A. the market fluctuation is comparatively mild	A. 市场波动较为温和
B. the financial industry is facing the anemic recovery	B. 金融行业正面临疲软复苏
C. the new regulation has taken effect in controlling the market volatility	C. 新规在控制市场波动方面已经产生了作用
D. the Federal Reserve Bank interfered the market	D. 联邦储备银行对市场进行了干预

【解题思路】**A**。逻辑关系题。根据题干关键词（pre-crisis revenue）定位到文章第四段第三句。本题考查原因。定位句指出"即便没有多德-弗兰克法案，银行也很难在一个数十年来波动性最小的市场中保持其在经济危机前的交易收入水平"，第四句指出只有市场存在大幅度波动的时候银行才能够通过交易取得巨大利益，综合这两句的意思可看出银行目前无法维持足够利润的原因在于市场波动性太小，因此选项 A 正确，该项中的 fluctuation 与原文中的 volatility 和 shifts 两词对应，comparatively mild 对应第三句中的 lowest。

【排他分析】选项 B 中的 anemic recovery 是本段最后一句的原词，但该短语所在从句的主语是美联储，而非该项中的金融业，且语意与该项无关，因此排除。本段首句已经把新规的因素放在一边，因此之后的内容应该与新规没有关系，且选项 C 中的"控制市场波动"之意在原文中并未出现，因此直接排除。选项 D 中的 Federal Reserve Bank 出现在本段最后一句中，根据常识可知，美联储是通过储备准备金的方式（商业银行放在美联储的押金）来减少社会流动资金，从而控制通货膨胀，这是一种宏观手段，并非对市场的直接干预，这不是题干所问的直接原因，因此选项 D 可以排除。

Para. 5 ①All of this leads to a self-perpetuating vicious cycle: the lack of access to banking services, loans and capital fuels America's growing wealth divide, which is particularly stark when it comes to race. ②A May study by the Center for Global Policy Solutions, a Washington-based consultancy, and Duke University found that the median amount of liquid wealth (assets that can

参考译文 ①所有这些都导致了一种永久存在的恶性循环：无法得到银行服务、贷款和资金加速了美国逐渐扩大的贫富差距，当涉及种族后，这种贫富差距则更加明显。②位于华盛顿的咨询机构全球政策方案中心和杜克大学于五月发布的研究发现，非洲裔美国家庭所持有

easily be turned into cash) held by African-American households was $200. ③ For Latino households it was $340. ④ Meanwhile, the median for white households was $23,000.

的平均流动资产(可变现的资产)是200美元。③拉丁裔的家庭是340美元。④而普通白人家庭的流动资产达到了23 000美元。

原文剖析 本段开始讨论银行迎合富人做法的结果。首句总结指出银行只迎合富人的举措会导致恶性循环,扩大贫富差距。第二句到最后用某研究结论对首句观点进行举例论证,突出少数族裔的美国家庭所持有的平均流动资产与普通白人家庭相比差距较大。

设题点睛 本段首句和其后内容构成"观点+例证"结构,因此首句是重要内容,可用来设置正确选项。

生词解析

self-perpetuating *adj.* 可永久存在的,永在的
stark *adj.* 明显的,突出的
median *adj.* 【统计学】中位数的
Latino *adj.* 拉丁美洲的;拉丁美洲人的

vicious *adj.* 恶意的;有错误的
consultancy *n.* 咨询公司
liquid *adj.* 【经济学】流动性的

4 The income comparison mentioned in paragraph 5 is used to _____.

A. stress the importance of liquid wealth in America
B. highlight the hardships faced by African-Americans
C. illustrate the harsh reality of the income gap in America
D. expose the increased wealth gap caused by ethnic inequality

第五段谈到收入差距是为了_____。

A. 强调流动资产在美国的重要性
B. 突出非洲裔美国人所面临的困难
C. 说明美国收入差距的残酷现实
D. 曝光由种族不平等导致的贫富差距扩大

【解题思路】D。例子功能题。根据题干要求定位到第五段。本题考查第五段给出收入对比的目的或作用。本段首句是观点句,指出"无法得到银行服务、贷款和资金加速了美国逐渐扩大的贫富差距,当涉及种族后,贫富差距则更加明显",从第二句开始给出美国不同族裔家庭所持有的平均流动资产,对比数据的目的是指出本段首句所谈到的美国人的贫富差距拉大的事实在不同种族家庭中体现得很明显,与选项D对应,该项中的 ethnic 对应文中的 race。

【排他分析】选项A中的 liquid wealth 出现在本段第二句,这只是一个指标,对比这个指标并非为了说明其重要性,因此排除该项。选项B谈到的 African-Americans 出现在该段第二句中,虽然非洲裔美国家庭所持有的平均流动资产在三者中是最少的,但其目的是突出美国不同种族间的贫富差距,因此选项B属于过度引申,可排除。选项C虽然谈到了本段的核心内容"贫富差距",但不涉及第二句有关不同种族家庭财富差距的比较,因此相对于选项D而言,并非最佳答案,因此排除。

Para. 6 ①Policymakers and banks need to

参考译文 ①政策制定者和银行需要重

rethink who is a "good" borrower. ② One 10-year study by the University of North Carolina, Chapel Hill, for example, found that poor buyers putting less than 5% down can be better-than-average credit risks if vetted by metrics aside from how much cash they have on hand. ③ If banks won't take the risk of lending to them, they may eventually find their own growth prospects in peril. ④ After all, 1% can you only so far.

新考虑谁才是"优质"借方。②比如,位于教堂山的北卡罗来纳州立大学曾经进行了一项为期十年的研究,该研究发现如果不考虑手头有多少现金,经指标审查后,首付低于5%的拮据型买家,其信用风险会优于平均水平。③如果银行不愿意承担贷款给他们的风险,最终银行可能会发现自己的未来发展处于危险之境。④毕竟,到目前为止只有1%的人是富人。

原文剖析 本段首句给出一个抽象的观点,其中的"good"加双引号表明此处要强调的并非是字面上的意思,需要根据后文确定含义。第二句用一个十年的研究成果举例说明所谓的"穷人"的贷款信用其实要优于一般人,暗示前文谈到的银行认为迎合富人会使自己风险降低的想法并不符合实际。第三句指出后果,即银行不为穷人提供贷款服务的做法将置自己的未来发展于危险之地。第四句是作者给出这样预测的理由,暗示银行如果只做富人的买卖就好像把鸡蛋放在了同一个篮子中,因为富人只占人群的1%。因此,句首处的"good"暗示原来银行所认为的富人群体并不是真正的优质客户。

设题点睛 本段后两句体现明确的观点和态度,可用来设置观点态度题。

生词解析

put down 买东西时先付(一部分钱)作为定金
vet *vt.* 审查;核实
take the risk of 冒……的风险

better-than-average *adj.* 中上等的
metric *n.* 衡量标准
in peril 危急;冒着危险

长难句解析

One 10-year study by the University of North Carolina, Chapel Hill, for example, found
  主语   定语   插入语   谓语
that poor buyers putting less than 5% down can be better-than-average credit risks
                              宾语从句
if vetted by metrics aside from how much cash they have on hand.
   条件状语从句   状语

本句为主从复合句。本句主干为 One 10-year study found that...,主干采用主谓宾结构,宾语为 that 引导的从句,该从句较长,主干为 poor buyers can be better-than-average credit risks if...,其中包含一个 if 引导的条件状语从句,putting 分词短语作 buyers 的后置定语,句末的 aside from 介词短语及其后的 how much 宾语从句构成 if 从句的状语。

5 The author's attitude toward the banks' current behavior is _____.

作者对银行目前举措的态度是_____。

A. contemptuous
B. biased
C. appreciated
D. disapproving

A. 鄙视的
B. 偏见的
C. 欣赏的
D. 反对的

【解题思路】D。观点态度题。根据顺序原则定位到文章最后一段,或可纵观全文后做出判断。第六段涉及作者的建议,第三句明确指出"如果银行不愿意承担贷款给他们(them)的风险,最终银行可能会发现自己的未来发展处于危险之境(in peril)",其中的 them 回指第二句例子中谈到的"首付低于5%的拮据型买家",说明作者认为银行目前只迎合富人的举措是在自掘坟墓,因此选项 D 正确。

【排他分析】作者全篇从客观角度(新规的实施、市场波动性小)和主观角度(银行想弥补损失、降低风险和成本)两个方面分析了银行目前迎合富人的做法,作者在某种程度上对银行的做法表示了理解,因此并没有"蔑视"银行或者对银行表示"偏见",排除选项 A 和 B。选项 C 与第六段第二句所体现的作者态度相反,可直接排除。

Text 6

At a recent hearing on drug prices, Representative Alexandria Ocasio-Cortez said that by funding federal research agencies such as the National Institutes of Health, "the public is acting as an early investor, putting tons of money in the development of drugs that then become privatized." The American people, she complained, receive "no return on the investment that they have made." The witness she was addressing, Harvard Medical School professor Aaron Kesselheim, confirmed the absence of "licensing deals that bring money back into the pockets of the NIH."

Direct licensing deals between companies and government labs are rare by design—a design that has fueled American economic, military and political power for the past seven decades. This structure has been a critical engine of U.S. economic growth since the end of World War II.

The American electronics, personal-computer and biotech industries all can trace their origin to federal research. The internet, genetic engineering, 3-D animation in movies, even the Siri voice assistant on iPhones—all sprang from federal research. Yet the government receives no royalties on Disney movies or iPhones.

Still, Ms. Ocasio-Cortez is wrong that taxpayers get no return on their investment. The resulting growth from these inventions generates significant government revenue in the form of income and capital-gains taxes on thousands of companies and their millions of employees. Leading the world in science and technology also enhances America's geopolitical power and strengthens national security.

The goal of the federal research system has always been to transfer new knowledge and laboratory results as quickly and seamlessly as possible to private industry, which can then translate them into useful products that can boost the economy. The NIH, for example, spends $3.9 billion annually on research conducted in national labs. Biotech and pharmaceutical companies spend more than $90 billion annually on drug discovery and development.

Quantifying the "return" of that taxpayer investment, and separating the contribution of private vs. public investment, is a famously difficult problem in science policy. But as one measure, economists have attributed roughly half of the trillions of dollars in U.S. gross domestic product growth since the end of World War II to technology improvements. Other countries have noticed the model's success and adopted it. To remain the world's leading power, the U.S. needs to invest more in federal research and to transfer its findings seamlessly to industry. Additional taxes on innovation would be a hindrance.

A lack of licensing deals between companies and national labs has nothing to do with high drug prices, which reflect the enormous development costs-in cancer studies, for example, more than 95% of drug candidates never make it past testing. Many smart people are trying to figure out how to develop effective treatments while keeping prices low. Some of their ideas were reviewed during last week's hearing. None, however, involve creating more friction between federal research and private industry. Taxing iPhones, Disney movies or cancer drugs for the federal research that enabled them won't do anyone any good.

(*The Wall Street Journal*, 2019.2)

1. Alexandria Ocasio-Cortez would most probably agree that _____.
   A. the NIH fails to protect the interests of its investors
   B. licensing deals are related to the issue of drug price
   C. the public expects too much of the federal research agencies
   D. the funding cuts would hinder the development of new drugs

2. Which of the following is true about the federal research system?
   A. Many industries benefit a lot from it.
   B. It earns profit through levying high income tax.
   C. Royalties should be charged for the use of its results.
   D. It has greatly ensured America's national security.

3. The author examines the federal research system by _____.
   A. illustrating its leading position
   B. analyzing the causes behind it
   C. comparing different views on it
   D. listing its remarkable influences

4. The U.S. science policy is suggested to _____.
   A. propagate its successful model to other countries
   B. divide the contribution of private vs. public research
   C. invest more in federal research to encourage innovation
   D. ease the tension between federal research and private industry

5. According to the last paragraph, high drug prices may be addressed by _____.
   A. intervening in market competition
   B. carrying out licensing deals
   C. adopting a taxation mechanism
   D. investing more in research

语篇分析与试题精解

Para. 1 ①At a recent hearing on drug prices, Representative Alexandria Ocasio-Cortez said that by funding federal research agencies such as the National Institutes of Health, "the public is acting as an early investor, putting tons of money in the development of drugs that then become privatized." ②The American people, she complained, receive "no return on the investment that they have made." ③The witness she was addressing, Harvard Medical School professor Aaron Kesselheim, confirmed the absence of "licensing deals that bring money back into the pockets of the NIH."

参考译文 ①在近期一次药价听证会上，众议员亚历山大·奥卡西奥-科特兹表示：通过资助诸如国立卫生研究院等联邦研究机构，"公众充当着早期投资人，投入大量资金来研发药物，而这些药物日后却归私人所有"。②她抱怨，美国人民"所做的投资得不到任何回报"。③她所质询的证人——哈佛医学院教授艾伦·克塞尔海姆证实没有"将资金回笼至国立卫生研究院的许可协议"。

原文剖析 本段首先介绍议员就药价问题的看法：联邦研究机构接受大量投资研发药物而将成果私有化，使得公众投入无回报；随后引用哈佛教授证词点明议员眼中药价问题出现的原因：缺乏许可协议；从而将下文语意重点落于联邦研究体制。

设题点睛 本段包含了该议员对药价问题的看法，属于个人观点态度，可设置题目。

生词解析

hearing *n.* 听证会
address *vt.* 与……讲话
license *vi.* 批准，许可

privatize *vt.* 使归私有，使私营化
confirm *vt.* 证实；确认（日期、安排或情况等）

长难句解析

<u>The witness</u> <u>she was addressing</u>, <u>Harvard Medical School professor Aaron Kesselheim</u>,
　　主语　　　定语从句1　　　　　　　　同位语

<u>confirmed</u> <u>the absence of</u> "licensing deals <u>that bring money back into the pockets of</u>
　谓语　　　宾语　　　　　后置定语　　　　　　定语从句2

the NIH."

本句是主从复合句。本句的主干为 The witness confirmed the absence of licensing deals，主语之后为省略了引导词 that 的定语从句，两个逗号中间的内容为主语的同位语，后面 that 引导的从句作定语修饰 licensing deals。

1 Alexandria Ocasio-Cortez would most probably agree that _____.

A. the NIH fails to protect the interests of its investors
B. licensing deals are related to the issue of drug price
C. the public expects too much of the federal research agencies
D. the funding cuts would hinder the development of new drugs

亚历山大·奥卡西奥－科特兹最有可能赞同_____。

A. 国立卫生研究院未能保护其投资者的利益
B. 许可协议与药品价格问题有关
C. 公众对联邦研究机构期望过高
D. 资金的削减将阻碍新药的开发

【解题思路】B。推理判断题。根据题干关键词（Alexandria Ocasio-Cortez）直接定位到第一段。第一段最后一句作者引用哈佛教授证词点明议员眼中药价问题出现的原因：缺乏许可协议，由此可以推出，许可协议与药品价格问题有关，选项B属于合理推断，故为正确答案。

【排他分析】文中第二句提到美国人所做的投资得不到任何回报，由此主观臆断出选项A，文中说公众充当着早期投资人，这只是一种比喻的说法，选项A错误，因此排除。文中并未提及公众对联邦研究机构的期望，选项C属于无中生有，因此排除。文中并未提及 funding cuts 相关内容，故选项D排除。

Para. 2 ① Direct licensing deals between companies and government labs are rare by design—a design that has fueled American economic, military and political power for the past seven decades. ②This structure has been a critical engine of U.S. economic growth since the end of World War Ⅱ.

参考译文 ①企业与政府实验室之间的直接许可协议在设计上是罕见的——这种设计在过去70年里推动了美国的经济、军事和政治力量发展。②自"二战"结束以来，这种结构一直是美国经济增长至关重要的引擎。

原文剖析 本段介绍当前联邦研究机制"直接许可协议少"并概述其重大作用：70年来推动美国经济、军事及政治力量发展；二战结束以来一直是美国经济增长至关重要的引擎。

设题点睛 本段较短且都是在陈述事实，不包含观点性内容，不适合单独设题。

生词解析
fuel *vt.* 增加；加强；刺激

Para. 3 ① The American electronics, personal-computer and biotech industries all can trace their origin to federal research. ② The internet, genetic engineering, 3-D animation in movies, even the Siri voice assistant on iPhones—all sprang from federal research. ③Yet the government

参考译文 ①美国的电子、个人计算机及生物技术产业都可溯源至联邦研究。②互联网、基因工程、电影中的3D动画，甚至是苹果手机上的Siri语音助手——所有这一切都源自联邦研究。③但是，政府并没有从迪士尼电影

receives no royalties on Disney movies or iPhones.　或苹果手机收取任何特许权使用费。

【原文剖析】 本段进一步介绍当前联邦研究机制：政府的确未曾收取技术创新的使用费。先铺陈联邦研究推动技术创新，后转而指出政府并不对此收费。

【设题点睛】 本段前两句陈述客观事实，最后一句虽然含有转折，但本段信息量较少，不适合单独设题。

【生词解析】

electronics *n.* 电子工业，电子学　　　　trace *vt.* 追溯，追查
spring from 源自……　　　　　　　　　royalty *n.* （发明等的）使用费，版税

Para. 4 ① Still, Ms. Ocasio-Cortez is wrong that taxpayers get no return on their investment. ② The resulting growth from these inventions generates significant government revenue in the form of income and capital-gains taxes on thousands of companies and their millions of employees. ③ Leading the world in science and technology also enhances America's geopolitical power and strengthens national security.

【参考译文】 ①尽管如此，奥卡西奥—科特兹女士关于"纳税人投资没有回报"的观点还是错了。②这些发明带来的增长以对数千家公司及其数百万员工征收所得税和资本利得税的形式为政府创造了可观的收入。③在科技方面领先世界也增强了美国的地缘政治实力，加强了国家安全。

【原文剖析】 本段针对议员"纳税人未获得任何回报"的观点做出驳斥，指出纳税人的获利形式借由国家财政收入实现，同时从侧面说明这一机制的重大作用——实现国富民强。

【设题点睛】 本段与上文联系密切，同样都在说明联邦研究的重大作用，可结合上文设题。

【生词解析】

generate *vt.* 产生；引起　　　　　　　revenue *n.* 财政收入；税收收入
capital-gain *n.* 资本收益　　　　　　geopolitical *adj.* 地缘政治学的

Para. 5 ① The goal of the federal research system has always been to transfer new knowledge and laboratory results as quickly and seamlessly as possible to private industry, which can then translate them into useful products that can boost the economy. ② The NIH, for example, spends $3.9 billion annually on research conducted in national labs. ③ Biotech and pharmaceutical companies spend more than $90 billion annually on drug discovery and development.

【参考译文】 ①联邦研究体系的目标一直以来都是将新知识和实验室成果尽可能快速、不间断地输送到能将这些成果转化为有用产品从而推动经济发展的私营产业中去。②比如国立卫生研究院每年要对在国家实验室进行的研究投入39亿美元。③生物科技公司和制药公司每年投入900多亿美元用于药品发现与开发。

【原文剖析】 本段首先说明联邦研究的目标，随后说明联邦研究机构与私人公司投入研发的情况。

【设题点睛】 本段为客观说明性内容，不适合单独设题，可结合上文设置题目。

生词解析

transfer vt. 迁移，搬运
translate（sth.）into sth. 使……转变成……
pharmaceutical adj. 制药的；配药的
seamlessly adv. 不停顿地，无缝地
conduct vt. 进行，实施

长难句解析

The goal of the federal research system has always been to transfer new knowledge
　主语　　　　后置定语　　　　　　　系动词　　　　　　表语
and laboratory results as quickly and seamlessly as possible to private industry, which
　　　　　　　　　　　　状语1　　　　　　　　　　状语2
can then translate them into useful products that can boost the economy.
　　　　　非限制性定语从句　　　　　　　　　定语从句

本句是主从复合句。本句的主干为 The goal has always been to transfer... to private industry, of 介词短语作主语的后置定语，as quickly and seamlessly as possible 作方式状语，which 引导的是非限制性定语从句，that 引导的是定语从句，修饰 useful products。

2	Which of the following is true about the federal research system?	关于联邦研究系统，下列哪项是正确的？
	A. Many industries benefit a lot from it.	A. 许多行业从中受益良多。
	B. It earns profit through levying high income tax.	B. 它通过征收高额所得税来盈利。
	C. Royalties should be charged for the use of its results.	C. 使用其研究成果应收取使用费。
	D. It has greatly ensured America's national security.	D. 它极大地确保了美国的国家安全。

【解题思路】A。事实细节题。根据题干关键词可判断涉及该关键词的段落较多，可定位到第二至五段。第二段提到当前联邦研究机制是推动美国经济、军事及政治的力量，第三段提到美国的电子、个人计算机及生物技术产业都可溯源至联邦研究。互联网、基因工程、电影中的3D动画，甚至是苹果手机上的 Siri 语音助手，所有这一切都源自联邦研究，由此可知许多行业都从中获益良多，选项 A 为正确答案。

【排他分析】第四段提到了 income taxes，但并未指出这种 income taxes 是高额的，选项 B 与原文不符，可排除。文章第三段最后一句提到了使用费，但是，政府并没有从迪士尼电影或苹果手机获取任何特许权使用费，选项 C 与原文事实不符，可排除。第四段最后一句指出，在科技方面领先世界也增强了美国的地缘政治实力，加强了国家安全，并非联邦研究系统确保了国家安全，选项 D 张冠李戴，故排除。

3	The author examines the federal research system by _____.	作者通过_____研究联邦研究系统。
	A. illustrating its leading position	A. 阐述其领先地位
	B. analyzing the causes behind it	B. 分析其背后的原因
	C. comparing different views on it	C. 比较不同的观点
	D. listing its remarkable influences	D. 列举其显著影响

83

【解题思路】D。事实细节题。根据题干可知本题的定位段比较广。第二至三段主要论述了联邦研究系统对各行业的深远影响,第四段从侧面说明这一机制的重大作用:实现国富民强,第五段也通过介绍联邦研究系统的目标侧面说明了其重大作用,由此可知,作者通过列举联邦研究系统的重要作用或影响来研究联邦研究系统,选项 D 为正确答案。

【排他分析】选项 A 将其对各行业的重大影响曲解为它的地位很重要,有失偏颇,故排除。文中并未提及联邦研究系统存在的原因,选项 B 排除。文中只提到了奥卡西奥-科特兹个人对联邦研究系统的观点,并不存在 different views,选项 C 排除。

Para. 6 ① Quantifying the "return" of that taxpayer investment, and separating the contribution of private vs. public investment, is a famously difficult problem in science policy. ② But as one measure, economists have attributed roughly half of the trillions of dollars in U.S. gross domestic product growth since the end of World War II to technology improvements. ③ Other countries have noticed the model's success and adopted it. ④ To remain the world's leading power, the U.S. needs to invest more in federal research and to transfer its findings seamlessly to industry. ⑤ Additional taxes on innovation would be a hindrance.

参考译文 ①量化纳税人投资的"回报",并将私人投资与公共投资的贡献分开,是科学政策上出了名的难题。②但是作为一种衡量标准,经济学家们已将"二战"后美国国内生产总值增长的数万亿美元中的大约一半归功于技术进步。③其他国家也注意到了该模式的成功并纷纷采用该模式。④为了保持世界领先的实力,美国需要在联邦研究上投入更多,并将其研究成果不间断地输送到产业中去。⑤对创新额外征税会成为阻碍。

原文剖析 本段首先指出美国当前联邦研究体制下科技进步贡献巨大,他国纷纷效仿;然后提出建议,应增加联邦研究投入,额外征税会阻碍创新。

设题点睛 本段最后两句为观点句,可用来设置考题。

生词解析

quantify *vt.* 量化
attribute sth. to... 把……归因于……
hindrance *n.* 障碍,妨害

4 The U.S. science policy is suggested to _____. | 美国的科学政策被建议_____。

A. propagate its successful model to other countries | A. 向其他国家宣传其成功模式

B. divide the contribution of private vs. public research | B. 区分私人和公共研究的贡献

C. invest more in federal research to encourage innovation | C. 加大对联邦研究的投入,鼓励创新

D. ease the tension between federal research and private industry | D. 缓解联邦研究和私营企业之间的紧张状态

【解题思路】C。推理判断题。根据题干关键词(The U.S. science policy)直接定位到第六段。根据这一段,为了保持世界领先的实力,美国需要在联邦研究上投入更多,并将其研究成果不间断地输送到产业中去。对创新额外征税会成为一个阻碍。由此可见作者建议增加联邦研究投入,额外征税会阻碍创新,也就是加大投入并鼓励创新,选项 C 为正确答案。

【排他分析】第三句提到,其他国家也注意到了该模式的成功并纷纷采用该模式,但并未提及主动去宣传,选项 A 错误。第一句只提到,将私人投资与公共投资的贡献分开是科学政策上出了名的难题,并不是作者所建议的内容,选项 B 排除。文中并未提及紧张状态等内容,选项 D 属于无中生有。

Para. 7 ① A lack of licensing deals between companies and national labs has nothing to do with high drug prices, which reflect the enormous development costs-in cancer studies, for example, more than 95% of drug candidates never make it past testing. ② Many smart people are trying to figure out how to develop effective treatments while keeping prices low. ③ Some of their ideas were reviewed during last week's hearing. ④ None, however, involve creating more friction between federal research and private industry. ⑤ Taxing iPhones, Disney movies or cancer drugs for the federal research that enabled them won't do anyone any good.

参考译文 ①企业和国家实验室之间缺乏许可协议与高药价没有关系,药价高反映的是开发成本巨大——比如癌症研究,超过 95% 的候选药物都没能通过测试。②许多聪明人都在努力想办法研发有效疗法,同时保持低价。③他们的一些想法在上周的听证会上得到了审议。④但没有一个涉及"在联邦研究和私营产业间制造更多摩擦"。⑤通过对苹果手机、迪士尼电影或抗癌药物征税来进行联邦研究,这对任何人都没有好处。

原文剖析 本段继续发表评论:药价高昂另有原因,加税反哺联邦研究可能危害创新。

设题点睛 本段第一句为观点句,且有例证,可用于设置正确选项。最后一句也为观点态度句,可用来设置正确选项。

生词解析

have nothing to do with 与……无关　　　figure out 想出;弄明白
friction n. 摩擦,矛盾

5 According to the last paragraph, high drug prices may be addressed by _____.

A. intervening in market competition
B. carrying out licensing deals
C. adopting a taxation mechanism
D. investing more in research

根据最后一段,高药价可以通过 _____ 来解决。

A. 干预市场竞争
B. 实施许可协议
C. 采用课税机制
D. 加大研究投入

【解题思路】D。推理判断题。根据题干直接定位到最后一段。首句说明药价高昂的真正原因不在于许可协议,而在于研发成本。第二句借助智人士做法明确作者观点:继续加大研究投入,以研发有效疗法(才可能解决药价问题),因此选项 D 为正确答案。

【排他分析】最后一段并未提及市场竞争，选项 A 无中生有，可排除。首句指出，企业和国家实验室之间缺乏许可协议与高药价没有关系，因此选项 B 与原文相悖，可排除。文末指出，对创新征税对任何人都没好处，选项 C 错误，可排除。

Text 7

Half of a typical family's spending today goes to transportation and housing, according to the latest Consumer Expenditure Survey, released by the Bureau of Labor Statistics. But Millennials have turned against both cars and houses in dramatic and historic fashion. Just as car sales have plummeted among their age cohort, the share of young people getting their first mortgage between 2009 and 2011 is half what it was just 10 years ago, according to a Federal Reserve study.

Needless to say, the Great Recession is responsible for some of the decline. But it's highly possible that a perfect storm of economic and demographic factors—from high gas prices, to re-urbanization, to stagnating wages, to new technologies enabling a different kind of consumption—has fundamentally changed the game for Millennials. The largest generation in American history might never spend as lavishly as its parents did—nor on the same things. Millennials may have lost interest in both.

From a distance, the sharing of cars, rooms, and clothes may seem a curiosity, more hippie than revolutionary. But technology is allowing these practices to go mainstream, and that represents a big new step for consumers. For decades, inventory management was largely the province of companies, not individuals, and continual efforts to reduce inventory helped companies improve their bottom line. But today, peer-to-peer software and mobile technology allow us all to have access, just when we need it, to the things we used to have to buy and hold. And the most powerful application is for cars.

The typical new car costs ＄30,000 and sits in a garage or parking spot for 23 hours a day. Zipcar gives drivers access to cars they don't have to own. Car ownership, meanwhile, has slipped down the hierarchy of status goods for many young adults.

Some automakers are slowly coming around to that view. Last year, Ford agreed to become Zipcar's largest supplier on more than 250 college campuses. Young people prize "access over ownership," said Sheryl Connelly, head of global consumer trends at Ford.

Subaru's publicist Doug O'Reilly told us, "The Millennial wants to tell people not just 'I've made it,' but also 'I'm a tech person.'" Smartphones compete against cars for young people's big-ticket dollars, since the cost of a good phone and data plan can exceed ＄1,000 a year. But they also provide some of the same psychic benefits—opening new vistas and carrying us far from the physical space in which we reside. "You no longer need to feel connected to your friends with a car when you have this technology that's so ubiquitous, it transcends time and space," Connelly said.

In other words, mobile technology has empowered more than just car-sharing. It has empowered friendships that can be maintained from a distance. The upshot could be a continuing shift from automobiles to mobile technology, and a big reduction in spending.

Millennials, of course, are sharing more than transportation. According to Harvard University's Joint Center for Housing Studies, between 2006 and 2011, the homeownership rate among adults younger than 35 fell by 12 percent, and nearly 2 million more of them—the equivalent of Houston's population—were living with their parents, as a result of the recession. The ownership society has been overrun by renters and squatters.

(*The Atlantic*, 2012.9)

1. It can be learned from the first paragraph that _____.
   A. Americans have lost interest in buying new cars
   B. car sales have experienced a retreat between 2009 and 2011
   C. transportation and housing consist a majority of Millennials' spending
   D. Millennials are less enthusiastic in consumerism

2. Which of the following contributes to the automobile consumption revolution occurred among Millennials?
   A. The advancement of technology.
   B. The sweeping tide of urbanization.
   C. The perfection of inventory management.
   D. The aggravated income inequality.

3. Car ownership, according to Sheryl Connelly, is _____.
   A. hard to get for the high price of cars
   B. vital for representing high social status
   C. replaced with accessibility by some large automakers
   D. less important than its access in young people's eyes

4. The smartphone is welcomed because of _____.
   A. its convenience in building up new friendship
   B. its competence compared with high-priced cars
   C. its power to outlive time and space
   D. its ability of pushing the users' physical and mental limits

5. It can be learned from the last paragraph that _____.
   A. Houston's young people like to stay with their parents
   B. renters and squatters are dominating the society
   C. homeownership is an important social index
   D. economic decline is partly responsible for Millennials' way of living

语篇分析与试题精解

Para. 1 ①Half of a typical family's spending today goes to transportation and housing, according to the latest Consumer Expenditure Survey, released by the Bureau of Labor Statistics. ②But Millennials have turned against both cars and houses in dramatic and historic fashion. ③Just as car sales have plummeted among their age cohort, the share of young people getting their first mortgage between 2009 and 2011 is half what it was just 10 years ago, according to a Federal Reserve study.

参考译文 ①美国劳动统计局最新公布的"消费者支出调查"显示,如今一个普通家庭的一半开支都用在了交通和住房上。②然而,千禧一代却以一种历史性和戏剧性的方式反其道而行。③美联储的一项研究显示,处于这个年龄段的客户中,汽车销量直线下滑,此外,2009年至2011年期间,获得首次贷款的年轻人的数量也只有十年前的一半。

原文剖析 本段前两句的语意形成转折,对比了美国普通家庭和千禧一代的不同消费热点(千禧一代不热衷于买车和购房)。第三句用具体数字举例说明第二句的观点。本文中提到的Millennials是指1980年以后出生,也就是所谓在2000年左右达到合法饮酒年龄,现在低于35岁的年轻一代,他们差不多与科技革命共同成长。

设题点睛 本段第二句为观点句,与首句构成转折,且被第三句支撑,属于重要内容,可用来设置题目。

生词解析
Millennials n. 千禧一代
dramatic adj. 戏剧性的;引人注目的
cohort n. 一批同时代的同龄人
turn against (使)转而反对(或反抗)
plummet vi. (价格、水平等)骤然下跌
mortgage n. 抵押借款,抵押贷款

长难句解析
Just as car sales have plummeted among their age cohort, the share of young people
　　　　　比较状语从句　　　　　　　　　　　　　　　　　主语
getting their first mortgage between 2009 and 2011　is　half what it was just 10 years ago,
　　　后置定语　　　　　　　时间状语　　　　　系动词　表语　　宾语从句
according to a Federal Reserve study.
　　　状语

本句为主从复合句。本句主干为the share of young people is half...,句首处为as引导的比较状语从句,将主句和从句的动作或状态进行比较,说明它们之间有相似之处,在从句中常省略与主句相同的部分。主句的表语后省略了介词of,可还原为half of what...,of及其之后的what宾语从句作half的后置定语,对其进行范围上的限定。

1 It can be learned from the first paragraph that _____.
　A. Americans have lost interest in buying new cars

从第一段可推断出_____。
　A. 美国人对购买新车已经失去了兴趣

B. car sales have experienced a retreat between 2009 and 2011
C. transportation and housing consist a majority of Millennials' spending
D. Millennials are less enthusiastic in consumerism

B. 汽车销量在2009至2011年之间经历了下滑
C. 千禧一代的大部分消费由交通和住房组成
D. 千禧一代对消费主义的热情并不高

【解题思路】D。推理引申题。根据题干要求定位到文章首段。本段第二句为重要的观点句,第三句用具体数据支撑该句。通过与首句(美国普通家庭的一半开支都用于交通和住房)对比后可看出,第二句意在表示千禧一代(Millennials)并不像普通家庭那样热衷于购房和购车(turned against both cars and houses)。选项D中的consumerism可指"专心于或倾向于购买消费品的消费主义",对应原文中的cars and houses,而less enthusiastic对应第二句中的turned against和第三句中所列举的具体数据,因此相较于其他选项而言,选项D最佳。且第二段最后一句总结谈到"(千禧一代)也许对烧钱的行为和这些消费品已经不感兴趣了",也可印证本项正确。

【排他分析】选项A中的Americans是泛指,指一般的美国人,而首段后两句是说千禧一代(年青一代)的美国人并没有那么热衷于买房和购车,不能代表一般美国人的行为,因此排除。选项B中的car sales和between 2009 and 2011虽然对应最后一句,但该项表意不严谨,原文是说"处于这个年龄段的客户中,汽车销量直线下滑",不一定是汽车的整体销量下滑,只不过年轻人购车的数量下降,因此排除。选项C是对首段第一句和第二句的随意拼凑,第二句已经明确指出年青一代并不热衷于买房和购车,因此排除该项。

Para. 2 ①Needless to say, the Great Recession is responsible for some of the decline. ②But it's highly possible that a perfect storm of economic and demographic factors—from high gas prices, to re-urbanization, to stagnating wages, to new technologies enabling a different kind of consumption—has fundamentally changed the game for Millennials. ③The largest generation in American history might never spend as lavishly as its parents did—nor on the same things. ④Millennials may have lost interest in both.

参考译文 ①毫无疑问,经济大萧条是下滑的原因之一。②然而,从高油价、再城镇化,到收入增长停滞和新科技催生新型消费,这些有关经济和人口因素的完美风暴,很有可能从根本上改变了千禧一代的游戏规则。③千禧一代,作为美国历史上人数最多的一代,可能再也不会像其父辈那样挥金如土了,他们的消费兴趣点也会有所转移。④他们也许已经对烧钱的行为和这些消费品不感兴趣了。

原文剖析 本段开始分析出现以上现象的原因,前两句给出导致年轻人对车、房消费热情下降的诸多外界(客观)原因。后两句描述千禧一代在消费方面与其父辈们的不同观念和消费产品变化。

设题点睛 本段第二句为带有转折语意和破折号的长难句,可用来设置正确选项。

生词解析
needless to say 不用说

demographic *adj.* 人口统计学的;人口学的

re-urbanization *n.* 再城市化
lavishly *adv.* 丰富地；浪费地
stagnate *vt.* 使停滞，使不发展

〖长难句解析〗

But it's highly possible that a perfect storm of economic and demographic factors—
　　　主系表　　　　　　　（主语从句）主语
from high gas prices, to re-urbanization, to stagnating wages, to new technologies enabling a
　　　　　　　　　　　　　　　　插入语
different kind of consumption—has fundamentally changed the game for Millennials.
　　　　　　　　　　　　（主语从句）谓语　　　（主语从句）宾语

本句为主从复合句。本句主干为 it's highly possible that…，it 是形式主语，真正的主语是后面的从句，主语从句中破折号之间的介词短语作插入语，对 economic and demographic factors 进行举例说明，采用了 from… to… 的结构，连接若干并列的名词性成分。

Para. 3 ①From a distance, the sharing of cars, rooms, and clothes may seem a curiosity, more hippie than revolutionary. ②But technology is allowing these practices to go mainstream, and that represents a big new step for consumers. ③For decades, inventory management was largely the province of companies, not individuals, and continual efforts to reduce inventory helped companies improve their bottom line. ④But today, peer-to-peer software and mobile technology allow us all to have access, just when we need it, to the things we used to have to buy and hold. ⑤And the most powerful application is for cars.

〖参考译文〗①从过去看来，分享车子、房子和衣服的行为似乎很稀奇，更具有嬉皮士而非革命的意味。②但技术的发展正在使这种行为成为主流，对消费者而言，这意味着一个全新的阶段。③几十年来，库存管理在很大程度上是企业的职责而与个人无关，不断努力降低库存量可帮助企业改善其财务盈亏情况。④而如今，有了对等软件和移动技术，我们可以在需要的时候获得过去不得不购买和持有的服务或产品。⑤汽车是最有力的例子。

〖原文剖析〗本段前两句构成语意转折关系，对比了人们过去与现在对分享个人用品行为的不同观点，解释目前年轻人所崇尚的这种消费理念与技术的发展有关，暗示这种转变具有革命性（代表全新的消费阶段）。第三句和第四句再次构成语意转折关系，从商家角度介绍了过去和现在的改变，暗示过去企业需要进行库存管理或去库存，如今技术使个人也可起到管理库存的作用。最后一句举例，用于引出下文对共享汽车的介绍，同时回应首段年青一代不再对购车感兴趣的内容。

〖设题点睛〗本段出现两处转折结构，转折后的观点内容可以用来设置正确的选项。

〖生词解析〗
hippie *adj.* 具有嬉皮士特点的
inventory *n.* 存货，存货清单
bottom line 结算盈亏的底线

go mainstream 成为主流
province *n.* 本分；职权；职责

长难句解析

But today, peer-to-peer software and mobile technology allow us all to have access,
　　状语　　　　　　　　主语　　　　　　　　　　　　谓语　宾语　宾语补足语
just when we need it, to the things we used to have to buy and hold.
　时间状语从句　　　　定语　　　　定语从句

本句为主从复合句。本句主干为 peer-to-peer software and mobile technology allow us to have access to the things，主语为并列结构，谓语为 allow sb. to do sth. 的用法，其中不定式作宾语 us 的补语，该不定式中还包含 have access to sth. 的结构，但被 when 引导的时间状语从句隔开；we used to... 为前边省略了 that 的定语从句，其先行词为 things。

2 Which of the following contributes to the automobile consumption revolution occurred among Millennials?

以下哪项推动了在千禧一代中发生的汽车消费革命？

A. The advancement of technology.
B. The sweeping tide of urbanization.
C. The perfection of inventory management.
D. The aggravated income inequality.

A. 技术的进步。
B. 城镇化浪潮。
C. 库存管理的优化。
D. 收入不平等的加剧。

【解题思路】A。事实细节题。根据题干关键词（automobile，revolution 和 contribute to）定位到第三段。由于该段旨在分析现象的成因，因此与题干中的 contribute to 对应。该段第二句指出"技术的发展正在使这种行为成为主流"（technology is allowing these practices to go mainstream），"这些行为"回指首句谈到的 sharing of cars，rooms，and clothes，该句后半部分指出"这意味着一个全新的阶段"，说明以分享代替消费的变化具有革命性质，对应题干中的 consumption revolution。该段第四句列举了科技进步所带来的改变，因此千禧一代消费行为改变的主要原因在于科技的发展，选项 A 正确。

【排他分析】选项 B 中的 urbanization 对应第二段第二句，原文提到的是"再城镇化"（re-urbanization），而非"城镇化"，且这只是"改变"年轻人消费习惯的因素之一，并非"促成"他们形成如今消费行为的因素，因此排除。选项 C 中的 inventory management 对应第三段第三句，原文只是谈到公司去库存的做法有助于改善其财务状况，因此是公司的职责，本项是对"去库存"和"改善"两个信息的杂糅，与原文意思无关，因此排除。选项 D 谈到的 income 只在第二段第二句中涉及（stagnating wages），首先"收入增长停滞"不等同于"收入不平等"（income inequality），其次该项中 aggravated 所表达的意思在原文中并未提到，因此排除。

Para. 4 ①The typical new car costs $30,000 and sits in a garage or parking spot for 23 hours a day. ②Zipcar gives drivers access to cars they don't have to own. ③Car ownership, meanwhile, has slipped down the hierarchy of

参考译文 ①一辆普通新车的售价约为 30 000 美元，一天中的 23 小时车都停在车库或者停车场里。②而热布卡公司（Zipcar）可让用户享有对他人汽车的使用权。③与此同时，很多年轻人认为，拥

status goods for many young adults.　　　　　　有汽车已不再是社会地位的象征。

原文剖析 本段承接上段尾句谈到的"车"。首句举例说明车昂贵,但一天中的大部分时间都没有派上用场。第二句指出共享车公司的出现改变了车没有得到充分利用的情况,体现其合理性。第三句指出汽车在年轻人看来已不是可以炫耀地位的奢侈品,体现共享车的出现符合年轻人的心理,具备了一定的主观条件和群众基础。

设题点睛 本段从客观和主观角度证明共享车的出现顺应消费者需求和年轻人的心理,可用来设置正确选项。

生词解析

give sb. access to 允许某人使用某物　　　　hierarchy n. 等级系统,分级系统
status n. 地位;身份

Para. 5 ① Some automakers are slowly coming around to that view. ② Last year, Ford agreed to become Zipcar's largest supplier on more than 250 college campuses. ③ Young people prize "access over ownership," said Sheryl Connelly, head of global consumer trends at Ford.

参考译文 ①一些汽车制造商也逐渐意识到这一点。②去年,福特与热布卡达成协议,成为热布卡在250多所大学里的最大供应商。③福特的全球消费趋势部门主管谢丽尔·康纳利(Sheryl Connelly)表示,年轻人很追捧"使用权优于所有权"的消费模式。

原文剖析 本段首句承接上一段谈到的共享车的出现,是观点句,指出传统的汽车制造商逐渐认识到了这一消费趋势。第二句以福特与共享车的合作举例说明传统汽车制造商顺应消费趋势的变通举措。第三句为个人观点,也用于论证第一句。

设题点睛 本段第三句是个人观点,明确支持首句内容,所谈到的抽象理论(使用权优于所有权)为重点内容,可用来设置正确选项。

生词解析

come around to 转变过来同意　　　　　　prize vt. 欣赏;重视
access n. 接近(或进入、享用)权

---

3 Car ownership, according to Sheryl Connelly, is _____.　　　　在谢丽尔·康纳利看来,汽车拥有权 _____。

A. hard to get for the high price of cars　　　　A. 因汽车价位太高而很难获得

B. vital for representing high social status　　　B. 因代表较高的社会地位而很重要

C. replaced with accessibility by some large automakers　　　C. 被一些大型汽车生产厂商以易得性取代

D. less important than its access in young people's eyes　　　D. 在年轻人眼中不如其使用权重要

【解题思路】D。事实细节题。根据题干关键词(Car ownership 和 Sheryl Connelly)定位到文章第五段最后一句。原文以谢丽尔·康纳利之口指出年轻人更加看重使用权而不是所有权(Young people prize "access over ownership"),由于本段在讨论汽车,

因此这里的 ownership 应指对汽车的所有权，与选项 D 的内容一致，该项中的 less important than its access 是对 prize "access over ownership" 的同义替换。

【排他分析】选项 A 对应第四段首句，原文指出买一部新车需要花约 3 万美金而且一天有 23 小时车都停在车库或停车场，是想表示新车价高且并未得到有效利用，该项中的"很难取得所有权"在原文中没有提到，因此排除。选项 B 对应第四段最后一句，原文用了 has slipped down 明确指出年轻人不再认为汽车所有权是身份的象征，与该项的意思直接相反，因此排除。选项 C 的干扰性较强，虽然第五段的前两句描述一些汽车制造商也转变了观点，成为汽车共享公司的供应方，可理解为这些制造商顺应年轻人的观念，开展了新的业务（汽车租赁或共享），但这种业务不可能代替其主营的汽车买卖的业务，因此排除该项，且 accessibility 指"容易获得的特点"，与 access（可表示"使用权"）的意思并不完全一致，因此排除。

Para. 6 ①Subaru's publicist Doug O'Reilly told us, "The Millennial wants to tell people not just 'I've made it,' but also 'I'm a tech person.'" ②Smartphones compete against cars for young people's big-ticket dollars, since the cost of a good phone and data plan can exceed \$1,000 a year. ③But they also provide some of the same psychic benefits—opening new vistas and carrying us far from the physical space in which we reside. ④"You no longer need to feel connected to your friends with a car when you have this technology that's so ubiquitous, it transcends time and space," Connelly said.

参考译文 ①斯巴鲁公司的公关人员道格·奥雷利（Doug O'Reilly）告诉我们："千禧一代想要向人们传达的意思不仅仅是'我成功了'，他们还想让人们知道'我还是一个技术达人'。"②智能手机在与汽车竞争年轻人大额消费的市场，因为一部好手机加上流量套餐的花费每年可超过 1 000 美元。③此外，智能手机还能够提供这样的精神慰藉——带来新视角，让我们远离所居住的物理空间。④康纳利说："移动科技无处不在，它突破了时间和空间的限制，有了这种科技，你不需要驾车也能探访朋友，享受友情。"

原文剖析 本段第一句借用汽车公司员工之口指出年轻人消费习惯所体现的新观念（希望展现自己的成功和对科技的熟悉程度）。第二句用智能手机举例说明，年轻人愿意花费大价钱（每年超过 1 000 美元）购买和使用智能手机，因为这种产品既能体现身份地位，又能体现科技性，因此符合年轻人的新观念。第三句虽然出现了 but，但实际体现递进的关系，指出智能手机一类的高科技产品可提供另一种优势（精神慰藉），之后的第四句用直接引语的方式指出这种精神优势的具体作用（突破时空限制，维持人际交往）。

设题点睛 本段首句为总观点句，后几句为具体说明，因此都是重要内容，可用来设置考题。

生词解析

publicist *n.* 广告员；宣传员；公关人员
data plan 流量套餐
vista *n.* （对未来）一连串的展望
transcend *vt.* 胜过，超越

big-ticket *adj.* 高价的
psychic *adj.* 精神的；心灵的
ubiquitous *adj.* 普遍存在的；无所不在的

4 The smartphone is welcomed because of _____.

A. its convenience in building up new friendship
B. its competence compared with high-priced cars
C. its power to outlive time and space
D. its ability of pushing the users' physical and mental limits

智能手机因其 _____ 而受欢迎。

A. 在帮助结交新朋友方面的便利性
B. 与高价汽车相比的竞争力
C. 比时空的存在更为长久
D. 突破使用者物理和精神局限的能力

【解题思路】D。事实细节题。根据题干关键词(smartphone)定位到文章第六段后三句。本题考查智能手机受欢迎的原因,也就是智能手机的特点和优势。本段第三句和第四句对智能手机进行了评价,第三句指出智能手机可通过带给人们新的视野和突破居住之地的限制(opening new vistas and carrying us far from the physical space in which we reside)而为使用者提供精神上的慰藉(psychic benefits),第四句与汽车相比进一步指出智能手机因跨越了时空的限制(it transcends time and space)在维持人际关系上具有优势(人们无须驾车去探亲访友),第三句中的 psychic benefits 对应选项 D 中的 mental,第四句中的 it transcends time and space 对应该项中的 physical,因此选项 D 体现了智能手机的优势。

【排他分析】选项 A 对应第六段最后一句,该句表示人们用智能手机就能足不出户地与朋友们保持联系,但并没有具体到"结交新朋友",因此排除。第六段第二句谈到智能手机在与汽车竞争年轻人的高价消费市场(Smartphones compete against cars for young people's big-ticket dollars),两者都属于高价消费品,因此智能手机相对于汽车的优势并非是其价格低廉,因此选项 B 与原文不符。选项 C 对应第六段最后一句的 it transcends time and space(跨越了时间和空间的界限),而该项中的 outlive 指"活得比……长",由常识可知,时空是永久存在的,智能手机的存在时间不可能超过时空的存在,因此排除该项。

Para. 7 ①In other words, mobile technology has empowered more than just car-sharing. ②It has empowered friendships that can be maintained from a distance. ③The upshot could be a continuing shift from automobiles to mobile technology, and a big reduction in spending.

参考译文 ①换句话说,移动科技不仅仅促成了汽车共享方式的出现。②它同时让远距离维持友谊成为可能。③最终,人们的消费对象会不断从汽车转向移动科技,且消费支出会大幅下降。

原文剖析 本段前两句对上段内容进行总结和评价,指出移动科技的影响(促进共享汽车出现,使长距离友情成为可能)。第三句做出预测,指出移动科技将取代汽车成为消费新宠,且人们的消费支出会在移动科技的帮助下大幅下降。

设题点睛 本段属于总结性内容,与前文观点有所重复,因此单独设题的概率非常小。

生词解析

empower vt. 允许;使能够

upshot n. 结果,结局;要点

Para. 8 ①Millennials, of course, are sharing more than transportation. ②According to Harvard University's Joint Center for Housing Studies, between 2006 and 2011, the homeownership rate among adults younger than 35 fell by 12 percent, and nearly 2 million more of them—the equivalent of Houston's population—were living with their parents, as a result of the recession. ③The ownership society has been overrun by renters and squatters.

参考译文 ①当然,千禧一代所分享的不只是代步工具。②哈佛大学住房研究联合中心发现,由于经济萧条,2006年到2011年间,在35岁以下的成年人中,置业率下降了12%,他们之中更有超过200万人(相当于休斯敦市的人口)与父母一起生活。③在这个所有权社会中,租房客和蹭房族反而更为常见。

原文剖析 本段首句承上启下,旨在引出新的讨论范围。第二句用数据具体说明这一新的共享领域是房屋(举例说明年轻人中买房的人少了,与父母一起生活的多了)。第三句为作者的评价,指出共享房屋的做法如今十分常见。本段回应首段提到的普通家庭的消费热点——房子和车子,将年轻人共享汽车和住房的做法与其做对比。

设题点睛 本段第二句虽然带有数据,看似是细节内容,但由于是明显的长难句,可用来设置正确选项。

生词解析
equivalent n. 等价物,相等物　　　　　　overrun vt. 风靡于,流行于
squatter n. 依法在公地上定居的人

长难句解析
According to Harvard University's Joint Center for Housing Studies, between 2006 and 2011,
　　　　　　　　　　　　　　　　　状语1
the homeownership rate among adults younger than 35　fell　by 12 percent, and
　　主语1　　　　　　　　后置定语　　　　　　　谓语1　　状语2
nearly 2 million more of them—the equivalent of Houston's population— were living
　　　主语2　　　　　　　　　　同位语　　　　　　　　　　　　谓语2
with their parents, as a result of the recession.
　　状语3　　　　　　状语4

本句为并列复合句。本句主干为 the homeownership rate fell and nearly 2 million more of them were living with…,本句由 and 连接的两个并列句构成,后一句两个破折号之间的内容作 nearly 2 million 的同位语,最后 as a result of 介词短语构成表示原因的状语。

5 It can be learned from the last paragraph that _____.

从最后一段可知_____。

A. Houston's young people like to stay with their parents

B. renters and squatters are dominating the society

C. homeownership is an important social index

D. economic decline is partly responsible for Millennials' way of living

A. 休斯敦的年轻人喜欢与父母待在一起

B. 租房客和蹭房族正在主导社会

C. 房屋拥有权是一项重要的社会指标

D. 经济衰退是千禧一代选择如此生活方式的原因之一

【解题思路】D。事实细节题。根据题干要求定位到最后一段,在题干没有提供更准确定位点的情况下,优先考查段落的观点信息或者特殊结构。本段第二句为长难句,指出他们中有 200 多万人和父母住在一起(nearly 2 million more of them were living with their parents),其中的 them 指代前半句中的"35 岁以下的成年人",也就是本文所讨论的年轻人(千禧一代),句末用 as a result of 引出原因,即 recession(经济萧条),选项 D 中的 economic decline 对应该句中的 recession,be responsible for 对应 as a result of,Millennials' 与原句中的 them 和 adults younger than 35 属于同义替换,因此该项正确。

【排他分析】选项 A 中的 Houston 出现在本段倒数第二句的同位语 equivalent of Houston's population 中,表示 200 万这一数量相当于休斯敦市的总人口,用类比的方式说明与父母同住的美国年轻人的数量很多,但与休斯敦市的年轻人没有多大关系,因此排除该项。选项 B 对应本段最后一句,原文中 overrun 的意思是"大量出现",本项中的 dominating 含有"成为主流或主导"的意思,将原文的意思拔高了,且从规模上看,千禧一代的数量还不足以构成社会的主体,因此排除该项。选项 C 所表达的意思在最后一段中并未涉及,因此属于干扰选项,可以直接排除。

Text 8

When it comes to oil, the question becomes how low can prices go. And with Iran back as a full player in world oil markets, the previously unthinkable—sub-$20-a-barrel crude—is looking more possible.

Iran's oil ministers say they intend to boost their oil production and ship 500,000 barrels a day initially, now that sanctions have been lifted in light of nuclear inspections deal, the Islamic Republic News Agency reported. Iran's goal is 2 million barrels a day. Those levels alone are big enough to further depress the price of oil, especially since Saudi Arabia has refused to cut its production levels. The result could lead to oil prices in the mid-$20s a barrel, and with occasional bouts of panic selling, briefly dip into the teens, said Tom Kloza, chief global analyst for the Oil Price Information Service.

Oil already plunged past one key threshold last week, falling past $30 a barrel. West Texas Intermediate, the benchmark U.S. crude, closed Friday at $29.42, down $1.78 for the day. Brent crude, an international benchmark, closed at $28.94, down $1.94. The low oil prices are reflected in the price of gasoline, which dipped Sunday to $1.90 a gallon nationally, down almost 7 cents in a week, according to AAA's Fuel Gauge Report. "The expectation is we're going to plumb new lows. Every oil investor and trader worth his salt has anticipated it," Kloza said.

Even though Iran was under sanctions, it was able to sell limited amounts of oil to a few select countries—China, India and a few other Asian nations. Now, it faces no limitations. Plus, Iran is able to produce oil at lower overall "lifting costs" than many other nations, as little as $10 a barrel. Even when oil prices are absurdly low, it is one of the countries that can still make money. That puts American producers at a huge disadvantage, pushing many out of the market.

Iran, Saudi Arabia and other big producers within the Organization of Petroleum Exporting Countries are "playing a longer game than our poor guys can play," said Ed Hirs, an economist at the University of Houston. "We need to step back and take a long perspective on this."

The long perspective is that Iran lacks the kind of oil technology and infrastructure that has led to the resurgence of the industry in the U.S. Some think that after an initial surge, Iran won't be able to sustain high levels of exports. "The likely increases in Iranian exports should not be a game changer," wrote Julian Jessop of Capital Economics in a note in to clients. Even with a surge of exports, there isn't much storage capacity or demand left in the world for the excess oil. "We do not believe that Iran would want to depress prices much further by rushing to dump its inventories," Jessop said. "The oil market is all about the short run at the moment. These oil prices are not sustainable in the long term, but anything goes in the next 40 days," he said.

(*USA Today*, 2016.1)

1. It can be inferred from the first two paragraphs that _____.
   A. people never expect the oil price to dip into teens
   B. Iran can largely boost its oil production due to the sanctions
   C. the nuclear-related sanctions on Iran once helped oil price stay high
   D. Saudi Arabia has launched a fierce oil battle against Iran

2. It is suggested in paragraph 3 that professionals believe _____.
   A. oil price can exert an influence on the sale of gasoline
   B. the oil price may not hit the bottom yet
   C. oil investors have anticipated the bottom point of oil price
   D. traders use the salt to predict the trend of oil price

3. Which of the following is true according to paragraph 4?
   A. U.S. oil producers are driven out of the market by Iran.
   B. Iran enjoys a cost advantage over many other oil producers.
   C. The sanctions totally banned the Iran's oil selling.
   D. The decline in oil price has largely influence Iran's profit.

4. Ed Hirs suggests that the U.S. oil producer should _____.
   A. be cautious about the industry's prospect
   B. join the longer game with other big producers
   C. prepare for a long period of competition
   D. not be pessimistic about OPEC's future

5. Julian Jessop would most likely agree that _____.
   A. Iran will increase the export to change the market

B. the whole world lacks storage capacity
C. Iran pays a high value on its oil inventory
D. the oil price crisis caused by Iran is temporary

语篇分析与试题精解

Para. 1 ①When it comes to oil, the question becomes how low can prices go. ②And with Iran back as a full player in world oil markets, the previously unthinkable—sub-$20-a-barrel crude—is looking more possible.

参考译文 ①每当谈到石油,人们总会关心油价到底会降到多低。②随着伊朗强势回归全球原油市场,之前不可想象的事情——原油价格低于每桶20美元——如今看来很有可能发生。

原文剖析 本段首句指出人们很关心油价的底线。第二句给出预测:随着伊朗的回归,油价会下降到每桶20美元以下。

设题点睛 本段可用来设置选项的信息太少,不会单独出题。

生词解析

unthinkable *adj.* 不可想象的   crude *n.* 原油

Para. 2 ①Iran's oil ministers say they intend to boost their oil production and ship 500,000 barrels a day initially, now that sanctions have been lifted in light of nuclear inspections deal, the Islamic Republic News Agency reported. ②Iran's goal is 2 million barrels a day. ③Those levels alone are big enough to further depress the price of oil, especially since Saudi Arabia has refused to cut its production levels. ④The result could lead to oil prices in the mid-$20s a barrel, and with occasional bouts of panic selling, briefly dip into the teens, said Tom Kloza, chief global analyst for the Oil Price Information Service.

参考译文 ①据伊朗伊斯兰共和国通讯社报道,伊朗石油部长表示,鉴于伊朗同意核调查,国际上解除了对伊朗的制裁,伊朗将增加石油生产,初步计划每天输出50万桶。②伊朗的目标是每天输出200万桶原油。③这一生产水平就足以进一步拉低油价,尤其在沙特阿拉伯拒绝减少本国石油生产的情况下。④油价资讯服务公司的首席全球分析师汤姆·克罗沙(Tom Kloza)指出,这一结果可能导致石油价格在每桶25美元上下浮动,而且伴随着间歇出现的恐慌性抛售,油价还会暂时跌破20美元大关。

原文剖析 本段开始解释上段最后一句预测的理由。前两句指出因为针对伊朗的制裁取消,所以伊朗决定从最初的每天50万桶的产量最终增加到每天产出200万桶。第三句继续指出由于沙特拒绝减产,油价会被进一步拉低。第四句回应首段第二句涉及的数字,借用人物观点指出油价会在25美元上下浮动,并可能暂时跌破20美元。

设题点睛 本段是对首段的进一步解释,首句(长难句)与上一段最后一句可能会结合出题。

生词解析

sanction *n.* 制裁   in light of 鉴于
depress *vt.* 使价格下跌   bout *n.* 发作

98

dip *vi.* 下降　　　　　　　　　　teens *n.* 十三至十九

长难句解析

Iran's oil ministers say they intend to boost their oil production and ship 500,000 barrels
　主语　　　　　谓语　　　　　　　宾语从句
a day initially, now that sanctions have been lifted in light of nuclear inspections deal,
　　　　　　　　　　原因状语从句
the Islamic Republic News Agency reported.
　　　　　　　插入语

本句最后的 the Islamic Republic News Agency reported 可看作插入语,本句主干采用主谓宾结构,宾语由一个从句构成。now that 表示"既然,由于",可引导原因状语从句。

1 It can be inferred from the first two paragraphs that _____ .　　　　从前两段可推知_____。

A. people never expect the oil price to dip into teens
B. Iran can largely boost its oil production due to the sanctions
C. the nuclear-related sanctions on Iran once helped oil price stay high
D. Saudi Arabia has launched a fierce oil battle against Iran

A. 人们从没期望油价会降到每桶十几美元
B. 由于遭受制裁,伊朗可能大幅提高其石油产量
C. 针对伊朗的核制裁曾经帮助油价稳定在高位
D. 沙特阿拉伯对伊朗发动了激烈的石油之战

【解题思路】C。推理引申题。根据题干要求定位到第一、二段,首段第二句指出伊朗回归原油市场,原油价格会下跌到每桶20美元。第二段第一句对首段第二句做了进一步解释,指出因为伊朗同意国际调查,因此对其进行的核制裁被解除,伊朗会大幅度提高自己的日均产油量,由此可以反推出之前由于核问题受到制裁,伊朗基本上被禁止输出石油,导致市场中石油缺少,自然也就拉高了油价,因此选项C是正确答案。

【排他分析】选项A对应第二段的最后一句,原文表达了汤姆·克罗沙的看法,他认为伊朗增加石油产量可能导致油价暂时跌破每桶20美元,虽然首段中用了 unthinkable 这个词,但不等同于人们从来没有设想过20美元以下的油价(不是没想过,是不敢相信),因此排除。选项B对应第二段第一句,但原文指出并不是因为制裁而使伊朗可以大幅提高其石油产量,而是因为制裁解除(sanctions have been lifted),因此排除。选项D对应第二段第三句,原文意思是沙特不减产会进一步拉低油价,而没有明确提出沙特对伊朗发动石油战争,选项D属于过度推断,所以排除。

Para. 3 ① Oil already plunged past one key threshold last week, falling past $30 a barrel. ② West Texas Intermediate, the benchmark U.S. crude, closed Friday at $29.42, down $1.78 for the day. ③ Brent crude, an

参考译文 ①上周油价暴跌,已经跌破每桶30美元的大关。②上周五,西德克萨斯州中质原油,即美国基准原油的收盘价格为29.24美元,当天下跌1.78美元。③国际基准布伦特原油的收盘

international benchmark, closed at $28.94, down $1.94. ④The low oil prices are reflected in the price of gasoline, which dipped Sunday to $1.90 a gallon nationally, down almost 7 cents in a week, according to AAA's Fuel Gauge Report. ⑤"The expectation is we're going to plumb new lows. ⑥Every oil investor and trader worth his salt has anticipated it," Kloza said.

价格为28.94美元,下跌1.94美元。④价格低迷体现在汽油价格上。美国汽车协会的《燃油计量报告》显示,上周日全国汽油价格跌至每加仑1.9美元,一周内价格下跌了将近7美分。⑤"现在大家的预测就是石油价格还会再创新低。⑥所有称职的石油投资商和贸易商都已经预见到了这一点。"克罗沙说道。

原文剖析 本段首句到第四句都是在列举数据,承接上一段,用目前的市场价格来反映原油价格的大幅下跌。第五句和第六句继续给出人物的观点:石油投资商和贸易商已预见石油价格会创新低。

设题点睛 本段前四句都是带有数据的细节内容,一般不会设置考点,最后两句是顺接上一段出现的新观点,如果设题,题目会相对比较简单。

生词解析

plunge vi. 突然下降
benchmark n. 基准
worth one's salt 称职;胜任
threshold n. 门槛;临界值
plumb vt. 达到……的最低点

2 It is suggested in paragraph 3 that professionals believe _____.

A. oil price can exert an influence on the sale of gasoline
B. the oil price may not hit the bottom yet
C. oil investors have anticipated the bottom point of oil price
D. traders use the salt to predict the trend of oil price

第三段表明专业人士认为_____。

A. 石油价格会对汽油的销售造成影响
B. 石油价格可能还未触底
C. 石油投资者已经预测到了石油价格的最低点
D. 贸易商用盐预测了油价走势

【解题思路】B。事实细节题。根据题干要求定位到第三段,professionals 可以对应原文中的克罗沙(油价资讯服务公司首席全球分析师)。其观点很明确,该段最后两句用直接引语指出石油价格会创新低,而且大家都已经预见到了。选项 B 明确可以对应原文,其中的 may not hit the bottom 等同于原文的 going to plumb new lows,因此选项 B 是正确答案。

【排他分析】选项 A 对应本段第四句,原文大意是原油价格的低迷体现在汽油价格上,可以说汽油价格的下跌是由原油价格下跌导致的,但是选项 A 所说的是原油价格会对汽油销量产生影响,两者的关系无法由原文推知,所以排除。选项 C 对应该段最后一句,原文提到石油投资商和贸易商预见到石油价格还将走低,而选项 C 指出他们预测到了最低点,和原文不同,因此排除。选项 D 对应本段最后一句中的 worth his salt(称职的),选项 D 完全曲解了该习语的意思,毫无逻辑,所以直接排除。

Para. 4 ① Even though Iran was under sanctions, it was able to sell limited amounts of oil to a few select countries—China, India and a few other Asian nations. ②Now, it faces no limitations. ③Plus, Iran is able to produce oil at lower overall "lifting costs" than many other nations, as little as $10 a barrel. ④Even when oil prices are absurdly low, it is one of the countries that can still make money. ⑤That puts American producers at a huge disadvantage, pushing many out of the market.

参考译文 ①尽管伊朗受到了制裁，但它可以向选定的部分国家出售限量石油——如中国、印度以及其他几个亚洲国家。②如今制裁解除，该国的出口量不再受限制。③而且，与许多其他国家相比，伊朗出产石油的综合采油成本更低，仅为每桶10美元。④因此，即便石油价格低得离谱，伊朗仍然是能从石油出售中获利的国家之一。⑤这会使美国的石油生产商处于极为不利的境地，甚至会让相当一部分生产商退出市场。

原文剖析 本段首句给出事实：尽管过去伊朗受到制裁，但还是可以定向出售少量石油。第二句过渡指出现在完全没有限制了。第三句和第四句继续给出新事实：伊朗开采原油的成本极低，即使油价下滑伊朗还是有利可图。第五句给出伊朗制裁解除造成的影响：美国的原油商被迫退出市场。

设题点睛 本段第三句和第四句给出伊朗作为石油产出国的一个巨大成本优势，属于新观点，一般会设置相应的考题。

生词解析

overall *adj.* 全部的，总体上的
lift *vt.* 挖出，提起
absurdly *adv.* 荒谬地

3 Which of the following is true according to paragraph 4?

根据第四段可知以下哪项正确？

A. U.S. oil producers are driven out of the market by Iran.
B. Iran enjoys a cost advantage over many other oil producers.
C. The sanctions totally banned the Iran's oil selling.
D. The decline in oil price has largely influence Iran's profit.

A. 美国石油生产商被伊朗挤出市场。
B. 与许多其他石油生产国相比，伊朗享有成本优势。
C. 制裁对伊朗的石油出售进行了绝对的限制。
D. 石油价格的下降对伊朗的利润产生了极大影响。

【解题思路】**B**。事实细节题。根据题干要求定位到文章第四段，在没有更加具体的定位点的情况下优先阅读本段的考点结构。通过语篇分析可知，本段的第三、四句为新观点。第三句指出伊朗的原油开采成本更低(produce oil at lower overall "lifting costs")，第四句进一步指出即使油价大幅度下降(absurdly low)，伊朗还是有利可图。选项B中的cost advantage是对原文at lower overall "lifting costs"的同义替换，因此是正确答案。

【排他分析】选项A对应第四段最后一句，文章只是指出因为油价大幅下滑可能使

得美国的石油生产商因无利可图最终被迫退出市场,尽管原油价格下滑和伊朗有关,但是前文也指出这和沙特坚持不减产也有关,因此不能说美国石油生产商的退出就是伊朗单方面的原因造成的,其本身较高的开采成本才是主要原因,所以排除。选项 C 对应本段首句,尽管制裁确实让伊朗的原油生产基本停滞,但是其还是可以向中国和印度等少数国家出售少量石油,因此选项 C 中的 totally banned 是错误的,所以排除。选项 D 对应本段第四句,原文只是提到伊朗在油价大幅下降的情况下还是有利可图(can still make money),并没有明确指出伊朗的利润受到严重影响(尽管这是自然的,但是本题不是推论题,正确选项一定要和文章本身能够对应),因此排除。

Para. 5 ①Iran, Saudi Arabia and other big producers within the Organization of Petroleum Exporting Countries are "playing a longer game than our poor guys can play," said Ed Hirs, an economist at the University of Houston. ②"We need to step back and take a long perspective on this."

参考译文 ①作为石油输出国组织成员的伊朗、沙特阿拉伯和其他一些大的石油出产国"正在进行长线角逐,而我们国家的生产商则无力参与。"休斯敦大学经济学家埃德·希尔什(Ed Hirs)说。②"我们该做的就是退后一步并且用长远的眼光审视现状。"

原文剖析 本段首句承接上段尾句,美国经济学家提出观点:几大原油国在长线竞争,而美国生产者无法与之匹敌。第二句继续补充观点:我们需要从长远来审视现状。

设题点睛 本段只有两个单句,均为个人观点。从考研英语历年真题上看,经常会有专门针对某人观点设置的考题,难度一般都不会太大,只要能排除错误选项即可。

生词解析

game n. (需要技能、勇气、耐力等的)比赛　　perspective n. 观点,视角

4 Ed Hirs suggests that the U. S. oil producer should _____ .

A. be cautious about the industry's prospect
B. join the longer game with other big producers
C. prepare for a long period of competition
D. not be pessimistic about OPEC's future

埃德·希尔什建议美国石油生产商_____。

A. 对行业前景持谨慎态度
B. 和其他石油生产大国一起进行长线角逐
C. 做好长期竞争的准备
D. 不要对石油输出国组织的未来持悲观态度

【解题思路】A。推理引申题。根据题干的人名 Ed Hirs 定位到文章第五段,本段为此人观点的陈述段,大意是美国在石油战争中处于弱势,只能先退出,再从长计议,选项 A 中的 be cautious about 对应本段第二句中的 step back and take a long perspective,因此选项 A 正确。

【排他分析】选项 B 对应第五段首句中的 playing a longer game than our poor guys can play,大意是伊朗、沙特等石油大国有能力进行长线角逐,而美国生产商则无力应对,选项 B 与此意相反,所以排除。选项 C 对应原文第二句,原文只提到要从更长远的角度去做打算(long perspective),没有提到为长期竞争做准备(况且已经退出了竞争),

因此排除。选项 D 的 OPEC 对应第五段首句,但是原文中此人没有对石油输出国组织的未来表达观点,选项 D 属于无中生有,所以排除。

Para. 6 ①The long perspective is that Iran lacks the kind of oil technology and infrastructure that has led to the resurgence of the industry in the U.S. ②Some think that after an initial surge, Iran won't be able to sustain high levels of exports. ③"The likely increases in Iranian exports should not be a game changer," wrote Julian Jessop of Capital Economics in a note in to clients. ④Even with a surge of exports, there isn't much storage capacity or demand left in the world for the excess oil. ⑤"We do not believe that Iran would want to depress prices much further by rushing to dump its inventories," Jessop said. ⑥"The oil market is all about the short run at the moment. ⑦These oil prices are not sustainable in the long term, but anything goes in the next 40 days," he said.

参考译文 ①从长远来看,伊朗缺乏石油技术和石油基础设施。而正是这两者的发展促成了美国石油行业的复苏。②有人认为产量激增的初始阶段过去之后,伊朗并不能长期保持高出口量。③"伊朗石油出口量很有可能提高,这不应成为游戏规则改变的因素。"资本经济公司的朱利安·杰索普(Julian Jessop)在致客户的一份报告中写道。④虽然伊朗的石油出口量激增,但世界各国对过剩的石油都没有存储能力和需求,⑤他说道:"我们确信伊朗不会急于采取倾销存货的方式进一步压低油价,⑥目前石油市场都是短期运转的。⑦当前的油价并不会长期走低,但至少在今后的 40 天会保持这一走向。"

原文剖析 本段首句指出伊朗的缺点:缺乏石油技术和基础设施。第二句和第三句顺接首句,指出人们并不相信伊朗可以长时间保持高出口量。第四句指出目前市场上的石油已经供过于求了。第五句、第六句、第七句是个人观点:从长远来看原油价格不会继续走低,但是最近还是会保持低位。

设题点睛 本段最重要的内容应该是朱利安·杰索普提出的观点性内容,因此第五句到第七句为考点。

生词解析
infrastructure *n.* 基础设施　　resurgence *n.* 复苏
dump *vt.* 倾销　　inventory *n.* 存货

5 Julian Jessop would most likely agree that _____.

朱利安·杰索普极有可能同意_____。

A. Iran will increase the export to change the market
B. the whole world lacks storage capacity
C. Iran pays a high value on its oil inventory
D. the oil price crisis caused by Iran is temporary

A. 伊朗会增加出口量来改变市场
B. 整个世界都缺少存储能力
C. 伊朗很重视其石油存货
D. 伊朗造成的石油价格危机只是暂时的

【解题思路】D。人物观点题。通过人名定位到文章最后一段,之前的语篇分析中已经指出本段第五句、第六句、第七句最为重要,大意是杰索普认为从长远来看石油价格不会持续走低,但是未来40天内还是会保持低位。选项D中的temporary对应原文最后一句的not sustainable,因此选项D是正确答案。

【排他分析】选项A对应最后一段的第五句,该句中杰索普明确表示不相信伊朗会采取倾销库存(dump its inventories)的方式进一步加大出口量来压低油价,该项与原文矛盾,所以排除。选项B对应本段第四句,原文指出世界对过剩的石油没有多少存储能力(isn't much storage capacity for the excess oil),并不是说世界完全没有存储能力,因此排除。选项C在本段中并未提及,属于干扰选项,所以排除。

第二节　政治文化类

Text 9

A recent survey conducted by the Pew Research Centre showed that a mere 16% of Americans think that a four-year degree course prepares students very well for a high-paying job in the modern economy. Some of this may be a cyclical effect of the financial crisis and its economic aftermath. But technology also seems to be complicating the picture.

A paper published by a trio of Canadian economists, Paul Beaudry, David Green and Benjamin Sand, questions optimistic assumptions about demand for non-routine work and shows that since 2000 the share of employment accounted for by high-skilled jobs in America has been falling.

This analysis buttresses the view that technology is already playing havoc with employment. Skilled and unskilled workers alike are in trouble. Those with a better education are still more likely to find work, but there is now a fair chance that it will be unenjoyable. Those who never made it to college face being squeezed out of the workforce altogether. This is the argument of the techno-pessimists.

There is another, less apocalyptic possibility. James Bessen, an economist at Boston University, finds that since 1980 employment has been growing faster in occupations that use computers than in those that do not. Partial automation can actually increase demand by reducing costs. But even though technology may not destroy jobs in aggregate, it does force change upon many people.

In many occupations it has become essential to acquire new skills as established ones become obsolete. Burning Glass Technologies, a Boston-based startup that analyses labor markets by scraping data from online job advertisements, finds that the biggest demand is for new combinations of skills—what its boss, Matt Sigelman, calls "hybrid jobs". The composition of new jobs is also changing rapidly.

　　A college degree at the start of a working career does not answer the need for the continuous acquisition of new skills, especially as career spans are lengthening. Vocational training is good at giving people job-specific skills, but those, too, will need to be updated over and over again during a career lasting decades. "Germany is often lauded for its apprenticeships, but the economy has failed to adapt to the knowledge economy," says Andreas Schleicher, head of the education directorate of the OECD, a club of mostly rich countries. "Vocational training has a role, but training someone early to do one thing all their lives is not the answer to lifelong learning."

　　Add all of this up, and it becomes clear that times have got tougher for workers of all kinds. A college degree is still a prerequisite for many jobs, but employers often do not trust it enough to hire workers just on the strength of that, without experience. In many occupations workers on company payrolls face the prospect that their existing skills will become obsolete, yet it is often not obvious how they can gain new ones. And a growing number of people are self-employed. In America the share of temporary workers, contractors and freelancers in the workforce rose from 10.1% in 2005 to 15.8% in 2015.

(*The Economist*, 2017.1)

1. We can learn from the paper conducted by the Canadian economists that _____.
   A. the traditional way of employment has been shaken by technology
   B. skilled workers are no longer required in the most American industries
   C. college degree is considered a crucial factor in career success
   D. techno-pessimism paves the way for future technology development

2. James Bessen believes that _____.
   A. computer has always been an essential factor in employment
   B. increased demand can bring about cost reduction
   C. technology advancement has a positive influence upon common people
   D. progressive automation has some merits for companies

3. Burning Glass Technologies is mentioned as an example to show that _____.
   A. online job advertisements require a precise data analyses
   B. acquisition of new skills is indispensable in current job market
   C. the composition of new jobs is shaped by technology
   D. Matt Sigelman envisions a bright future of job market

4. It can be learned from paragraph 6 that _____.
   A. apprenticeships are fundamental for current German economy
   B. vocational training hinders the personal career advancement
   C. job-specific training is inadequate for lifelong career
   D. college degrees need to be upgraded during a career span

5. Which of the following is the best title for the text?
   A. Lifelong Learning: an Economic Imperative
   B. Technology Revolution: the Only Way to Success
   C. College Degree: a Guarantee for Career Change
   D. Vocational Training: a Blessing for the Job-Losers

语篇分析与试题精解

Para. 1 ①A recent survey conducted by the Pew Research Centre showed that a mere 16% of Americans think that a four-year degree course prepares students very well for a high-paying job in the modern economy. ②Some of this may be a cyclical effect of the financial crisis and its economic aftermath. ③But technology also seems to be complicating the picture.

参考译文 ①最近,皮尤研究中心所进行的一项调查显示,仅有16%的美国人认为四年制的学位课程能使学生做好在现代经济社会中获得高薪的准备。②这种结果出现的原因可能是金融危机的周期性影响,也可能是其经济余波。③而技术的发展也让情况变得更为复杂了。

原文剖析 本段首句叙述了一项调查结果,指出大多数人认为本科四年获得的知识是不足以获得高薪工作的。第二句和第三句给出可能的原因(经济危机和科技发展)。

设题点睛 本段第三句虽然带有转折连词But,但从语意上看是对前文的递进说明,两者都可用来设置正确选项。

生词解析

cyclical *adj.* 周期的,循环的   aftermath *n.* 后果;余波
complicate *vt.* 使复杂化;使恶化

Para. 2 ①A paper published by a trio of Canadian economists, Paul Beaudry, David Green and Benjamin Sand, questions optimistic assumptions about demand for non-routine work and shows that since 2000 the share of employment accounted for by high-skilled jobs in America has been falling.

参考译文 ①三位加拿大经济学家保罗·博德里(Paul Beaudry)、大卫·格林(David Green)和本杰明·桑德(Benjamin Sand),在一篇共同发表的论文中质疑了对非常规性工作需求的乐观推测,他们在文中指出,自2000年来,美国熟练技术岗位在就业中的比重一直在下降。

原文剖析 本段给出三位经济学家的观点,即美国熟练工岗位数处于下滑中,与上一段的关系并不十分明确,需要参考下文确定。

设题点睛 本段由一句话构成,属于体现人物观点的长难句,可用来设置考点。

生词解析

trio *n.* 三人一组   routine *n.* 日常工作,日常事务
account for (比例)占

长难句解析

<u>A paper</u> <u>published by a trio of Canadian economists</u>, <u>Paul Beaudry, David Green and</u>
 主语   后置定语1   同位语
<u>Benjamin Sand</u>, <u>questions</u> <u>optimistic assumptions</u> <u>about demand for non-routine work</u> and
                  谓语1   宾语   后置定语2
<u>shows</u> <u>that since 2000 the share of employment accounted for by high-skilled jobs in America</u>
 谓语2   宾语从句
<u>has been falling</u>.

本句是主从复合句。本句主干为 A paper questions optimistic assumptions and shows that...，出现了两个并列的谓语，第二个谓语后为 that 引导的宾语从句，该从句中的 accounted for by 中有两个介词连用，语序较乱，by 引出的实际是 accounted for 的动作发出者，可还原为 high-skilled jobs accounted for the share of employment。

Para. 3 ①This analysis buttresses the view that technology is already playing havoc with employment. ②Skilled and unskilled workers alike are in trouble. ③Those with a better education are still more likely to find work, but there is now a fair chance that it will be unenjoyable. ④Those who never made it to college face being squeezed out of the workforce altogether. ⑤This is the argument of the techno-pessimists.

参考译文 ①这一分析支持了技术的发展正在破坏就业的观点。②熟练和非熟练员工同处困境之中。③受教育程度较高的人虽然更容易就业，但获得的工作很可能并不尽如人意。④那些未能接受大学教育的人面临着被整体挤出劳动力市场的危险。⑤这其实也是技术悲观主义者的论点。

原文剖析 本段首句指出前两段观点之间的联系，即第二段的研究支持了第一段最后谈到的"技术的发展也让情况变得更为复杂了"。本段第二句到第四句具体从受教育程度较高的人和较低的人的角度分析技术的发展对就业具有相同的破坏性影响，再次回应首段第二句谈到的本科四年获得的知识不足以获得高薪工作的看法，也就是说高薪工作与教育程度的关系并没有过去那么大了，可理解为科技甚至代替了高级知识分子的作用。

设题点睛 本段首句和剩余内容构成总分关系，首句观点可用来设置题目。

生词解析

buttress *vt.* 支持，支撑
fair chance 机会均等；公平的机会
techno-pessimist *n.* 技术悲观主义者
play havoc with（对……）造成严重破坏
make it to 赶上，到达

1 We can learn from the paper conducted by the Canadian economists that _____.

　　A. the traditional way of employment has been shaken by technology
　　B. skilled workers are no longer required in the most American industries

加拿大经济学家所发表的论文表明_____。

　　A. 传统的就业方式已经被技术动摇
　　B. 美国的大多数产业已不再需要熟练工

C. college degree is considered a crucial factor in career success
D. techno-pessimism paves the way for future technology development

C. 大学学历是获得职业成功的关键因素
D. 技术悲观主义为未来的技术发展铺平了道路

【解题思路】 A。事实细节题。根据题干关键词(Canadian economists)定位到原文第二段。该段介绍了三位加拿大经济学家的研究成果,即"质疑了对非常规性工作需求的乐观推测……自2000年以来,美国熟练技术岗位在就业中的比重一直在下降",但并未明确该研究要说明什么观点。第三段首句的主语 this analysis 回指该研究,指出这项研究说明技术发展已经给就业带来了毁灭性的打击,也就是本题的答案,与选项A的内容一致,选项A中的 has been shaken by technology 对应原文中的 technology is already playing havoc with,因此选项A正确。

【排他分析】 选项B中的 skilled workers 出现在第三段第二句,该句指出熟练工和非熟练工都陷入了困境(Skilled and unskilled workers alike are in trouble),这里的"困境"应指就业受限,但并不能说不再被行业所需要,且前一段谈到的是熟练工岗位数量下滑,并没有消失,因此该项属于过度推断,可排除。选项C对应第三段第三句,原文后半句转折指出这些高学历人群可能也找不到好工作(but there is now a fair chance that it will be unenjoyable),说明大学文凭并非获得高薪工作的必要条件,与该项相反,因此排除。选项D中的 techno-pessimism 对应第三段最后一句,指出"技术的发展正在破坏就业的观点"也是技术悲观主义者的看法(This is the argument of the techno-pessimists),这些人应该将技术发展看作威胁,并非支持者,与该项相反,因此排除。

Para. 4 ①There is another, less apocalyptic possibility. ②James Bessen, an economist at Boston University, finds that since 1980 employment has been growing faster in occupations that use computers than in those that do not. ③Partial automation can actually increase demand by reducing costs. ④But even though technology may not destroy jobs in aggregate, it does force change upon many people.

参考译文 ①另一种可能是,情况并没有这么糟糕。②来自波士顿大学的经济学家詹姆斯·贝森(James Bessen)发现,自1980年以来,在就业率的增长速度这一方面,使用计算机的行业比不使用计算机的行业快。③半自动化事实上通过降低成本的方式增加了需求。④或许技术的发展不会影响总体的就业形式,但会迫使许多人做出改变。

原文剖析 本段转折前文,给出另一种可能性(技术进步对就业的冲击也许并没这么大)。首句是观点句。后两句利用人物观点(研究成果)给出理由(某些行业中的就业出现增长),这两句的逻辑关系或可理解为:半自动化降低了成本,使公司有更多资金招聘员工。最后一句体现让步关系,给出总体评价和预测(技术变革或许不会影响总体就业,但会促使人们做出改变)。

设题点睛 本段首句观点句与最后一句的总结句都是重要内容,可用来设置考点。

生词解析

apocalyptic *adj.* 像世界末日的；可怕的
automation *n.* 自动化；自动操作
occupation *n.* 职业；工作；行业
in aggregate 总计；总的来说

2 James Bessen believes that _____.　　　詹姆斯·贝森认为_____。

A. computer has always been an essential factor in employment
B. increased demand can bring about cost reduction
C. technology advancement has a positive influence upon common people
D. progressive automation has some merits for companies

A. 计算机一直是就业的关键因素
B. 需求增长可能降低成本
C. 科技进步对普通人有积极影响
D. 先进的自动化技术对公司而言有好处

【解题思路】D。推理引申题。根据题干关键词（James Bessen）定位到第四段。本题实际考查此人的研究结果。第四段第二句和第三句是对此人研究的描述，其中第三句指出"半自动化实际上通过降低成本的方式增加了需求"（Partial automation can actually increase demand by reducing costs），这里的 increase demand 回指前一句中的 employment has been growing，即就业人数的增长，"半自动化"代表技术发展，"降低成本"可看作是技术发展给公司带来的好处，因此选项 D 正确，该项中的 merits 表示"优点，价值；功绩"。

【排他分析】选项 A 中的 computer 出现在第四段第二句中，原文指出需要使用计算机的岗位所雇用的人数增多，用"计算机"对岗位性质和特点进行了限定，以便引出后面所说的"半自动化"的好处，但该项所说的"关键因素"在文中并未体现，因此属于过度引申，可排除。选项 B 对应第四段第三句，原文 by 引出方式（reducing costs），应理解为通过降低成本的方式增加了工作岗位，与该项的动宾关系正好相反，因此排除。选项 C 对应第四段最后一句，原文后半句指出技术革新迫使人们做出改变，force 含有迫使他人改变看法或做本不愿做的事的意思，因此无法体现出是"积极的影响"，因此排除该项。

Para. 5 ①In many occupations it has become essential to acquire new skills as established ones become obsolete. ②Burning Glass Technologies, a Boston-based startup that analyses labor markets by scraping data from online job advertisements, finds that the biggest demand is for new combinations of skills—what its boss, Matt Sigelman, calls "hybrid jobs." ③The composition of new jobs is also changing rapidly.

参考译文　①在许多行业中，由于现有技能变得过时，因此掌握新技能很有必要。②总部位于波士顿的创业公司燃镜科技通过分析从在线招聘广告中获取的数据，发现劳动力市场对新型组合型技能的需求量最大；燃镜科技的老板马特·西格尔曼（Matt Sigelman）称之为"混合型工作"。③而新工作的技能构成也处于迅速变化之中。

原文剖析 本段承接上一句末尾谈到的新的就业情况对人的要求和影响。首句为观点句,指出人们需要掌握更多新技能,并给出原因(旧技能过时)。第二句通过某一公司的数据分析,论证首句观点,指出职场目前最需要的是"混合型技能"。第三句递进指出这种技能构成还处于不断变化之中。

设题点睛 本段前两句构成"观点+例证"的结构(例证中带有人物观点),属于重要内容,可用来设置正确选项。

生词解析

obsolete *adj.* 废弃的;老式的   startup *n.* 新创办的小公司

scrape *vt.* 刮掉   hybrid *adj.* 混杂而成的;合成的

composition *n.* 组成;构成

长难句解析

Burning Glass Technologies, a Boston-based startup that analyses labor markets by scraping
　　　主语　　　　　　　　同位语　　　　　　　　定语从句
data from online job advertisements, finds that the biggest demand is for new combinations of
　　　　　　　　　　　　　　　　　　谓语　　　　宾语从句
skills—what its boss, Matt Sigelman, calls "hybrid jobs".
　　　　　　同位语从句

本句为主从复合句。本句主干为 Burning Glass Technologies finds that…,主语后为同位语成分,该同位语中还包括一个定语从句,宾语也由一个从句构成,破折号后的内容为 what 引导的同位语从句,对 combinations of skills 的内容进行说明,what 在句中作宾语。

③ Burning Glass Technologies is mentioned as an example to show that _____.	作者以燃镜科技为例说明_____。
A. online job advertisements require a precise data analyses	A. 在线招聘广告要求精确的数据分析
B. acquisition of new skills is indispensable in current job market	B. 在目前的就业市场里有必要掌握新技能
C. the composition of new jobs is shaped by technology	C. 新工作的组成由科技决定
D. Matt Sigelman envisions a bright future of job market	D. 马特·西格尔曼看好就业市场的未来

【解题思路】**B**。例子功能题。根据题干关键词(Burning Glass Technologies)定位到第五段第二句。通过分析可知,该段首句为观点句,出现例子的第二句是为了论证首句观点,理解首句意思则理解了该例子的功能。本段首句指出"在许多行业中,由于现有技能变得过时,因此获取新技能十分必要"(it has become essential to acquire new skills)。第二句进一步指出劳动市场对新型组合型技能的需求最大,重复第一句中的"获取新技能"的观点。因此选项 B 是对首句内容的正确理解,其中 acquisition of new skills 对应原文中的 acquire new skills,indispensable 对应原文中的 essential。

【排他分析】选项 A 中的 online job advertisements 出现在第五段第二句的例证描述中,属于例子的细节内容,并非是该例子想要证明的观点,因此排除。选项 C 中的

composition 出现在第五段最后一句中,原文指出"新工作的技能构成也处于迅速变化之中",并没有谈到"技能构成"与科技的关系,而且该句也不是例子想要说明的观点,因此排除。选项 D 中的人名对应第五段第二句,原文只是表达此人对"新型组合型技能"给出了另一种表述 hybrid jobs,并未对"就业市场的未来"进行预测,因此排除。

Para. 6 ① A college degree at the start of a working career does not answer the need for the continuous acquisition of new skills, especially as career spans are lengthening. ② Vocational training is good at giving people job-specific skills, but those, too, will need to be updated over and over again during a career lasting decades. ③ "Germany is often lauded for its apprenticeships, but the economy has failed to adapt to the knowledge economy," says Andreas Schleicher, head of the education directorate of the OECD, a club of mostly rich countries. ④ "Vocational training has a role, but training someone early to do one thing all their lives is not the answer to lifelong learning."

参考译文 ①在职业生涯初期,大学文凭并不能满足岗位对新技能的持续性要求,尤其是在人们的职业生涯也在延长的情况下。②职业培训擅长传授人们特定的职业技能,但这些技能也需要在长达几十年的职业生涯中不断更新。③主要由富裕国家组成的经合组织(OECD)的教育署主管安德烈亚斯·施莱歇尔(Andreas Schleicher)说:"德国因其学徒制度备受赞誉,然而德国的经济未能适应知识经济的发展。"④"职业培训有一定作用,但过早训练人们一辈子只做一件事,这并不符合终身学习的要求"。

原文剖析 本段首句回应首段内容,指出大学教育具有局限性(不能满足持续获取新技能的要求)。第二句顺承指出用于弥补大学教育的职业培训也有类似的局限性(只传授特定技能)。后两句利用人物观点进行举例论证,以德国的学徒制度为例说明职业培训所涉及的技能也需要不断更新。

设题点睛 本段第四句是含有观点的转折句,可用来设置正确选项。

生词解析

laud *vt.* 赞美;称赞   apprenticeship *n.* 学徒期;见习,训练

4 It can be learned from paragraph 6 that _____.   从第六段可知_____。

A. apprenticeships are fundamental for current German economy

B. vocational training hinders the personal career advancement

C. job-specific training is inadequate for lifelong career

D. college degrees need to be upgraded during a career span

A. 学徒制度是目前德国经济的基础

B. 职业培训阻碍了个人的职业发展

C. 特定的职业培训不足以满足终身事业的需要

D. 在整个职业生涯中,需要提升大学文凭

【解题思路】C。事实细节题。根据题干要求定位到文章第六段。在没有准确定位点的情况下,优先利用对应段中的观点或者重要逻辑结构解题。本段最后一句体现人物观点,且含有转折结构,指出"职业培训有一定作用,但过早训练人们一辈子只做一件事,这并不符合终身学习的要求"(training someone early to do one thing all their lives is not the answer to lifelong learning),answer to 有"适合于,符合"之意;本段第二句指出"职业培训擅长传授人们特定的职业技能,但这些技能也需要在长达几十年的职业生涯中不断更新",选项 C 是对这两句话的综合概括,其中 inadequate 对应原文的 not the answer to,因此选项 C 正确。

【排他分析】选项 A 中的 apprenticeships 出现在该段第三句,原文后半句转折,为本句重点,指出"德国的经济未能适应知识经济的发展"(but the economy has failed),与该项的褒义色彩相反,因此排除。选项 B 的 vocational training 出现在该段第二句,原文前半句指出"职业培训擅长传授人们特定的职业技能",说明职业培训对个人职业发展有帮助,只是需要不断更新,与该项中的"阻碍"之意矛盾,因此排除。选项 D 中的 college degrees 对应本段前两句,原文明确指出需要"更新"的是 skills,而不是"大学文凭"(college degrees),因此排除。

Para. 7 ①Add all of this up, and it becomes clear that times have got tougher for workers of all kinds. ②A college degree is still a prerequisite for many jobs, but employers often do not trust it enough to hire workers just on the strength of that, without experience. ③In many occupations workers on company payrolls face the prospect that their existing skills will become obsolete, yet it is often not obvious how they can gain new ones. ④And a growing number of people are self-employed. ⑤In America the share of temporary workers, contractors and freelancers in the workforce rose from 10.1% in 2005 to 15.8% in 2015.

参考译文 ①综上所述,可明显看出各类工种的日子都更不好过了。②大学文凭仍是获得很多工作的必要前提,但若无工作经验,很多雇主不会仅凭一纸文凭就雇用一个人。③在许多行业,公司雇员面临自己的现有技能即将过时,但又常常不清楚该如何获得新技能的情况。④还有越来越多的人不受雇于他人。⑤在美国,临时工、承包人和自由职业者的比重由 2005 年的 10.1% 上升到了 2015 年的 15.8%。

原文剖析 本段首句总结指出职场上各类人的日子都不会好过了。第二句从刚毕业大学生的角度论证首句观点,指出大学文凭并非高薪工作的保证(文凭和工作经验同等重要)。第三句从在职者的角度论证首句观点,指出很多公司雇员面临技能过时但找不到更新途径的问题。第四句和第五句通过数据指出有越来越多的人不受雇于他人,这也是对首句观点的论证,可理解为很多人因找不到长期稳定的工作而成为"临时工、承包人和自由职业者"。

设题点睛 本段第三句为带有转折语意的长难句,最后两句体现就业困难产生的结果,都属于重要内容,可用来设置考点。

生词解析

prerequisite *n.* 先决条件　　　　on the strength of 基于;凭借……

on the payroll 在职
freelancer n. 自由职业者
self-employed adj. 个体经营的；不受雇于他人的

长难句解析

In many occupations workers on company payrolls face the prospect that their existing skills
　　状语　　　　　　主语　　　后置定语　　　　　谓语　　宾语　　　定语从句
will become obsolete, yet it is often not obvious how they can gain new ones.

本句为主从复合句。本句主干为 workers face the prospect that...，宾语后为 that 引导的定语从句，对其进行补充说明。该定语从句由 yet（可作连词，表示"但是；然而"）连接的两个句子构成，后半句采用了 it is adj. how 的结构，it 作形式主语，真正的主语是 how 引导的表示方式的主语从句。

5 Which of the following is the best title for the text?

以下哪项是本文最佳标题？

A. Lifelong Learning: an Economic Imperative
B. Technology Revolution: the Only Way to Success
C. College Degree: a Guarantee for Career Change
D. Vocational Training: a Blessing for the Job-Losers

A. 终身学习：经济的需要
B. 技术革命：成功的唯一道路
C. 大学文凭：改变职业的保证
D. 职业培训：失业者的福音

【解题思路】A。主旨大意题。解答本题要求对全文核心内容有所把握。作者在首段到第三段的内容中，主要叙述技术发展对就业产生的破坏，促使人们做出改变和调整。第四段和第五段指出人们调整和改变的方法，即不断掌握新技能。第六段谈到掌握新技能的方式（通过终身学习）。最后一段对全文进行总结，重申目前就业环境对求职者和在职者的严峻挑战，突出技能更新、学历、工作经验同等重要。因此全文想要说明的核心观点是：在如今的就业环境下，要想获得职业上的成功，必须通过终身学习的方式不断掌握新技能，与选项 A 所提取的关键词相符，economic 回应技术发展影响经济和就业的大环境，imperative 体现终身学习的重要性，因此选项 A 正确。

【排他分析】原文虽然谈到了技术变革，但这只是需要进行终身学习的大环境和原因，因此选项 B 提炼的主题错误，可以排除。选项 C 所谈到的"大学文凭"在文中被多次否定，原文将其描述为找到工作的敲门砖，工作经验也很重要，且原文并未谈到"改变职业"这个内容，因此排除。选项 D 所谈到的职业培训主要出现在倒数第二段中，原文提到职业培训也需要不断更新，是针对在职员工而言的，并未谈到失业者接受职业培训这一话题，因此该项与原文无关，可排除。

Text 10

Human beings are not born with the knowledge that others possess minds with different contents. Children develop such a "theory of mind" gradually, and even adults have it only imperfectly.

But a study by Samantha Fan and Zoe Liberman at the University of Chicago, published in *Psychological Science*, finds that bilingual children, and also those simply exposed to another language on a regular basis, have an edge at the business of getting inside others' minds.

In a simple experiment, Dr. Fan and Dr. Liberman sat monolingual, bilingual and "exposure" children aged between four and six with a grid of objects placed between them and an experimenter.

Some objects were blocked from the experimenter's sight, a fact the children could clearly see. With a large, a medium and a small car visible to the child, but the small car hidden from the adult, the adult would ask "I see a small car" and ask the child to move it. Both bilingual and those in the exposure group moved the medium-sized car (the smallest the experimenter could see) about 75% of the time, against 50% for the monolinguals. The successful children were less likely even to glance at the car the experimenter could not see.

This study joins a heap of others suggesting that there are cognitive advantages to being bilingual. Researchers have found that bilinguals have better executive function (control over attention and the planning of complex tasks). Those that suffer dementia begin to do so, on average, almost five years later than monolinguals. Full bilinguals had previously been shown to have better theory-of-mind skills. But this experiment is the first to demonstrate that such benefits also accrue to those merely exposed to other languages.

It has become fashionable to consider multilingualism as a kind of elite mental training. The question is not settled, though, for many studies have not been successfully replicated. Nor is it yet clear precisely which kinds of language skills and exposure make people better at exactly which tasks. For example, in Dr. Fan's and Dr. Liberman's experiment the bilingual children had better executive function than the exposure ones, while all three groups had similar vocabularies, fluid intelligence (the ability to reason quickly and think abstractly) and nonverbal visual-spatial skills. This makes it surprising that the exposure group resembled the bilinguals more than the monolinguals when it came to taking the experimenter's point of view.

If the bilingual advantage is to hold up, more clever research design is needed. Some advantages may accrue only to bilinguals who switch languages often. Some may apply only to those who live in mixed communities. While some advantages, such as lack of dementia, appear late in life, others may appear early only to disappear thereafter. Research on multilingual minds is, itself, still in a kind of adolescence, but it is a promising one.

(*The Economist*, 2015.5)

1. The expression "'exposure' children"(Para. 3) refers to _____.
   A. children who possess minds with different contents
   B. children who can get inside others' minds
   C. children who have imperfect mental ability
   D. children who periodically get in touch with a second language
2. By describing the result of the experiment, the author intends to show that _____.
   A. bilingual children have a better understanding of others' thought
   B. visual capacity largely influences the result of the experiment
   C. monolinguals have a problem with their mental function
   D. the successful group has no interest in the smallest car
3. Multiple researches have shown that _____.
   A. executive function is a key criteria in judging cognitive ability
   B. dementia has a more significant impact on monolinguals
   C. bilinguals still need to prove their theory-of-mind skills
   D. bilinguals possess a superior mental capacity
4. It is indicated in paragraph 6 that _____.
   A. bilinguals performed much better in understanding the experimenter's purpose
   B. the relevance between certain linguistic ability and mental function is obscure
   C. monolinguals are always inferior to the exposure ones
   D. few people concentrate on employing multilingualism in mind-training
5. What is the author's attitude toward the research?
   A. Uncertain and confused.   B. Immature yet worthy.
   C. Analytical and sophisticated.   D. Irregular yet promising.

语篇分析与试题精解

Para. 1 ①Human beings are not born with the knowledge that others possess minds with different contents. ②Children develop such a "theory of mind" gradually, and even adults have it only imperfectly.

参考译文 ①人类并非天生就知道每个人的想法不同。②孩子们在成长过程中才会逐渐认识到这一"心智理论",即便是成人也不敢说能完全掌握这一理论。

Para. 2 ①But a study by Samantha Fan and Zoe Liberman at the University of Chicago, published in *Psychological Science*, finds that bilingual children, and also those simply exposed to another language on a regular basis, have an

参考译文 ①然而,美国芝加哥大学的萨曼莎·法恩(Samantha Fan)和佐伊·利伯曼(Zoe Liberman)的研究表明,双语儿童,以及那些只定期接触第二种语言的儿童,能更好地理

edge at the business of getting inside others' minds.

解他人的思想。该研究发表在《心理科学》杂志上。

原文剖析 首段和第二段可放在一起分析。首段先给出基本观点：人类并非天生就能够知道人与人的思维是不同的；小孩在成长过程中可以慢慢地形成这种认识，但也许直到成年这种认识都未发展成熟。第二段出现转折，引出了萨曼莎·法恩和佐伊·利伯曼的新观点：双语儿童或者定期接触第二语言的儿童会比同龄人更好地理解他人的想法。

设题点睛 只有第二段的转折和人物观点可用来设题，因为这也是引领全文的核心观点。

生词解析

possess vt. 拥有　　　　　　　imperfectly adv. 有缺点地,不完美地
bilingual adj. 双语的　　　　　have an edge（略）占优势

Para. 3 ①In a simple experiment, Dr. Fan and Dr. Liberman sat monolingual, bilingual and "exposure" children aged between four and six with a grid of objects placed between them and an experimenter.

参考译文 ①在一个简单的实验中,法恩博士和利伯曼博士分别找来了年龄为4～6岁的单语儿童、双语儿童和规律性接触第二语言的儿童,并在他们和一位主试者之间放置了一些呈网格状分布的物品。

原文剖析 该段承接前一段谈到的研究,描述了两位研究者进行的一项简单的实验,谈到了实验的对象。

设题点睛 本段基本不具备可用来设置题目的内容,但其中带有引号的"exposure"可以用来考查指代类或语意理解类题目。

生词解析

sit vt. 使就座　　　　　　　a grid of 一个网格状的……

1 The expression "'exposure' children" (Para. 3) refers to _____.

A. children who possess minds with different contents
B. children who can get inside others' minds
C. children who have imperfect mental ability
D. children who periodically get in touch with a second language

"'exposure' children"（第三段）指的是_____。

A. 想法不同的儿童
B. 能洞悉他人想法的儿童
C. 心智有缺陷的儿童
D. 定期接触第二语言的儿童

【解题思路】D。语意理解题。根据题干要求定位到文章第三段。"exposure" children 的含义无法通过其后的内容得知,最多只知道小孩的年龄在四到六岁之间。而 exposure 是和 monolingual 以及 bilingual 并列的内容,推断该词应和语言有关系。第二段观点句中的 those simply exposed to another language on a regular basis 曾出现与此处 exposure 照应的内容,且与之前的 bilingual 并列,可以推断出与"exposure" children 所指相同,选项 D 中的 periodically 对应原文的 on a regular basis,因此选项 D 是正确答案。

【排他分析】选项 A 对应文章首段,首段谈到的内容与第三段中的实验无关,所以选项

A错误。选项B对应第二段,但能够理解他人思维的孩子不仅仅是"exposure" children,也包括了bilingual children,选项B存在指代不明的情况,因此排除。选项C是利用第一段第二句中的imperfectly一词设置的干扰项,与原文谈到的人群无关,可直接排除。

Para. 4 ①Some objects were blocked from the experimenter's sight, a fact the children could clearly see. ②With a large, a medium and a small car visible to the child, but the small car hidden from the adult, the adult would ask "I see a small car" and ask the child to move it. ③Both bilingual and those in the exposure group moved the medium-sized car (the smallest the experimenter could see) about 75% of the time, against 50% for the monolinguals. ④The successful children were less likely even to glance at the car the experimenter could not see.

参考译文 ①有些物品是主试者看不见的,这点孩子们都知道。②孩子们能看见一辆大型车、一辆中型车和一辆小型车,但是主试者是看不见小型车的。主试者可以说:"我看见一辆小型车",并请孩子们移动它。③双语和规律性接触第二语言的孩子们四次中有三次都移动了中型车(这是主试者能够看见的最小型的车),而单语儿童两次中只有一次移动了中型车。④实验成功的孩子们几乎看都不看小型车,因为他们知道主试者看不见。

原文剖析 本段与上一段一起构成了对该实验的完整介绍,上一段给出实验参与者,本段描述实验方式和实验结果。其中最后两句是比较关键的内容,谈到双语和规律性接触第二语言的孩子可能更了解主试者的意图。

设题点睛 第四段中最重要的信息应该是实验结果,因此作者一般可利用实验的结果设置一个例子功能题进行考查。

生词解析
block vt. 阻止;限制　　　　　　　medium adj. 中等的
glance vi. (匆匆地)看一眼;扫视

2 By describing the result of the experiment, the author intends to show that _____.
　A. bilingual children have a better understanding of others' thought
　B. visual capacity largely influences the result of the experiment
　C. monolinguals have a problem with their mental function
　D. the successful group has no interest in the smallest car

通过描述实验结果,作者想要说明的是_____。
　A. 双语儿童能更好地理解他人的想法
　B. 视觉能力对实验结果产生很大影响
　C. 单语者在心智功能方面有问题
　D. 成功的一组对小型车没有兴趣

【解题思路】A。例子功能题。描述实验结果的内容出现在文章第四段。文章第二段提出了萨曼莎·法恩和佐伊·利伯曼的观点,认为学习双语的小孩在理解他人想法的能力上更加突出。第三段是对实验的介绍,第四段给出实验结论,该结论应该和第二段两人的观点一致。第四段第三句和第四句给出的实验结果是双语和规律性接触第二语言的小孩比单语种小孩更能够为主试者考虑,从事实上支持了第二段专家提出的观点(have an edge at the business of getting inside others' minds),所以选项A符合原文大意,是正确答案。

【排他分析】选项B对应第四段第一句及第二句,虽然第一句中出现clearly see,第二句出现visible to,但是不等同于视觉能力会影响实验结果,这种安排有特定目的,所以排除。第四段的实验结果谈到双语小孩能够站在主试者的角度来思考问题,只能推测出单语种小孩很难站在他人角度思考问题,不等同于其心智功能存在问题,所以排除选项C。选项D对应第四段最后一句,文章中并没有说实验的成功组对小尺寸的汽车不感兴趣,他们之所以完全不关注小尺寸汽车(less likely even to glance at)纯粹是因为他们知道主试者无法看见,所以排除。

Para. 5 ① This study joins a heap of others suggesting that there are cognitive advantages to being bilingual. ② Researchers have found that bilinguals have better executive function (control over attention and the planning of complex tasks). ③ Those that suffer dementia begin to do so, on average, almost five years later than monolinguals. ④ Full bilinguals had previously been shown to have better theory-of-mind skills. ⑤ But this experiment is the first to demonstrate that such benefits also accrue to those merely exposed to other languages.

参考译文 ①该项研究和其他诸多研究一起,表明了双语人群拥有认知能力上的优势。②研究人员发现,双语人群的执行能力(对注意力的控制能力和对复杂任务的计划能力)更强。③双语人群患痴呆症的平均年龄也比单语人群晚五年。④之前已证实,完全双语人群拥有更好的心智理论技能。⑤但该实验第一次说明,这种优势也存在于仅仅接触第二语言的人身上。

原文剖析 本段承接上文的实验结果提出新观点,首句指出双语人群拥有更高的认知能力。第二句、第三句和第四句对首句观点进行了具体解释,指出双语使用者的执行力更强且患痴呆症的时间更晚,同时心智理论技能也更强大。第五句转折提出本段段内的一个新观点:这是首个证明接触第二语言的人群同样也会出现上述优势的研究。

设题点睛 从考点设置来说,本段首句为观点句,第二句、第三句、第四句是对首句的细化展开,这四句话构成局部的总分结构,可以设置考点。第五句虽然出现转折,但并不否定首句的观点,所以设置正确选项的概率不大。

生词解析

a heap of 一大堆,许多　　　　　　cognitive *adj.* 认知的
executive *adj.* 执行的　　　　　　dementia *n.* 痴呆
accrue to 适用于

长难句解析

But　this experiment　is　the first　to demonstrate　that such benefits also accrue to those
连词　　主语　　　　系动词　表语　　后置定语1　　　　　宾语从句

merely exposed to other languages.

后置定语2

本句主干结构为 this experiment is the first to demonstrate that…，动词不定式 to demonstrate… 作后置定语修饰 the first，that 引导的从句作 demonstrate 的宾语，宾语从句中非谓语动词 exposed to other languages 作后置定语，修饰 those（people）。

3 **Multiple researches have shown that _____.** 　　大量研究已表明_____。

A. executive function is a key criteria in judging cognitive ability 　　A. 执行力是评判认知能力的一个重要标准

B. dementia has a more significant impact on monolinguals 　　B. 痴呆对单语人群的影响更大

C. bilinguals still need to prove their theory-of-mind skills 　　C. 双语者仍旧需要证明他们的心智理论技能

D. bilinguals possess a superior mental capacity 　　D. 双语者拥有更强的心智能力

【解题思路】D。事实细节题。根据题干的 multiple researches 定位到第五段首句的 This study joins a heap of others（联合其他研究），本题考查多个研究得出的共同结论。本段第一句和第二句都有明确的结论性内容，首句的 cognitive advantages 等同于选项 D 中的 superior mental capacity，所以选项 D 是正确答案。

【排他分析】选项 A 的 executive function 对应第五段第二句，原文表示双语使用者的执行能力更强，并没有明确指出执行力是辨别认知能力高低的重要标准，所以排除。选项 B 对应的是第五段第三句，原文指出双语使用者患痴呆症的平均年龄要比单语使用者晚五年（时间早晚的影响），并没有提到痴呆症对单语使用者的影响更大（程度高低的影响），所以排除。选项 C 对应第五段第四句，原文的意思是已证实完全双语人群有更强的心智理论技能，与该项的意思不同，所以排除。

Para. 6 ①It has become fashionable to consider multilingualism as a kind of elite mental training. ②The question is not settled, though, for many studies have not been successfully replicated. ③Nor is it yet clear precisely which kinds of language skills and exposure make people better at exactly which tasks. ④For example, in Dr. Fan's and Dr. Liberman's experiment the bilingual children had better executive function than the exposure ones, while all three groups had similar vocabularies, fluid intelligence (the ability to reason quickly and think abstractly) and nonverbal visual-spatial skills. ⑤This makes it surprising that the exposure group resembled the

参考译文 ①把多语理论看作一种卓越的心理训练方法已经成为时尚。②然而，该问题还没有盖棺定论，因为很多研究还未被成功复制，③而且我们也没有完全弄清楚，哪些语言技能和接触哪种语言能够帮助人们在哪些任务中脱颖而出。④例如，在法恩博士和利伯曼博士的实验中，双语儿童比单纯接触第二语言的儿童拥有更好的执行能力，而三组孩子在词汇、流体智力（快速推理和抽象思维能力）和非语言空间视觉能力上不相上下。⑤这就让人费解，为什么单纯接触第二语言的儿童能够和双语儿

bilinguals more than the monolinguals when it came to taking the experimenter's point of view.

童一样,比单语儿童更能理解主试者的意图呢?

原文剖析 本段首句描述现象:越来越多的人开始关注多语种训练对培养心智能力的作用。第二句和第三句对此提出质疑:此结论并未被其他研究论证,且对于哪一种语言可以帮助人提高哪一种能力也不是很清楚。第四句举例论证第三句,说明双语儿童、接触第二语言的儿童和单语儿童这三类孩子在不同能力上的表现不同(语言多样性不一定同步提高各项能力)。最后一句提出一个未被解释的疑惑:为何第二语言接触者在揣测他人意图上的能力与双语小孩类似。

设题点睛 从考点设置来说,本段第二句、第三句、第四句构成"疑问+例证"的结构,是最适合出题的,可以利用第二句或者第三句设置正确选项,因为否定结构容易出考点。

生词解析

elite *adj.* 卓越的   replicate *vt.* 复制
nonverbal *adj.* 非语言的   visual-spatial 空间视觉
resemble *vt.* 像,类似

长难句解析

This makes it surprising that the exposure group resembled the bilinguals more than
主语 谓语 宾语 宾语补足语   真正宾语
the monolinguals when it came to taking the experimenter's point of view.
                            状语从句

本句主干结构为 This makes it surprising that... when...,句中 it 为形式宾语,that 引导的从句为真正的宾语。

4 It is indicated in paragraph 6 that _____ .   第六段暗示了_____。

A. bilinguals performed much better in understanding the experimenter's purpose
B. the relevance between certain linguistic ability and mental function is obscure
C. monolinguals are always inferior to the exposure ones
D. few people concentrate on employing multilingualism in mind-training

A. 双语者能更好地理解主试者的目的
B. 某种语言能力和心智功能之间的关系并不清楚
C. 单语者总是比接触第二语言者差
D. 很少有人专注于将多语理论应用于心智训练

【解题思路】**B**。推理引申题。根据题干要求定位到原文第六段,本段第三句和第四句构成"疑问+举例"的结构,大意是我们对于哪些语言技能和接触哪种语言能够帮助人们在哪些任务中脱颖而出还不是很清楚(Nor is it yet clear),言下之意是这三者间的关联是模糊不清的,且第四句举例指出语言能力与执行能力的高低有关,但其与词汇、快速推理、抽象思维和空间视觉能力的高低并无对等关系,即选项 B 谈到的语言能力与心智能力的关系并不清楚,该项正确。

【排他分析】选项 A 对应本段最后一句,原文大意是单纯接触第二语言的小孩在理解主试者意图上与双语小孩是一样强的(resembled),选项 A 的表述不严谨,所以排除;

选项 C 对应的是本段第四句的举例内容,原文后半句的意思是三组小孩在词汇、流体智力和非语言空间视觉上的能力不相上下,单语儿童并不总是比接触第二语言的儿童差,所以排除;选项 D 对应本段的首句,原文大意是现在越来越多的人(become fashionable)认为多语理论可用于训练心智能力,选项 D 与之相反,所以排除。

Para. 7 ① If the bilingual advantage is to hold up, more clever research design is needed. ②Some advantages may accrue only to bilinguals who switch languages often. ③Some may apply only to those who live in mixed communities. ④ While some advantages, such as lack of dementia, appear late in life, others may appear early only to disappear thereafter. ⑤Research on multilingual minds is, itself, still in a kind of adolescence, but it is a promising one.

参考译文 ①如果要确认双语优势,还需要有更精妙的研究设计。②有些优势只有在双语者不断转换语言的情况下才存在。③有些优势可能只适用于住在混合族裔社区中的人。④还有些优势在生命中出现得较晚,比如说不易患痴呆症,而其他优势可能只在早期具有,后期就消失了。⑤虽然对多语人群心智的研究还在起步阶段,但前景光明。

原文剖析 本段承接上一段的疑问,指出需要更多的研究来论证双语的优势。第二、三、四句指出双语带来的优势存在不确定性。而最后一句给出作者观点,谈到虽然针对双语人群的心智研究尚处于起步阶段,但前途是光明的。

设题点睛 从考点设置来说,本段最重要的单句应该是最后一句,这句话明确给出作者的态度,可以设置观点态度题。

生词解析

hold up 证明属实
thereafter *adv.* 从那以后
promising *adj.* 有希望的

switch *vt.* 转换
adolescence *n.* (文化、语言的)发育成形阶段

长难句解析

While some advantages, such as lack of dementia, appear late in life, others may appear
　　　　　　　　　让步状语从句　　　　　　　　　　　　　主语　　谓语
early only to disappear thereafter.
　　　结果状语

本句是主从复合句,本句主干为 others may appear early…。句首为 while 引导的让步状语从句,其主干为 some advantages appear late…,包含 such as 引导的插入语,主句后还有个 only to do 结构的状语,体现结果。

5 What is the author's attitude toward the research?

A. Uncertain and confused.
B. Immature yet worthy.
C. Analytical and sophisticated.
D. Irregular yet promising.

作者如何看待这一研究?

A. 不确定并感到困惑。
B. 不成熟但认为值得。
C. 重分析且复杂。
D. 无规律但有希望。

【解题思路】**B**。观点态度题。根据顺序原则,本题定位到最后一段的可能性较大。本段最后一句带有让步结构,大意是对于多语人群的心智研究虽然尚处在起步阶段(still in a kind of adolescence),但是前途是光明的(promising one),选项 B 的 immature 对应原文的 adolescence,worthy 对应原文的 promising,因此选项 B 是正确答案。

【排他分析】选项 A 的 uncertain 可以等同于 adolescence(处于发展初期确实难以判断之后的情况),但是 confused 表达的是一种不认可的态度,与原文的 promising 相违背,所以排除;选项 C 的 analytical 和 sophisticated 都为中性词,无法反映原文所说研究尚处于初期但有希望的态度,所以排除;选项 D 的 irregular 在文中没有体现,且如果没有规律,则不存在研究的必要,所以排除。

Text 11

Europeans can sometimes seem like a miserable bunch. The continent has produced downbeat writers such as Jean-Paul Sartre and philosophers such as Slavoj Zizek. But although there are many reasons for Europeans to feel gloomy at present—from a migration crisis stretching from Greece to Germany to the possibility that Britain, one of the fastest-growing economies in Europe, may leave the European Union—many, instead, seem to be becoming ever cheerier.

Most Europeans are, on average, at their happiest since the financial crisis. In 2008 76% of EU citizens said they were satisfied with their lives. That number is now 80%, according to the Eurobarometer survey, which has tracked self-reported happiness for over four decades. Those in northern European countries, such as Denmark and Sweden, are consistently the most content. But some countries have bucked the trend. According to Ruut Veenhoven, a professor at Erasmus University in Rotterdam who has been analysing data on happiness for decades, people in Greece and Portugal have become gloomier over the past three decades (although they have started to perk up over the past few years).

Some general themes stand out. According to Eurostat, the EU's statistical office, the only metric consistently correlated with European happiness is relative income. Moving one step up the income ladder increases happiness in every country in the EU; the difference in happiness between the bottom quintile and the second quintile is the largest. European men tend to be slightly happier than women, though not in Britain or Denmark. Those who go to university tend to be happier (not controlling for income).

But some big differences also emerge. Europeans are generally happier when they are younger. However, richer countries see an uptick of joyfulness in old age: Germans are happier when they are over 75 years old than when they are between 25 and 34, and the Swiss are happier when they are over 75 than when they are teenagers. (Britons, Swedes and Danes are happiest when they are between 65 and 74.) The Portuguese seem to have the worst mid-life crises, whereas Greeks, Bulgarians, Romanians and Slovenians all become glummer as they get older.

Where and how Europeans live also determines their happiness. In all countries, people are least happy if they live on their own. By the same token, in most countries those with children tend to be happier, with the exception of Britain, Denmark, Ireland and Switzerland, where people tend to be happier when childless. Overall, Europeans tend to be most content if they live in towns or suburbs as opposed to cities or rural areas. Northern Europeans tend to be cheerier the farther they are from cities (and hence from other people). In most parts of southern and eastern Europe, however, the opposite is true.

What makes city-dwellers happier varies from one city to the next. According to the most recent data from Eurobarometer, most city-dwellers have become slightly happier. The highest correlation with life satisfaction in cities is a feeling of safety. But in Stockholm, Amsterdam and Vienna it is those who think foreigners are well integrated who tend to be happiest. Parisians and Berliners who rate their cities' cleanliness highly are the most content. In Reykjavik, curiously, the telltale sign of happiness is being satisfied with the public transport system.

Those places which are happiest appear to have good governance. This may suggest a lesson to politicians: reducing unemployment and boosting wages will undoubtedly increase happiness. But clean pavements are important, too.

(*The Economist*, 2016.2)

1. The current gloominess of the Europeans _____.
   A. is mainly due to the possible departure of Britain from EU
   B. is accelerating the breakdown of EU
   C. may be a misinterpretation of the situation
   D. breeds the outburst of the downbeat writers

2. Which of the following elements may bring a continuous feeling of wellbeing to the Europeans?
   A. Education background.
   B. Gender difference.
   C. Income improvement.
   D. Income inequality.

3. It can be inferred from paragraph 4 and 5 that _____.
   A. suburbanization is well-developed in Northern Europe
   B. Europeans are less dependent on their children
   C. age plays a pivotal role in determining happiness
   D. Europeans have diversified definitions about happiness

4. Which of the following is not a key element in deciding Europeans' happiness?
   A. A fair way of wealth distribution.
   B. A sense of security.
   C. A harmonious atmosphere.
   D. A conscientious government.

5. The best title for this passage is _____.
   A. Governance Improvement: the Only Way to Raise the Happiness for Europeans
   B. Multiple Factors in Deciding the Happiness for Europeans
   C. A Gloomy Future: Europe Is Dominated by Downbeat Writers
   D. Europeans' Feeling of Happiness Reaches a Record High

语篇分析与试题精解

Para. 1 ①Europeans can sometimes seem like a miserable bunch. ②The continent has produced downbeat writers such as Jean-Paul Sartre and philosophers such as Slavoj Zizek. ③But although there are many reasons for Europeans to feel gloomy at present—from a migration crisis stretching from Greece to Germany to the possibility that Britain, one of the fastest-growing economies in Europe, may leave the European Union—many, instead, seem to be becoming ever cheerier.

参考译文 ①欧洲人有时看上去似乎有点悲观。②这片大陆上诞生过保罗·萨特(Jean-Paul Sartre)这样的忧郁作家以及斯拉沃热·齐泽克(Slavoj Zizek)这样的悲观哲学家。③而如今，移民危机从希腊一直蔓延到德国，甚至欧洲增速最快国家之一的英国也可能因此离开欧洲，尽管这些理由足以让欧洲人民不那么乐观，但很多人却变得比以前更加欢乐。

原文剖析 本段前两句为"观点+例证"的关系，指出欧洲人有时很悲观。第三句用But转折指出即便目前欧洲面临着复杂情况，但很多欧洲人非但不感到悲观，反而还比以前更为乐观。

设题点睛 本段第三句是带有"转折+双破折"的长难句，是本段的观点性内容，可用来设置题干或正确选项。

生词解析

miserable *adj.* 悲惨的；痛苦的
downbeat *adj.* （对现实）悲观的，忧郁的
bunch *n.* ［口语］一群，一帮，一伙
gloomy *adj.* 沮丧的；阴郁的

长难句解析

But although there are many reasons for Europeans to feel gloomy at present—from a migration
　　　　　　　让步状语从句
crisis stretching from Greece to Germany to the possibility that Britain, one of the fastest-
　　　　后置定语　　　　　　　　　　　　　　　同位语从句　　　　同位语
growing economies in Europe, may leave the European Union—many, instead,　seem
　　　　同位语从句　　　　　　　　　　　　　　　　主语　　　　　　系动词
to be becoming ever cheerier.
　　表语

本句是主从复合句。本句主干为although..., many seem to be cheerier, 句首although引导让步状语从句，破折号之间的部分较长，实际上可看作对让步状语从句中many reasons的举例说明，使用了介词短语from...to...的结构(from a migration crisis to the possibility),表示范围,其中 possibility 后的 that 从句作同位语,其主干为 Britain may leave the European Union,破折号后的部分才是本句的主句。

1 The current gloominess of the Europeans _____.   目前欧洲人的沮丧感 _____。

A. is mainly due to the possible departure of Britain from EU
B. is accelerating the breakdown of EU
C. may be a misinterpretation of the situation
D. breeds the outburst of the downbeat writers

A. 主要源于英国可能离开欧盟
B. 加速了欧盟的解体
C. 可能是对形势的误解
D. 促使忧郁型作家大量涌现

【解题思路】C。推理引申题。根据题干关键词(gloominess of the Europeans)定位到文章首段第三句。原文第三句较长,但其主干内容为"但很多人却变得比以前更欢乐"(many, instead, seem to be becoming ever cheerier),明确指出即便欧洲面临诸多危机和风险,但欧洲人的悲观情绪并没有想象的那么严重。选项 C 中的 misinterpretation 表示"对……的错误解释",只有该项可体现出事实与想象有出入,因此该项正确。

【排他分析】选项 A 中的 possible departure of Britain from EU 对应第三句双破折号之间的内容,英国可能脱欧只是欧洲面临的众多问题中的一个,因此选项 A 中的 mainly 不符合原文,排除该项。选项 B 所表达的"欧盟解体"之意在原文中并未提及,且不符合实际,可以直接排除。选项 D 中的 downbeat writers 出现在首段第二句,原文虽然谈到欧洲人有时感到悲观,并产生了一些悲观作家,但并未提到与 outburst(数量激增)有关的内容,且这种现象和题干所问的目前(current)情况无关,因此排除。

Para. 2 ①Most Europeans are, on average, at their happiest since the financial crisis. ②In 2008 76% of EU citizens said they were satisfied with their lives. ③ That number is now 80%, according to the Eurobarometer survey, which has tracked self-reported happiness for over four decades. ④ Those in northern European countries, such as Denmark and Sweden, are consistently the most content. ⑤ But some countries have bucked the trend. ⑥According to Ruut Veenhoven, a professor at Erasmus University in Rotterdam who has been analysing data on happiness for decades, people in Greece and Portugal have become gloomier over the past three decades (although they have started to perk up over the past few years).

参考译文 ①总体上看,大部分欧洲人处于金融危机以来最幸福的时期。②2008 年,76% 的欧洲人表示,他们对自己的生活感到满意。③欧洲晴雨表的调查结果显示,这个数字目前上升到了 80%,该调查记录了被调查者在过去四十多年中的自我幸福感。④丹麦和瑞典等北欧人的幸福感依然最强。⑤而有些国家则大相径庭。⑥鹿特丹伊拉斯姆斯大学的卢特·范荷文(Ruut Veenhoven)教授数十年来致力于对幸福感相关数据的分析,他指出,在过去的三十年里,希腊和葡萄牙的国民幸福感在下降(尽管最近几年这两国的国民幸福感指数有所上升)。

原文剖析 本段首句承接上段最后一句的观点，继续指出目前欧洲人并非像人们想象的那么悲观。第二句到第四句都对首句进行举例论证。第五句开始转折，引出相反的情况，即第六句所说的希腊和葡萄牙的国民幸福感在下降，但括号里的内容又表明这种情况也在改善之中。

设题点睛 本段只在最后两句中转折指出某些欧洲国家的国民幸福感指数在过去的几十年中有所下降，但整段的观点与前文较为一致，不适合用来设置题目。

生词解析
track *vt.* 跟踪；追踪；掌握（动向等）　　buck the trend 反潮流
perk up 增加，上涨

长难句解析
According to Ruut Veenhoven, a professor at Erasmus University in Rotterdam who has
　　　　　状语　　　　　　　　　　　　　　同位语
been analysing data on happiness for decades, people in Greece and Portugal have become
　　　　　定语从句　　　　　　　　　　　　主语　　　后置定语　　　　系动词
gloomier over the past three decades (although they have started to perk up over the past few years).
表语　　　　时间状语　　　　　　　　　　让步状语从句

本句是主从复合句。本句主干为 people have become gloomier...，句首状语中出现的人名被之后较长的同位语和定语从句修饰，句末括号之中为 although 引导的让步状语从句，是对主句语意的转折。

Para. 3 ①Some general themes stand out. ②According to Eurostat, the EU's statistical office, the only metric consistently correlated with European happiness is relative income. ③Moving one step up the income ladder increases happiness in every country in the EU; the difference in happiness between the bottom quintile and the second quintile is the largest. ④European men tend to be slightly happier than women, though not in Britain or Denmark. ⑤Those who go to university tend to be happier (not controlling for income).

参考译文 ①有一些显而易见的一般性因素。②欧盟统计局的数据显示，相对收入是唯一一项始终与欧洲幸福度有关的度量指标。③任何一个欧洲国家，只要收入上升一个台阶，其国民幸福度就会增加；用五分位数统计法测算后发现，处于数据金字塔底层81%~100%和第二层21%~40%的两个人群间的幸福度差别最大。④除了英国和丹麦，相对于女性而言，欧洲男性的幸福感略高。⑤而在不考虑收入的情况下，受过大学教育的人群也会感到更加幸福。

原文剖析 本段首句为总起句，属于抽象观点，提示下文要开始讨论原因。第二句和第三句用"观点+例证"的结构给出第一个最重要的因素（收入）。第四句给出第二个因素（性别）。最后一句给出第三个因素（教育程度）。其中，第三句中的 quintile 是统计学专用词，一个五分位数是一组数据集，整体呈金字塔形，每个代表特定人口中的20%，则第一个五分位数（the first quintile）代表最少的五分之一（1%~20%），第二个五分位数（the second quintile）代表21%~40%，以此类推。

设题点睛 本段抽象观点之后给出三个因素，可用来设置细节题的正确选项。

生词解析

stand out 突出，显眼
be correlated with 与……有关
metric n. 衡量标准
quintile n.【统计学】五分位数

2 Which of the following elements may bring a continuous feeling of wellbeing to the Europeans?

以下哪种因素可能给欧洲人带来持续的幸福感？

A. Education background.
B. Gender difference.
C. Income improvement.
D. Income inequality.

A. 教育背景。
B. 性别差异。
C. 收入改善。
D. 收入不平等。

【解题思路】C。事实细节题。本题考查能让欧洲人感到持续幸福的原因。本文第三段总体介绍了欧洲人一般幸福感的来源，即题干中的 elements。该段第二句强调"相对收入是唯一一项始终与欧洲幸福度有关的度量指标"（the only metric consistently correlated with European happiness is relative income），其中的 consistently 与题干中的 continuous 对应，因此该句可看作定位句，其内容与选项 C 和选项 D 中的"收入"有关，第三句继而谈到"收入上升一个台阶，其国民幸福度就会增加"，说明定位句所强调的不仅仅是"收入"，而且可具体到"收入改善"，因此选项 C 正确。

【排他分析】选项 A 对应本段最后一句，虽然该句提到学历确实和人们的幸福感有关，但是括号中补充了限定条件，即"在不考虑收入的情况下"（not controlling for income），且最后一句与题干中的"持续的"没有对应部分，因此排除。选项 B 对应本段第四句，虽然原文谈到"欧洲男性的幸福感略高"，但也指出英国和丹麦并非如此，且该句也没有涉及题干中 continuous 的内容，因此排除。选项 D 在本段中并没有涉及，但根据常识，收入不平等一定不会让所有人都有持续的幸福感，因此排除该项。

Para. 4 ① But some big differences also emerge. ② Europeans are generally happier when they are younger. ③ However, richer countries see an uptick of joyfulness in old age: Germans are happier when they are over 75 years old than when they are between 25 and 34, and the Swiss are happier when they are over 75 than when they are teenagers. (Britons, Swedes and Danes are happiest when they are between 65 and 74.) ④ The Portuguese seem to have the worst mid-life crises, whereas Greeks, Bulgarians, Romanians and Slovenians all become glummer as they get older.

参考译文 ①然而，也存在一些较大的差异。②在欧洲，人们往往在其年轻时感觉更幸福。③但在较富裕的国家，老年人的幸福感有所提升：大于75岁的德国人比他们25岁到34岁时更加快乐；在瑞士，75岁以上的人群比他们十几岁时更加欢乐。（英国人、瑞典人和丹麦人在他们65到74岁时感觉最幸福。）④葡萄牙人的中年危机最严重，而在希腊、保加利亚、罗马尼亚和斯洛文尼亚，随着年龄的增长，人们的幸福感会越来越低。

原文剖析 本段首句指出欧洲各国的国民在幸福感方面也存在差异。后面三句探讨了不同年龄段与幸福感的关系，分别以欧洲整体、较富裕国家、葡萄牙和希腊等国的情况为例,进行对比说明。

设题点睛　本段第三句含有转折语意和冒号,句子较长,信息量较多,虽然可以用来设置细节题的选项,但是由于整段大多为细节内容,所以不适合单独设置题目。

生词解析

emerge *vi.* 显露;(事实、意见等)被知晓　　　　uptick *n.* 上升;兴旺;增大;提高

glum *adj.* 阴沉的;忧郁的(比较级 glummer)

长难句解析

However, richer countries　see　an uptick of joyfulness in old age: Germans　are
　　　主语1　　　谓语1　宾语　　后置定语　　　状语　　主语2　系动词1

happier when they are over 75 years old than when they are between 25 and 34, and
表语1　　时间状语从句1　　　　　　比较状语1

the Swiss　are　happier when they are over 75 than when they are teenagers.
主语3　系动词2　表语2　　时间状语从句2　　　比较状语2

(Britons, Swedes and Danes　are　happiest when they are between 65 and 74.)
　　主语4　　　系动词3　表语3　　时间状语从句3

本句为并列复合句。本句主干为 rich countries see an uptick: Germans are happier when... than..., and the Swiss are happier when... than...。冒号两边为两个完整的句子,冒号后的部分用于解释冒号前的句子。冒号后为两个并列句,都可看作主系表结构,由 and 连接,每个句子的结构相同,都含有时间状语从句和 than 引导的比较状语。

Para. 5 ①Where and how Europeans live also determines their happiness. ②In all countries, people are least happy if they live on their own. ③By the same token, in most countries those with children tend to be happier, with the exception of Britain, Denmark, Ireland and Switzerland, where people tend to be happier when childless. ④ Overall, Europeans tend to be most content if they live in towns or suburbs as opposed to cities or rural areas. ⑤Northern Europeans tend to be cheerier the farther they are from cities (and hence from other people). ⑥In most parts of southern and eastern Europe, however, the opposite is true.

参考译文　①决定欧洲人幸福感的还有他们的居住地以及生活方式。②在所有欧洲国家里,独居人群的幸福指数最低。③出于同样的原因,在大多数欧洲国家中,有小孩的家庭感觉更幸福,但英国、丹麦、爱尔兰和瑞士除外,因为在这些国家中,无子女家庭的幸福感更强。④总体而言,与居住在城市或农村的人相比,居住在欧洲城郊的居民感觉最幸福。⑤而在北欧,居住地离城市越远(也就是离其他人越远)的居民的幸福感更强。⑥然而,在南欧和东欧的绝大部分地区,情况恰恰相反。

原文剖析　本段承接前两段内容,首句总结指出影响欧洲各国幸福感的另外两个因素,即居住地点和居住方式。第二句到第六句分别以欧洲相关国家和地区的情况为例进行举例论证,相对于上一段而言内容更加细碎,信息点更密集。

设题点睛　本段与前一段呈并列关系,都在讨论影响欧洲人幸福感的因素,由于两者的细节内容较多,且话题类似,可合并出题。

生词解析

live on one's own 独立生活；独自生活
with the exception of 除了……以外
by the same token 由此，由于同样的原因
as opposed to 与……截然相反；对照

3 It can be inferred from paragraph 4 and 5 that _____ .

A. suburbanization is well-developed in Northern Europe
B. Europeans are less dependent on their children
C. age plays a pivotal role in determining happiness
D. Europeans have diversified definitions about happiness

从第四段和第五段可看出_____。

A. 北欧国家的郊区化发展得很好
B. 欧洲人对自己的子女依赖较少
C. 年龄在决定幸福感方面起关键作用
D. 欧洲人对幸福的定义不同

【解题思路】D。推理引申题。根据题干要求定位到第四段和第五段。在没有准确定位点的情况下，优先考虑段落主旨和特殊逻辑结构。分析后可看出，这两段从欧洲人的年龄、居住地和生活方式三个因素出发讨论了欧洲不同国家的国民幸福感情况，由其中的具体内容可看出地区不同、年龄段不同和生活方式不同的欧洲人对幸福的感受不同，选项 D 中的 diversified 和 happiness 分别对应这里的不同因素和幸福感，因此是正确答案。

【排他分析】选项 A 对应第五段第五句，原文指出"在北欧，离城市越远（也就是离其他人越远）的居民的幸福感更强"，但并不能由此推断出北欧国家的郊区化（suburbanization）发展得好，因此排除。选项 B 有关孩子的内容对应第五段第二句和第三句，这两句虽然指出在欧洲的大多数国家里有小孩的家庭感觉更幸福，但并不能由此看出欧洲人对孩子的依赖程度，且这是第五段的内容，无法概括第四段，因此排除。选项 C 对应第四段的内容，虽然该段第二句指出"在欧洲，人们往往在其年轻时感觉更幸福"，但也举了反例，此外，第三段第二句明确指出"欧盟统计局的数据显示，相对收入是唯一一项始终与欧洲幸福度有关的度量指标"，说明"收入"才是左右幸福度的关键因素，与该项给出的关键因素不同，因此排除。

Para. 6 ①What makes city-dwellers happier varies from one city to the next. ②According to the most recent data from Eurobarometer, most city-dwellers have become slightly happier. ③The highest correlation with life satisfaction in cities is a feeling of safety. ④But in Stockholm, Amsterdam and Vienna it is those who think foreigners are well integrated who tend to be happiest. ⑤Parisians and Berliners who rate their cities' cleanliness highly are the most

参考译文 ①不同城市的居民，感到幸福的原因也各不相同。②欧洲晴雨表的最新数据显示，大部分城市居民的幸福度略有提升。③安全感与城市生活满意度有着最直接的联系。④然而，在斯德哥尔摩、阿姆斯特丹和维也纳，那些认为外国人能很好地融入当地社会的居民会感到最幸福。⑤在巴黎和柏林，对所在城市洁净度评价较高的市民对自己的生活最满意。⑥而

content. ⑥In Reykjavik, curiously, the telltale sign of happiness is being satisfied with the public transport system.

在雷克雅未克，幸福感取决于人们对城市公共交通系统的满意程度，这一点着实令人惊讶。

原文剖析　本段承接前文,从欧洲不同城市的角度探讨居民幸福感的来源,范围更加小。第二句总结指出大部分欧洲城市居民的幸福度都有所提升。第三句总结指出欧洲城市居民的幸福感与安全感有关。第四句到第六句递进指出另外三个特殊的因素(社会融合度、清洁度、交通系统)。

设题点睛　本段首句和其后部分构成了总分结构,可以利用分论点的内容进行正确选项的设置。

生词解析

dweller n. 居民,居住者　　　　　　correlation n. 相互关系,关联
rate vt. 评定等级;认为　　　　　　telltale adj. 说明问题的

Para. 7 ①Those places which are happiest appear to have good governance. ②This may suggest a lesson to politicians: reducing unemployment and boosting wages will undoubtedly increase happiness. ③But clean pavements are important, too.

参考译文　①幸福感最强地区的政府似乎有较高的管理水平。②这也提示政客,要提升民众的幸福度,降低失业率和涨薪是不二之选。③此外,保持街道清洁也很重要。

原文剖析　本段承接前文所谈到的居民幸福感来源,暗示这些因素都是政府管理水平的体现,并以此向政府官员提出建议。

设题点睛　本段第二句为带有冒号的长难句,起到总结全文的作用,可以利用其设置正确选项,但是由于和前文观点存在重复的地方,因此单独设置考题的概率不大。

生词解析

governance n. 管理;统治方式　　　　pavement n. 人行道

4　Which of the following is not a key element in deciding Europeans' happiness?

以下哪项不是决定欧洲人幸福感的关键因素?

A. A fair way of wealth distribution.
B. A sense of security.
C. A harmonious atmosphere.
D. A conscientious government.

A. 对财富的公平分配。
B. 安全感。
C. 和谐的氛围。
D. 尽责的政府。

【解题思路】A。事实细节题。本题考查原文没有提及的因素。根据选项内容定位到第六段。选项A提到的"财富分配"方式在该段中没有出现,因此是正确答案。

【排他分析】选项B所涉及的"安全感"因素对应第六段第三句,原文指出"安全感与城市生活满意度有着最直接的联系",因此该项属于因素之一。第六段第四句谈到"在斯德哥尔摩、阿姆斯特丹和维也纳,那些认为外国人能很好地融入当地社会的居民会感到更幸福","融入当地社会"可理解为选项C所提到的"和谐氛围",因此该项也属于因素之一。第六段第六句谈到"在雷克雅未克,幸福感取决于人们对公共交通系统的满意程度","公共交通系统"可理解为政府责任,对交通系统满意说明当地政

府尽责,且第七段首句直接点明"幸福感最强地区的政府似乎有较高的管理水平",与选项 D 的内容一致,因此该项也属于因素之一。

5 The best title for this passage is _____. 本文的最佳标题是_____。

A. Governance Improvement: the Only Way to Raise the Happiness for Europeans
B. Multiple Factors in Deciding the Happiness for Europeans
C. A Gloomy Future: Europe Is Dominated by Downbeat Writers
D. Europeans' Feeling of Happiness Reaches a Record High

A. 管理改进:欧洲人提升幸福感的唯一方式
B. 决定欧洲人幸福感的诸多因素
C. 悲凉的未来:欧洲由悲观主义作家主导
D. 欧洲人的幸福感达到历史新高

【解题思路】B。主旨大意题。需纵观全文找出本文大意。文章前两段指出欧洲人实际比较幸福。从第三段开始具体讨论欧洲人幸福的不同标准或使欧洲各国和各城市居民感到幸福的不同因素,提到了富裕程度、年龄、居住地、生活方式、安全感、和谐氛围和政府管理等多个方面,选项 B 分别谈到了本文主题"幸福感"和"诸多因素",因此选项 B 是概括本文的最佳标题。

【排他分析】选项 A 只涉及文章最后一段,属于以偏概全,因此排除。选项 C 对应文章首段,文章讨论的并不是欧洲人的悲观态度,而是其幸福感,该项主题抓取错误,因此排除。选项 D 对应第二段首句"总体上看,大部分欧洲人处于金融危机以来最幸福的时期",但这只是一个细节,并未概括后文用较大篇幅对幸福感来源进行的分析,因此排除。

Text 12

Reality television provides all sorts of pretexts for traveling to exotic places and gawking at quaint (but wise) local cultures: learning to cook, winning a race, saving wildlife, detailing cars, drinking beer. "Human Weapon," which has its premiere tonight on the History Channel, adds a new quest to that list: learning to bash someone's brains out.

There are two main characters in the show. Actually, the mission of Jason Chambers and Bill Duff, the show's Mutt-and-Jeff stars—Mr. Chambers is a normal-size "mixed-martial-artist and professional fighter," Mr. Duff a quite large and bullet-headed "former professional football player and wrestler"—is to "fold back the rich historical and cultural layers" of various martial arts.

In the first two episodes, which cover the Asian disciplines of muay thai and eskrima, that folding back involves donning workout clothes and shuttling around Thailand and the Philippines to absorb the lessons, and beatings, of various Yoda-like masters. This is all in preparation for a final bout in which one of the travelers tests his newly acquired skills against a local hero. The trend so far is a graceful loss to a much smaller and quieter opponent; we'll see if that holds when the show moves on to savate in France or krav maga in Israel.

Along the way Mr. Chambers and Mr. Duff absorb history lessons—muay thai's role in ancient wars with the Burmese, the use of eskrima against Spanish and Japanese invaders—and soak up the local color. Apparently it's a rule that martial arts schools be near picturesque temples or waterfalls. (Though don't expect the local color to include the demure Asian beauties this sort of show usually lingers over: "Human Weapon" is all about sweaty, grimacing men.)

As a travelogue and an exercise in improving foreign relations, the show is charming and, despite its subject matter, harmless. Mr. Chambers and Mr. Duff are ever respectful, marveling at their hosts' skills and at the beauty and traditions of the countries they visit. If you're not a martial-arts fan, though, things can bog down a bit during the long training sequences, when we're shown how to knee our opponent in the solar plexus or pummel him in the side with a metal rod. And in those scenes, the show's gee-whiz energy can edge away from comfortably multicultural topics and toward the universal desire to inflict pain. In one of Mr. Duff's more enthusiastic moments, he exclaims during an eskrima session, "It's the same injury-producing force as being hit in the temple by a hammer!"

Like most hourlong reality shows, "Human Weapon" would be better at a half-hour; cut down the training sessions, but leave intact the attempt to practice eskrima throws on a water buffalo. (Final score: water buffalo 3, Filipino guy 0.) Still, it proves itself more useful than, say, "The Amazing Race" or "Anthony Bourdain: No Reservations." Those shows never taught us the skills to take out an Abu Sayyaf terrorist cell.

(*The New York Times*, 2016.1)

1. Reality television has often been characterized by the _____.
   A. multiformity in its theme
   B. focus on eccentric local culture
   C. nature of violence
   D. creativity in its content

2. It can be learned from paragraph 2 and 3 that _____.
   A. both Jason Chambers and Bill Duff are familiar with martial arts
   B. the aim of the show is to realize the final victory against a local hero
   C. the attraction of the show originates from the uniqueness of the local clothing
   D. the show intends to reveal the appealing of the martial arts

3. Why is "Human Weapon" different from other reality shows?
   A. It emphasizes more on local colors.
   B. It concentrates on the delivery of history lesson.
   C. It highly values the demonstration of manliness.
   D. It contains natural landscape in the show.

4. The example of Mr. Duff's learning of eskrima is cited to _____.
   A. show the enthusiasm provoked by the training of eskrima
   B. illustrate a detrimental deviation from the main topic
   C. criticize Mr. Duff's aggressiveness displayed in the show
   D. prove that the show is entertaining while harmless
5. According to the last paragraph, the author suggests that _____.
   A. water buffalo is a key factor in elevating the quality of "Human Weapon"
   B. other reality shows have cut their time by half
   C. some reality shows provide few practical elements to their audiences
   D. "Human Weapon" is crucial in helping audience to survive a terrorist attack

语篇分析与试题精解

Para. 1 ①Reality television provides all sorts of pretexts for traveling to exotic places and gawking at quaint (but wise) local cultures: learning to cook, winning a race, saving wildlife, detailing cars, drinking beer. ②"Human Weapon," which has its premiere tonight on the History Channel, adds a new quest to that list: learning to bash someone's brains out.

参考译文 ①真人秀节目提供了各种各样的借口,可以去有异国情调的地方旅游,拍摄当地离奇(但高明)的文化,让观众感到惊异。节目选题包括厨艺学习、比赛竞技、拯救野生动物、汽车设计以及喝啤酒。②在以上选题的基础上,历史频道今晚首播的真人秀《人体武器》又加入了新的元素:学习如何打爆别人的头。

原文剖析 本段首句对真人秀的题材进行了介绍:有异国情调的地方以及离奇的当地文化。第二句介绍一档全新的真人秀:学习如何打爆别人的头。

设题点睛 本段首句是一个长句,一般会设置细节题。

生词解析
pretext *n.* 托词
gawk *vt.* 呆呆地看着
premiere *n.* 首映
exotic *adj.* 异国情调的
quaint *adj.* 古怪的
bash *vt.* 猛击,痛击

1 Reality television has often been characterized by the _____.
   A. multiformity in its theme
   B. focus on eccentric local culture
   C. nature of violence
   D. creativity in its content

真人秀常以_____为特色。
   A. 主题多样
   B. 对怪异地方文化的关注
   C. 暴力的本质
   D. 有创意的内容

【解题思路】A。事实细节题。根据题干中的Reality television及顺序原则定位到文章首段,本题考查真人秀的特征。该段首句介绍真人秀在题材方面的多样性:通常选择有异国情调的地方并让观众对其文化感到惊异,之后罗列了多种不同的节目主题或内容。第二句引出了一档新的真人秀,涉及和之前完全不同的题材:学习如何用武力征服对方。综合两句的意思,选项A是正确答案。

【排他分析】选项 B 对应首句,原文表示真人秀会带领观众领略陌生之地并且为其怪异(或者高明)的文化而感到惊异,并不等同于所有真人秀都会重点关注奇怪的地方文化,选项 B 属于以偏概全,所以排除。选项 C 对应首段第二句中的 learning to bash someone's brains out,暴力性只是针对这一档《人体武器》的真人秀而言,并非所有真人秀都是如此,所以排除。选项 D"内容上的创新"暗指《人体武器》这档真人秀有别于其他真人秀,但原文并没有强调所有真人秀的内容都独具创意,且第一句已明确指出大部分真人秀都遵循一种套路,所以排除。

Para. 2 ①There are two main characters in the show. ②Actually, the mission of Jason Chambers and Bill Duff, the show's Mutt-and-Jeff stars—Mr. Chambers is a normal-size "mixed-martial-artist and professional fighter," Mr. Duff a quite large and bullet-headed "former professional football player and wrestler"—is to "fold back the rich historical and cultural layers" of various martial arts.

参考译文 ①节目中有两位主角。②杰森·钱伯斯(Jason Chambers)体型适中,是个"职业综合格斗士";比尔·达夫(Bill Duff)留着光头、体形硕大,是"前美式足球运动员及摔跤手"。两人在本节目中的任务就是寻访各类武术蕴含的"丰富的历史根源和文化背景"。

原文剖析 本段介绍该真人秀的两位主角以及两个人在真人秀中的主要任务:寻访各类武术蕴含的历史与文化背景。

设题点睛 本段两句内容不存在内在关联性,且各自的意思表达明确,虽然第二句是长难句并介绍了该节目的设计初衷和目的,但是由于可供设计干扰选项的信息太少,所以一般不会单独设题,但是也可能会结合下一段出题。

生词解析
bullet-headed *adj.* 光头的   wrestler *n.* 摔跤手
fold back 追寻   martial *adj.* 尚武的

长难句解析
Actually, the mission of Jason Chambers and Bill Duff, the show's Mutt-and-Jeff stars—
     主语   后置定语1   同位语
Mr. Chambers is a normal-size "mixed-martial-artist and professional fighter," Mr. Duff a
            插入语
quite large and bullet-headed "former professional football player and wrestler"—is to "fold
                    系动词
back the rich historical and cultural layers" of various martial arts.
     表语   后置定语2
本句较长,但并非复合句。本句主干为 the mission is to…,主语之后为同位语,破折号之间的内容可看作插入语,对主语进行进一步说明。谓语采用系表结构,不定式作表语。

Para. 3 ①In the first two episodes, which cover the Asian disciplines of muay thai and

参考译文 ①节目前两集讲的是属于亚洲武术项目的泰拳和截拳。节目中两位

eskrima, that folding back involves donning workout clothes and shuttling around Thailand and the Philippines to absorb the lessons, and beatings, of various Yoda-like masters. ② This is all in preparation for a final bout in which one of the travelers tests his newly acquired skills against a local hero. ③ The trend so far is a graceful loss to a much smaller and quieter opponent; we'll see if that holds when the show moves on to savate in France or krav maga in Israel.

主角身穿武术服装，穿梭在泰国和菲律宾，观摩像尤达大师一样的各路武术大师的拳脚功夫，从中学习。②所有的学习过程都是为了最终的较量。在最终较量的环节里，其中一位主角挑战一位当地的高手以检验自己学到的武术技能。③到目前为止，较量的结果通常是主角惜败给身量更小、更不起眼的当地对手。当节目播到法国自由搏击术和以色列搏击防身术时，较量的结果能否发生变化，我们将拭目以待。

原文剖析 本段主要对节目内容进行具体介绍。首句介绍前两集的内容：学习泰拳和截拳的过程。第二句继续指出学习的最终目的是为了和当地的高手进行比赛。第三句继续指出目前为止比赛的结果都是主角输，并期待在接下来的法国站和以色列站能发生改变。

设题点睛 本段承接上段对这档真人秀主角的描述，对节目内容和过程进行介绍，从内容上说，本段没有什么特别重要的内容，一般会结合上段内容出细节题。

生词解析

episode n. （电影、戏剧等的）连续剧的一集   muay thai 泰拳
eskrima 截拳   don vt. 穿上
bout n. 拳击比赛   savate n. 法国自由搏击术
krav maga 搏击防身术

长难句解析

In the first two episodes, which cover the Asian disciplines of muay thai and eskrima,
　　　　状语　　　　　　　　非限制性定语从句
that folding back　involves　donning workout clothes and shuttling around Thailand
　　主语　　　　　谓语　　　　　　　　　　宾语
and the Philippines to absorb the lessons, and beatings, of various Yoda-like masters.
　　　　　　　　　　　目的状语

本句为主从复合句，主干结构为 that folding back involves A and B to…，非限制性定语从句解释说明 two episodes 的内容。宾语 A 和 B 分别是动名词短语 donning workout clothes 和 shuttling around Thailand and the Philippines。

2 It can be learned from paragraph 2 and 3 that _____.　　从第二段和第三段中可知_____。

 A. both Jason Chambers and Bill Duff are familiar with martial arts　　A. 杰森·钱伯斯和比尔·达夫两人都对武术很熟悉
 B. the aim of the show is to realize the final victory against a local hero　　B. 这个真人秀的目的是最终战胜当地的一位高手
 C. the attraction of the show originates from　　C. 这个真人秀的吸引力来自地

135

the uniqueness of the local clothing
方服装的独特性

D. the show intends to reveal the appealing of the martial arts
D. 这个真人秀旨在展示武术的魅力

【解题思路】D。事实细节题。根据题干要求定位到文章第二段和第三段。结合语篇分析,第二段第二句为观点类长难句,其主干是 the mission of Jason Chambers and Bill Duff is to "fold back the rich historical and cultural layers" of various martial arts(两人的任务就是展现多种武术丰富的文化及历史内涵),可以直接对应选项 D,选项 D 中的 appealing 是对文中 rich historical and cultural layers 的抽象概括。

【排他分析】选项 A 对应的是文章第二段第二句中插入语的介绍,谈到两位主角的身份:一个是职业格斗家,一个是前美式足球运动员和摔跤手,但并没有提到两个人对武术是否熟悉,选项 A 属于过度推断,所以排除。选项 B 对应第三段第二句,原文只是说两人接受观摩培训后,最终的任务是和当地高手比武,检验自己的技能。这只是真人秀的一个环节,不是真人秀的真实目的(真实目的是第二段第二句),所以排除。选项 C 的 local clothing 对应第三段首句中的 workout clothes,原文指出两位主角要穿上当地武术的行头,但没有提到这是节目吸引人之处,本项属于过度推断,也可排除。

Para. 4 ① Along the way Mr. Chambers and Mr. Duff absorb history lessons—muay thai's role in ancient wars with the Burmese, the use of eskrima against Spanish and Japanese invaders—and soak up the local color. ② Apparently it's a rule that martial arts schools be near picturesque temples or waterfalls. ③ (Though don't expect the local color to include the demure Asian beauties this sort of show usually lingers over: "Human Weapon" is all about sweaty, grimacing men.)

参考译文 ①一路上,钱伯斯和达夫不仅了解了武术的历史渊源——泰拳在古代对抗缅甸的战争中所发挥的作用,截拳在反抗西班牙和日本侵略者中的应用——还领略了当地的风土人情。②显然,武馆通常建在风景如画的寺庙或瀑布附近,这几乎是一条铁律。③(但不要指望风土人情中会包含端庄娴静的亚洲美女,尽管同类的其他节目通常都会对这一元素着墨较多:《人体武器》讲的是流血流汗的男子汉。)

原文剖析 本段首句为长句,主干指出两人的任务就是了解武术历史和当地的风土人情。第二句和第三句对"风土人情"做出解释:这是真人秀必不可少的,但是这档真人秀中却没有美女,只有猛男。

设题点睛 本段第三句为带有括号的长句,用于解释说明,一般为出题点。

生词解析
soak up 吸收
demure adj. 端庄的
sweaty adj. 出汗的;吃力的
picturesque adj. 风景如画的
linger over 没完没了地说某事
grimace vi. (因痛苦)脸部扭曲

3 Why is "Human Weapon" different from other reality shows?
为什么《人体武器》和其他真人秀节目不同?

A. It emphasizes more on local colors.
A. 它更关注地方特色。

B. It concentrates on the delivery of history lesson.
C. It highly values the demonstration of manliness.
D. It contains natural landscape in the show.

B. 它专注于传授历史知识。
C. 它高度展现男子汉气概。
D. 它在节目中加入了自然风景类元素。

【解题思路】C。事实细节题。题干没有给出明确的定位点,通过顺序原则(上题考查第二段和第三段,下题考查第五段)判断本题考查第四段的可能性最大。通过语篇分析,可以确定本段最后一句括号内的内容涉及《人体武器》节目与其他真人秀节目的区别(其他有关风土人情的真人秀都会着重谈到端庄的亚洲美女,而《人体武器》则只讲流血流汗的男子汉),因此选项 C 是正确答案。

【排他分析】选项 A 的 local colors 在第四段的前两句话中都有体现,但是文章中并没有提到《人体武器》相比其他真人秀会更加关注风土人情,相反,第三句的言下之意是类似的节目都关注风土人情,并且会强调当地美女,而该档节目与之不同,所以排除。选项 B 对应第四段首句,原文确实提到两位主人公需要了解武术的历史,但是选项 B 没有说"武术历史",而只是"历史",自然其他真人秀节目中也会有以传承历史为内容的,所以排除。选项 D 对应第四段第二句,确实《人体武器》的拍摄地也很可能选在风景如画之地,但是文章没有明确说这是它与其他真人秀不同的地方,所以排除。

Para. 5 ① As a travelogue and an exercise in improving foreign relations, the show is charming and, despite its subject matter, harmless. ② Mr. Chambers and Mr. Duff are ever respectful, marveling at their hosts' skills and at the beauty and traditions of the countries they visit. ③ If you're not a martial-arts fan, though, things can bog down a bit during the long training sequences, when we're shown how to knee our opponent in the solar plexus or pummel him in the side with a metal rod. ④ And in those scenes, the show's gee-whiz energy can edge away from comfortably multicultural topics and toward the universal desire to inflict pain. ⑤ In one of Mr. Duff's more enthusiastic moments, he exclaims during an eskrima session, "It's the same injury-producing force as being hit in the temple by a hammer!"

参考译文 ①作为一档有利于改善外交关系的旅行见闻类节目,《人体武器》相当精彩有趣。尽管选题暴力,但节目内容却是无害的。②钱伯斯和达夫对他们所造访的主人恭敬有加,对其高超的武术技艺叹为观止,对所到国家的风土人情惊叹不已。③然而,对于不是武术爱好者的观众来说,演示如何用膝盖踢对手的心口或用金属棒击打其一侧身体的漫长训练过程则使节目略显拖沓。④播放此类场景时,节目的惊人能量可能会偏离轻松的多元文化主题,转向人类心中普遍存在的对施虐的渴望。⑤在达夫学习截拳的一个精彩片段中,他大呼:"这一攻击的力度不亚于用锤子击打太阳穴!"

原文剖析 本段首句给出作者观点:节目很有趣且无害。第二句承接首句指出两位主角对节目中自身经历的喜爱。第三句和第四句则指出节目的不足:第三句认为漫长训练过程对非武术爱好者而言略显无聊,第四句进一步指出,随着暴力场景的播放,人类心中的施虐心理得以释放。最后一句举例论证了第四句的内容。

设题点睛 本段最重要的考点结构应该是第四句(观点)与第五句(举例)构成的总分结构。此处一般会设置考研英语阅读常见的例子功能题。

生词解析

travelogue *n.* 旅行见闻
bog down 停顿
solar plexus 心口；腹腔神经丛
gee-whiz *adj.* 惊人的

marvel at 对……感到惊奇
knee *vt.* 用膝盖撞
pummel *vt.* 击打
inflict *vt.* 造成，使遭受

长难句解析

If you're not a martial-arts fan, though, things can bog down a bit during the long
条件状语从句　　　　　　　连词　　主语　　谓语　　状语1　　状语2
training sequences, when we're shown how to knee our opponent in the solar plexus
　　　　　　　　　　　时间状语从句
or pummel him in the side with a metal rod.

本句主干结构为 things can bog down，句中包含一个 if 引导的条件状语从句和一个 when 引导的时间状语从句。时间状语从句中包含 how to do 结构作 show 的宾语。

4 The example of Mr. Duff's learning of eskrima is cited to _____.　　引用达夫学习截拳的例子是为了_____。

A. show the enthusiasm provoked by the training of eskrima
B. illustrate a detrimental deviation from the main topic
C. criticize Mr. Duff's aggressiveness displayed in the show
D. prove that the show is entertaining while harmless

A. 展示训练截拳激发出的热情
B. 例证节目向有害的方向发展，偏离了主题
C. 批评达夫在节目中展现出的攻击性
D. 证明这个节目既具娱乐性又无害处

【解题思路】B。例子功能题。根据题干关键词 Mr. Duff's learning of eskrima 定位至第五段最后一句，该句描述了此人习武的一个片段，高呼"这一攻击的力度不亚于用锤子击打太阳穴"。本句顺承前文，可看作是对前文观点的举例说明。第三句和第四句谈到播放暴力训练过程会让观众感觉不是在看一个了解武术知识的真人秀，可能激发他们内心施虐的冲动(desire to inflict pain)，指出这种施虐的心理与节目轻松的文化主题相违背，说明节目的主题此时发生了有害偏离，因此选项 B 正确。

【排他分析】选项 A 对应第五段最后一句，是对例子内容的字面理解，属于就事论事，所以排除。最后一句例子中达夫的言语虽然含有攻击的意味，但是文中并没有对此进行评价，所以排除选项 C。选项 D 对应的是第五段的首句，首句中确实提到这档节目是有趣而且无害的，并且在第二句对此观点进行了支持，但是从第三句开始就已经在谈这个节目的不足了，最后一句的例子明显是支撑不足的观点的，因此排除。

Para. 6 ①Like most hourlong reality shows,　　参考译文　①与多数时长为一小时左右

"Human Weapon" would be better at a half-hour; cut down the training sessions, but leave intact the attempt to practice eskrima throws on a water buffalo. ② (Final score: water buffalo 3, Filipino guy 0.) ③Still, it proves itself more useful than, say, "The Amazing Race" or "Anthony Bourdain: No Reservations." ④Those shows never taught us the skills to take out an Abu Sayyaf terrorist cell.

的真人秀节目一样,《人体武器》最好能将节目的时长控制在半小时左右。删减训练环节,但尝试使用截拳与水牛对抗的环节要完整保留。②(最后比分:水牛3分,菲律宾选手0分。)③事实证明,该节目还是比《极速前进》或《安东尼·波登:美味情缘》更具有实际意义。④那些节目从来没有教我们如何打败一帮阿布沙耶夫恐怖分子。

原文剖析 本段首句提出建议:《人体武器》应该将时间减至半个小时,但保留攻击水牛的部分,回应上一段,以迎合非武术爱好者的需求。第二句括号中的内容属于插入语。第三句转折,指出它还是比一些其他的真人秀更有用。第四句对其他真人秀做了评价:它们无法帮助人们对抗恐怖分子(言下之意是学不到有用的东西)。

设题点睛 从考点设置来看,本段第一句的转折和第三句的解释比较适合设置考点。

生词解析

intact *adj.* 完整的
take out 毁灭,消除

throw *n.* 摔倒对手的方法
cell *n.* (党派、团体的)基层组织

5 According to the last paragraph, the author suggests that _____.

A. water buffalo is a key factor in elevating the quality of "Human Weapon"
B. other reality shows have cut their time by half
C. some reality shows provide few practical elements to their audiences
D. "Human Weapon" is crucial in helping audience to survive a terrorist attack

在最后一段内容中,作者暗示_____。

A. 水牛环节是提升《人体武器》节目质量的重要因素
B. 其他真人秀节目已将播出时长减半
C. 有些真人秀节目并不能为其观众带来多少实用的东西
D.《人体武器》对于帮助观众从恐怖袭击中逃生至关重要

【解题思路】C。事实细节题。根据题干要求定位到原文最后一段。本段第三句指出,该节目比《极速前进》或《安东尼·波登:美味情缘》更具有实际意义,第四句进一步解释,暗指从观看《人体武器》节目中可以学到一些有用的东西(如对抗恐怖分子),而其他真人秀节目没有这个好处。所以选项 C 是正确答案。

【排他分析】选项 A 对应该段第一句转折之后的内容,原文中只说需要保留有关使用截拳对抗水牛的片段,但是并没有提出水牛对提升节目质量的作用,该项是对原文字面意思的过度推断,所以排除。选项 B 对应该段首句前半句内容,文章观点是,与其他时长为一个小时的真人秀一样,《人体武器》的节目时长也最好减至半个小时,但是作者并没有指明其他节目已经这么做了,且这一内容并非本段重点,因此排除。选项 D 对应本段最后一句,明显属于对内容的字面理解,最后一句只是举例,证明作者认为《人体武器》是有实用价值的,所以排除。

Text 13

Do Americans hate science? They certainly seem to hate it more than they used to, as they rage against experts in every field. This is more than a traditional American distaste for eggheads and intellectuals. Americans, increasingly, are acting on myths and misinformation about science, and placing themselves at significant risk.

Of course, Americans don't really hate science: they rely on it every day in ways they don't even notice. Rather, it is more accurate to say that the American public distrusts *scientists*, rather than *science* itself. Scientists, however, should be consoled by the fact that they are disdained not for their work, but for being part of an undifferentiated mass of "experts" whom a fair number of Americans now view as, at best, a suspect political class, and, at worst, as an enemy.

In one sense, this attack on the defenders of established knowledge was inevitable. It is not only fueled by an obvious culprit—the internet—but also by the unintended side effects of otherwise positive social changes. Universal education and increased social mobility, among other changes, have thrown America's experts and citizens into direct contact after nearly two centuries in which they lived segregated lives and rarely interacted with each other. As for the current relation between the two, both the professional community and the public it serves bear some responsibility for our parlous condition.

For its part, the American public is in the grip of a sullen, almost paranoid, narcissism about science and experts. This is not a function of education. Indeed, ignorance has become hip, with some Americans now wearing their rejection of expert advice as a badge of cultural sophistication.

Instead, the public rejection of science is an extension of our politics, which in turn have become an expression of our constant outrage about everything that offends our deepest beliefs about ourselves. As social scientist David Dunning has put it: "Some of our most stubborn misbeliefs arises... from the very values and philosophies that define who we are as individuals." When those misbeliefs are challenged, laypeople take it not as correction but as a direct attack on their identity.

The expert community, however, must shoulder some of the blame for the collapse of the relationship between science and the public. Experts often trespass across from empirical knowledge to normative demands and thus validate the suspicions of laypeople that the real goal of expert advice is to force compliance with expert policy preferences.

At the same time, experts cannot withdraw from a public arena increasingly controlled by opportunistic demagogues who seek to discredit empiricism and rationality. Instead, the expert community must help to lead laypeople back along the road to a better day when the citizens of the United States valued scientists and other professionals as essential parts of the American story.

(*Scientific American*, 2017.3)

1. It can be learned from the first two paragraphs that _____.
   A. Americans have hated science for long
   B. intellectuals have a worse reputation than scientists
   C. science has a subtle impact on Americans' daily life
   D. there is no distinction between scientist and politician

2. What does the author think of the attack on the defenders of traditional knowledge?
   A. It is caused mainly by the rise of internet.
   B. Positive social changes are the main culprit behind it.
   C. Universal education has a more serious influence than social mobility.
   D. Multiple factors are responsible for its occurrence.

3. The public's rejection of science originates from _____.
   A. the schism between self-perception and reality
   B. personal outrage against politics
   C. individual ignorance of education
   D. Americans' cultural sophistication

4. It is suggested that the expert community _____.
   A. should be completely responsible for the current crisis
   B. actively promotes the normative demands and empirical knowledge
   C. should discredit empiricism and rationality
   D. is in some way representative of government policies

5. The author's attitude toward scientists is _____.
   A. supportive   B. critical   C. tolerating   D. biased

语篇分析与试题精解

Para. 1 ①Do Americans hate science? ②They certainly seem to hate it more than they used to, as they rage against experts in every field. ③This is more than a traditional American distaste for eggheads and intellectuals. ④Americans, increasingly, are acting on myths and misinformation about science, and placing themselves at significant risk.

参考译文 ①美国人讨厌科学吗？②他们对各个领域的专家都满腹牢骚，似乎比过去更讨厌科学了。③美国人有不待见书呆子和知识分子的传统，现在对科学的厌恶更是有过之而无不及。④美国人目前越来越迷信玄学和伪科学，这样做会置自己于极大的风险之中。

原文剖析 本段用一个问句引入主题。后三句对此进行回答，指出美国人目前对科学的态度是非常危险的(鄙视科学，相信玄学和伪科学)。

设题点睛 本段首句设问之后的解答属于重要的观点性内容，可以用来设置考点。

生词解析
rage against 对……非常气愤   distaste n. 厌恶；讨厌
egghead n. 受过高等教育的人；书呆子

Para. 2 ①Of course, Americans don't really hate science; they rely on it every day in ways they don't even notice. ②Rather, it is more accurate to say that the American public distrusts *scientists*, rather than *science* itself. ③Scientists, however, should be consoled by the fact that they are disdained not for their work, but for being part of an undifferentiated mass of "experts" whom a fair number of Americans now view as, at best, a suspect political class, and, at worst, as an enemy.

参考译文 ①当然,美国人并非真的厌恶科学:他们每天都依赖科学生活,只是以他们根本没有留意的方式而已。②美国公众并非怀疑科学,只是不信任科学家,这样说或者更加确切。③然而,科学家们应当感到庆幸,因为事实上他们并不是因为自己的工作而遭到蔑视,而是因为他们是"专家"这个无差别群体中的一员,很多美国人觉得"专家"说得好听点疑似政客,说得难听点就是敌人。

原文剖析 本段前两句否定了第一段的回答,指出美国人实际上并非不信任科学,而是不相信科学家。第三句再次转折指出美国人并非不信任科学家的工作,而是不信任其所在的专家群体,并解释美国人对专家这一群体的评价(觉得他们更像是政客或者敌人)。本段语意层层递进,互相解释,对首段进行了补充。

设题点睛 本段对前一段内容进行了部分否定,且第三句是带有转折语意的长难句,对第二句内容进行解释,因此属于重要的观点性内容,可用来设置考点。

生词解析
console *vt.* 安慰;慰藉
undifferentiated *adj.* 无差别的;一致的
at worst 在最坏的情况下;坏到极点
disdain *vt.* 蔑视,鄙视,轻视
at best 充其量;说得再好也只是

长难句解析
Scientists, however, should be consoled by the fact that they are disdained not for their
  主语   谓语   方式状语   同位语从句
work, but for being part of an undifferentiated mass of "experts" whom a fair number of
                                                                        定语从句
Americans now view as, at best, a suspect political class, and, at worst, as an enemy.

本句为主从复合句。本句主干为 Scientists should be consoled by the fact that…,主句方式状语中的 fact 后接 that 从句作其同位语,具体解释"事实"的内容,该同位语中包含一个 not for… but for… 的选择结构作原因状语,还包含一个由 whom 引导的定语从句,其先行词是"experts",由于该从句的连接词在句中作 view as 的宾语而非主语,因此用 whom 代替 who。

1 It can be learned from the first two paragraphs that _____.
  A. Americans have hated science for long
  B. intellectuals have a worse reputation than scientists

从前两段可知 _____。
  A. 美国人憎恶科学很久了
  B. 知识分子的名声比科学家的还要坏

C. science has a subtle impact on Americans' daily life

D. there is no distinction between scientist and politician

C. 科学对美国人日常生活所产生的影响不明显

D. 科学家和政客之间毫无区别

【解题思路】C。推理引申题。根据题干要求定位到文章前两段。在没有准确定位点的情况下,优先利用段落观点或者重要逻辑结构解题。第二段转折首段内容,给出了更为确切的答案,因此是重点段。该段首句指出美国人没有意识到自己在日常生活中会依赖科学(they rely on it every day in ways they don't even notice),说明科学对美国人的生活会产生影响和作用,只不过他们并未意识到,与选项C的表述一致,该项中的 subtle 含有"不明显的,无法察觉的"之意,对应原文中的 they don't even notice,因此该项是对原文的同义替换。

【排他分析】首段第三句谈到"美国人有不待见书呆子和知识分子的传统",说明美国人一直以来厌恶的对象是人(书呆子和知识分子),并非选项A所说的"科学",可直接排除。原文第一段第三句涉及比较,指出美国人对科学的厌恶比以往对书呆子和知识分子的厌恶更为严重(This is more than a traditional American distaste for eggheads and intellectuals),this 回指前一句所说的"(美国人)似乎比过去更讨厌科学了",比较对象为知识分子和科学,而非科学家,因此排除选项B。选项D对应第二段最后一句的转折内容,原文指出相当一部分美国人现在把包括科学家在内的专家群体看作可疑的政客或敌人,这是美国人的主观看法,也是从某种角度进行的类比,并不代表实际情况,也不代表两者之间完全没有区别,因此排除选项D。

Para. 3 ① In one sense, this attack on the defenders of established knowledge was inevitable. ② It is not only fueled by an obvious culprit—the internet—but also by the unintended side effects of otherwise positive social changes. ③ Universal education and increased social mobility, among other changes, have thrown America's experts and citizens into direct contact after nearly two centuries in which they lived segregated lives and rarely interacted with each other. ④ As for the current relation between the two, both the professional community and the public it serves bear some responsibility for our parlous condition.

参考译文 ①某种意义上,既有知识体系的捍卫者难免遭人攻击。②互联网显然是肇事者之一,另外,其他一些原本积极的社会变革,也产生了出乎意料的副作用,煽动了这种攻击。③过去两个世纪以来,美国专家和民众过着相互隔离的生活,极少进行互动,而如今,一些包括全民教育和社会流动性增强在内的社会变化使两者有了直接接触。④就目前这两个群体间的关系而言,专家们和他们所服务的公众都要为这棘手的局面承担一定的责任。

原文剖析 本段首句中作者对前文描述的现象表示理解。后两句对此观点做出解释,即分析科学家遭到普通民众鄙视的客观原因(互联网和一些积极社会变革带来的负面影响),其中第三句可看作对第二句中积极社会变革的举例说明(全民教育和社会流动性增强属于积极的社会变化,其负面影响是使民众和专家接触变多,距离接近反而使关系紧张)。最后一句是作者的观点和评价,指出两者都要为目前出现的问题负责,可判断下文将从专家和公众的角度分析原因。

设题点睛 本段重在解释原因,在结构上属于总分关系,可用来设置正确选项。

生词解析

culprit *n.* 犯人,罪犯
throw... into 使……(突然)陷入某一状态
bear some responsibility 承担某种责任
unintended *adj.* 无意识的;非计划中的
live segregated lives 过隔离的生活
parlous *adj.* 危险的;不易对付的

长难句解析

<u>Universal education and increased social mobility</u>, <u>among other changes</u>, <u>have thrown</u>
　　　　　　主语　　　　　　　　　　　　　　　　后置定语　　　　　　　谓语
<u>America's experts and citizens</u> <u>into direct contact after nearly two centuries</u> <u>in which they lived</u>
　　　　宾语　　　　　　　　　　　　　　　状语　　　　　　　　　　　　　定语从句
segregated lives and rarely interacted with each other.

本句为主从复合句。本句主干为 Universal education and increased social mobility have thrown America's experts and citizens into..., 主干的谓语使用了 throw... into... 的结构, into 介词短语作状语, after 介词短语也作状语, 表示时间, 其后接一个由 in which 引导的定语从句(因有先行词 two centuries, 故为定语从句), 当"介词+which"在定语从句中作时间、地点和原因状语时, 可以用相应的关系副词 when, where 和 why 来替换。

2 What does the author think of the attack on the defenders of traditional knowledge?

　　作者如何看待传统知识捍卫者所受到的攻击?

A. It is caused mainly by the rise of internet.
B. Positive social changes are the main culprit behind it.
C. Universal education has a more serious influence than social mobility.
D. Multiple factors are responsible for its occurrence.

A. 主要是互联网的兴起引起的。
B. 积极的社会变革是罪魁祸首。
C. 全民教育的负面影响比社会流动性要大。
D. 多种因素应为这种现象的出现负责。

【解题思路】D。事实细节题。根据题干关键词(defenders of traditional knowledge)定位到第三段。浏览选项内容后可发现,本题实际考查原因。本段第二句和第三句分别列举了一些因素。第二句谈到互联网的出现以及积极社会变革所产生的出乎意料的副作用"煽动了这种攻击"。第三句做进一步解释,认为教育的普及和社会流动性的增强所产生的负面影响在于拉近了专家和民众的距离,增加了双方的互动。综上所述,可看出造成民众对专家进行攻击的原因是多方面的。因此选项 D 正确。

【排他分析】选项 A 和选项 B 都对应本段第二句,原文提到互联网和积极的社会变革所带来的副作用是并列的两个原因,并不能相互包含,而且选项 B 中缺失了原文提到的"出乎意料的副作用"这层信息,因此排除这两项。选项 C 对应本段第三句,原文中"教育普及"和"社会流动性"也是一组并列的因素,属于积极社会变革的内容,但作者并未在两者之间进行比较,因此该项所提出的观点与原文无关,可排除。

Para. 4 ①For its part, the American public is in the grip of a sullen, almost paranoid, narcissism about science and experts. ②This is not a function of education. ③Indeed, ignorance has become hip, with some Americans now wearing their rejection of expert advice as a badge of cultural sophistication.

参考译文 ①就美国公众而言,他们在看待科学和专家时受到一种沉闷、甚至带有偏执色彩的自恋心理的控制。②这可不是教育的作用。③实际上,无知已经成为时髦,当下一些美国人将对专家意见的排斥当作自己具有文化教养的标志。

原文剖析 本段承接上段最后的观点,先从美国公众身上寻找原因。首句指出美国公众太过自恋。第二句指出这并非是因为他们受到了良好的教育(或拥有较高的文化素养)。第三句进一步指出造成前两句所述现象的原因,即目前美国人有将无知当时髦的倾向。本段可理解为美国公众对科学的了解实际并不深,采取攻击或否定专家意见的方式是为了假装自己有文化。

设题点睛 本段承接上段,从美国公众的角度加以分析,属于上段谈论的一个方面,可与后文综合设题。

生词解析

in the grip of 受……控制
paranoid *adj.* 偏执狂的;类似妄想狂的
hip *n.* 时髦
sophistication *n.* 有教养,有经验,老练

sullen *adj.* 闷闷不乐的,不高兴的
narcissism *n.* 自恋,自我陶醉
badge *n.* 徽章;证章;标记

Para. 5 ① Instead, the public rejection of science is an extension of our politics, which in turn have become an expression of our constant outrage about everything that offends our deepest beliefs about ourselves. ② As social scientist David Dunning has put it: "Some of our most stubborn misbeliefs arises… from the very values and philosophies that define who we are as individuals." ③ When those misbeliefs are challenged, laypeople take it not as correction but as a direct attack on their identity.

参考译文 ①事实上,对科学的公然抵触正是我们政治主张的延伸,这种抵触反过来成为我们长期以来发泄对触犯内心深处自我信仰的所有事物所产生的怒气的方式。②正如社会学家大卫·邓宁(David Dunning)所说的那样:"某些我们最顽固的错误信念正是来自那些定义我们是谁的价值观和哲学思想"。③当错误信念遭到质疑时,外行人就会认为这种质疑不是为了纠正,而是对他们自身定位的一种攻击。

原文剖析 本段承接上段内容,继续分析公众对科学产生抵触情绪的根源。首句是个长难句,指出公众对科学的抵触是为了发泄某种怒气。第二句借用社会学家的观点指出这种怒气产生的根源在于科学对个人进行了重新定义,与个人的自身定义产生了冲突,民众因此厌恶科学。第三句暗示公众对科学的抵触是错误的,此处的 misbelief 为关键词,含有贬义,说明作者对民众自身错误看法的否定。

设题点睛 本段对公众抵触科学的心理进行了深入探究,是全文的核心,适合设置考点。

生词解析

extension n. 延伸；广度
misbelief n. 错误的信仰；信仰邪说
laypeople n. 外行；非专业人员
outrage n. 愤怒，愤慨
arise...from 由……引起，起因于
take it as 把……看作

长难句解析

Instead, the public rejection of science is an extension of our politics,
　　　　　　主语　　　　　　　　　系动词　　　表语
which in turn have become an expression of our constant outrage about everything
　　　　　　　　　　　　非限制性定语从句
that offends our deepest beliefs about ourselves.
　　　　　　　定语从句

本句是主从复合句。本句主干为 the public rejection of science is an extension of our politics…，采用了主系表结构，逗号后为非限制性定语从句，其中 which 指代主句内容，其中还有个 that 引导的定语从句，其先行词为 everything。

3 The public's rejection of science originates from _____.　　公众对科学的抵触来源于_____。

A. the schism between self-perception and reality　　A. 自我认知和现实之间的差距
B. personal outrage against politics　　B. 个人对政治的愤慨
C. individual ignorance of education　　C. 个人对教育的无知
D. Americans' cultural sophistication　　D. 美国人的文化教养

【解题思路】A。推理引申题。根据题干关键词（public's rejection of science）和顺序原则定位到第五段首句。本题考查原因。本段首句指出这种抵触是政治看法的延伸，是人们怒气的发泄方式。后两句对这种怒气的来源做进一步说明。第二句谈到人们具有与"我们是谁"有关的"顽固的错误信念"（most stubborn misbeliefs），第三句指出当这种"错误信念遭到质疑时"，公众会将其看作科学或专家对人们自身定位的一种攻击。由第二句可看出公众对自身的看法是错误的，也就是和现实不符，在科学纠正大众自身错误观点的过程中，大众产生了对科学的抵触情绪，因此选项 A 是对这两句话的正确解读。

【排他分析】选项 B 对应本段首句，该句只是说公众对科学的抵触是"政治主张的延伸"，并未具体谈到公众对政治的态度，可理解为是与领导人或政策制定者的政治主张不一致，且该项并非公众抵触科学的根源，因此排除。选项 C 对应第四段中的 education 和 ignorance，但这两个词分别出现在第二句和第三句中，两句意思并不一致，因此该项属于随意拼凑，可以排除。选项 D 中的 cultural sophistication 对应第四段最后一句，该句是说美国公众将自己对科学的抵触看作有文化教养的表现，该项属于表现而非根源，可排除。

Para. 6 ①The expert community, however, must shoulder some of the blame for the collapse of the　　参考译文 ①然而，科学和公众关系的坍塌应部分归咎于专家

relationship between science and the public. ② Experts often trespass across from empirical knowledge to normative demands and thus validate the suspicions of laypeople that the real goal of expert advice is to force compliance with expert policy preferences.

群体。②专家们常常无视经验型知识,而直接给出标准化要求,这样做反而证实了民众的怀疑,即专家意见的真正目的是迫使民众服从其政策偏向。

【原文剖析】本段从事件的另一方(专家)的角度讨论原因。第一句是观点句,指出专家也有责任。第二句对首句进行论述,指出专家有时太过急躁,没有考虑到公众经验型知识的影响和作用,直接给出科学的标准,由于两者间可能产生矛盾(回应上段内容),从而使民众对科学产生了敌对情绪,并认为专家和政客一样,只是为了达成一定目的。

【设题点睛】本段第二句为长难句,用于解释首句观点并回应前文内容,属于重点信息,可用来设置考点。

【生词解析】
trespass *vi.* 擅自进入;违反;冒犯
normative *adj.* 规范的,标准的
compliance *n.* 顺从,服从
empirical *adj.* 经验主义的,完全根据经验的
validate *vt.* 证实;确认;使生效

【长难句解析】
Experts often trespass across from empirical knowledge to normative demands and thus
 主语   谓语1   状语
validate the suspicions of laypeople that the real goal of expert advice is to force compliance
 谓语2   宾语   同位语从句
with expert policy preferences.

本句为主从复合句。本句主干为 Experts trespass and validate the suspicions that…,有两个并列谓语,第一个谓语 trespass 后的 across from… to… 介词短语作状语,体现范围,第二个谓语后的 suspicions 为抽象名词作宾语,其后的 that 从句作其同位语,对内容进行限定和说明。

4 It is suggested that the expert community _____.

A. should be completely responsible for the current crisis
B. actively promotes the normative demands and empirical knowledge
C. should discredit empiricism and rationality
D. is in some way representative of government policies

从文中可得知,专家群体_____。

A. 应为目前的危机负全责
B. 积极宣传标准化要求和经验型知识
C. 应该怀疑经验主义和理性
D. 在某些方面代表了政府政策

【解题思路】D。推理引申题。根据题干关键词(expert community)定位到文章第六段。本段首句直接指出这些专家也应负责。第二句进行解释说明,指出专家并未考虑大众的经验型知识,太过急躁地推行标准化要求的后果是"证实了民众的怀疑,即专家意见的真正目的是迫使民众服从其政策偏向"。由此可知,民众认为专家这样做的真正的目标是让民众听从其观点,以符合政府的政策导向,说明专家与政府政策站在同一立场,也符合前文谈到的民众认为专家与政客并无二致的说法,选项 D 是对此

意的正确推断。

【排他分析】第六段首句明确指出 shoulder some of the blame(承担一些责任)，因此排除选项 A。选项 B 对应本段第二句，原文中的 trespass 一词含有否定用法，表示"违反，冒犯"，因此原文表示否定 empirical knowledge 而肯定 normative demands，并非本项所表达的并列关系，且原文并未提到与 actively promotes 有关的内容，因此排除。选项 C 对应第七段首句，属于无中生有的选项，可以直接排除。

Para. 7 ①At the same time, experts cannot withdraw from a public arena increasingly controlled by opportunistic demagogues who seek to discredit empiricism and rationality. ②Instead, the expert community must help to lead laypeople back along the road to a better day when the citizens of the United States valued scientists and other professionals as essential parts of the American story.

参考译文 ①与此同时，机会主义的煽动者愈发控制了公众这一竞技场，这些煽动者企图诽谤经验主义和理性，专家却不能因此退缩。②相反，专家群体必须起到引领外行公众的作用，使他们能沿路回到当初的美好时光，那时美国公民将科学家和其他专业人士看作美国历史的重要部分。

原文剖析 本段重在体现作者对解决目前公众和专家分歧的态度和建议。首句指出调和两者矛盾的困难所在(机会主义者煽动民众)。第二句作者利用 Instead 转折谈到自己的观点和建议(专家应该引领美国大众回到当初)，明显体现作者对科学家作用的积极看法。

设题点睛 本段首句和第二句构成"A. Instead, B."的重要逻辑结构，第二句体现重要信息，可用来设置考点。

生词解析

arena *n.* 舞台；竞技场   opportunistic *adj.* 机会主义的；投机取巧的

demagogue *n.* 煽动者；煽动政治家

长难句解析

Instead, the expert community must help to lead laypeople back along the road to a better day
         主语   谓语   宾语   状语

when the citizens of the United States valued scientists and other professionals as essential
                                    定语从句

parts of the American story.

本句是主从复合句。本句主干为 the expert community must help to lead...，谓语后的不定式作宾语，back along... to... 的介词结构作状语，体现方式和途径，其中 day 后由 when 引导的定语从句对其作具体说明，该从句谓语采用了 value... as... 的结构。

5 The author's attitude toward scientists is _____.

A. supportive

B. critical

作者对于科学家的态度是_____。

A. 支持的

B. 批评的

C. tolerating
D. biased

C. 容忍的
D. 偏颇的

【解题思路】A。观点态度题。根据本题考查内容(作者态度)以及顺序原则定位到文章最后一段。本段第二句是作者对科学界的建议,可从中体会作者的态度,该句指出"专家群体必须起到引领外行公众的作用"(the expert community must help to lead laypeople),并将美国公民看重科学家和其他专业人士的时期描述为"美好时光"(a better day)。由此看出作者对专家和科学界的态度是非常肯定的,因此选项 A 正确。

【排他分析】选项 B 与本段最后一句所体现的态度直接矛盾,可排除。选项 C 在文中并无体现,可排除。本文既指出了科学界的问题,也指出了民众的问题,因此是比较客观的分析,因此排除选项 D。

Text 14

Environmentalists have had a rough year, but over the past week the Environmental Protection Agency (EPA) and the Fifth Circuit Court of Appeals gave them some hope. On Dec. 23 the agency announced a schedule for setting greenhouse gas standards for power plants and oil refineries over the next two years, and on Wednesday the court refused to halt the implementation of the EPA's carbon-cutting program pending legal challenge. Congress hasn't passed a sensible, comprehensive energy policy. EPA regulation of greenhouse gases is one way the government can cut emissions now, using current law. Over the next year, the president should defend his administration's authority to do so.

With the Supreme Court's blessing, the EPA has deemed greenhouse emissions threats to public health under the Clean Air Act. That means the agency can require emitters to arrest those gases' release in various ways. What the EPA will force plant operators to do, though, isn't yet clear. The guidance it produced for state regulators last month stresses the value of efficiency improvements, such as turbines that convert more of the energy released from burning fossil fuels into usable electricity.

Agency officials insist that requirements will be "cost-effective" and "common-sense." In a legally distinct but nonetheless related effort, the EPA is also preparing to clamp down on other nasty things that coal-fired power plants spew into the air, such as mercury, which would require other emissions control technologies.

Critics such as Rep. Fred Upton (R-Mich.), the incoming chairman of the House Energy and Commerce Committee, insist that both regulatory avenues will seriously harm the economy. They are exaggerating, but it's true that EPA regulation absent some overarching congressional carbon policy isn't ideal. While such a rule raises no revenue, it can't compensate those consumers who have to pay more for their energy. Moreover, it depends on the policy preferences of the president, new administrations might move to gut the policies, leading to the sort of regulatory uncertainty that is punishing to business.

Above all, it relies on federal mandate, it's not likely to put America on the cheapest path to sustainable energy production even if it became America's primary carbon-reducing program.

But Mr. Upton's GOP colleagues killed the efficient solution: putting a price on carbon and unleashing market forces in the fight against climate change. And carbon dioxide continues to accumulate in the atmosphere. If critics want to be helpful, they should propose a realistic emissions-reduction scheme instead of simply picking on the EPA.

In the long term, this attenuated sort of EPA regulation alone isn't likely to result in the carbon reductions that America needs to participate seriously in the global response to climate change; it might cut emissions by 5 percent of 2005 levels by 2020, not the 17 percent that is Obama's stated policy. Congress will have to act, and sooner is better. In the meantime, modest EPA regulation can achieve some valuable ends and keep pressure on Congress to do more. The president must resist lawmakers' efforts to limit the EPA's power.

(*The Washington Post*, 2010.12)

1. Environmentalists' pressure is eased by _____.
   A. the absence of a comprehensive energy policy
   B. the joint efforts of certain government sectors
   C. the reduction of greenhouse gas emissions
   D. the president's defense of EPA regulation

2. The "turbines" cited in paragraph 2 could be used to _____.
   A. largely enhance the energy conversion ratio
   B. directly reduce the greenhouse gas emissions
   C. quickly produce clean air for the public
   D. efficiently convert fossil fuels into electricity

3. Fred Upton contends that EPA regulation is imperfect because _____.
   A. it relies on the policy preference of the business
   B. it cannot generate cost-effective energy
   C. it bears no economic merits to America
   D. it cannot cut the energy consumption

4. The phrase "picking on" (Para. 5) is closest in meaning to _____.
   A. reaffirming   B. dishonoring
   C. upholding   D. denouncing

5. According to the last paragraph, the author suggests that _____.
   A. global climate change imposes a huge pressure on Congress
   B. Congress should exert more efforts on environmental policy-making
   C. EPA regulation can hardly reduce the greenhouse gas emissions
   D. the president is resistant in the protection of EPA regulation

语篇分析与试题精解

Para. 1 ① Environmentalists have had a rough year, but over the past week the Environmental Protection Agency (EPA) and the Fifth Circuit Court of Appeals gave them some hope. ②On Dec. 23 the agency announced a schedule for setting greenhouse gas standards for power plants and oil refineries over the next two years, and on Wednesday the court refused to halt the implementation of the EPA's carbon-cutting program pending legal challenge. ③Congress hasn't passed a sensible, comprehensive energy policy. ④EPA regulation of greenhouse gases is one way the government can cut emissions now, using current law. ⑤ Over the next year, the president should defend his administration's authority to do so.

参考译文 ①今年对于环保人士来说是艰难的一年,但上周美国环境保护署(EPA)和第五巡回上诉法院(FCCA)却给了他们一线希望。②12月23日,环保署宣布了为电厂及炼油厂此后两年温室气体排放制定标准的计划。本周三,巡回上诉法院驳回了关于停止实施环保署碳减排计划的上诉。③国会尚未通过合理、全面的能源政策。④环保署的规则是政府根据现行法律减少温室气体排放的一种途径。⑤在未来一年内,总统应捍卫这一政府职能部门实施监管的权威。

原文剖析 本段首句给出观点:环保署和第五巡回上诉法院给了环保人士一线希望。第二句描述环保署及第五巡回上诉法院的具体做法:环保署宣布对电厂和炼油厂的温室气体排放量制定标准。而第五巡回上诉法院驳回了关于停止减排计划的上诉。第三句指出国会尚未通过合理的能源政策。第四句继而说明目前政府仍主要依靠环保署来减排。第五句承接第四句:正因为如此,总统需要维护环保署的权威。

设题点睛 本段第一句(观点)与第二句构成总分的结构,一般会设置相应的考点。

生词解析

Circuit Court of Appeals 巡回上诉法院   refinery *n.* 精炼厂,提炼厂
pending *prep.* ……期间

长难句解析

On Dec. 23   the agency   announced   a schedule   for setting greenhouse gas standards for
时间状语1   主语1   谓语1   宾语1   后置定语1

power plants and oil refineries over the next two years,   and   on Wednesday   the court
                                                            连词   时间状语2   主语2

refused   to halt the implementation   of the EPA's carbon-cutting program pending legal
谓语2   宾语2   后置定语2

challenge.

本句由 and 连接的两个并列句组成。两句都为主谓宾结构,第一句的主干为 the agency announced a schedule;第二句的主干为 the court refused to halt the implementation,由不定式结构作 refused 的宾语。

1 Environmentalists' pressure is eased by _____.
A. the absence of a comprehensive energy policy
B. the joint efforts of certain government sectors
C. the reduction of greenhouse gas emissions
D. the president's defense of EPA regulation

环保人士的压力得以缓解的原因是_____。
A. 全面能源政策的缺失
B. 政府相关部门的共同努力
C. 温室气体排放量的减少
D. 总统对环保署规则的捍卫

【解题思路】B。推理引申题。根据题干 Environmentalists 定位到文章首段首句,题干考查环保人士的压力通过何种方式减弱了。文章首段首句内的转折结构提示美国政府的两个部门(环保署及第五巡回上诉法院)给予了环保人士一些希望,而第二句具体描述环保署和第五巡回上诉法院做了什么事来促进环保,因此选项 B 是正确答案,选项 B 中的 certain government sectors 指的就是环保署和第五巡回上诉法院两个部门。

【排他分析】选项 A 对应原文首段第三句。原文大意是国会尚未通过合理全面的能源政策,而这会给环保人士推进环保运动带来压力,而非题干所问的"减压",所以排除。选项 C 对应原文首段第四句,原文意思是政府现在就是通过环保署的规则来帮助减少温室气体的排放,并不等于温室气体排放已经少到可使环保人士放心的程度,所以排除。选项 D 对应本段最后一句,原文大意是总统在未来一年内应该捍卫其政府部门(即环保署)的监管权力,虽然这样做可能减轻环保人士的压力,但该做法并未发生,所以排除。

Para. 2 ① With the Supreme Court's blessing, the EPA has deemed greenhouse emissions threats to public health under the Clean Air Act. ② That means the agency can require emitters to arrest those gases' release in various ways. ③ What the EPA will force plant operators to do, though, isn't yet clear. ④ The guidance it produced for state regulators last month stresses the value of efficiency improvements, such as turbines that convert more of the energy released from burning fossil fuels into usable electricity.

参考译文 ①根据《清洁空气法案》的规定,在最高法院庇护之下的环保署已将温室气体的排放列为威胁公共健康的因素。②这就意味着环保署可以要求排放者采用多种方法停止该类气体的排放。③但是,环保署具体将迫使电厂运营商有何动作,目前尚不明确。④上个月环保署为各州监管机构制定的指南强调了提高能源使用效率的重要意义,如推荐可以将燃烧矿物燃料产生的更多能量转化为可用电能的涡轮机。

原文剖析 本段首句指出环保署已经将温室气体定义为有害气体(threats to public health)。第二句解释首句的意义:环保署可以因此要求排放者停止此类气体的排放。第三句和第四句指出环保署可能采取的措施:虽然目前还不清楚环保署具体会要求运营商做什么,但是上个月已经开始强调采取能提高能源使用效率的改进措施。

设题点睛 本段最重要的内容应该是最后一句(对第三句做解释、本身为长难句、句内存在例子),可能会针对本句设置考题。

生词解析

blessing *n.* 庇佑
arrest *vt.* 使停止，阻止
deem *vt.* 认为，视作
turbine *n.* 涡轮机

长难句解析

The guidance | it produced for state regulators last month | stresses | the value of efficiency
主语　　　　　定语从句1　　　　　　　　　　　　　　　　谓语　　　宾语　　　后置定语
improvements, such as turbines | that convert more of the energy released from burning
　　　　　　　插入语　　　　　　　　　定语从句2
fossil fuels into usable electricity.

本句主干结构为 The guidance stresses the value…，句中定语从句1解释说明先行词 guidance。such as 引出插入语，对 efficiency improvements 进行举例说明，其中还包含一个定语从句。

2 The "turbines" cited in paragraph 2 could be used to _____.　　第二段谈到的"turbines"可用来_____。

A. largely enhance the energy conversion ratio　　A. 大幅提高能量转化率
B. directly reduce the greenhouse gas emissions　　B. 直接减少温室气体的排放
C. quickly produce clean air for the public　　C. 快速为公共环境制造清洁空气
D. efficiently convert fossil fuels into electricity　　D. 有效地将化石燃料转化成电能

【解题思路】**A**。语意理解题。根据题干要求定位到第二段第四句，turbines 为本句例子当中的内容，原句表示 turbines 可以将燃烧矿物燃料产生的更多热量转化为可用的电能，说明 turbines 可以提高能量的转化率，支持本句主句中的 stresses the value of efficiency improvements（强调提高能源使用效率的重要意义），因此选项 A 是正确答案。此题实际上考查 turbines 定语从句的内容。

【排他分析】选项 B 对应第二段第二句，根据分析，turbines 并不能阻止温室气体的排放，它本身的功能是提高能量转化效率，进而间接减少温室气体的排放，所以排除。选项 C 对应本段首句，原文并没有指出 turbines 可以制造清洁的空气，选项 C 是利用原文无关细节编造的干扰项，所以排除。选项 D 对应本段最后一句，原文意思是可以将燃烧燃料产生的热量最大限度地转化为电能，而不是如选项 D 所说将燃料直接转化成电能，因此排除。

Para. 3 ① Agency officials insist that requirements will be "cost-effective" and "common-sense." ② In a legally distinct but nonetheless related effort, the EPA is also preparing to clamp down on other nasty things that coal-fired power plants spew into the air, such as mercury, which would require other emissions control technologies.

参考译文 ①环保署官员坚持认为，这些要求将符合"成本效益"和"常识"。②在一次法律上不同但又与法律密切相关的努力之下，环保署还准备严格限制火力发电厂排放到大气中的其他污染物，如汞，这就需要其他控制排放的技术。

原文剖析 本段首句给出环保署官员的看法：环保署的规定或要求符合成本效益和常识性。第二句进一步指出环保署还要限制其他空气污染物（如汞）的排放。

设题点睛 本段两句话的内在关联不是很强。第二句虽然是长难句，但是核心大意就是除去温室气体之外，环保署还要控制其他污染物的排放，直接针对此段设置干扰选项的难度较大，因此这样的段落一般不会设置考题，但可能会结合下一段共同设置考题。

生词解析

cost-effective *adj.* 成本效益好的
clamp down 取缔，施加压力
spew *vi.* 喷涌；呕吐
distinct *adj.* 有区别的
nasty *adj.* 肮脏的

长难句解析

<u>In a legally distinct but nonetheless related effort</u>, <u>the EPA</u> <u>is also preparing</u> <u>to clamp</u>
　　　　　状语　　　　　　　　　　　　　　　　主语　　　　谓语　　　　宾语
<u>down on other nasty things</u> <u>that coal-fired power plants spew into the air</u>, <u>such as</u>
　　　　　　　　　　　　　　　　　定语从句　　　　　　　　　　　　　　　　插入语
<u>mercury</u>, <u>which would require other emissions control technologies</u>.
　　　　　　　　　　　非限制性定语从句

本句主干结构为 the EPA is also preparing to clamp down on...，句中动词不定式结构为 prepare 的宾语，其中还包含一个定语从句，解释说明 other nasty things。非限制性定语从句中 which 指代前面整个句子，并对其进行解释说明。

Para. 4 ①Critics such as Rep. Fred Upton (R-Mich.), the incoming chairman of the House Energy and Commerce Committee, insist that both regulatory avenues will seriously harm the economy. ②They are exaggerating, but it's true that EPA regulation absent some overarching congressional carbon policy isn't ideal. ③While such a rule raises no revenue, it can't compensate those consumers who have to pay more for their energy. ④Moreover, it depends on the policy preferences of the president, new administrations might move to gut the policies, leading to the sort of regulatory uncertainty that is punishing to business. ⑤Above all, it relies on federal mandate, it's not likely to put America on the cheapest path to sustainable energy production even if it became America's primary carbon-reducing program.

参考译文 ①即将出任能源和商务委员会主席的佛瑞德·厄普顿（Fred Upton）（密歇根州，共和党）是其中一名批评人士，他坚持认为两种监管途径都会严重损害经济发展。②他们夸大了事实，但有一点却是正确的，在缺乏由国会通过的支配性的碳排放政策的情况下，环保署的规则并不理想。③因为该规则不能提升任何收入，也不能补偿那些必须为能源支付更多钱的消费者。④此外，这一规则所仰仗的是总统的政策偏好，而新政府可能会废止一些政策，这就导致了对企业不利的监管的不确定性。⑤同时，该规则还依靠联邦授权，因此，即使该规则成为美国碳减排的首要计划，也不可能为美国找到价格最低廉的可再生能源的生产途径。

原文剖析 本段首句给出批评方观点：上段所提及的两种监管渠道都将损害经济发展。第二句的重点在句内转折之后，指出环保署的规则确实不是很理想（isn't ideal）。第三句、第四句、第五句为递进结构，阐述环保署规则不理想的理由：首先不能提高任何收入，因此不能补偿消费者的额外支出；其次是这种政策要看总统的偏好，如果换了总统可能也就得换政策，这种不确定性对公司不利；最后指出即使该计划成为碳减排的优选方案，也不能帮助美国找到价格最低的可再生能源。

设题点睛 本段后三句对第二句做了解释，其中最后一句从逻辑上看程度最深，因此为考点设置处。

生词解析

exaggerating *adj.* 夸大的　　　　　　　absent *vt.* 使缺席
overarching *adj.* 支配一切的　　　　　　gut *vt.* 破坏……的主要力量
punishing *adj.* 给予沉重打击的　　　　　mandate *n.* 授权

长难句解析

Moreover, it depends on the policy preferences of the president, new administrations
状语　　主语1　谓语1　　　　宾语　　　　　后置定语　　　　　　主语2
might move to gut the policies, leading to the sort of regulatory uncertainty
谓语2　　　目的状语　　　　　　　　　　结果状语
that is punishing to business.
　定语从句

本句由逗号隔开的两个完整的句子组成。前一句为主谓宾结构，主干结构为 it depends on the policy preferences；后一句为主谓结构，其中包含非谓语动词作表示结果的伴随状语，其中的定语从句解释说明先行词 regulatory uncertainty。

3 Fred Upton contends that EPA regulation is　　　佛瑞德·厄普顿称环保署的规则
imperfect because ＿＿＿＿.　　　　　　　　　　　并不完美的原因在于＿＿＿＿。

A. it relies on the policy preference of the　　　A. 其依赖于公司的政策偏好
　　business
B. it cannot generate cost-effective energy　　　B. 其不能生产出划算的能源
C. it bears no economic merits to America　　　C. 其不能给美国带来经济方面
　　　　　　　　　　　　　　　　　　　　　　　　的好处
D. it cannot cut the energy consumption　　　　D. 其不能减少能源消耗量

【解题思路】C。事实细节题。根据题干人名 Fred Upton 和 imperfect 定位到第四段第二句（isn't ideal）。通过语篇分析，从第三句到第五句都是对 isn't ideal 原因的描述，第五句大意是即使该规则成为碳减排的首要计划（primary carbon-reducing program），也无法为美国找到价格最低廉的可再生能源的生产途径（not likely to put America on the cheapest path to sustainable energy production），the cheapest path 呼应选项 C 的意思。同时在第三句中提到该规则既不能产生收入也不能补偿那些必须为能源支付更多钱的消费者，也是在表达选项 C 的意思，所以该项是正确答案。

【排他分析】选项 A 对应第四段第四句，原文大意是这种规则有赖于总统的偏好，总统更换可能政策也要跟着换，而不是选项 A 说的依靠公司的政策偏好，所以排除。选项

B 的 cost-effective 对应第三段的首句,而整体内容对应第四段第五句,本段第五句只谈到不能为美国找到最廉价的可再生能源的生产途径,而对于能不能生产出性价比高的能源却并没有谈到,选项 B 是无中生有,所以排除。选项 D 对应本段第三句,原文的意思是不能补偿美国人增长的能源花费(暗指美国人要为能源掏更多的钱)而非增长的能源消耗,选项 D 属于对原文的错误理解,所以排除。

Para. 5 ① But Mr. Upton's GOP colleagues killed the efficient solution: putting a price on carbon and unleashing market forces in the fight against climate change. ② And carbon dioxide continues to accumulate in the atmosphere. ③ If critics want to be helpful, they should propose a realistic emissions-reduction scheme instead of simply picking on the EPA.

参考译文 ①然而,厄普顿的共和党同僚却扼杀了有效的解决方案:为碳定价并充分释放市场力量来应对气候变化。②与此同时,二氧化碳在大气中持续累积。③如果批评人士想要施以援手,他们应该提出现实可行的减排计划,而不只是对环保署横加批评。

原文剖析 本段首句指出厄普顿的同僚扼杀了一个有效的解决方案:为碳定价并释放市场力量。第二句指出现在二氧化碳的排放还在增加(暗示急需出台解决方案)。第三句承接第二句指出批评人士应该提出可行的减排方案,而不是仅仅进行指责。

设题点睛 本段第一句带有冒号用于解释,第三句带有否定结构,可用来出题。

生词解析

unleash vt. 解除对……的束缚 scheme n. 计划,规划
pick on 老是挑剔(某人)

4 The phrase "picking on" (Para. 5) is closest in meaning to _____.

A. reaffirming
B. dishonoring
C. upholding
D. denouncing

词组"picking on"(第五段)与以下哪项的意思最接近?

A. 再次确认
B. 使丢脸
C. 支持
D. 谴责

【解题思路】D。语意理解题。根据题干精确定位到第五段最后一句。picking on 存在于一个否定结构中,instead of 表明前后内容应该相反。前半句的大意是批评者们应该提出现实的减排措施,之后转折应指出他们不应该对环保署做某事,因此答案应该是偏负面的,所以是在选项 B 和选项 D 中选一个。而本句的主语是 critics,所以他们做出的动作更可能是 denouncing,因此选项 D 是正确答案。

【排他分析】选项 A 和选项 C 为含义偏正面的选项,不符合 instead of 所体现的转折语意逻辑,可以直接排除。选项 B 表示"使丢脸",态度过于偏激,一般在考研英语阅读理解涉及态度题的考查中,态度过于偏激的选项一般为错,因此排除。

Para. 6 ①In the long term, this attenuated sort of EPA regulation alone isn't likely to result in the

参考译文 ①长期看来,仅靠环保署的此类规则不可能达到美国认真参

carbon reductions that America needs to participate seriously in the global response to climate change; it might cut emissions by 5 percent of 2005 levels by 2020, not the 17 percent that is Obama's stated policy. ②Congress will have to act, and sooner is better. ③In the meantime, modest EPA regulation can achieve some valuable ends and keep pressure on Congress to do more. ④The president must resist lawmakers' efforts to limit the EPA's power.

与应对全球气候变化工作所需要的碳减排量。到2020年,碳的排放量可能比2005年降低5%,而不是奥巴马推行政策中所说的17%。②国会必须有所作为,而且越快越好。③在此期间,环保署制定合适的规则也能达到一些可喜的结果,同时还可向国会施压,使其有更多作为。④总统必须抵抗住来自立法者要求限制环保署权力的压力。

【原文剖析】 本段首句给出观点:只依靠环保署无法帮助美国达到碳减排的长期要求。后三句给出作者建议:国会应该尽早行动起来;环保署制定适度规则,并向国会施压;总统必须力挺环保署。

【设题点睛】 本段首句为长难句,但是当中有半句话是由数据组成的,一般不会设置考点。而最后一句的总统需要力挺环保署和首段最后一句内容重合,也不会设置考点。第二句和第三句针对国会的作者建议为新观点,此处为考点设置处。

【生词解析】

attenuate vt. 使变细;减轻   end n. 宗旨,目的

5	According to the last paragraph, the author suggests that _____.	在最后一段中,作者暗示_____。
	A. global climate change imposes a huge pressure on Congress	A. 全球气候变化给国会施加了巨大的压力
	B. Congress should exert more efforts on environmental policy-making	B. 国会应当加大制定环境政策的力度
	C. EPA regulation can hardly reduce the greenhouse gas emissions	C. 环保署的规则很难减少温室气体的排放量
	D. the president is resistant in the protection of EPA regulation	D. 总统在保护环保署规则方面持反对态度

【解题思路】B。事实细节题。根据题干要求定位到文章最后一段,通过语篇分析确定本段第二句和第三句相对而言比较重要,分别指出国会应该尽早行动起来,环保署的规则也能产生作用并对国会施压。选项B可以对应这两句话体现的言外之意,即第二句谈到的"国会必须有所作为",以及第三句中的keep pressure on Congress to do more,所以选项B是正确答案。

【排他分析】选项A的global climate change在最后一段首句中出现,但是本段中并没有任何信息指出全球气候变化能够对美国国会产生巨大压力,只是在第三句中提到环保署规则产生效果后能给国会施压,因此选项A属于无中生有,所以排除。选项C对应本段第三句,原文明确提到环保署的规则是可以达到一些效果的(modest EPA regulation can achieve some valuable ends),与选项C矛盾,所以排除。选项D对应最后一句,作者在最后一句指出总统应该抵抗住(resist)来自立法者要

求限制环保署权力的压力,言下之意就是总统应该保护环保署的权力,和选项 D 的大意相反,因此排除。

Text 15

Schools of higher education in the United States are no doubt in a reflective mood about the meaning of institutional integrity. On Monday, the FBI announced 50 indictments related to fraud and bribery in the admissions process of several elite universities. More indictments are expected.

The federal charges point a finger at both wealthy parents who cheated to get their children into prestigious schools as well as school workers who assisted them, especially athletic coaches. Yet while the institutions seem blameless, they do bear ultimate responsibility for the incentives that drove the scandal—and the solutions to prevent a similar one.

Few universities today see themselves as a vehicle for learning virtues to live a full life. Most now aim to ensure a lucrative career for graduates and to signal social worth for them. Education has become more a consumer commodity and less a guide to civic values and moral progress. The mere acceptance into a top-flight school has become an end in itself followed by receiving a diploma that bestows status.

In 1966, The American Freshman Survey found 86 percent of entering students saw higher education a way to discover a meaningful approach to life. Less than half wanted to be "very well off financially." By 2015, the survey found 82 percent preferred the aim of making money while only 45 percent sought meaning. No wonder so many parents try to rig the admissions process to give a child an unfair leg-up.

The competitive incentives to cheat on applications, testing, and other parts of the process are huge. In addition, many schools give preferences for admission not based on merit. In a 2015 survey by Kaplan Test Prep, a quarter of admission officers said they felt pressure from their schools to accept an applicant who didn't meet the requirements.

The answer to the illegal or unethical manipulation of admissions is to make sure schools are a community of learners—including teachers—dedicated to character formation, not just intellectual achievements. The message must go out to all staff in higher education that values such as honesty and trust are part of the entire school experience. They are a public good that can be nurtured in the thinking of young people. Some colleges, such as Tulane University in New Orleans, promote the "core values" expected in campus life, including in the admissions process.

When schools provide constant models for integrity, they can inspire staff, students, and parents to see education as developing qualities of thought. The incentives to cut corners should go away.

(*The Washington Post*, 2019.3)

1. According to paragraph 1, the author may agree that _____.
   A. schools are accountable for cheating in admissions
   B. elite schools are generally more likely to cheat in exams
   C. measures should be taken immediately to eliminate this issue
   D. admission processes of higher education schools need improving
2. Education now is regarded as a consumer commodity partly due to _____.
   A. the influence of consumer culture
   B. school's change of function orientation
   C. the moral deficiency of college teachers
   D. students' complex of famous schools
3. The author reveals the excessive utility trend of higher education by _____.
   A. investigating students' life goals
   B. analyzing the causes behind it
   C. illustrating different views on it
   D. listing data at different times
4. According to the passage, the "core values" (Para. 6) refers to _____.
   A. equal development of virtue and intellect
   B. a fairer and more just admission process
   C. students-centered education views
   D. critical thinking of young people
5. Which of the following is the best title for the text?
   A. How to increase college admission rate?
   B. What are the "core values" concerning education?
   C. How to de-corrupt college admissions?
   D. What is the fundamental functions of education?

语篇分析与试题精解

Para. 1 ①Schools of higher education in the United States are no doubt in a reflective mood about the meaning of institutional integrity. ②On Monday, the FBI announced 50 indictments related to fraud and bribery in the admissions process of several elite universities. ③More indictments are expected.

参考译文 ①美国高等教育院校无疑正在对学校诚信的含义进行反思。②周一,联邦调查局公布了和多所名校招生舞弊受贿相关的五十份刑事起诉书。③预计会有更多的起诉书被公布。

原文剖析 本段提出讨论话题——高校招生舞弊案,暗示作者对高校的批评态度,交代事件的严重性。第一句由高校反思学校诚信入手,暗示作者态度:高校对招生舞弊案负有责任,应进行反思。第二句和第三句交代案件阶段性调查结果,以涉案人员之多(50 indictments, more indictments are expected)说明招生舞弊问题的严重性。

设题点睛 本段首句暗含作者的观点态度,可据此设置题目。

生词解析

reflective *adj.* 深思的;沉思的
integrity *n.* 诚实正直
fraud *n.* 欺诈罪;欺骗罪
institutional *adj.* 机构的
indictment *n.* 刑事起诉书;公诉书
bribery *n.* 行贿;受贿

1 According to paragraph 1, the author may agree that _____.

A. schools are accountable for cheating in admissions
B. elite schools are generally more likely to cheat in exams
C. measures should be taken immediately to eliminate this issue
D. admission processes of higher education schools need improving

根据第一段,作者可能赞同_____。

A. 学校要为其招生中的作弊行为负责
B. 精英学校通常更容易在考试中作弊
C. 应立即采取措施根除这一问题
D. 高等教育院校招生流程有待改进

【解题思路】A。推理引申题。根据题干要求定位到第一段。该段首句指出高校无疑正在反思学校诚信问题,暗示作者态度:高校对招生舞弊案负有责任,应进行反思,选项 A 中的 cheating in admissions 与文中的 fraud and bribery in the admissions process 为同义替换,故选项 A 为正确答案。

【排他分析】首段提到联邦调查局公布了和多所名校招生舞弊受贿相关的五十份刑事起诉书,可能说明名校招生舞弊受贿现象更常见,但选项 B 曲解为在考试中作弊,明显与文章内容不符,选项 B 排除。首段并未提及措施(measures)等内容,且选项 C 中的 eliminate 过于绝对,选项 C 排除。招生舞弊不一定说明是招生流程有问题,且首段也未提及流程存在问题等内容,选项 D 排除。

Para. 2 ①The federal charges point a finger at both wealthy parents who cheated to get their children into prestigious schools as well as school workers who assisted them, especially athletic coaches. ② Yet while the institutions seem blameless, they do bear ultimate responsibility for the incentives that drove the scandal—and the solutions to prevent a similar one.

参考译文 ①联邦调查局不仅对协助家长舞弊的学校工作人员,尤其是运动员教练提出了指控,而且对通过作弊将孩子送进名校的富裕家长也提出了指控。②然而,虽然学校看起来无可指责,但是他们却对促使丑闻发生的动机——以及提出防止历史重演的解决方案——负有首要责任。

原文剖析 本段提出作者观点:学校在招生舞弊案中负有首要责任。第一句让步,交代家长和学校职员在案件中的责任。第二句转折,提出作者观点:学校看似无辜,实则是责任主体。

设题点睛 本段含有转折句,也包含了作者的观点态度,但是观点态度过于明显,不适宜设题。

生词解析

point a finger at 指控;指责
prestigious *adj.* 有威望的;声誉高的

blameless *adj.* 无过错的；无可指责的
ultimate *adj.* 最根本的；最原始的
scandal *n.* 丑闻；流言蜚语

bear responsibility for sth. 对某事负责
incentive *n.* 动机；刺激

[长难句解析]

The federal charges point a finger at both wealthy parents who cheated to get their
　　主语　　　　　谓语　　　　　　宾语1　　　　　定语从句1
children into prestigious schools as well as school workers who assisted them,
　　　　　　　　　　　　　　　　宾语2　　　　　　　定语从句2
especially athletic coaches.
　　同位语

本句是主从复合句。本句主干为 The federal charges point a finger at both wealthy parents as well as school workers，句子中包含两个由 who 引导的定语从句，分别修饰 wealthy parents 和 school workers。

Para. 3 ①Few universities today see themselves as a **vehicle** for learning virtues to live a **full** life. ②Most now aim to ensure a **lucrative** career for graduates and to signal social worth for them. ③Education has become more a consumer **commodity** and less a guide to **civic** values and moral progress. ④The mere acceptance into a **top-flight** school has become an end in itself followed by receiving a diploma that **bestows** status.

[参考译文] ①如今很少有大学将自身视为学习美德从而过上充实生活的媒介。②大多数大学旨在确保毕业生在职业生涯中能赚大钱，并表明学生的社会价值。③教育与其说是公民价值观和道德进步的向导，不如说已经变成了一种消费品。④仅仅是被顶级大学录取本身就变成了最重要的事，接着拿到文凭就获得了社会地位。

[原文剖析] 本段分析当前校界和外界对学校的看法：好学校象征着名利地位，而不再是传道解惑的场所。前两句从学校角度出发，指出当前大多数学校的自我定位有误，比起传授美德，更重视对学生谋取金钱和社会地位的帮助。第三句和第四句递进，指出学校错误的自我定位导致外界更注重教育的功利性：现在教育更像是一种商品，顶级大学的入场券变成了社会地位的直通车。

[设题点睛] 本段首句的 few 含有否定意义，可说明事件的严重性及外界更注重教育的功利性的原因，可用来设置正确选项。

[生词解析]
vehicle *n.* (实现目的的)工具；媒介
lucrative *adj.* 赚大钱的；获利多的
civic *adj.* 公民的；市民的
bestow *vt.* 给予；授予

full *adj.* (生活)充实的；多姿多彩的
commodity *n.* 商品
top-flight *adj.* 一流的；最佳的

2 Education now is regarded as a consumer commodity partly due to _____.

A. the influence of consumer culture
B. school's change of function orientation
C. the moral deficiency of college teachers
D. students' complex of famous schools

教育现在被认为是一种消费品，部分原因在于_____。

A. 消费文化的影响
B. 学校功能定位的转变
C. 高校教师道德的缺失
D. 学生的名校情结

【解题思路】B。事实细节题。根据题干中的"a consumer commodity"可定位到第三段。本段第三句说，不如说教育已经变成了一种消费品，那么原因有可能在本段前两句。前两句从学校角度出发，指出当前大多数学校的自我定位有误，比起传授美德，更重视对学生谋取金钱和社会地位的帮助。第三句和第四句递进，指出学校错误的自我定位导致外界更注重教育的功利性，由此导致教育更像是一种消费品，可见部分原因是学校对自我的定位更功利了，因此选项B为正确答案。

【排他分析】选项A利用文中的 consumer 一词作干扰，文中并未提及 consumer culture（消费文化）等内容，选项A排除。选项C利用文中的 moral 一词作干扰，文中并未提及 moral deficiency（道德缺失）等内容，选项C排除。本段最后确实指出，顶级大学的入场券变成了社会地位的直通车，但并未提及学生们具有名校情结，学生家长也有可能存在名校情结，选项D排除。

Para. 4 ①In 1966, The American Freshman Survey found 86 percent of entering students saw higher education a way to discover a meaningful approach to life. ②Less than half wanted to be "very well off financially." ③By 2015, the survey found 82 percent preferred the aim of making money while only 45 percent sought meaning. ④No wonder so many parents try to rig the admissions process to give a child an unfair leg-up.

参考译文 ①1996年，美国新生调查发现百分之八十六的新生将高等教育视为发现有意义的生活态度的途径。②只有不到一半的学生想变得"非常富有"。③到2015年，该调查发现百分之八十二的学生更乐意以挣钱为目标，而只有百分之四十五的学生是为了寻求意义。④难怪这么多家长试图操纵招生过程，给予孩子不公平的帮助。

原文剖析 本段通过对比现在和过去的数据，说明当前社会更看重教育的功利作用，指出招生舞弊是这一大环境的产物。前三句通过对比，用调查数据明确说明，从前学生更注重学校的教育意义，而今却更注重金钱回报。第四句归纳总结，指出家长对招生过程的干预是学校教育功能弱化、功利作用凸显的产物，暗示学校是招生舞弊案的根本责任人。

设题点睛 本段有现在和过去的数据对比，可得出相应的结论，可设置题目考查作者得出结论的方式。

生词解析
approach n. (待人接物或思考问题的)态度，方式
rig vt. (以不正当手段)操纵，控制
well off 境况良好的
give sb. a leg-up 帮助、援助某人(改善境况)

3 The author reveals the excessive utility trend of higher education by _____.

A. investigating students' life goals
B. analyzing the causes behind it
C. illustrating different views on it
D. listing data at different times

作者通过_____揭示了高等教育过度功利的趋势。

A. 调查学生的人生目标
B. 分析背后的原因
C. 阐述不同的观点
D. 列出不同时间的数据

【解题思路】D。事实细节题。根据出题顺序可定位到第四段。前三句通过对比,用调查数据明确说明,从前学生更注重学校的教育意义,而今却更注重金钱回报,说明当前社会更看重教育的功利作用,因此选项 D 为正确答案。

【排他分析】第四段调查的是学生对于接受教育的意义的看法,而不是学生的人生目标,选项 A 偷换概念,可排除。选项 B 干扰性较强,因为上段分析了教育功利性的原因,但本题干问的是过度功利的趋势,说的是一种变化的趋势,因此选项 B 排除。文中并未提及不同的人对教育功利性的不同观点,选项 C 排除。

Para. 5 ①The competitive incentives to cheat on applications, testing, and other parts of the process are huge. ②In addition, many schools give preferences for admission not based on merit. ③In a 2015 survey by Kaplan Test Prep, a quarter of admission officers said they felt pressure from their schools to accept an applicant who didn't meet the requirements.

参考译文 ①在申请学校、考试及招生过程的其他环节中,作弊的竞争动机是巨大的。②另外,很多学校招生时并不看重学生的品质。③在卡普兰考试培训学校2015年的一项调查中,四分之一的招生人员表示,他们感受到了来自学校的压力,要求他们录取不符合条件的考生。

原文剖析 本段从学生和学校两方面,说明教育功利化是招生舞弊的重要原因。第一句从学生角度出发,说明竞争压力巨大是招生舞弊的一个重要原因。第二句指出学校招生也并非全然择优录取。第三句以调查数据论证第二句。

设题点睛 本段为"观点+例证"的结构,可用来设置正确选项。

生词解析
preference n. 偏爱
merit n. 优点;美德
meet the requirements 符合要求;满足条件

Para. 6 ①The answer to the illegal or unethical manipulation of admissions is to make sure schools are a community of learners—including teachers—dedicated to character formation, not just intellectual achievements. ②The message must go out to all staff in higher education that values such as honesty and trust are part of the entire school experience. ③They are a public good that can be

参考译文 ①解决非法或不道德地操纵招生问题的答案在于,确保学校是一个为学习者(包括老师)打造的社区,不仅致力于智慧成就,而且致力于品行培养。②高等教育的全体教职员工都应意识到,诚实和信任等价值观是整个学校经历的一部分。③他们是可以从年轻人的思想

nurtured in the thinking of young people. ④Some colleges, such as Tulane University in New Orleans, promote the "core values" expected in campus life, including in the admissions process.

上培养的公共美德。④一些大学,如位于新奥尔良的杜兰大学便宣传大学生活(包括入学申请过程中)所期待的"核心价值观"。

原文剖析 本段提出建议,指出解决问题的途径在于学校德智并重,并举例说明。第一句提出论点,明言解决问题之道在于大学德智并重,强调品德塑造的重要性。第二句和第三句递进,解释说明德育的方式和意义。第二句阐释德育的方式,强调诚信等价值观教育应作为校园经历的一部分被所有教职工重视。第三句阐释德育的现实意义:从思想上培养年轻人的公共美德。第四句举例论证第一句。

设题点睛 本段为"观点+例证"的结构,可利用例证设置题目;或利用其中带引号的"core values"考查指代类或语意理解类题目。

生词解析
unethical adj. 不道德的
dedicated adj. 专心致志的;一心一意的
manipulation n. (暗中)操纵;控制
nurture vt. 培养(人等)

长难句解析

The answer to the illegal or unethical manipulation of admissions is to make sure
 主语   后置定语   系动词 表语
schools are a community of learners—including teachers—dedicated to character
      宾语从句   插入语   后置定语
formation, not just intellectual achievements.

本句是主从复合句,本句主干为 The answer is to make sure…。to the illegal or… of admissions 为主语 The answer 的后置定语,make sure 后面省略了引导词 that 的宾语从句,作 make sure 的宾语。宾语从句中,including teachers 为插入语,对 community 的内容进行补充说明,dedicated to… achievements 为 learners 的后置定语,对 learners 的性质进行补充说明。

4 According to the passage, the "core values" (Para. 6) refers to _____.

A. equal development of virtue and intellect
B. a fairer and more just admission process
C. students-centered education views
D. critical thinking of young people

根据文章,"核心价值观"(第六段)指的是_____。

A. 德智发展并重
B. 一个更公平公正的招生过程
C. 以学生为中心的教育观
D. 年轻人的批判性思维

【解题思路】A。推理引申题。根据题干中的"core values"定位到第六段。该关键词出现在本段的最后一句,且是例证句,那么本题考查的其实是论点。本段第一句即为论点,第一句明确指出解决问题之道在于大学德智并重,强调品德塑造的重要性,因此"core values"应该是指大学要德智并重,选项A为正确答案。

【排他分析】第六段并未涉及招生过程(admission process)等内容,选项B属于无中生有,故排除。本段内容主要阐述要以培养学生的道德思想为重,而不是以学生为中心,选项C错误。选项D利用第三句中的 the thinking of young people 作干扰,文中并未提及 critical,故排除。

Para. 7 ①When schools provide constant models for integrity, they can inspire staff, students, and parents to see education as developing qualities of thought. ②The incentives to cut corners should go away.

参考译文 ①学校若不断培养出诚信楷模,便可激励教职员工、学生和家长将教育视为发展思想素质的途径。②走捷径的动机也就消失了。

原文剖析 本段总结,再次强调学校的道德指示作用,指出学校道德培养价值的树立是杜绝舞弊的根本途径。第一句指出学校诚信教育的成果能使各方认可教育的道德培养功能。第二句递进,指出若各方都尊重教育,则舞弊自然消失。两句话呈现出"学校诚信→各界尊重教育→杜绝舞弊"三者之间环环相扣的因果关系。

设题点睛 本段承接上段强调学校的道德指示作用,段落较短且本段的两句话为递进的关系,一般不会单独设题,可以结合上文出题。

生词解析

constant adj. 持续不断的;一直存在的　　　cut corners (做事)走捷径

5. Which of the following is the best title for the text?　　以下哪项是本文的最佳标题?

A. How to increase college admission rate?　　A. 如何提高大学录取率?
B. What are the "core values" concerning education?　　B. 什么是教育的核心价值?
C. How to de-corrupt college admissions?　　C. 如何消除高校招生腐败现象?
D. What is the fundamental functions of education?　　D. 教育的基本功能是什么?

【解题思路】C。主旨大意题。需纵观全文找出本文大意。本文作者从对近期美国名校招生舞弊案的反思和阶段性调查结果切入,指出高校要对此负首要责任,并提出高校要明确自身教书育人的职责、加强自身道德建设,这样才能从根本上解决问题,各选项中只有选项 C 涉及了招生舞弊的相关表达,且符合文章大意,因此选项 C 为正确答案。

【排他分析】文章并未提及大学录取率低与高的问题,选项 A 属于无中生有,故排除。选项 B 中的"core values"只在第六段提到,属于以偏概全,因此排除。本文部分内容涉及学校自身定位的错误,但文章的主题词是围绕招生舞弊展开的,因此选项 D 可排除。

Text 16

It may poison the 2016 election, but the Supreme Court should strike down Texas's restrictive abortion law.

As if next year's presidential election were not shaping up to be contentious enough, the Supreme Court has picked 2016 to issue its most consequential ruling on abortion in 20 years. This will add fresh impetus to a cultural battle that has raged, unresolved, on America's national stage for almost half a century. That is regrettable. It is also necessary.

At issue is whether a law passed by the Texas legislature called HB2 is constitutional. The state has piled regulations on abortion clinics with the aim (so far rather successful) of closing them down. The number of such clinics in the state has dropped from 41 in 2012 to 18 at the last count. If the court rules next year that HB2 is constitutional, that number will shrink further. Other states keen to restrict legal access to abortion would follow suit. Already there are four that have only one clinic for the whole state, making the legal termination of a pregnancy a right that exists in theory but not in practice.

A clear majority of Americans have, for decades, told pollsters that abortion should be legal in most cases. More recently, a narrower majority has emerged for outlawing abortion after 20 weeks, with some exceptions. That position—access to abortion that is legal and unrestricted until late in the second trimester, with some restrictions thereafter—is not unlike the compromise reached in other countries. In more secular Britain abortion is banned after 24 weeks, with exceptions in cases where to continue the pregnancy would threaten the life of the mother, or where the child is likely to be severely disabled. The Supreme Court itself has already endorsed limits after 24 weeks, the point at which a fetus is considered to be viable outside the womb, putting it squarely alongside public opinion.

The best way forward would be to pass legislation to this effect. But there is no chance of that, because the two sides are farther apart than ever, with some pro-choice groups arguing that abortion is an absolute right that cannot be restricted under any circumstances, and their pro-life opponents retorting that all abortions are acts of murder. The shift to the extremes has been most noticeable among Republicans. Marco Rubio, who currently looks a good bet to win his party's presidential nomination, is in favour of any law that promises to reduce the number of abortions, even one without exclusions for rape or incest. In the past four years state legislatures have put in place 231 restrictions on abortions—more than in the whole of the previous decade.

That nine unelected justices can do a better job of reflecting what America, in aggregate, favors than thousands of elected politicians in Washington or state capitols—as they did when ruling for gay marriage—is a painful indictment of American politics. It is nevertheless true. Despite the reaction it will provoke, the court should strike down.

(*The Economist*, 2015.11)

1. It can be inferred from the first two paragraphs that _____.
   A. the Supreme Court has imposed a poisonous impact on the 2016 election
   B. Americans have fiercely debated the legitimacy of abortion for a long time
   C. the 2016 election has prompted the abolishment of Texas's abortion law
   D. it is regrettable that Texas launched a cultural battle against the Supreme Court

2. What will happen if HB2 is legitimized by the constitution?
   A. It will invalidate the legal right to terminate pregnancy.
   B. It will eliminate all the abortion clinics in the state of Texas.
   C. It will bring another baby boom in America.
   D. It will expand the abortion clinics' business in other states.
3. Britain is cited as an example in paragraph 4 to show _____.
   A. that American pollsters pose a profound influence on abortion law
   B. that timing is a crucial factor in the legitimacy of abortion in America
   C. the necessity of abortion under urgent circumstances
   D. that religion plays an essential role in Americans' compromise of abortion
4. Why is it impossible to solve the divergence on abortion through legislation?
   A. Republicans have taken the leading position in the establishment of laws.
   B. There is an insurmountable gap between the two sides.
   C. Abortion is not an absolute right under the circumstances of rape or incest.
   D. Too many restrictions on abortion have been put into effect.
5. Which of the following is the best title for the text?
   A. HB2: Come to an End
   B. The Only Way out for Texas
   C. HB2 and Its Supporters
   D. Pros and Cons of Abortion Law

语篇分析与试题精解

Para. 1 ①It may poison the 2016 election, but the Supreme Court should strike down Texas's restrictive abortion law.

Para. 2 ①As if next year's presidential election were not shaping up to be contentious enough, the Supreme Court has picked 2016 to issue its most consequential ruling on abortion in 20 years. ②This will add fresh impetus to a cultural battle that has raged, unresolved, on America's national stage for almost half a century. ③That is regrettable. ④It is also necessary.

参考译文 ①尽管可能对2016年选举产生不利影响,最高法院还是应该废除得克萨斯州的限制堕胎法。

参考译文 ①似乎明年的总统选举还没有引起足够大的争议,最高法院选定在2016年发布近二十年来最为重要的关于堕胎问题的裁决。②这将再次激起一场全美文化战争,这场悬而未决的激烈争辩已经在美国持续了快半个世纪了。③虽然有些可悲。④却很有必要。

原文剖析 第一段和第二段可以合并理解,第二段内容可看作对第一段的具体说明。首段由一句话构成,后半句转折指出观点:最高法院应该废除得州的限制堕胎法。第二段首句细化了第一段内容,指出最高法院这样做的一个影响是会给下一年的总统选举添乱(好像总统选举带来的话题性还不够强烈),第二句指出另一个影响:再次挑起长达半个世纪的文化争辩。最后两句给出作者评价:虽然可悲,但有必要。

设题点睛 第二段的第二句适合设置相关考题。第二段第三、四句的内容虽然重要,但是观点明确,很难针对其设置干扰项,所以一般不设置试题。

生词解析

poison *vt.* 阻碍，败坏
abortion *n.* 流产
contentious *adj.* 引起争论的
rage *vi.* 发怒
restrictive *adj.* 限制性的，约束的
shape up 顺利发展
consequential *adj.* 重要的
unresolved *adj.* 悬而未决的

1 It can be inferred from the first two paragraphs that _____.

A. the Supreme Court has imposed a poisonous impact on the 2016 election
B. Americans have fiercely debated the legitimacy of abortion for a long time
C. the 2016 election has prompted the abolishment of Texas's abortion law
D. it is regrettable that Texas launched a cultural battle against the Supreme Court

从文章前两段可以推知_____。

A. 最高法院对2016年选举产生了不利影响
B. 美国人就堕胎是否合法激烈争论了很长时间
C. 2016年选举促使得克萨斯州堕胎法被废除
D. 可悲的是得克萨斯州挑起了对抗最高法院的文化战争

【解题思路】B。推理引申题。根据题干要求定位到文章前两段。首段只有一句，后半句提出观点，指出最高法院应该废除得州的限制堕胎法。第二段首句基本等同于首段，再次强调最高法院做出这个决定的时机在政治上较为敏感，第二句中的that定语从句对有关堕胎的全美文化辩论进行说明，从that has raged, unresolved, on America's national stage for almost half a century的描述中可看出这场辩论历时长久但还没有结果，这与选项B的内容基本相同，既然涉及法律，那么一定是在讨论堕胎这一问题的合法性，所以选项B是正确答案。

【排他分析】选项A对应首段的前半句话，原文使用了may poison，体现对未来情况的假设，而选项A用完成时态体现出这是一个既定事实，所以排除。选项C对应文章前两段，文中指出最高法院废除得州限制堕胎法的做法可能影响总统选举并激起社会讨论，但总统选举和该法案的废除没有直接的因果关系，该项属于张冠李戴，可以排除。选项D对应第二段，倒数第二句所说的regrettable应指前一句谈到的美国人对堕胎是否合法的问题进行了长达半个世纪的争论，且激起文化战争的不是得州，而是最高法院的裁决，所以排除。

Para. 3 ①At issue is whether a law passed by the Texas legislature called HB2 is constitutional. ②The state has piled regulations on abortion clinics with the aim (so far rather successful) of closing them down. ③The number of such clinics in the state has dropped from 41 in 2012 to 18 at the last count. ④If the court rules next year that HB2 is constitutional, that number will

参考译文 ①争论的焦点在于得克萨斯州立法机构颁布的一项名为HB2的法案是否符合宪法。②此法案旨在对堕胎诊所采取一系列管制措施以使它们无法继续经营，并且到目前为止取得了不错的效果。③得克萨斯州堕胎诊所的数量从2012年的41家减少到最新统计的18家。④如果明年最

shrink further. ⑤ Other states keen to restrict legal access to abortion would follow suit. ⑥Already there are four that have only one clinic for the whole state, making the legal termination of a pregnancy a right that exists in theory but not in practice.

高法院裁决HB2合宪,这个数字还会继续缩水。⑤其他打算限制合法堕胎途径的州也会纷纷效仿。⑥现在已有四个州将堕胎诊所的数量控制在全州只有一家,使得合法终止妊娠成了一项名存实亡的权利。

【原文剖析】 本段对前文提到的得州限制堕胎法案进行说明。首句指出该法案的合宪性是问题的关键,也是需要最高法院裁决的。第二句介绍该法案的具体内容和目的:利用行政手段,间接减少堕胎诊所的数量。第三句描述了该法案目前的影响:得州堕胎诊所数量锐减。从第四句开始到最后一句是作者对最高法院判决该法案合宪所产生影响的预测:合法堕胎将名存实亡。

【设题点睛】 本段最重要的内容应该是该法案一旦合宪之后可能产生的影响(事件产生的影响比事件本身重要),所以可能会针对最后一句提问。

【生词解析】
at issue 争论中的   follow suit 效仿
termination n. 终止

2 What will happen if HB2 is legitimized by the constitution?
如果宪法认可HB2法案,那么会发生什么?

A. It will invalidate the legal right to terminate pregnancy.
A. 终止妊娠的合法权利就无效了。

B. It will eliminate all the abortion clinics in the state of Texas.
B. 得克萨斯州所有的堕胎诊所都会被取缔。

C. It will bring another baby boom in America.
C. 会引发美国出现新的生育高峰。

D. It will expand the abortion clinics' business in other states.
D. 会帮助其他州的堕胎诊所拓展业务。

【解题思路】A。事实细节题。根据题干关键词HB2和constitution可定位到第三段第一句。该句的内容与题干一致,但并不涉及本题考查的结果和影响。从第三段第四句开始,对该法案如果合宪所产生的结果进行了预测:诊所数量继续减少(第四句)、其他州将效仿(第五句)、合法终止妊娠的权利将名存实亡(第六句)。其中第六句是总结和概括,是选项A的同义替换,选项A中的invalidate等于文中的exists in theory but not in practice。

【排他分析】选项B对应第三段第四句,该句指出如果法案合宪,得州堕胎诊所的数量还会减少,但并未指出会全部消失,因此该项中的eliminate意思太过绝对,所以排除。根据第三段的描述,虽然可推断一旦该法案合宪,美国的女性就不能随意堕胎,婴儿出生率会有所增加,但是文章中没有明确提到这会带来生育高峰,选项C属于过度推断,所以排除。第三段第五句指出如果该法案合宪,其他州会效仿得州的做法(follow suit),即其他州也会限制堕胎诊所的数量,因此其他州堕胎诊所的生意自然会受到影响,而不会扩大,所以选项D排除。

Para. 4 ①A clear majority of Americans have, for decades, told pollsters that abortion should be legal in most cases. ②More recently, a narrower majority has emerged for outlawing abortion after 20 weeks, with some exceptions. ③That position—access to abortion that is legal and unrestricted until late in the second trimester, with some restrictions thereafter—is not unlike the compromise reached in other countries. ④In more secular Britain abortion is banned after 24 weeks, with exceptions in cases where to continue the pregnancy would threaten the life of the mother, or where the child is likely to be severely disabled. ⑤The Supreme Court itself has already endorsed limits after 24 weeks, the point at which a fetus is considered to be viable outside the womb, putting it squarely alongside public opinion.

参考译文 ①根据民意调查，绝大多数美国人几十年来一直认为堕胎在大多数情况下应该是合法的。②最近，将近一半美国人主张禁止怀孕20周以后堕胎，但允许有例外情况。③受孕六个月之前都可以合法、不受限制地堕胎，但六个月以后将会有所限制，这种立场与其他国家所做出的妥协相似。④在受宗教影响较小的英国，怀孕满24周就禁止进行人工流产，除非继续怀孕会威胁到母体生命，或者胎儿有患严重残疾的可能。⑤最高法院早已同意了24周这个限制，因为24周正是胎儿被视为可以在子宫外独立存活的时间点，这正好顺应了民意。

原文剖析 本段前两句用民意调查的结果指出大多数美国人对堕胎看法的变化：一直以来大多数美国人认为堕胎在大多数情况下是合法的，最近近一半人认为不应在怀孕20周之后堕胎。由此可以看出人们对堕胎行为提出了一定限制和要求。第三句和第四句就前一句谈到的20周的时间点进行讨论，指出很多国家规定24周之后堕胎违法，并以英国为例进行说明。第五句指出美国的最高法院也同意24周这个时间限制，并科学阐释了这个时间点的合理性（胎儿24周后可在母体外生存，因此不会威胁母体健康，不应被强制剥夺生命）。

设题点睛 本段有两个部分可以用来设置考点，一个是前两句体现的观点变化对比，另外一个是第三句和第四句构成的"观点＋例证"的结构。

生词解析

pollster *n.* 民意测验专家　　　　trimester *n.* 三个月
is not unlike 与……相似　　　　secular *adj.* 世俗的，非宗教的
endorse *vt.* 支持，赞同　　　　　fetus *n.* 胎儿
viable *adj.* 能养活的，可行的　　womb *n.* 子宫
squarely *adv.* 正好，干脆地

长难句解析

[句1] That position—access to abortion that is legal and unrestricted until late in
　　　　主语　　　　插入语　　　　　　　　　　定语从句
the second trimester, with some restrictions thereafter—is　not unlike the compromise
　　　　　　　　　　状语　　　　　　　　　系动词　　　　表语
reached in other countries.
后置定语

本句主干结构为 That position is not unlike the compromise。破折号中间的部分为插入语，

对 that position 进行解释说明,该插入语中包含一个 that 引导的定语从句,修饰 abortion。

[句2]In more secular Britain abortion is banned after 24 weeks, with exceptions in cases
　　　　　状语　　　　　　　主语　　 谓语　　　时间状语　　　　　 伴随状语
where to continue the pregnancy would threaten the life of the mother, or where the child
　　　　　　　　　　　　　　　　　定语从句
is likely to be severely disabled.

本句主句部分采用了被动语态,主干结构为 abortion is banned。该句包含一个"with + 名词"结构,作伴随状语,该状语中包含两个 where 引导的定语从句,采用了"先行词(抽象名词 cases)+关系副词(where)+定语从句"的用法,从句中不缺少主谓宾成分。

3 **Britain is cited as an example in paragraph 4 to show _____.**　　第四段列举英国的例子是为了说明_____。

A. that American pollsters pose a profound influence on abortion law
B. that timing is a crucial factor in the legitimacy of abortion in America
C. the necessity of abortion under urgent circumstances
D. that religion plays an essential role in Americans' compromise of abortion

A. 美国民意调查者对堕胎法产生了深远的影响
B. 时间对美国堕胎的合法性而言是重要因素
C. 在紧急情况下堕胎的必要性
D. 美国人之所以在堕胎问题上妥协,宗教发挥了重要作用

【解题思路】D。例子功能题。根据题干要求明确定位到第四段第四句,本句举例指出英国作为一个更加世俗的(more secular)国家,对于堕胎所限制的时间点为24周,相对于第二句谈到的美国一些人主张怀孕20周以后禁止堕胎而言更为宽松。结合第四句对英国特点的评价(更为世俗)可以推测出正是由于美国是一个更加宗教化的国家(美国清教徒不允许堕胎),才会出现美国公众在对待堕胎问题上不如英国宽松的现状。所以选项D是正确答案。

【排他分析】选项A中的 pollsters 对应本段首句,但该句只是说大部分美国民众对民意调查人员谈到应在大多数情况下认定堕胎合法,本项不符合原文意思,且与英国事例没有任何关系,所以排除。选项B中的 timing 针对该段第二句到最后一句中提到的不同的堕胎时间点(20 weeks, 24 weeks),但原文中时间点只是体现不同国家的要求,从英国所规定的24周的时间点无法推断出其与堕胎合法性之间的关系(即不能说24周合法,20周就不合法),因此排除。选项C中的 urgent circumstances 对应本段第四句有关英国事例中的 threaten the life of the mother 和 severely disabled,原文是说英国规定怀孕满24周禁止堕胎,除非有危险的情况出现,这是对选择24周作为时间节点的补充说明,并非例子想说明的观点,所以排除。

Para. 5 ①The best way forward would be to pass legislation to this effect. ②But there is no chance of that, because the two sides are farther

参考译文 ①最好的方式是通过立法来解决争议,②但现在看来似乎没有机会了,因为双方的分歧比以

apart than ever, with some pro-choice groups arguing that abortion is an absolute right that cannot be restricted under any circumstances, and their pro-life opponents retorting that all abortions are acts of murder. ③The shift to the extremes has been most noticeable among Republicans. ④Marco Rubio, who currently looks a good bet to win his party's presidential nomination, is in favour of any law that promises to reduce the number of abortions, even one without exclusions for rape or incest. ⑤In the past four years state legislatures have put in place 231 restrictions on abortions—more than in the whole of the previous decade.

往任何时候都大,主张堕胎合法的人们认为在任何情况下都不该约束这一绝对权力,然而反对堕胎合法化的人们认为任何时候的堕胎都与谋杀无异。③这种极端的转变在共和党中最为明显。④极有可能赢得党内提名的总统候选人马尔科·鲁比奥(Marco Rubio)就是一个例子,他赞同所有能降低堕胎率的法案,甚至强奸和乱伦造成怀孕的情况也不例外。⑤在过去的四年里,州立法机关已经通过了231条对堕胎的限制条令,这个数字超过了前十年的总和。

原文剖析 本段首句提出观点:最佳途径是通过立法达到规范的目的。第二句立刻用But转折,对这一观点表示了否定并且给出原因:支持方和反对方的分歧已经到了难以调和的地步(支持方认为堕胎是绝对权力,不应受限;反对方认为任何时候进行堕胎都无异于谋杀)。第三句到第五句对第二句的反对派观点进行举例说明,第三句指出共和党属于明显的反对派,第四句用该党未来可能的总统候选人的观点举例说明第三句,最后一句给出事实:州立法机关实施了231条堕胎限制令,来证明反对派态度的坚定。

设题点睛 本段第二句为带有"转折+原因"结构的长难句,最适合设置题目。

生词解析
to this effect 为此目的   nomination n. 任命,提名
incest n. 乱伦,近亲通婚

长难句解析
But there is no chance of that, because the two sides are farther apart than ever,
　　　there be 句型　　主语　　　　　　原因状语从句
with some pro-choice groups arguing that abortion is an absolute right that cannot be
　　　　伴随状语1　　　　　　　　宾语从句1　　　　　　定语从句
restricted under any circumstances, and their pro-life opponents retorting that all abortions
　　　　　　　　　　　　　　　　　　伴随状语2　　　　　　　　　宾语从句2
are acts of murder.

本句是主从复合句,本句主干为there is no chance of that, because…,"with+名词+现在分词"的结构作伴随状语,表示主动和进行状态,该结构的主干为with some pro-choice groups arguing… and their pro-life opponents reporting…,包含两个宾语从句和一个定语从句。

4 Why is it impossible to solve the divergence on abortion through legislation?

为什么不可能用立法的方式来解决堕胎分歧?

A. Republicans have taken the leading position in the establishment of laws.

A. 共和党在立法上居于主导地位。

B. There is an insurmountable gap between the two sides.

C. Abortion is not an absolute right under the circumstances of rape or incest.

D. Too many restrictions on abortion have been put into effect.

B. 两方有不可跨越的鸿沟。

C. 堕胎在强奸或乱伦情况下不是绝对权力。

D. 关于堕胎的很多限令已经开始生效。

【解题思路】B。事实细节题。根据顺序原则和题干关键词 divergence 和 legislation，基本可定位在第五段，本题旨在询问原因。该段第二句转折指出通过立法无法解决分歧的原因：双方分歧已经太大（the two sides are farther apart than ever），直接对应选项 B 的 insurmountable gap（难以逾越的鸿沟），因此该项正确。

【排他分析】选项 A 谈到的 Republicans 在第五段第三句中出现，原文指出共和党对于堕胎的态度明显走向极端，但并没有提到该党派在立法上的地位，所以排除。选项 C 中的 rape or incest 对应第五段第四句，该句阐述共和党人马尔科·鲁比奥的观点，指出即便是在强奸和乱伦造成怀孕的情况下，也不能实施堕胎，该项中 absolute right 出现在第二句中，支持者认为堕胎是一种绝对权力，任何情况都不应约束该权力，原文两句间并无关系，且无法解释题干所问，因此该项是利用原文细节编造的干扰项，可排除。选项 D 对应第五段最后一句，文中指出，州立法机关已经通过了231条堕胎限制令，这一事实只能说明反对方的努力程度，而不能直接解释为何无法通过立法解决堕胎争议，所以排除。

Para. 6 ①That nine unelected justices can do a better job of reflecting what America, in aggregate, favors than thousands of elected politicians in Washington or state capitols—as they did when ruling for gay marriage—is a painful indictment of American politics. ② It is nevertheless true. ③Despite the reaction it will provoke, the court should strike down.

参考译文 ①总体而言，还未选出的九位大法官在反映美国人心声方面，可以做得比几千位国会或州议会政客当初裁决同性婚姻时更好些，这是对美国政治的痛苦控诉。②确实如此。③最高法院应该废除限制堕胎法，即便这样做会一石激起千层浪。

原文剖析 本段首句表明作者的观点：还未选出的九名大法官能比目前的政客更好地代表民意。第二句为过渡句。第三句总结，重申作者对于得州限制堕胎法案的看法：理应被最高法院废除。

设题点睛 本段内容中最重要的是最后一句总结，已经在文章首段提出，此处用于呼应，所以本段并没有太重要的值得考查的新信息存在。

生词解析

in aggregate 总体而言，归结起来　　capitol *n.* 国会大厦；州议会大厦

indictment *n.* 起诉，控诉

长难句解析

That nine unelected justices can do a better job of reflecting what America, in aggregate,

　　　　主语从句　　　　　　　　　　　后置定语　　　　宾语从句

173

favors than thousands of elected politicians in Washington or state capitols—
比较状语
as they did when ruling for gay marriage— is a painful indictment of American politics.
插入语　　　　　系动词　　　　　表语

本句主干为 That nine unelected justices can do a better job than… is a indictment,为主系表结构,主语是由 that 引导的名词性从句(不应将 that 看作修饰 nine unelected justices,否则应使用 those),该从句宾语 job 后为 of 介宾短语作后置定语,其中 what 引导的从句作 reflecting 的宾语,破折号之间的部分为插入语。

5 Which of the following is the best title for the text?　以下哪项最适合作本文的标题?

A. HB2: Come to an End　　　　　　A. HB2 法案:将被废除
B. The Only Way out for Texas　　　 B. 得克萨斯州的唯一出路
C. HB2 and Its Supporters　　　　　 C. HB2 法案及其支持者
D. Pros and Cons of Abortion Law　　D. 堕胎法案的正反双方

【解题思路】A。主旨大意题。选择最佳标题的题目也应看作是对全文主旨的考查。如果文章中作者的观点十分明确,则此类题的正确选项往往和作者观点一致。本文首段和最后一段首尾呼应,反复表达了作者认为最高法院应该废除得州限制堕胎法,即 HB2 法案,只有选项 A 的意思贴近这一主旨,因此该项正确。

【排他分析】文中只对得州 HB2 法案产生的效果进行了描述,并没有谈到得州的"出路"在哪,选项 B 在文中没有涉及,直接排除。选项 C 存在一定迷惑性,因为第三段和第五段确实提到了一些州和共和党人士对于限制堕胎法案的支持,但是根据作者所阐述的观点,文章最终要表达的是最高法院应该废除限制堕胎的法案,而非支持,该项只涉及原文部分内容,且并非主旨,可排除。选项 D 主要针对第五段的内容,虽然该段谈到了对堕胎问题的支持者和反对者,但并未体现作者对该问题的看法,该项也只涉及部分内容,所以排除。

Text 17

　　Perhaps the oldest management cliché is that "people are our most important asset". If that were true, companies would rigorously assess their own hiring practices, and their record, to ensure that they are indeed recruiting the best people. Remarkably, many fail miserably at this task. Only a third of American companies check whether their recruitment process produces good employees. That is one of the striking revelations in a recent survey of hiring by Peter Cappelli, professor of management at the Wharton School in Philadelphia.

　　When companies are asked why they do not monitor the effectiveness of hiring, the most common response is that measuring employee performance is too difficult. Given that staff costs are the single biggest expense item at many companies, this is a startling admission.

And, as Mr. Cappelli points out, there are some simple things employers could do: check how long newly hired workers stay at the company, or ask a supervisor whether they regret the hiring decision.

Companies often seem to be channelling Groucho Marx in their approach to applicants: they won't hire someone who is actively looking for work. Employers seem to operate on the principle that there must be something wrong with someone who is unhappy with their current job. Instead they aim to lure "passive" candidates who have shown no sign of wanting to move. Inevitably, this is time-consuming. <u>It can also come back to bite companies</u>, as rival firms compete to lure away each other's staff.

In turn, the employment merry-go-round leads to an arms' race, and thus higher costs. After all, employees happy with their current job are likely to need a greater inducement to move. Mr. Cappelli has not discovered any evidence that hiring outsiders is more cost-effective than hiring other workers, or that passive candidates make better employees.

The best interview strategy is to ask all applicants the same set of predetermined questions. That way answers can be fairly compared. Managers, though, tend to improvise, looking for workers who will be a "<u>cultural fit</u>", with questions like "what would you do if stranded on a desert island?" Unsurprisingly, this technique is subject to the biases of the interviewers, who then tend to recruit people most like themselves. Automated hiring algorithms reproduce this effect if they are trained on the characteristics of existing employees.

So how can companies improve? Mr. Cappelli suggests that firms post all job openings internally, check how many positions are filled from within, and make a greater effort to see how outside hires perform.

(*The Economist*, 2019.5)

1. According to paragraph 1, the author may agree that _____.
    A. few believe the oldest management cliché
    B. companies should improve their hiring strategy
    C. many companies may fail to hire the right people
    D. strict recruitment process equals to good employee

2. Companies' answer is surprising because _____.
    A. they could have took some plain steps
    B. they neglected the high cost of employees
    C. they failed to assess their own hiring practices
    D. they think little of employees' performance

3. By saying "It can also come back to bite companies", the author means that _____.
    A. passive job seekers are harmful to the company
    B. rival firms will win in the hiring arms' race

C. what employers do will result in higher costs

D. outsiders generally have a high salary requirement

4. Hiring arms' race causes higher costs because _____.

A. passive candidates proved to be greedy

B. a better employee is qualified for a greater pay

C. outsiders are said to be more cost-efficient

D. a higher salary is a kind of incentives

5. According to paragraph 5, the "cultural fit" is more likely to accord with that of _____.

A. the interviewees   B. the interviewers

C. the companies   D. the trainers

语篇分析与试题精解

Para. 1 ①Perhaps the oldest management cliché is that "people are our most important asset". ②If that were true, companies would rigorously assess their own hiring practices, and their record, to ensure that they are indeed recruiting the best people. ③Remarkably, many fail miserably at this task. ④Only a third of American companies check whether their recruitment process produces good employees. ⑤That is one of the striking revelations in a recent survey of hiring by Peter Cappelli, professor of management at the Wharton School in Philadelphia.

参考译文 ①也许最古老的管理方面的陈词滥调是"人是我们最重要的资产"。②如果这是真的,公司将严格评估自己的招聘行为和招聘记录,以确保他们确实在招聘最优秀的人才。③值得注意的是,许多公司在这项任务上惨败。④只有三分之一的美国公司检查了他们的招聘过程是否能引进优秀的员工。⑤这是费城沃顿商学院管理学教授彼得·卡佩里(Peter Cappelli)在最近一项招聘调查中令人震惊的发现之一。

原文剖析 本段借一项调查研究结果指出多数公司都没有监测招聘过程是否能引进优秀员工。文章首句引用一句俗语开篇,第二句指出按照俗语公司应该怎么做,第三、四句指出只有少数公司做到了,该结果令人震惊。

设题点睛 本段第一句中有带引号的内容,可根据其与下文之间的关系设题;本段还引用了一项调查结果,可考查其引用目的或产生该结果的原因等。

生词解析

cliché n. 陈词滥调,老生常谈   rigorously adv. 严厉地;残酷地

practice n. 通常的做法;惯例;常规   recruit vt. 招聘;聘用

remarkably adv. 显著地;引人注目地   striking adj. 惊人的,显著的

revelation n. 启示;揭露

长难句解析

If that were true, companies would rigorously assess their own hiring practices, and
条件状语从句   主语   状语   谓语   宾语1

their record, to ensure that they are indeed recruiting the best people.
宾语2　　目的状语　　　　　　　宾语从句

本句是主从复合句。本句主干为 companies would rigorously assess their own hiring practices and record,主句有两个并列宾语,不定式结构 to ensure… 作目的状语,that 引导的从句作 ensure 的宾语。

1 According to paragraph 1, the author may agree that _____ .　　根据第一段,作者可能赞同_____。

A. few believe the oldest management cliché
B. companies should improve their hiring strategy
C. many companies may fail to hire the right people
D. strict recruitment process equals to good employee

A. 很少有人相信最古老的管理方面的陈词滥调
B. 公司应该改进他们的招聘策略
C. 许多公司可能没有招到合适的人
D. 严格的招聘程序等于优秀的员工

【解题思路】C。推理判断题。根据题干关键词定位到第一段。第二、三句指出,如果这是真的,公司将严格评估自己的招聘行为和招聘记录,以确保他们确实在招聘最优秀的人才。值得注意的是,许多公司在这项任务上惨败。这项任务就是严格评估自己的招聘行为和招聘记录,任务失败也就是没有严格评估自己的招聘行为和招聘记录,也就可能会导致招聘不到最优秀的人才,选项 C 属于合理推断,故为正确答案。

【排他分析】文中第二句说的是在这种陈词滥调下,公司应该怎么做,第四句指出三分之一的美国公司是这么做的,选项 A 中的 few 错误,因此排除。文中说的是公司应严格评估自己的招聘行为,并非其招聘策略有问题,选项 B 曲解文意,因此排除。优秀的员工是由多种因素决定的,选项 D 过于绝对,因此排除。

Para. 2 ①When companies are asked why they do not monitor the effectiveness of hiring, the most common response is that measuring employee performance is too difficult. ②Given that staff costs are the single biggest expense item at many companies, this is a startling admission. ③And, as Mr. Cappelli points out, there are some simple things employers could do: check how long newly hired workers stay at the company, or ask a supervisor whether they regret the hiring decision.

参考译文　①当公司被问及为何不监测招聘的有效性时,最常见的回答是,衡量员工的表现太难了。②考虑到员工成本是许多公司最大的支出项目,这个回答令人吃惊。③而且,正如卡佩里先生所指出的那样,雇主可以做一些简单的事情:检查新员工在公司待了多长时间,或者问问主管是否后悔当初的聘用决定。

原文剖析　本段承接上文,指出公司不监测招聘有效性的原因以及作者对此原因的态度,第三句引用卡佩里的话再次表达作者吃惊的态度。

设题点睛　本段包含明显的态度观点句,可设置题目考查态度背后的原因。

> 生词解析

monitor *vt.* 监视；跟踪调查　　　　　startling *adj.* 令人吃惊的
supervisor *n.* 主管人；监督人

> 长难句解析

When companies are asked　why they do not monitor the effectiveness of hiring, the
　　　时间状语从句　　　　　　　　宾语从句
most common response　is　that measuring employee performance is too difficult.
　主语　　　　系动词　　　　　　表语从句

本句是主从复合句，本句主干为 the most common response is that…，when 引导的时间状语从句中包含一个由 why 引导的宾语从句，主句为主系表结构，表语由 that 引导的表语从句充当。

2 Companies' answer is surprising because _____. | 公司的回答令人惊讶，因为_____。

A. they could have took some plain steps
B. they neglected the high cost of employees
C. they failed to assess their own hiring practices
D. they think little of employees' performance

A. 他们本可以采取一些简单的措施
B. 他们忽视了员工的高成本
C. 他们没有评估自己的招聘行为
D. 他们很少考虑员工的表现

【解题思路】A。事实细节题。根据题干及顺序原则定位到第二段。第一句说明了公司的回答，第二句表明了作者吃惊的态度，第三句作者引用卡佩里的话指出，雇主可以做一些简单的事情，显然雇主都没有做，这也是作者感到吃惊的一方面原因，因此选项 A 为正确答案。

【排他分析】第二句提到考虑到员工成本是大多数公司最大的支出项目，这个回答令人吃惊。这里说的是作者考虑到员工成本，并未提及公司有没有考虑员工成本，选项 B 属于无中生有，因此排除。评估招聘行为是首段的内容，与本题无关，选项 C 排除。文章指出，公司认为衡量员工的表现太难了，并非没有考虑员工的表现，选项 D 与原文不符，因此排除。

Para. 3 ① Companies often seem to be channelling Groucho Marx in their approach to applicants: they won't hire someone who is actively looking for work. ②Employers seem to operate on the principle that there must be something wrong with someone who is unhappy with their current job. ③ Instead they aim to lure "passive" candidates who have shown no sign of wanting to move. ④Inevitably, this is time-consuming. ⑤It

> 参考译文

①公司在对待求职者的方式上，似乎经常采用格劳乔·马克思（Groucho Marx）的方法：他们不会聘用那些找工作特别积极的人。②雇主们的经营原则似乎是：对目前的工作不满意的人肯定有什么问题。③相反，他们的目标是吸引那些没有表现出要跳槽迹象的"被动"求职者。④这样做难免会非

can also come back to bite companies, as rival firms compete to lure away each other's staff.

常费时。⑤当竞争对手相互竞争以吸引对方的员工时,它也会反过来咬公司一口。

原文剖析 本段叙述了公司对待求职者的方式、雇主们的经营原则以及他们的招聘目标。最后两句作者表明观点:这种做法既费时,可能还会给公司带来负面影响。

设题点睛 本段最后两句包含作者的观点态度,可用来设置正确选项,也可设题考查"反过来咬公司一口"到底是什么意思。

生词解析

channel *vt.* 引导;把……用于
lure *vt.* 吸引(其他公司或地方的顾客、工人、资金等)
approach *n.* 方法,方式
rival *n.* 对手;竞争者

3 By saying "It can also come back to bite companies", the author means that _____.

A. passive job seekers are harmful to the company
B. rival firms will win in the hiring arms' race
C. what employers do will result in higher costs
D. outsiders generally have a high salary requirement

通过说"它也会反过来咬公司一口",作者认为_____。

A. 被动的求职者对公司是有害的
B. 竞争对手将在招聘的军备竞赛中获胜
C. 雇主的做法将增加成本
D. 外部员工通常对薪水要求很高

【解题思路】C。事实细节题。根据题干关键词定位到第三段最后一句。第四句和最后一句都在说雇主的做法的弊端。那么第五句所指的弊端到底是什么,接着看下一段。第四段首句指出,反过来,就业的旋转木马引发了军备竞赛,从而导致更高的成本。第四段首句中的 in turn 与 come back to 为同义,因此雇主的做法增加了成本,选项 C 符合文意,是正确答案。

【排他分析】文章说吸引"被动"求职者是耗时的,选项 A 中的 harmful 程度过于严重,可排除。选项 B 利用第五句中的 rival firms 作干扰,但选项 B 所述内容原文未提及,属于无中生有,因此排除。文中并未提及 high salary 相关内容,选项 D 排除。

Para. 4 ① In turn, the employment merry-go-round leads to an arms' race, and thus higher costs. ② After all, employees happy with their current job are likely to need a greater inducement to move. ③ Mr. Cappelli has not discovered any evidence that hiring outsiders is more cost-effective than hiring other workers, or that passive candidates make better employees.

参考译文 ①反过来,雇用的旋转木马引发了军备竞赛,从而使成本更高了。②毕竟,对目前工作感到满意的员工可能需要更大的动力才会跳槽。③卡佩里先生还没有发现任何证据表明雇用外部员工比雇用其他员工更划算,或者证明被动的候选人能成为更好的员工。

原文剖析 本段承接上文，首句指出雇主的做法引发军备竞赛，给公司带来更高的成本。第二句解释带来更高的成本的原因，第三句作者借卡佩里先生的研究发现反面表明他对雇主的做法的怀疑或是不赞同。

设题点睛 本段与上文联系密切，首句可以根据上文内容设置正确答案，还可以设置题目考查成本更高的原因；或者根据最后一句，考查作者的观点态度。

生词解析

in turn 反过来；转而
arms' race 军备竞赛
cost-effective adj. 有成本效益的
merry-go-round n. 旋转木马；一连串的繁忙活动
inducement n. 诱因，刺激物

长难句解析

Mr. Cappelli has not discovered any evidence that hiring outsiders is more cost-effective
　　主语　　　　　谓语　　　　宾语　　　　　　同位语从句1
than hiring other workers, or that passive candidates make better employees.
　　比较状语　　　　　　　　同位语从句2

本句是主从复合句，本句主干为 Mr. Cappelli has not discovered any evidence that…, or 连接的两个从句作宾语 any evidence 的同位语，介词短语 than hiring… 作同位语从句1 的比较状语。

4 Hiring arms' race causes higher costs because _____ .	雇用军备竞赛会导致成本增加，因为_____。
A. passive candidates proved to be greedy	A. 被动的候选人被证明是贪婪的
B. a better employee is qualified for a greater pay	B. 一个更好的员工有资格获得更高的薪水
C. outsiders are said to be more cost-efficient	C. 雇用外部员工据说更划算
D. a higher salary is a kind of incentives	D. 更高的薪水是一种激励

【解题思路】D。推理判断题。根据题干关键词定位到第四段。第一句，即题干表明，反过来，雇用的旋转木马引发了军备竞赛，从而使成本更高了。第二句表明，毕竟，对目前工作感到满意的员工可能需要更大的动力才会跳槽，这说明，对于那些对目前工作感到满意的员工而言，更高的薪资可能是一种跳槽的动力，这也就导致了雇用公司更高的成本，选项D属于合理推断，故为正确答案。

【排他分析】选项A中的greedy(贪婪的)文章未提及，属于无中生有，故排除。选项B所述内容本身可能是对的，但与本文无关，且这场军备竞赛中，竞争的是外部员工，根据第三句，卡佩里先生还没有发现任何证据表明雇用外部员工比雇用其他员工更划算，可知外部员工并不一定就是 a better employee，选项B排除。选项C明显与第三句文意相悖，故排除。

―――――――――――――――――――――――――――――

Para. 5 ①The best interview strategy is to ask all applicants the same set of predetermined questions. ②That way answers can be fairly compared.

参考译文 ①最好的面试策略是问所有求职者相同的预先确定的问题。②这样答案就可以比较。

③Managers, though, tend to improvise, looking for workers who will be a "cultural fit", with questions like "what would you do if stranded on a desert island?" ④Unsurprisingly, this technique is subject to the biases of the interviewers, who then tend to recruit people most like themselves. ⑤Automated hiring algorithms reproduce this effect if they are trained on the characteristics of existing employees.

③然而,经理们往往会即兴发挥,寻找"文化契合度"高的员工,提出诸如"如果被困在荒岛上,你会怎么做?"等问题。④不出所料,这种方法会受到面试官的偏见影响,而面试官往往会招聘最像自己的人。⑤如果根据现有员工的特点进行培训,自动招聘算法会重现这种效果。

【原文剖析】 本段前两句作者指出他认为的最好的面试策略。第三句指出经理们的实际做法,第四、五句说明这种做法的弊端及弊端的必然性。

【设题点睛】 本段中含有转折及观点态度的相关内容,可设置正确选项;第三句中还含有带引号的内容,可用来设置题目。

【生词解析】
predetermined *adj.* 预先确定的
strand *vt.* 使陷于困境;使搁浅
reproduce *vt.* 使再次发生;再现
improvise *vi.* 即兴创作;即兴表演
algorithms *n.* [计]算法

5. According to paragraph 5, the "cultural fit" is more likely to accord with that of _____.

A. the interviewees
B. the interviewers
C. the companies
D. the trainers

根据第五段,"文化契合度"更可能符合_____的"文化"。

A. 面试者
B. 面试官
C. 公司
D. 训练员

【解题思路】B。事实细节题。根据题干关键词直接定位到第五段。第三句指出,然而,经理们往往会即兴发挥,寻找"文化契合度"高的员工;第四句接着说道,不出所料,这种方法会受到面试官的偏见影响,而面试官往往会招聘最像自己的人。面试官招聘最像自己的人,所以"文化契合度"更符合面试官自己,因此选项 B 为正确答案。

【排他分析】根据以上分析可知,选项 A 与选项 C 均与原文不符,故排除。文中并未提及选项 D,选项 D 利用文中的 trained 作干扰,故排除。

Para. 6 ①So how can companies improve? ②Mr. Cappelli suggests that firms post all job openings internally, check how many positions are filled from within, and make a greater effort to see how outside hires perform.

【参考译文】①那么,企业该如何改进呢?②卡佩里先生建议公司在内部发布所有的职位空缺,检查有多少职位是由内部填补的,并且更加努力地观察外部员工的表现。

【原文剖析】 本段相当于一个转折指出卡佩里先生所认为的公司招聘的正确做法。

【设题点睛】 本段较短,且属于陈述客观事实,不包含观点态度,不适合设题。

生词解析

job opening 职位空缺

长难句解析

Mr. Cappelli suggests that firms post all job openings internally, check how many
　　主语　　　谓语　　　　　宾语从句1　　　　　　　从句谓语1
positions are filled from within, and make a greater effort to see how outside hires
　　　　宾语从句2　　　　　　从句谓语2　　宾语　　状语　　宾语从句3
perform.

本句是主从复合句，本句主干为 Mr. Cappelli suggests that…, that 引导的从句较长，作 suggests 的宾语。that 引导的宾语从句1由三个并列的谓宾结构构成，三个并列谓语分别为 post, check 和 make，且宾语从句1省略了 should。how 引导的从句2作 check 的宾语，从句3作 see 的宾语。

Text 18

　　Britain's top universities have long been among the world's most sought-after destinations for study and research, drawing the brightest minds from all corners of the globe. But since Britons voted in June to leave the 28-nation EU, many in the science community say the U. K. risks losing the money, the international influence—and crucially, the talent—to sustain that enviable position.

　　More than one-tenth of research funding at British universities has come from the EU in recent years. Some fields are more dependent on EU funding than others, according to a report by technology firm Digital Science. From 2007 to 2013, Britain received 8.8 billion euros ($9.4 billion) in direct EU investment in research.

　　Scientists and researchers argue that being part of the EU has given British science a huge boost because it allows Britain to recruit the best talent across Europe and take part in important research collaborations and student exchanges without being constrained by national boundaries. The bloc's freedom of movement means its 500 million people can live and work visa-free in any member state.

　　No one knows yet what form Britain's exit from the EU—commonly known as Brexit—is going to take, but immigration was a key issue for "Leave" voters. Many believe some limit should be put on the number of EU citizens moving to Britain.

　　Prime Minister Theresa May has vowed to reassert control over British borders. She has offered no firm guarantees for the rights of Europeans already living in Britain, an uncertainty that weighs heavily over the 32,000 Europeans who make up 16 percent of the academic workforce in British universities. Many universities say the rhetoric over immigration control is also jeopardizing recruitment of researchers and students from further afield.

　　Adam Durrant, a British entrepreneur who founded an aerospace startup supplying climate data to airlines and aircraft manufacturers, says he's now considering moving some of his business to a EU country outside of Britain. Part of the reason, he says, is that Brexit will likely make hiring the right people much harder than before.

Similar anxieties are being felt at the undergraduate level. The 125,000 European students studying at British universities now pay the same fees as locals and have access to the same government loans. Officials have promised this will not change for those applying next year—but no one knows what will happen after that.

"It's not all doom and gloom—but it will be harder," Ramakrishnan said, who is a Nobel Prize-winning biologist and president of Britain's prestigious Royal Society. "We could make a go of it outside the EU. But for that to happen, we have to attract talent and fund science. And those two things are critical."

(*The Christian Science Monitor*, 2016.12)

1. According to the first paragraph, what has EU brought to Britain?
   A. Britain's separation with the other 27 nations.
   B. Construction of Britain's science community.
   C. Britain's international financial influence.
   D. Britain's importance in the academic world.

2. It can be learned from the text that British immigration _____.
   A. should have more guaranteed rights after the Brexit
   B. is the paramount component in British universities
   C. would jeopardize the recruitment of researchers from abroad
   D. is a pivotal cause for the realization of Brexit

3. Why dose Adam Durrant want to move his business out of Britain?
   A. Britain's climate data is harder to detect.
   B. Brexit can pose a threat to his aircraft manufacture.
   C. Brexit may hinder the free flow of talented workers.
   D. Brexit makes it impossible to hire the right people.

4. By citing the example of the 125,000 European students, the author intends to _____.
   A. show a potential threat faced by them
   B. stress the benefit from the government loans
   C. highlight the promise made by the local officials
   D. illustrate the anxieties of the British undergraduates

5. Which of the following is the best title for the text?
   A. Brexit, the Doom for the British Business Men
   B. Brexit, an Alarm for the British Academic World
   C. Brexit, Risk and Opportunity Combined
   D. Brexit, a Gloomy Future for the Talented over the World

语篇分析与试题精解

Para. 1 ① Britain's top universities have long been among the world's most sought-after destinations for study and research, drawing the brightest minds from all corners of the globe. ② But since Britons voted in June to leave the 28-nation EU, many in the science community say the U.K. risks losing the money, the international influence—and crucially, the talent—to sustain that enviable position.

参考译文 ①英国诸多顶尖大学一直是求学者和研究者们最推崇的学术圣地之一,吸引着世界各地的优秀人才。②但自从六月份英国进行全民公投,确定退出已有二十八个成员国的欧盟之后,许多科学界人士认为,英国为了维持其让人称羡的地位而选择脱欧,是冒着经济损失、国际影响力下滑以及人才流失的风险而做出的举措,其中人才流失这一后果最为严重。

原文剖析 本段首句用现在完成时指出英国的大学自古以来一直被优秀人才广为推崇。第二句出现"转折+双破折"的结构,指出英国脱欧的决定可能带来的一系列负面影响。

设题点睛 第二句含有"转折+双破折"结构,可用来设置正确选项。

生词解析

sought-after adj. 受欢迎的,很吃香的
crucially adv. 关键地;至关重要地
risk doing sth. 冒险做某事
enviable adj. 值得羡慕的;引起忌妒的

长难句解析

But since Britons voted in June to leave the 28-nation EU, many in the science community
　　　　原因状语从句　　　　　　　　　主语　　　后置定语
say the U.K. risks losing the money, the international influence—and crucially, the talent—
谓语　　　　　宾语从句　　　　　　　　　　　　　　　　　　　插入语
to sustain that enviable position.
　　　目的状语

本句是主从复合句。本句主干为 But since…, many say…,句首出现 since 引导的原因状语从句,指出主句发生的条件和理由,主句的主语 many 可作代词,表示"许多人",由 in 引导的介词短语作后置定语对其修饰。谓语 say 后为省略 that 的宾语从句,破折号之间的内容作插入语,用于强调,最后的不定式作 risk doing sth. 的目的状语。

1 According to the first paragraph, what has EU brought to Britain?

A. Britain's separation with the other 27 nations.
B. Construction of Britain's science community.
C. Britain's international financial influence.
D. Britain's importance in the academic world.

根据第一段的内容,欧盟曾给英国带来过什么?

A. 英国与其他27个国家的分离。
B. 英国科学界的组建。
C. 英国在金融方面的国际影响力。
D. 英国在学术界的重要性。

【解题思路】D。推理引申题。根据题干要求定位到文章首段。本题实际考查欧盟为英国带来的好处。本段第二句描述了英国脱欧可能带来的坏处,可以以此反推出欧盟曾给英国带来的好处。原句指出如果离开欧盟, the U.K. risks losing the money, the international influence—and crucially, the talent(钱没了,国际影响力没了,人才也没了),涉及选项 D 学术重要性的相关内容,因此该项正确。

【排他分析】选项 A 所述的 separation with the other 27 nations(暗指英国的脱欧行为)是英国自己的决定,不是欧盟带给英国的,与所问不符,可排除。选项 B 为易混选项,文中确实出现了很多科学界的人士(many in the science community)对英国脱欧的担忧,但是并没有提到欧盟在建立英国学术界方面的作用,该项属于无端猜测,可排除。选项 C 中的 international financial influence(国际金融影响力)是对原文中 the money 和 the international influence 的拼凑,原文谈到的是两个方面,不能混为一谈,因此排除该项。

Para. 2 ①More than one-tenth of research funding at British universities has come from the EU in recent years. ②Some fields are more dependent on EU funding than others, according to a report by technology firm Digital Science. ③From 2007 to 2013, Britain received 8.8 billion euros ($9.4 billion) in direct EU investment in research.

参考译文 ①近年来,在英国高校的科研基金中,有超过十分之一的份额来自欧盟的资助。②一家名为数码科学的科技公司所做的报告显示,一些科研领域尤其依赖欧盟的赞助。③从 2007 年到 2013 年,欧盟对英国科研的直接投资高达 88 亿欧元(94 亿美元)。

原文剖析 本段从欧盟给予英国科研领域巨大经济支持的角度分析了英国的欧盟成员国身份是如何帮助其推动学术研究发展的,支持了欧盟对于英国学术界有好处的论断。

设题点睛 本段内容主要用数据举例,支持上段,段内单句内容简单,不宜设置考题。

Para. 3 ①Scientists and researchers argue that being part of the EU has given British science a huge boost because it allows Britain to recruit the best talent across Europe and take part in important research collaborations and student exchanges without being constrained by national boundaries. ②The bloc's freedom of movement means its 500 million people can live and work visa-free in any member state.

参考译文 ①科研人员认为,英国的欧盟成员国身份极大地推动了本国的科研发展,因为英国不仅可以利用这个身份广纳全欧洲最优秀的人才,而且可以突破国界的限制,在重大研究上开展合作,学生之间也可以进行交流。②欧盟成员国的公民可自由往来,这意味着五亿人可以在任意成员国内生活和工作,而不受签证的限制。

原文剖析 本段承接上段,从人才流动更为便利的角度指出英国的欧盟成员国身份对其学术研究发展有帮助。

设题点睛 本段与上一段一起作为支撑段落,但由于首句为带有原因状语从句的长难句,可以利用其原因部分设置正确选项。

生词解析

give sb. a boost 给予某人支持;提升
constrain vt. 束缚;驱使;强迫
visa-free(作形容词或副词)免签证;免护照
collaboration n. 合作,协作
bloc n. 集团(或政治组织)

长难句解析

Scientists and researchers argue that being part of the EU has given British science a huge boost because it allows Britain to recruit the best talent across Europe and take part in important research collaborations and student exchanges without being constrained by national boundaries.

（主语：Scientists and researchers；谓语：argue；宾语从句：that being part of the EU has given British science a huge boost；原因状语从句：because it allows Britain to recruit the best talent across Europe and take part in important research collaborations and student exchanges；状语：without being constrained by national boundaries）

本句为主从复合句。本句主干为 Scientists and researchers argue that... because...，其中谓语 argue 后为 that 引导的宾语从句，because 引导的状语从句解释主句的原因，句末的 without 介词短语作状语，体现伴随语意。

Para. 4 ① No one knows yet what form Britain's exit from the EU—commonly known as Brexit—is going to take, but immigration was a key issue for "Leave" voters. ② Many believe some limit should be put on the number of EU citizens moving to Britain.

参考译文 ①英国将采取何种形式脱离欧洲（即通常所说的"脱欧"）尚未可知，但对于支持脱欧的英国选民而言，"移民问题"是一个关键的考量因素。②很多人认为，英国应该限制欧盟公民入境的数量。

原文剖析 本段指出促成英国脱欧的重要原因之一是移民问题，与上一段结合理解后可看出，欧盟成员国身份所带来的人口流动性既有好处也有坏处。

设题点睛 本段首句转折，第二句解释原因，强调了移民因素，可利用这一关键内容设置题目。

生词解析

exit n. 退出，离开，退去　　　　　　immigration n. 外来移民；移居

some limit should be put on（=should put some limit on）应在……上设限

长难句解析

No one knows yet what form Britain's exit from the EU—commonly known as Brexit—is going to take, but immigration was a key issue for "Leave" voters.

（主语1：No one；谓语：knows；宾语从句：what form Britain's exit from the EU ... is going to take；插入语：commonly known as Brexit；主语2：immigration；系动词：was；表语：a key issue；状语：for "Leave" voters）

本句属于并列复合句。由 but 连接的两个并列的句子构成，第一个句子是主从复合句，含有由 what 引导的宾语从句，该从句被破折号引出的插入语隔开，其主干可完整理解为 No one knows what form Britain's exit... is going to take，使用了表示"具有一定形式，成形"的固定短语 take form。第二个句子为主系表结构，"Leave"加双引号含有特定含义，指支持"离开"的选民。

Para. 5 ①Prime Minister Theresa May has vowed to reassert control over British borders. ②She has offered no firm guarantees for the rights of

参考译文 ①英国首相特蕾莎·梅（Theresa May）宣布要重新控制英国边界。②但对居住在英国境内的

Europeans already living in Britain, an uncertainty that weighs heavily over the 32,000 Europeans who make up 16 percent of the academic workforce in British universities. ③ Many universities say the rhetoric over immigration control is also jeopardizing recruitment of researchers and students from further afield.

欧盟其他国家的公民的权利,她并未提供有力的保障,这一不确定性让32 000名欧洲学者(在英国高校的学术队伍中,他们占16%)如履薄冰。③许多大学表示,限制移民的说辞阻碍了它们招聘境外研究人员和招收留学生。

【原文剖析】 本段首句承接上段最后提到的"移民因素",表明英国政府的立场是要控制移民。第二句指出针对目前居住在英国的移民,现在政府对其权利并未提供确切的保障,第三句继而指出这种不确定性给英国的大学造成的影响,其中的rhetoric一词含有"花言巧语"的意思,明显体现大学对政府举措的消极态度。

【设题点睛】 本段第二句为长难句,提出了脱欧让英国境内的欧盟移民(尤其是研究人员)感到担忧这一新观点,可以利用其设置考点。

【生词解析】
vow vi. 郑重宣告;发誓
rhetoric n. 华丽的辞藻,花言巧语
from further afield 远道而来
weigh over(=weigh on) 使苦恼;重压于
jeopardize vt. 危及;使处于危险境地

【长难句解析】
She has offered no firm guarantees for the rights of Europeans already living in Britain, an
主语   谓语   宾语   状语   后置定语
uncertainty that weighs heavily over the 32,000 Europeans who make up 16 percent of the
                   定语从句1   定语从句2
academic workforce in British universities.

本句是主从复合句。本句主干为 She has offered no firm guarantees...,宾语后为 for 引出的状语,表示"为了……",living 为现在分词作后置定语修饰 Europeans。an uncertainty 可看作省略了 which is 的非限制性定语从句,an uncertainty 指代前面整句话,受其后的 that 引导的定语从句限定,最后 who 引导的定语从句的先行词是 the 32,000 Europeans。

2 It can be learned from the text that British immigration _____.

A. should have more guaranteed rights after the Brexit
B. is the paramount component in British universities
C. would jeopardize the recruitment of researchers from abroad
D. is a pivotal cause for the realization of Brexit

从文中可以了解到英国的移民_____。

A. 应在英国脱欧后享有更有保障的权利
B. 在英国大学里是最重要的组成部分
C. 将影响对外国研究员的招聘
D. 是导致英国脱欧的重要因素

【解题思路】D。事实细节题。根据题干关键词(British immigration)定位到第三段至第五段(四、五两段明显出现了immigration一词)。第四段第一句破折号之后谈到

but immigration was a key issue for "Leave" voters(对于支持脱欧的英国选民而言,"移民问题"是一个关键的考量因素),与选项 D 的内容一致。该项中的 pivotal cause 对应原文的 key issue,the realization of Brexit 对应原文中的"Leave",故选项 D 正确。【排他分析】选项 A 与第五段第二句的内容不一致,该句指出英国首相对居住在英国境内的欧盟其他国家公民的权利并未提供有力的保障,可推断英国一旦脱欧,英国内其他欧盟国家的移民的权利可能受到影响,因此排除该项。选项 B 与第五段第二句所谈到的 16% 的比例并不相符,因此 paramount component 的说法并无根据,排除该项。选项 C 直接对应第五段最后一句中的 jeopardizing recruitment of researchers(影响对研究人员的招聘),但是造成这一问题的并不是移民,而是对移民的限制政策,本项属于张冠李戴,可排除。

Para. 6 ①Adam Durrant, a British entrepreneur who founded an aerospace startup supplying climate data to airlines and aircraft manufacturers, says he's now considering moving some of his business to a EU country outside of Britain. ②Part of the reason, he says, is that Brexit will likely make hiring the right people much harder than before.

参考译文 ①英国企业家亚当·杜兰特(Adam Durrant)说他正在考虑把公司从英国挪到其他欧洲国家,他的公司是一家为航空公司和飞机制造商提供天气数据的初创公司。②他表示,这样做的原因之一在于英国脱欧可能会增加其招收合适人才的难度。

原文剖析 本段首句列举了某一公司考虑将业务搬离英国的例子。第二句解释其这样做的原因,与前一段英国大学的抱怨一致,本段从英国本土用人单位的角度分析英国脱欧对人才流失的影响。

设题点睛 第二句用于解释原因,可利用其设置正确选项。

生词解析

entrepreneur n. 企业家 aerospace adj. 宇宙空间的,宇宙航行的
startup n. 新兴公司(尤指新兴网络公司)

3	Why dose Adam Durrant want to move his business out of Britain?	亚当·杜兰特为何想将其公司撤出英国?
	A. Britain's climate data is harder to detect.	A. 英国的气候数据更难探测。
	B. Brexit can pose a threat to his aircraft manufacture.	B. 脱欧可对其飞机制造业务产生威胁。
	C. Brexit may hinder the free flow of talented workers.	C. 脱欧可能阻碍人才自由流动。
	D. Brexit makes it impossible to hire the right people.	D. 脱欧使其招聘不到合适的人才。

【解题思路】C。事实细节题。根据题干关键词(Adam Durrant)定位到文章第六段首句。题干考查此人将公司业务撤出英国的原因。第六段第二句解释原因之一为"英国脱欧会增加其招收合适人才的难度"(Brexit will likely make hiring the right people much harder),造成这一结果的根本原因即为选项 C 的分析,该项中的 hinder 是对原

文中 make harder 的同义替换，talented workers 即指原文中的 right people，故选项 C 正确。

【排他分析】选项 A 中的 climate data 虽然在第六段第一句中出现（supplying climate data），但原文并未提到天气数据获取的难易程度，且原句只用于介绍该企业，与题干所问的原因无关，所以排除。选项 B 中的 aircraft manufacture 也在第六段第一句中出现，但根据介绍，此人的公司并不直接从事飞机制造业务，该项是利用原文细节编造的无关项，可排除。选项 D 虽然与第六段第二句内容相关，但 impossible 所表达的意思太过绝对，与原文意思有出入，可排除。

Para. 7 ①Similar anxieties are being felt at the undergraduate level. ② The 125,000 European students studying at British universities now pay the same fees as locals and have access to the same government loans. ③Officials have promised this will not change for those applying next year—but no one knows what will happen after that.

参考译文 ①大学本科生也有相似的焦虑。②目前，有 125 000 名欧洲大学生在英国学习，他们和本地同学一样，交同样的学费，可获得同样的政府贷款。③虽然官员们承诺，脱欧不会影响明年申请的学生，但明年之后，一切就不得而知了。

【原文剖析】本段首句提出观点（本科生也有焦虑），后两句对首句谈到的"焦虑"进行解释说明。

【设题点睛】本段三个句子之间构成"观点＋细节证明"的关系，可用来设置例子功能题。

【生词解析】

anxiety n. 焦虑；令人焦虑的事　　　　　have access to sth. 有权使用；可以利用

4 By citing the example of the 125,000 European students, the author intends to _____.

A. show a potential threat faced by them
B. stress the benefit from the government loans
C. highlight the promise made by the local officials
D. illustrate the anxieties of the British undergraduates

通过列举 125 000 名欧洲学生的例子，作者想要_____。

A. 指出他们所面临的潜在威胁
B. 强调政府贷款的好处
C. 突出当地官员做出的承诺
D. 说明英国本科生的焦虑

【解题思路】A。例子功能题。根据题干中的数字（125,000）定位到第七段第二句。题干考查作者通过举例想要表达的观点。第七段第二句指出目前在英国学习的这 125 000 名大学生与当地学生的学费一样，也可以申请同样的助学贷款，但由该段最后一句破折号后的 but no one knows what will happen after that 推断，明年之后，脱欧可能会使这些来自欧洲其他国家的学生在英国的留学费用增加，也解释了首句谈到的"焦虑"的来源。选项 A 中的 potential threat 对应了首句中的 anxieties，也对应了后文谈到的可能出现的学费上涨的问题，因此是正确选项。

【排他分析】第七段第二句中虽然出现了 government loans，但原文只用于介绍背景和情况，并非是该例子要说明的观点，因此排除选项 B。选项 C 中的 promise made by the local officials 在第七段第三句中出现，但该句的重点在于破折号之后的转折部分，即"但明年之后，一切就不得而知了"，说明当地官员的承诺可能并不长久，可排除。

选项 D 的内容虽然和第七段首句类似，但是原文所述的感到焦虑的不包括英国本国的学生，只是来自欧盟其他成员国家的留学生，该项扩大了范围，可排除。

Para. 8 ① "It's not all doom and gloom—but it will be harder," Ramakrishnan said, who is a Nobel Prize-winning biologist and president of Britain's prestigious Royal Society. ② "We could make a go of it outside the EU. ③ But for that to happen, we have to attract talent and fund science. ④ And those two things are critical."

参考译文 ①诺贝尔奖得主、著名的英国皇家学会主席、生物学家拉马克里希南(Ramakrishnan)表示："虽然不至于走投无路，但情况肯定会更加艰难。"②"脱欧之后，我们也许能做出点成绩。③但前提是能吸引人才和获得科研经费。④这两点最为关键。"

原文剖析 本段首句给出某位英国科学家的观点，该句破折号之后的转折部分为重点，总结指出英国脱欧之后情况会更加艰难的观点，体现英国科学界的态度。后三句之间也存在转折关系，谈到也许可通过吸引人才和获得资助的方式获得成功，但根据上文所述，这两点正是脱欧后受到影响的重要因素，因此回应首句观点，再次说明目前英国科学界将面临脱欧所带来的困境。

设题点睛 本段为英国某位科学家的观点，从中可看出作者对脱欧一事的态度，可用来设置观点态度题或主旨大意题。

生词解析

doom and gloom 凄惨，前景不妙　　　　prestigious *adj.* 受尊敬的，有声望的
make a go of 使成功

5. Which of the following is the best title for the text?

以下哪项为本文最佳标题？

A. Brexit, the Doom for the British Business Men
B. Brexit, an Alarm for the British Academic World
C. Brexit, Risk and Opportunity Combined
D. Brexit, a Gloomy Future for the Talented over the World

A. 英国脱欧，英国商人的末日到来
B. 英国脱欧，为英国学术界拉响警报
C. 英国脱欧，风险与机遇并存
D. 英国脱欧，全世界人才的暗淡未来

【解题思路】**B**。主旨大意题。本文从一开始就点明主题，指出后文将围绕英国脱欧对其学术界所产生的影响展开讨论，中间部分多为举例，分别谈到英国脱欧对大学、科学界招生、招聘和获得资助以及英国企业招聘等方面带来的负面影响，最后一段利用人物观点进行总结，指出英国脱欧之后，英国科学界"虽然不至于走投无路，但肯定会更艰难"，选项 B 中的 alarm 和 academic world 与全文的关键词"负面影响"和"学术界"对应，因此是最佳标题。

【排他分析】选项 A 中的 British Business Men 虽然对应原文第六段中列举的人物 Adam Durrant，但属于单一的细节内容，不能概括全文。选项 C 中 Opportunity 所体现的正面意义在全文中都没有涉及，可以快速排除。选项 D 中的 over the World 随意扩大了原文的讨论范围，且 Gloomy Future 的说法太过极端，原文主要谈到英国脱

欧后将面临人才流失的后果，并不意味着全世界的人才都会因为英国脱欧而找不到施展才华的舞台，因此排除该项。

Text 19

Grace McDonnell's parents gave one of her paintings to Barack Obama. The seven-year-old, who dreamed of being a painter, was shot dead in her classroom last month. The picture now hangs in the president's study as a reminder to act. Even in a country as accustomed to gun violence as America, the murder of 26 people, including 20 children, in a Newtown, Connecticut school last month was especially shocking.

On that day a tearful Mr. Obama said serious action was needed to prevent any more tragedies. On January 16th Mr. Obama, along with Vice-President Joe Biden, who headed the president's gun task-force, unveiled the most sweeping gun-control proposals Washington, DC has seen for two decades.

But Mr. Obama will need congressional backing for the main part of his plan: a proposal to renew an assault-weapons ban that went into effect in 1994 but expired ten years later. The ban would include, as it did back in 1994, a ban on high-capacity ammunition magazines, containing more than ten rounds. The trouble is that ban, especially the magazine part of it, proved impossible to enforce.

States, meanwhile, have jumped the gun. Andrew Cuomo, New York's governor and a gun-owner, signed the NY Safe Act on January 15th. The state, which already had strong gun laws, has now banned military-style assault weapons, and has mandated universal background checks, including on buyers of ammunition. Martin O'Malley, Maryland's governor, is about to introduce a sweeping gun-control package which echoes many of New York's measures. Colorado's governor has called for background checks for private gun sales, which are currently exempt.

Cities, too, are taking a stand. Since the Newtown shooting, more than 100 more mayors have joined Mayors Against Illegal Guns, the 800-strong coalition founded by Michael Bloomberg, New York's mayor.

Welcome as these state and city actions are, without federal backup they are not much use. They may also be vulnerable to revision by the Supreme Court. Would-be killers need only cross state lines to places with weak gun laws to get access to weapons. Nor is it clear whether the president's plan would have prevented the Newtown massacre. There, the shooter did not have a background check; he used his mother's guns.

Mr. Obama faces steep opposition, and not just from congressional opponents: even his fellow Democrat, Harry Reid, the majority leader of the Senate, has indicated that the assault-weapons ban will be a hard sell. While states like New York and California are moving to strengthen gun laws, other states are doing the opposite. Lawmakers in Arizona and Texas, for instance, intend to introduce bills that would loosen gun restrictions. A

Kentucky sheriff has said he will not enforce any new gun laws that he deems unconstitutional.

Most shockingly, gun sales have soared in recent weeks. In the month since the Newtown shooting 250,000 more people have joined the National Rifle Association, which has vowed to oppose the ban. The group is getting so cocky that it launched a free shooting app this week. For an extra 99 cents, players can use a MK-11 sniper rifle to shoot coffin-shaped targets.

(*The Economist*, 2013.1)

1. The author introduces his topic by _____.
   A. making a comparison
   B. posing a contrast
   C. presenting an instance
   D. showing a metaphor
2. According to paragraph 3, the assault-weapons ban _____.
   A. had proved impossible to enforce more than one time
   B. may be a barrier in realizing Obama's gun-control proposal
   C. had taken effect before Obama's presidential term
   D. can survive without the backing of the Congress
3. It is suggested in paragraph 4 that _____.
   A. buyers of ammunition in Colorado need background checks
   B. Maryland will follow the NY Safe Act on gun-purchasing
   C. Andrew Cuomo sets a good example for New York gun-owners
   D. background check is almost indispensable in gun-control regulation
4. Which of the following might fully comply with Obama's gun-control plan?
   A. The Supreme Court.
   B. Fellow Democrat in the Senate.
   C. Sheriffs outside Kentucky.
   D. Victims in the massacre.
5. It can be inferred from the last paragraph that the increase in gun sales may be due to _____.
   A. the enhanced sense of self-defense
   B. the attraction of the free shooting app
   C. the influence exerted by the National Rifle Association
   D. the shockingly low price of a MK-11 sniper rifle

语篇分析与试题精解

Para. 1 ① Grace McDonnell's parents gave one of her paintings to Barack Obama. ② The seven-year-old, who dreamed of being a painter, was shot dead in her classroom last month. ③The picture

参考译文 ①格蕾丝·迈克唐奈(Grace McDonnell)的父母将女儿的一幅画送给了巴拉克·奥巴马(Barack Obama)总统。②上个月,这个一直梦想成为一名画家的年仅七岁的小女孩在教室中被枪杀了。

now hangs in the president's study as a reminder to act. ④Even in a country as accustomed to gun violence as America, the murder of 26 people, including 20 children, in a Newtown, Connecticut school last month was especially shocking.

③现在,这幅画就悬挂在总统的书房中,提醒他要采取行动。④上个月在康涅狄格州纽镇一所学校中发生的枪击案导致26人遇害,其中20人是儿童——即便在美国这样一个对枪支暴力习以为常的国家,这起事件也格外令人震惊。

原文剖析 本段前三句是对事实的描述,为后文观点作背景和铺垫,第三句同时也谈到了作者的观点,即政府需要有所行动。第四句继续补充前文所涉案件的过程和结果,体现美国枪支泛滥的严重恶果。

设题点睛 本段整体以事实描述为主,虽然不存在特别重要的观点性信息,但是可以结合下一段内容设置例子功能题或写作手法题。

生词解析
study n. 书房　　　　　　　　　　　reminder n. 提醒者;提醒物
accustomed adj. 习惯的;通常的;独有的

Para. 2 ①On that day a tearful Mr. Obama said serious action was needed to prevent any more tragedies. ②On January 16th Mr. Obama, along with Vice-President Joe Biden, who headed the president's gun task-force, unveiled the most sweeping gun-control proposals Washington, DC has seen for two decades.

参考译文 ①案发当天,奥巴马含泪表示,必须采取严厉的行动,以避免类似悲剧再次发生。②1月16日,奥巴马和负责总统控枪工作小组的副总统乔·拜登(Joe Biden)共同颁布了20年来美国政府所见证过的最为彻底的枪支管控计划。

原文剖析 本段首句呼应上段谈到的政府需要有所行动。第二句具体说明这一举措的主要内容(颁布枪支管控计划),并对此计划的严格性进行说明(20年来最彻底)。

设题点睛 本段是对上段内容的回应,可综合这两段内容设置考题。

生词解析
task-force 工作小组　　　　　　　unveil vt. 揭示,展露
sweeping adj. 彻底的;广泛的

长难句解析

On January 16th Mr. Obama, along with Vice-President Joe Biden, who headed the president's
　状语　　　　　　主语　　　　　　插入语　　　　　　　　非限制性定语从句
gun task-force, unveiled the most sweeping gun-control proposals Washington, DC has seen
　　　　　　　谓语　　　　　　　宾语　　　　　　　　　　　　定语从句
for two decades.

本句是主从复合句。本句主干为 Mr. Obama unveiled the gun-control proposal, 主语 Mr. Obama 后接 along with 介词短语引导的插入语,谓语动词应与主语一致,该插入语后还有一个由 who 引导的非限制性定语从句,修饰 Joe Biden。本句宾语较长,其后为省略引导词的定语从句,其先行词为 gun-control proposals。

193

1 The author introduces his topic by _____.

A. making a comparison
B. posing a contrast
C. presenting an instance
D. showing a metaphor

作者通过 _____ 的方式引入话题。

A. 类比
B. 对比
C. 举例
D. 比喻

【解题思路】**C**。写作手法题。根据题干所问定位到前两段。本题考查作者引入话题的方式。首段的第一句、第二句和第四句完整描述了康涅狄格州发生的一次严重的枪击事件及一名受害小女孩父母的举动。首段第三句中的 as a reminder to act 和第二段首句中的 serious action was needed 展现出奥巴马政府对此事的态度（控枪势在必行），因此作者是通过举例的方式引出本文话题的，选项 C 正确。

【排他分析】虽然类比、对比和比喻这三种写作手法也较为常见，且往往位于文章开始处，用于引入主题，但并非本文所使用的方法，因此排除。

Para. 3 ① But Mr. Obama will need congressional backing for the main part of his plan: a proposal to renew an assault-weapons ban that went into effect in 1994 but expired ten years later. ② The ban would include, as it did back in 1994, a ban on high-capacity ammunition magazines, containing more than ten rounds. ③ The trouble is that ban, especially the magazine part of it, proved impossible to enforce.

参考译文 ①但奥巴马总统需要得到国会对其控枪计划中主要部分的支持，这一主要部分提议重新恢复1994年出台的攻击型武器禁令，此禁令于2004年失效。②这一禁令将延续1994年禁令的内容，规定禁止安装容量在10发子弹以上的高容量弹夹。③问题是，当时该禁令，尤其是关于弹夹容量方面的规定，被证实无法实施。

原文剖析 本段前两句指出前文所述的奥巴马控枪计划得以实施的条件和主要内容（需要国会支持限制弹夹容量的禁令）。第三句谈到这个有关弹夹容量的规定在过去无法实施，为以下其他解决方案的讨论做铺垫。

设题点睛 本段第三句对前两句所谈到的控枪计划的可行性进行了否定，虽然此处并没有立刻给出解决方案，但也可用来设置正确选项。

生词解析

backing *n.* 支持，赞同
go into effect 生效
high-capacity 高容量；大功率
magazine *n.* （枪的）弹仓；弹盒
assault-weapon 攻击性武器
expire *vi.* 失效
ammunition *n.* 弹药；军火
round *n.* 一发子弹（或炮弹）

长难句解析

The ban would include, as it did back in 1994, a ban on high-capacity ammunition magazines,
　　主语　　谓语　　　方式状语从句　　　宾语　　　　　后置定语1
containing more than ten rounds.
　　　后置定语2

本句为主从复合句。本句的主干为 The ban would include a ban，谓语和宾语之间被 as 引导的方式状语从句隔开，as 表示"像……一样，正如"，宾语 a ban 后的 on 介词短语作后置定语，现在分词形式的 containing 与之前的 magazines 属于主动关系，可看作一个由 which 引导的定语从句，对 ammunition magazines 进行修饰。

2 According to paragraph 3, the assault-weapons ban _____.

A. had proved impossible to enforce more than one time
B. may be a barrier in realizing Obama's gun-control proposal
C. had taken effect before Obama's presidential term
D. can survive without the backing of the Congress

根据第三段的内容，有关攻击型武器的禁令 _____。

A. 不止一次被证明无法实施
B. 可能成为实现奥巴马控枪计划的障碍
C. 在奥巴马上任前就已经生效
D. 无须获得国会支持即可通过

【解题思路】B。推理引申题。根据题干要求定位到文章第三段。由于该段第三句为否定句，可看作本段的重要内容。该句指出禁令被证明无法实施（The trouble is that ban proved impossible to enforce），而第二句谈到1994年出台的这一禁令是奥巴马控枪计划的重要组成部分，需要得到国会的支持（congressional backing for the main part of his plan），因此推断奥巴马控枪计划的实施可能会受到这一过去无法实施的有关攻击型武器禁令的影响而无法获得国会支持，与选项 B 的推断一致。

【排他分析】选项 A 中的 proved impossible to enforce 在第三段最后一句中出现过，虽然原文指出当时这个禁令无法实施，但并不代表以后也无法实施，且该项中的 more than one time（不止一次）在原文中并未提及，因此可以排除。选项 C 用过去完成时表示这一有关攻击型武器的禁令在奥巴马上任之前就已经产生效果，但第三句明确指出当时该禁令并没有得到有效实施，且原文并未说明该禁令推行的时间与奥巴马上任时间的关系，因此该项既与原文矛盾，又在原文中没有涉及，可排除。选项 D 与第三段首句谈到的"奥巴马总统需要得到国会对其控枪计划中主要部分的支持"直接相反，因此排除。

Para. 4 ①States, meanwhile, have jumped the gun. ②Andrew Cuomo, New York's governor and a gun-owner, signed the NY Safe Act on January 15th. ③The state, which already had strong gun laws, has now banned military-style assault weapons, and has mandated universal background checks, including on buyers of ammunition. ④Martin O'Malley, Maryland's governor, is about to introduce a sweeping gun-control package which echoes many of New York's measures. ⑤Colorado's governor has called for background checks for private gun sales, which are currently exempt.

参考译文 ①同时，各州也早早开始行动了。②1月15日，纽约州州长安德鲁·库摩（Andrew Cuomo）（他同时是一名枪支所有者）签署了《纽约州安全法案》。③纽约州之前已执行了严格的枪支管制法律，现在又禁止拥有军式攻击性武器，并且要求对包括弹药购买者在内的人进行全面的背景调查。④马里兰州的州长马丁·奥马利（Martin O'Malley）也将引入一个全面的枪支管制计划，这与纽约州实行的许多措施遥相呼应。⑤而科罗拉多州州长也已要求开始对目前得到豁免的私人枪支销售进行背景调查。

原文剖析 本段首句为总起句,用比喻的方式给出一个抽象观点,jump the gun 原指未听发令枪就起跑,可用来比喻过早行动,巧妙地和本文主题 gun(枪支)呼应,暗示各个州也早早开始采取控枪行动了。第二句开始到本段结束都是对各州举措的举例,共同论证首句观点。

设题点睛 本段首句和其后内容构成总分关系,由于观点本身比较浅显,不适合设置考点,但并列的例证结构可用来设置细节题选项。

生词解析

jump the gun 过早行动;提前行动
background check 背景调查
echo vt. 发出回声,产生回响

mandate vt. 责令,强制执行
package n. 一套建议;一揽子交易
exempt adj. 被豁免的;被免除的

3 It is suggested in paragraph 4 that _____.　　第四段的内容表明 _____。

A. buyers of ammunition in Colorado need background checks
B. Maryland will follow the NY Safe Act on gun-purchasing
C. Andrew Cuomo sets a good example for New York gun-owners
D. background check is almost indispensable in gun-control regulation

A. 科罗拉多州的弹药购买者需要接受背景调查
B. 马里兰州将在枪支买卖方面遵循《纽约州安全法案》
C. 安德鲁·库摩为纽约州的枪支所有者树立了良好的榜样
D. 背景调查几乎是枪支管控规定中的必备项

【解题思路】D。推理引申题。根据题干要求定位到文章第四段,在没有准确定位点的情况下优先考查本段的观点句或者特殊结构句。本段首句指出各个州已经开始实施控枪措施了,剩下的部分都是在举例说明。第二句和第三句举例说明纽约州的做法,其中包括"要求对包括弹药购买者在内的人进行全面背景调查"(universal background checks)。第四句谈到马里兰州所执行的措施"与纽约州实行的许多措施遥相呼应",暗示也可能包括背景调查的条款。第五句指出科罗拉多州"要求开始对目前得到豁免的私人枪支销售进行背景调查",再次出现"背景调查"。三个例子中的两个都谈到了"背景调查",由此推断 background checks 应该属于控枪措施中非常重要的一环,因此选项 D 正确。

【排他分析】选项 A 中的 Colorado 对应第四段最后一句,但原文要求"对目前得到豁免的私人枪支销售(private gun sales)进行背景调查",而非"弹药购买者"(buyers of ammunition),因此排除该项。选项 B 中的 Maryland 对应本段第四句,原文只是提到马里兰州的枪支管制计划与纽约州实行的许多措施遥相呼应(echoes many of New York's measures),但不等同于两者将实行同一个法案,因此排除该项。选项 C 中的 Andrew Cuomo 对应本段第二句,该句谈到 Andrew Cuomo 是一个枪支拥有者(a gun-owner),但"良好的榜样"之意在文中并未提到,因此排除该项。

Para. 5 ①Cities, too, are taking a stand. ②Since the Newtown shooting, more than

参考译文 ①各个城市也纷纷表明立场。②自纽镇枪击案以来,已有超过 100 名市

100 more mayors have joined Mayors Against Illegal Guns, the 800-strong coalition founded by Michael Bloomberg, New York's mayor.

长新加入了纽约市市长迈克尔·布隆伯格(Michael Bloomberg)成立的"美国反对非法枪支市长协会"这一由800位市长组成的强大联盟。

原文剖析 本段与前一段结构类似,首句为总起句,体现抽象观点,指出市长们也开始积极响应控枪行动,第二句举例说明。

设题点睛 本段两句构成总分关系,为考点结构,但由于所述内容较为简单,不适合单独设置考题。

生词解析

take a stand 表态;采取立场 coalition n. （尤指个人或党派间）临时结成的联盟

Para. 6 ①Welcome as these state and city actions are, without federal backup they are not much use. ②They may also be vulnerable to revision by the Supreme Court. ③Would-be killers need only cross state lines to places with weak gun laws to get access to weapons. ④Nor is it clear whether the president's plan would have prevented the Newtown massacre. ⑤There, the shooter did not have a background check; he used his mother's guns.

参考译文 ①尽管各州和市的举措深得民心,但如果没有得到联邦政府的支持,这些方案很难起到实效。②这些措施也很容易被最高法院修改。③想要杀人的人只需跨过州界,来到控枪法律薄弱的州市就能买到武器。④而如果实行总统的控枪计划,是否就能避免纽镇枪击屠杀事件的发生,这一点也不得而知。⑤因为在这次事件中,持枪者并未经过背景调查,他所使用的是其母亲的枪。

原文剖析 本段前两句存在语意上的转折关系,指出前两段所提到的相关州和市领导人提出的控枪方案在没有联邦政府和最高法院的支持下很难执行,可联系到第三段奥巴马控枪计划想要获得通过也需要国会的支持这一内容。第三句到第五句指出了这些控枪措施的漏洞所在,即犯罪分子可以跨州买枪,也可以使用他人的枪支作案,因此这些措施是否有效还不得而知。

设题点睛 本段前两句对前文所举例子进行反驳,属于重要的考点内容,暗示联邦政府和最高法院的支持是这些举措得以实施的关键(而这两者很可能不支持这些做法)。

生词解析

backup n. 支持;后援 be vulnerable to 易受……的伤害
revision n. 修改;修订;校订 would-be adj. 想要成为……的;自称……的
get access to 有接触(或进入)的机会 massacre n. 大屠杀;残杀

长难句解析

[句1] Welcome as these state and city actions are, without federal backup they are not much use.
　　　　　　让步状语从句　　　　　　　　　　状语　　　主语 系动词
表语

本句是主从复合句。本句主干为they are not much use。句首处的让步状语从句使用了部分倒装的形式,即" *adj.* +as +主语 +be 动词"。主句部分也采取了倒装,即将 without 引导的条件状语前置,主系表后置。

[句2]Nor is it clear whether the president's plan would have prevented the Newtown massacre.
　　　　主句　　　　　　　　　　　　名词性从句

本句是主从复合句。it 作形式主语,真正的主语是 whether 引导的名词性从句。本句 nor 提前,表示"也不",其后内容使用完全倒装的形式,whether 引导的从句部分使用了虚拟语气(would have done),表示现实可能与假设的情况相反。

Para. 7 ①Mr. Obama faces steep opposition, and not just from congressional opponents: even his fellow Democrat, Harry Reid, the majority leader of the Senate, has indicated that the assault-weapons ban will be a hard sell. ②While states like New York and California are moving to strengthen gun laws, other states are doing the opposite. ③Lawmakers in Arizona and Texas, for instance, intend to introduce bills that would loosen gun restrictions. ④A Kentucky sheriff has said he will not enforce any new gun laws that he deems unconstitutional.

参考译文 ①奥巴马总统还面临着严峻的反对浪潮,这种声音不仅来自国会中的反对派,甚至其民主党同僚兼参议院多数党领袖哈里·里德(Harry Reid)也指出,攻击型武器禁令恐怕难以推行。②当纽约、加利福尼亚等州忙于加强枪支管制法案时,其他州却背道而驰。③如亚利桑那州和得克萨斯州的立法者们打算采用放宽枪支限制的法案。④一位肯塔基州的治安官曾表示,他将不会执行任何看似违宪的新的枪支管制法。

原文剖析　本段首句承接上段,继续指出奥巴马总统所主导的控枪计划难以实施的原因(反对派和同僚的反对)。第二句与其后的内容构成总分关系,指出有些州也对控枪举措表示反对,并以亚利桑那州、得克萨斯州和肯塔基州为例进行说明。

设题点睛　本段首句为带有冒号的长难句,第二句到最后为总分结构,都是设置正确选项的重要内容。

生词解析

steep *adj.* 严峻的;陡峭的　　　　　　　hard sell 强行推销
loosen *vt.* 放宽(限制);放松　　　　　　sheriff *n.* 郡治安官;州长
deem *vt.* 认为,视作　　　　　　　　　　unconstitutional *adj.* 违反宪法的

4 Which of the following might fully comply with Obama's gun-control plan?

A. The Supreme Court.
B. Fellow Democrat in the Senate.
C. Sheriffs outside Kentucky.
D. Victims in the massacre.

以下哪项会完全遵从奥巴马的控枪计划?

A. 最高法院。
B. 参议院的民主党同僚。
C. 肯塔基州以外的治安官们。
D. 屠杀中的受害者。

【解题思路】D。推理引申题。题干中不存在明确的定位点。本题考查可能支持奥巴马控枪计划的人。首段所描述的案例中,提到了受害人的父母将受害人的一幅画赠予奥巴马总统,提醒总统要采取行动。受害人的父母也属于枪击案的受害者,他们自

然完全支持奥巴马的控枪计划,因此选项D正确。

【排他分析】选项A出现在第六段第二句,原文指出各州、市的控枪举措很可能被最高法院修改,说明最高法院不一定是控枪举措的支持者。选项B出现在第七段首句,原文谈到奥巴马总统还面临着来自国会反对派和民主党内部的反对声音,因此该项并非题干所问的支持方,可排除。选项C中的Sheriffs和Kentucky出现在第七段最后一句,原文是说肯塔基州的一位治安官反对违宪的控枪法案,无法推知其他州治安官的态度,因此排除。

Para. 8 ①Most shockingly, gun sales have soared in recent weeks. ②In the month since the Newtown shooting 250,000 more people have joined the National Rifle Association, which has vowed to oppose the ban. ③The group is getting so cocky that it launched a free shooting app this week. ④For an extra 99 cents, players can use a MK-11 sniper rifle to shoot coffin-shaped targets.

参考译文 ①最令人震惊的是,枪支销售量在近几周扶摇直上。②纽镇枪击事件之后的一个月内,已有超过25万人新加入了美国步枪协会,该协会立誓反对该枪支管控禁令。③该组织狂妄到在本周发布了一个免费的射击应用程序。④玩家只要多花99美分就能用MK-11式狙击步枪射击棺材形状的靶子。

原文剖析 本段首句用most shockingly转折指出枪支销量反而出现了增长。后三句以美国步枪协会为例,指出该协会的新入会人数增长迅速,以及该协会鼓励人们使用枪支的做法。本段都是对事实的描述,表明公众对枪击事件的奇怪反应,可推断很大一部分原因在于群众对前文所述各界政府的控枪能力和措施并不放心,他们可能出于自卫的需求而购买枪支。

设题点睛 本段是对事实的描述,由于体现了较为"令人震惊"的内容,因此可用来设置正确选项。

生词解析

soar vi. 猛增,剧增   rifle n. 步枪;来复枪
cocky adj. 狂妄自信的;自大的;骄傲的   sniper n. 狙击手

5. It can be inferred from the last paragraph that the increase in gun sales may be due to _____.

   A. the enhanced sense of self-defense
   B. the attraction of the free shooting app
   C. the influence exerted by the National Rifle Association
   D. the shockingly low price of a MK-11 sniper rifle

从最后一段可推断出枪支销售的增长可能是因为_____。

A. 人们自卫感的增强
B. 免费射击应用软件的吸引力
C. 美国步枪协会施加的影响
D. MK-11式狙击步枪令人惊讶的低价

【解题思路】A。推理引申题。根据题干要求定位到最后一段。本题考查原因。第一句和第二句都是对事实的描述,第一句指出"枪支销售量在近几周扶摇直上",第二句指出

"已有超过25万人新加入了美国步枪协会"。两句都体现了民众对枪击事件的反应——并非要求控制枪支，反而积极购买枪支，可由这种反差推断出民众出于对枪击事件的恐惧，为了自卫，他们选择购买枪支或加入美国步枪协会，因此选项A的推断正确。

【排他分析】选项B中的free shooting app对应本段第三句，这是一种安装在手机或电脑上的软件，应和枪支销量上升的现象没有根本性的关系，因此排除。选项C中的National Rifle Association对应本段第二句，该句虽然指出该协会反对控枪禁令，但并不能由此推断出更多人购买枪支是受其影响，且原文明确限定了现象发生的背景是"纽镇枪击事件之后的一个月内"，因此排除该项。选项D中的MK-11 sniper rifle对应本段最后一句，属于典型的对文章细节的误解，原文谈到人们只要"多花99美分就能用MK-11式狙击步枪射击棺材形状的靶子"，并非购买这种步枪需要99美分，因此排除该项。

第三节 科技研究类

Text 20

　　Automakers are racing to ramp up their digital offerings, linking in-dash systems to smartphones and services like traffic monitors faster than ever before. Contrary to what some overwhelmed shoppers may think, the car companies are not doing this because they have run dry of new ideas for luxury features and styling embellishments. Rather, it's a response to demand: according to a recent study by I.B.M., buyers will increasingly select their new cars based on the digital gadgetry they contain.

　　In the next eight years, shoppers will focus more on options like live traffic reports and the personalization of connected services rather than brand names and reliability, according to the report, titled *Transforming Retail*. While fuel economy is expected to remain paramount for many buyers, the emphasis on connected services is creating a digital debate among automakers over how to deliver these services. Should such in-car systems take an open, flexible approach to connecting with software and services, or should these services be tightly controlled and restricted by the automakers? It's shaping up as a battle similar to that between Google and Apple in smartphone operating systems.

　　The automakers' opinions are about evenly divided. "About 50 percent of U.S. auto executives expect that things will become mostly open," said Kalman Gyimesi, author of the six-month I.B.M. project. Mr. Gyimesi said he believed that the auto industry was at a tipping point in the technology tug of war, which could favor the open approach taken by companies like Ford. It lets outside companies more quickly create new apps and services that can then be used via smartphones, he says. On the other side are automakers like Mercedes-Benz that prefer to differentiate their systems and maintain customer loyalty by keeping tighter control over what connects to the car.

There's also the safety issue. "You don't want Angry Birds to set off an air bag," said Jake Sigal, chief executive of Livio Radio. Livio creates the software that connects cars like the Chevrolet Spark to cellphones and services like Internet music channels. Some car companies take the position that by doing the development themselves, they can focus on reliability and safety, Mr. Sigal said. But a disadvantage of that approach is that services may not appear in some cars until long after their popularity has waned. Underpinning these issues is an even more fundamental technical concern from the early days of personal computing: the lack of compatibility. In general, software and services across different vehicles are not consistent and often require that drivers download multiple apps, particularly in tightly controlled systems. It also means software developers may need to create separate versions for different automakers and car models.

According to the I. B. M. study, nearly one-fourth of buyers consider digital connectivity across models important when it comes to buying multiple vehicles. In other words, traffic reports and personalized streaming music channels should look and work the same in all cars. In the open versus controlled technology debate, the former usually wins, according to analysts. "The open approach tends to drive an industry," Mr. Gyimesi said. As evidence, one need only look at smartphone operating systems. According to the market research firm IDC, Android's 2012 market share through October was about 68 percent of the global market; Apple was a distant second, at nearly 15 percent.

(*The New York Times*, 2013. 1)

1. According to paragraph 1, automakers are increasingly focusing on _____.
   A. stylish auto decorations
   B. I. B. M.'s professional advice
   C. multiple digital devices
   D. overwhelmed auto consumers
2. The author mentions the battle between Google and Apple to illustrate _____.
   A. the difference between two types of in-car system
   B. the shoppers' preference for digital services over brand names
   C. the consumers' paramount need for fuel economy
   D. a better way of delivering digital services
3. It can be inferred from paragraph 3 that _____.
   A. there is a fierce business competition between Ford and Benz
   B. automakers should embrace the digital technology
   C. outside companies react more quickly to new technology
   D. a restrictive approach might hurt the automakers' long-term interests
4. According to paragraph 4, what hinders the progress of auto digital services?
   A. The software's compatibility.
   B. The auto company's reliability.
   C. The software's popularity.
   D. The driver's personal appetite.
5. Regarding Gyimesi's comment, the author feels _____ about open technology.
   A. pessimistic   B. optimistic   C. puzzled   D. enthusiastic

语篇分析与试题精解

Para. 1 ①Automakers are racing to ramp up their digital offerings, linking in-dash systems to smartphones and services like traffic monitors faster than ever before. ②Contrary to what some overwhelmed shoppers may think, the car companies are not doing this because they have run dry of new ideas for luxury features and styling embellishments. ③Rather, it's a response to demand: according to a recent study by I.B.M., buyers will increasingly select their new cars based on the digital gadgetry they contain.

参考译文 ①汽车制造商正争相推出自己的数字产品,这些产品可以前所未有的速度将内置系统与智能手机和交通监测服务相连接。②与不知所措的消费者的想法截然相反,汽车公司之所以这样做并不是因为它们在汽车奢侈部件及别具一格的造型装饰方面灵感枯竭。③恰恰相反,这是对客户需求的反馈:I.B.M公司近期所做的调查显示,根据数码配置选购汽车的消费者日益增多。

原文剖析 本段首句描述了一个现象:汽车制造商在争相推出自己的数字产品。第二句和第三句为两个转折句,采用了"A. Rather, B."的结构,其中 B 句体现观点,因此更为重要。第二句指出汽车公司这么做的原因并非是因为对汽车奢侈部件和造型装饰的灵感枯竭,第三句用调查结果阐述汽车制造商这样做的根本原因在于广大消费者的需求。

设题点睛 本段中带有否定结构的后两句话为重点内容,可用来设置细节题。

生词解析

ramp up 增加
overwhelmed *adj.* 不知所措的
gadgetry *n.* 小配件
in-dash 内置式
embellishment *n.* 装饰

长难句解析

Contrary to what some overwhelmed shoppers may think, the car companies are not doing
　状语　　　　宾语从句　　　　　　主语　　　谓语
this because they have run dry of new ideas for luxury features and styling embellishments.
宾语　　　　　　原因状语从句

本句的主干结构为 the car companies are not doing this because…。句首的 contrary to… 结构作状语,修饰整个句子,其中 what 引导的名词性从句作介词 to 的宾语。

1 According to paragraph 1, automakers are increasingly focusing on _____.

A. stylish auto decorations
B. I.B.M.'s professional advice
C. multiple digital devices
D. overwhelmed auto consumers

通过第一段可知,汽车制造商正越来越关注_____。

A. 时髦的汽车装饰
B. I.B.M.公司的专业建议
C. 各种数字装置
D. 不知所措的汽车消费者

【解题思路】C。事实细节题。根据题干要求定位到文章首段。本段首句谈到汽车制造商争相推出数字产品(digital offerings)的现象,其中 are racing to ramp up… than ever before 与题干中的 are increasingly focusing on 相对应,因此是本题的定位句,该句中的 digital offerings 即是本题答案,对应选项 C 中的 digital devices,因此该项正确。

【排他分析】选项 A 对应第一段第二句,原文是说汽车公司这么做不是因为缺少创造奢侈部件(luxury features)或别具一格的造型装饰(styling embellishments)的灵感,说明汽车制造厂商一直都在关注这两个方面,只不过现在又有了新的关注点(电子设备),因此排除。选项 B 中的 I.B.M. 出现在第一段最后一句中,原文是说 I.B.M. 最近的调查指出越来越多的消费者开始关注汽车的数码配置这一现象,并不是说汽车制造商越来越关注 I.B.M. 的建议,选项 B 属于张冠李戴,所以排除。选项 D 对应第一段第二句,虽然原文中提到了不知所措的消费者(overwhelmed shoppers),但原文意在指出他们对汽车制造商关注电子装置的行为动机判断错误,与题干所问无关,因此排除。

Para. 2 ①In the next eight years, shoppers will focus more on options like live traffic reports and the **personalization** of connected services rather than brand names and reliability, according to the report, titled *Transforming Retail*. ②While fuel **economy** is expected to remain **paramount** for many buyers, the emphasis on connected services is creating a digital debate among automakers over how to deliver these services. ③Should such in-car systems take an open, flexible approach to connecting with software and services, or should these services be tightly controlled and restricted by the automakers? ④It's shaping up as a battle similar to that between Google and Apple in smartphone operating systems.

参考译文 ①根据一篇题为《转变中的零售》的报告,今后八年,汽车购买者的注意力会更多集中在诸如实时路况报告以及个性化的连接服务等方面,而不是汽车品牌及其可靠性。②目前节约燃油仍然是许多购买者的首要考虑因素。而购买者对于连接服务的重视在汽车制造商之中引发了如何提供数字服务的讨论。③是否应该采用开放、灵活的途径实现车载系统与软件和服务的关联?或者,汽车制造商是否应严格控制或限制这些服务?④一场类似于谷歌与苹果关于智能手机操作系统之争的战役正在逐渐打响。

原文剖析 本段首句给出一篇报告的观点:未来汽车消费者更关注汽车的电子设备配置情况,而非汽车的品牌和可靠性,与上一段最后一句的调查结果相呼应。第二句让步指出尽管燃油率仍是消费者考虑的最重要指标,但首句谈到的现象依旧引发了有关汽车数字配置的讨论。第三句提出讨论的关键问题:是否应该提供开放灵活的车载数字服务和设备。第四句没有给出正面回答,而是通过与谷歌和苹果有关操作系统的争论进行类比(谷歌的操作系统是开放的,而苹果的则是限制的),引出后文讨论。

设题点睛 本段第一句存在句内否定(rather than)结构,第二句存在让步(while)关系,第三句和第四句又构成了"观点+例证"的结构,几乎每一句都有比较重要的考点结构,所以用来设置题目的可能性非常大。

生词解析

personalization *n.* 个性化
paramount *adj.* 最主要的
economy *n.* 节约,充分利用

2 The author mentions the battle between Google and Apple to illustrate _____.

A. the difference between two types of in-car system
B. the shoppers' preference for digital services over brand names
C. the consumers' paramount need for fuel economy
D. a better way of delivering digital services

作者提到谷歌和苹果之战是为了说明_____。

A. 两种车载系统的不同之处
B. 消费者对数字服务的关注超过了品牌
C. 消费者对节约燃油的巨大需求
D. 提供数字服务的更好办法

【解题思路】A。例子功能题。根据题干关键词 Google 和 Apple 定位到第二段第四句。该句与上一句属于顺承关系，因此是对第三句谈到的汽车生产厂商之间的争论进行的解释说明，第三句谈到汽车制造商争论的焦点在于是提供开放灵活的车载连接服务，还是应严格控制或限制此类服务。在理解第四句与第三句语意关系时，需要考生具有一定的背景知识，即谷歌采用的安卓操作系统较为开放和兼容，而苹果的操作系统 IOS 的限制较多，正好对应了第三句的两种不同的车载系统，因此选项 A 是正确答案。

【排他分析】选项 B 中的 brand names 对应第二段首句，原文表示消费者现在更加关注的是车载数字服务而不是汽车的品牌和可靠性，虽然该项与本句意思对应，但并非作者用谷歌和苹果操作系统之争为例要表达的观点，属于答非所问，因此排除。同理可证选项 C 错误，该项内容对应第二段第二句，但并非例子要支撑的观点。选项 D 对应第二段第二句的后半句，虽然谈到了汽车制造商如何提供数字服务的关键点，但原文并未指出哪种方法更好，因此该项中的 a better 并无原文语意支撑，可排除。

Para. 3 ① The automakers' opinions are about evenly divided. ② "About 50 percent of U. S. auto executives expect that things will become mostly open," said Kalman Gyimesi, author of the six-month I. B. M. project. ③ Mr. Gyimesi said he believed that the auto industry was at a tipping point in the technology tug of war, which could favor the open approach taken by companies like Ford. ④ It lets outside companies more quickly create new apps and services that can then be used via smartphones, he says. ⑤ On the other side are automakers like Mercedes-Benz that prefer to differentiate their systems and maintain customer loyalty by keeping tighter control over what connects to the car.

参考译文 ①汽车制造商的观点均匀分为两派。②"美国汽车制造企业的执行官中有约50%的人认为应采用开放的技术"，I. B. M 为期六个月的项目主持者卡尔曼·吉美西（Kalman Gyimesi）说道。③吉美西相信，汽车制造业在技术的拔河比赛中正处于一个临界点，而这场比赛对于采用开放技术的公司更为有利，如福特公司。④开放的方式可以让外部公司更快地开发能通过智能手机使用的新应用软件和服务。⑤而另一派则是以梅赛德斯—奔驰为代表的汽车制造商。这类制造商更趋向于区别化车载系统，通过对连接汽车系统软件或设备的严格控制来保持顾客忠诚度。

原文剖析 本段前两句承接上一段提出的汽车厂商间的争论,指出目前两派势均力敌,约一半的厂家认为应该使用开放的技术。第三句提出观点:虽然两派人数各占一半,但目前看来对开放派更加有利。第四句解释说明第三句谈到的"有利"的原因,即可以将外部公司的发明创造更快地为己所用。第五句介绍另一派的代表及其观点:奔驰汽车公司更看重通过限制连接汽车系统的设备或软件来使自己有别于他人,并最终保持客户忠诚度。

设题点睛 本段第二句和第三句为人物观点,一般会被用来设置考点。最后一句与之前谈到的观点构成对比,也可能用来设置考点。

生词解析

evenly *adv.* 均匀地　　　　　　　tipping point 临界点
tug of war 拔河,两派间激烈的竞争　　differentiate *vt.* 区分,区别

长难句解析

On the other side are automakers like Mercedes-Benz that prefer to differentiate their systems
　　　倒装句　　　　　　　后置定语　　　　　　　定语从句
and maintain customer loyalty by keeping tighter control over what connects to the car.
　　　　　　　　　　　　　　　　　状语　　　　　　　宾语从句

本句主句介词短语放在句首,采用了完全倒装的形式,实际上是主系表结构。that 引导的定语从句修饰先行词 automakers,by 引出方式状语,其后的 what 名词性从句作 over 的宾语。

3 It can be inferred from paragraph 3 that 　　从第三段可推断出_____。
_____.

A. there is a fierce business competition between Ford and Benz
B. automakers should embrace the digital technology
C. outside companies react more quickly to new technology
D. a restrictive approach might hurt the automakers' long-term interests

A. 福特和奔驰之间存在激烈的竞争
B. 汽车制造商应该欣然接受数字技术
C. 外部公司对新技术的反应更快
D. 采用限制的方式可能有损汽车制造商的长期利益

【解题思路】D。推理引申题。根据题干要求定位到第三段。在没有更准确的定位点的情况下优先阅读本段中的考点结构。本段第三句提出了明确的人物观点,该句后半句的非限制性定语从句指出这场拉锯战对支持开放技术的制造商更有利(favor the open approach taken by companies),也就是说支持限制技术的制造商可能会处于下风或遭受损失,与选项 D 的推断一致。

【排他分析】选项 A 中的 Ford 和 Benz 分别对应该段第三句和第五句中的两个例子,虽然从常理上判断两者必然存在商业竞争,但原文中并没有对此加以阐述,只是说两家公司分别代表了对立的两种方式,因此排除。本文讨论的焦点是车载数字系统是否应该开放,而非是否应该在汽车中安装数字设备,且文章首段已经表明汽车制造商现在都在推出自家的车载数字设备,因此选项 B 错误。选项 C 中的 outside companies 出现在本段第四句,该句用于解释采用开放技术的企业更有利的原因在于可以利用外部公司更快速地开发新的应用和服务(more quickly create new apps and services)，与选项 C 的说法不符，且外部公司并非本文要讨论的关键因素，因此排除。

Para. 4 ① There's also the safety issue. ② "You don't want Angry Birds to set off an air bag," said Jake Sigal, chief executive of Livio Radio. ③ Livio creates the software that connects cars like the Chevrolet Spark to cellphones and services like Internet music channels. ④ Some car companies take the position that by doing the development themselves, they can focus on reliability and safety, Mr. Sigal said. ⑤ But a disadvantage of that approach is that services may not appear in some cars until long after their popularity has waned. ⑥ Underpinning these issues is an even more fundamental technical concern from the early days of personal computing: the lack of compatibility. ⑦ In general, software and services across different vehicles are not consistent and often require that drivers download multiple apps, particularly in tightly controlled systems. ⑧ It also means software developers may need to create separate versions for different automakers and car models.

参考译文 ①还有安全问题。②"你不会希望因为玩愤怒的小鸟这一游戏而使安全气囊弹出。"利维奥广播公司首席执行官杰克·西格尔（Jake Sigal）说。③利维奥公司开发出连接雪佛兰乐驰等车型与移动电话的软件，以及类似互联网音乐频道的服务。④西格尔说，一些汽车公司认为，通过自行开发此类软件和服务，他们会关注可靠性和安全性。⑤但该方法有一个弊端：这些服务可能已经过时很久后，才会出现在一些车型中。⑥此外还有更为基本的技术问题：缺乏兼容性，这一问题在个人电脑出现之初就已存在。⑦总体来说，不同汽车所提供的软件和服务并不一致。驾驶者需要下载多个应用程序，尤其是使用严格控制的车载系统时。⑧这也意味着软件开发商需要为不同汽车制造商和不同车型开发不同版本的程序。

原文剖析 本段首句给出新的观点：安全问题。第二句和第三句进一步解释这一问题，借外部软件开发公司负责人之口指出用户肯定不希望连接系统出现命令错误或程序错乱的现象，暗示这种开放的系统可能存在安全隐患。第四句和第五句再次提及此人的观点，指出虽然汽车企业也可自行开发软件（更安全），但会赶不上市场的流行趋势，与第三段第四句（开放技术可以让外部公司更快地开发新应用软件和服务）对应。第六句谈到车载连接服务的另一个根本性问题：兼容性。第七句和第八句对这一问题的影响展开叙述：用户需要下载多个应用，软件开发商需要开发不同版本。

设题点睛 本段第五句出现转折，第六句的 even more 体现递进关系，其中递进关系是更重要的考点。

生词解析
take the position 采取立场
underpin vt. 巩固，支持
consistent adj. 一致的
wane vi. 衰落；变小
compatibility n. 兼容性

4 According to paragraph 4, what hinders the progress of auto digital services?

根据第四段的内容，是什么阻碍了汽车数字服务的进步？

A. The software's compatibility.

A. 软件的兼容性。

B. The auto company's reliability.
C. The software's popularity.
D. The driver's personal appetite.

B. 汽车公司的可靠性。
C. 软件的流行程度。
D. 驾驶者的个人喜好。

【解题思路】A。事实细节题。根据题干要求定位到第四段。本段第五句转折指出汽车厂家自行开发车载系统配套软件的弊端在于速度太慢,第六句用 even more 递进指出另一个根本性的弊端(fundamental technical concern),即缺乏兼容性(the lack of compatibility),也就是说不同的汽车要用不同的软件和服务,这一弊端与选项 A 一致,因此属于阻碍汽车数字服务进步的一个因素。

【排他分析】选项 B 中的 reliability 对应第四段第四句,根据常识,汽车的可靠性涉及安全,应该是重中之重,不可能成为阻碍汽车进步或发展的障碍,而应成为车载数字系统需要保障的因素,因此排除该项。选项 C 中的 popularity 对应本段第五句,原文只是提到汽车制造商自行制造的软件会在此类软件已不再流行之后才被应用在汽车上,因此与软件的流行度无关,而与汽车制造商开发软件的速度有关,因此排除。选项 D 在本段中没有出现,属于无中生有,直接排除。

Para. 5 ① According to the I.B.M. study, nearly one-fourth of buyers consider digital connectivity across models important when it comes to buying multiple vehicles. ② In other words, traffic reports and personalized streaming music channels should look and work the same in all cars. ③ In the open versus controlled technology debate, the former usually wins, according to analysts. ④ "The open approach tends to drive an industry," Mr. Gyimesi said. ⑤ As evidence, one need only look at smartphone operating systems. ⑥ According to the market research firm IDC, Android's 2012 market share through October was about 68 percent of the global market; Apple was a distant second, at nearly 15 percent.

参考译文 ①I.B.M. 研究结果表明,近四分之一的汽车购买者认为,如果他们购买多辆汽车,那么不同车型间的数码连接很重要。②换言之,路况报告和个性化的流媒体音乐频道在所有车内的外观和功能应保持一致。③分析师表示,在关于开放和控制两种技术的讨论中,通常是前者获胜。④"开放的技术能推动行业的发展。"吉美西如此说道。⑤事实上,智能手机的操作系统就能证明这一点。⑥根据市场研究公司 IDC 的研究结果,2012 年 10 月,安卓系统约占全球市场份额的 68%,而位列第二的苹果以近 15% 的份额远远落在后面。

原文剖析 本段首句承接上段最后谈到的兼容性问题,通过 I.B.M. 的研究指出:近四分之一的汽车购买者在购车时很看重车载数字系统的兼容性。第二句用 in other words 重申首句观点,指出数码服务应该统一。第三句和第四句呼应第二段引出的关于车载系统开放性或限制性的论战,再次指出开放性技术对行业发展有推动作用。第五句和第六句举例论证前两句观点:安卓系统作为开放性系统,占据了全球市场的一多半份额,相比之下,以限制性为特征的苹果操作系统只拥有近 15% 的市场份额。

设题点睛 本段第三句和第四句出现了人物观点,第五句和第六句为举例论证,均为重要内容,一般会用来设置相应考点。

生词解析

connectivity *n.* 连接性 streaming *n.* 串流传播
versus *prep.* 与……比较

5	Regarding Gyimesi's comment, the author feels _____ about open technology.	就吉美西的评论而言，作者对于开放技术的态度是_____。
A. pessimistic	A. 悲观的
B. optimistic	B. 乐观的
C. puzzled	C. 困惑的
D. enthusiastic	D. 热情的

【解题思路】**B**。观点态度题。根据顺序原则及题干中的人名定位到最后一段第四句。本题考查作者对于开放技术的态度。第四句为直接引语，吉美西指出开放的方式能推动行业的发展。后两句作者用安卓和苹果智能手机操作系统所占的市场份额为例，对比说明开放的技术更受用户欢迎，支持了吉美西的观点，因此选项 B 是正确答案。

【排他分析】第三段第三句、第四段和第五段有关兼容性重要程度的讨论内容都可说明作者对开放技术的支持态度，因此排除体现反对态度的选项 A 和选项 C。而选项 D 体现的态度过于赞同，原文第四段也谈到开放技术会存在安全隐患的问题，因此该项表意极端，因此排除。

Text 21

Most Australians have heard of wombats, but few could place the numbat. Both marsupials are among 315 mammal species that roamed Australia at the time of the first European settlement in the late 18th century. The wombat has thrived. The smaller numbat, once widespread, clings on in only a few colonies in Western Australia. There it is listed as endangered, because of predation by feral cats. At least it survives. Australia has one of the world's highest rates of mammal extinctions—29 have been recorded over more than two centuries. Feral cats are reckoned to be culprits in 27 of those disappearances: among them the desert bandicoot, the crescent nail tail wallaby and the large-eared Hopping mouse.

Cats probably arrived in Australia on British ships carrying convicts. Unlike the convicts, their descendants have grown wilder and more menacing. The feral-cat population today is estimated at between 4m and 20m, most of them prowling out back habitats. They are often huge, weighing 15 kilograms. And they eat perhaps 75m Australian animals a day.

A parliamentary inquiry and a scientific report on mammals called for governments to step in. Last year Greg Hunt, the federal environment minister, launched a "threatened species strategy" to stop mammals' decline. Fire, loss of habitat and foxes, another alien predator, have played a part. But, Mr. Hunt says, feral cats are "the number-one killers."

Ten cat-free sanctuaries are planned across Australia over the next four years. The Australian Wildlife Conservancy, an NGO, is to start fencing 650 square kilometres (250 square miles) in April to create the biggest one at Newhaven, in the desert in Northern Territory. Atticus Fleming, the outfit's head, calls this region the "epicenter of the extinction crisis." His colleagues aim to reintroduce several threatened mammals there, including the mala, a winsome creature resembling a tiny wallaby, which disappeared from mainland Australia 25 years ago. The project will also give jobs to the local Ngalia Warlpiri aboriginal clan. Its senior women, says Mr. Fleming, are "extremely good cat hunters."

The government wants 2m feral cats culled across Australia by 2020. It is funding trials on cat-specific baits, as well as an app allowing humans who venture into the outback to report cat sightings. Mr. Hunt insists the baits would work "humanely." If they eventually killed even half the cat population, "it would be the most important action for Australian wildlife in 100 years."

The planned feticide has greatly upset some cat people, notably Brigitte Bardot, a French former sex goddess, and Morrissey, a miserable British singer. But conservationists say killing cats and fencing enclosures have already saved several species from extinction, including the Gilbert's potoroo in Western Australia and the bridled nail tail wallaby in New South Wales. Mr. Fleming admits an Australia free of feral cats is a long way off: "But the fence strategy can buy time until a silver bullet is found."

(*The Economist*, 2016.1)

1. The word "culprits" (Para. 1) is closest in meaning to _____.
   A. criminal　　　　B. survivor　　　　C. victim　　　　D. mammal
2. It can be learned from paragraph 2 and 3 that the feral cats _____.
   A. were brought to Australia by convicts from Britain
   B. were much wilder than the descendants of the convicts
   C. are a major threat to the survival of local mammals
   D. have a fierce competition with another alien predator
3. The Australian Wildlife Conservancy intends to _____.
   A. create a harmonious surrounding for local clans
   B. recruit professionals to capture feral cats
   C. keep the endangered mammals alive
   D. protect the cat-free sanctuary for mammals
4. According to the passage, the planned feticide has _____.
   A. aroused anger all over the world
   B. hardly fulfilled its ultimate purpose
   C. saved the Australian mammals from extinction
   D. caused a serious financial damage

5. The author's attitude toward the cat-killing action is _____.
   A. confused
   B. tolerating
   C. contemptuous
   D. approving

语篇分析与试题精解

Para. 1 ①Most Australians have heard of wombats, but few could place the numbat. ②Both marsupials are among 315 mammal species that roamed Australia at the time of the first European settlement in the late 18th century. ③The wombat has thrived. ④The smaller numbat, once widespread, clings on in only a few colonies in Western Australia. ⑤There it is listed as endangered, because of predation by feral cats. ⑥At least it survives. ⑦Australia has one of the world's highest rates of mammal extinctions—29 have been recorded over more than two centuries. ⑧Feral cats are reckoned to be culprits in 27 of those disappearances; among them the desert bandicoot, the crescent nail tail wallaby and the large-eared Hopping mouse.

参考译文 ①大部分澳大利亚人都听说过袋熊,但没有多少人知道袋食蚁兽。②18世纪晚期,当欧洲人首次移居澳大利亚时,袋熊和袋食蚁兽属于当时已经漫步在澳大利亚土地上的315种哺乳动物中的两种。③袋熊兴旺至今。④而曾分布广泛的体型较小的袋食蚁兽,目前只存在于西澳大利亚州为数不多的几个种群中。⑤在那里,由于野猫的捕食,袋食蚁兽已被列为濒危物种。⑥但至少得以幸存。⑦澳大利亚是世界上哺乳动物灭绝率最高的地区之一——记录显示,两个多世纪以来,29种哺乳动物已经消失。⑧其中27种哺乳动物的灭绝被认为是拜野猫所赐,包括荒漠袋狸、新月甲尾袋鼠和大耳窜鼠。

原文剖析 本段前四句介绍了袋熊和袋食蚁兽两种有袋类哺乳动物的不同命运(袋熊数量越来越多,而袋食蚁兽则越来越少)。第五句和第六句解释了袋食蚁兽数量减少的原因,结合对袋食蚁兽的描述,可理解为袋食蚁兽体型较袋熊小,容易被野猫捕食。最后两句进一步将野猫的捕食范围推广至其他27种已经灭绝的哺乳动物,由此突出野猫对澳洲哺乳动物的生存造成了严重威胁。

设题点睛 本段后半部分解释了澳洲一些哺乳动物灭绝的原因,属于重点内容,可用来设置考点。

生词解析
wombat *n.* 袋熊
marsupial *n.* 有袋类动物
roam *vt.* 在……漫步,漫游
feral *adj.* 野生的;凶猛的
bandicoot *n.* 袋狸
wallaby *n.* 小袋鼠
numbat *n.* 袋食蚁兽
mammal *n.* 哺乳动物
predation *n.* 捕食;掠夺
culprit *n.* 犯人;被控犯罪的人
crescent *adj.* 新月形的

1 The word "culprits" (Para. 1) is closest in meaning to _____.

A. criminal
B. survivor
C. victim
D. mammal

单词"culprits"(第一段)的意思最接近于_____。

A. 罪犯
B. 幸存者
C. 受害者
D. 哺乳动物

【解题思路】A。语意理解题。根据题干要求定位至首段最后一句。本句可直译为"野猫被认为是其中27种动物灭绝的……"(Feral cats are reckoned to be culprits in 27 of those disappearances),其中those回指前一句所说的已经灭绝的哺乳动物,说明野猫和这27种哺乳动物的灭绝有关。feral cats也出现在该段第五句,原文指出野猫捕食袋食蚁兽使其被列为濒危物种。结合两句话的意思,可知野猫是某些哺乳动物的天敌,可能导致了最后一句所谈到的27种哺乳动物的灭绝,因此culprits与选项A的意思最为接近。

【排他分析】选项C与分析的意思相反,可直接排除。选项B和选项D是利用第一段原词设置的干扰项,没有语意支撑,也可排除。

Para. 2 ①Cats probably arrived in Australia on British ships carrying convicts. ②Unlike the convicts, their descendants have grown wilder and more menacing. ③The feral-cat population today is estimated at between 4m and 20m, most of them prowling out back habitats. ④They are often huge, weighing 15 kilograms. ⑤And they eat perhaps 75m Australian animals a day.

参考译文 ①猫很有可能是搭载英国押送犯人的船只抵达澳洲的。②与犯人不同的是,这些猫的后代们更具野性,并且更危险。③如今,澳洲野猫的数量约在四百万到两千万之间,大部分在栖息地出没。④野猫通常体型巨大,重约15公斤。⑤每天死于野猫之口的澳洲动物可达7 500万。

原文剖析 本段首句介绍澳洲猫的来源。第二句用unlike转折指出这些猫的后代(也就是野猫)更具野性和攻击性。第三句和第四句分别就澳洲野猫的数量、活动范围和体型进行了介绍。最后一句回应第二句,用数据体现澳洲野猫的凶残。

设题点睛 本段的观点性内容只出现在第二句,之后的内容均为细节描述,因此一般不单独用来设置考点,但可以利用第二句的观点设置选项。

生词解析
convict n. 囚犯,服刑的人
be estimated at 据估计
menacing adj. 危险的,威胁的
habitat n. 栖息地,产地

Para. 3 ① A parliamentary inquiry and a scientific report on mammals called for governments to step in. ②Last year Greg Hunt, the federal environment minister, launched a "threatened species strategy" to stop

参考译文 ①一项议会质询和一份关于哺乳动物的科学报告呼吁政府介入。②去年,为了防止哺乳动物数量继续减少,联邦环境部长格雷格·亨特(Greg Hunt)提出了"濒危物种战略"。③火

mammals' decline. ③Fire, loss of habitat and foxes, another alien predator, have played a part. ④But, Mr. Hunt says, feral cats are "the number-one killers."

灾、栖息地的减少和另一个外来捕食者狐狸的出现,也是导致澳洲哺乳动物数量锐减的几个因素。④但是,亨特先生认为,野猫是"头号杀手"。

原文剖析 本段前两句介绍了解决以上问题的方案之一(政府介入,发起保护行动)。后两句之间存在转折语意关系,通过对比其他危害澳洲哺乳动物的因素,强调野猫的危害性最大。

设题点睛 本段前两句介绍了政府的态度,第四句转折重申野猫的危害性(与第二段的核心观点重合),可合并设置考点。

生词解析

inquiry n. 质询;探究;调查　　　　　　step in 介入,插手,干涉
alien adj. 外来(种)的　　　　　　　　 play a part 起作用;有影响

2 It can be learned from paragraph 2 and 3 that the feral cats _____.　　从第二段和第三段中可知,野猫_____。

A. were brought to Australia by convicts from Britain
B. were much wilder than the descendants of the convicts
C. are a major threat to the survival of local mammals
D. have a fierce competition with another alien predator

A. 由犯人从英国带到澳大利亚
B. 要比犯人的后代更具野性
C. 是当地哺乳动物生存所面临的主要威胁
D. 与另一种外来捕食者竞争激烈

【解题思路】C。推理引申题。根据题干要求定位到第二段和第三段,本题考查这两段中有关野猫的内容。第二段最后一句指出"每天死于野猫之口的澳洲动物可达7 500万",第三段最后一句转折强调野猫是澳洲哺乳动物的"头号杀手"。这两处内容相互呼应,可看出野猫对澳洲当地哺乳动物的生存威胁极大,对应选项C中的major threat,因此该项正确。

【排他分析】选项A对应第二段首句,原文指出猫(cats)可能是和英国的流放犯人一同乘船来到澳洲的,主语是"猫"而不是"野猫",由后一句可看出这些猫的后代才是本文谈到的澳洲野猫,因此该项与题干所问的野猫无关。选项B对应第二段第二句"与犯人不同的是,这些猫的后代们更具野性,并且更危险",作者将人与野猫两者之间进行对比的作用是暗示这些犯人的后代(如今的澳洲人)并不具有危险性,应看作一种写作手法,但与本文主题关系不大,因此排除。选项D中的alien predator对应第三段第三句,原文谈到的"火灾、栖息地的减少和另一个外来捕食者狐狸的出现"是与"野猫"并列的造成澳洲哺乳动物减少的因素,且最后一句明确指出"野猫"是"头号杀手",因此"狐狸"与"野猫"不存在同等的竞争关系,因此排除。

Para. 4 ①Ten cat-free sanctuaries are planned 　　**参考译文** ①接下来的四年里,澳大利

across Australia over the next four years. ②The Australian Wildlife Conservancy, an NGO, is to start fencing 650 square kilometres (250 square miles) in April to create the biggest one at Newhaven, in the desert in Northern Territory. ③Atticus Fleming, the outfit's head, calls this region the "epicenter of the extinction crisis." ④His colleagues aim to reintroduce several threatened mammals there, including the mala, a winsome creature resembling a tiny wallaby, which disappeared from mainland Australia 25 years ago. ⑤The project will also give jobs to the local Ngalia Warlpiri aboriginal clan. ⑥Its senior women, says Mr. Fleming, are "extremely good cat hunters."

亚计划在全国建立十个无猫保护区。②非政府组织澳大利亚野生动物管理委员会准备4月份在北领地沙漠地带的纽黑文围地650平方千米（250平方英里），建造一个最大的无猫保护区。③该机构的负责人阿迪克斯·弗莱明（Atticus Fleming）称这个地区为"灭绝危机的震中地带"。④他的同伴们想在这里重新引进几种濒危的哺乳动物，包括mala，一种形似沙袋鼠的可爱生物，这种动物早在25年前就从澳洲大陆上消失了。⑤该项目也会给当地的纳加里亚华普利原住民部落提供就业机会。⑥弗莱明说，当地的老年妇女可是"捉猫能手"。

原文剖析 本段承接上一段提到的政府措施，前四句介绍具体的解决方案及其目的（建立十个无猫保护区，用于引入濒危的哺乳动物）。第五句和第六句指出此类保护区的另一种作用，即利用当地人捉猫的技能安排其在保护区就业。第三句引号中的内容为比喻用法，epicenter 表示"震中"，指地震感受最明显的地点，在此处用于表示保护区所在的区域目前受野猫威胁最为严重。

设题点睛 本段涉及细节，最后两句关于人物观点的内容可用来设置正确选项。

生词解析

sanctuary n. 自然保护区 NGO 非政府组织
fence vt. 把……用栅栏围起来 outfit n. （部队等的）单位；有组织的机构
epicenter n. 震中 winsome adj. 可爱的；迷人的
wallaby n. 沙袋鼠 aboriginal adj. 土著的；原始的
clan n. 部落；氏族

| 3 | The Australian Wildlife Conservancy intends to _____. | 澳大利亚野生动物管理委员会想要_____。 |

A. create a harmonious surrounding for local clans
B. recruit professionals to capture feral cats
C. keep the endangered mammals alive
D. protect the cat-free sanctuary for mammals

A. 为当地部落创造一个和谐的环境
B. 雇用专业人士来捕捉野猫
C. 让濒危哺乳动物生存下去
D. 保护为哺乳动物设立的无猫保护区

【解题思路】B。事实细节题。根据题干关键词（Australian Wildlife Conservancy）定位到第四段，本题考查该组织的目的和做法。该段介绍了该组织建立无猫保护区的计划，详细介绍了计划中最大的一个保护区。该段第五句提到了保护区的另一个功能是"给当地的……原住民部落提供就业机会",最后一句指出原因,即该部落的老年妇女非常善于捕猫("extremely good cat hunters"),此处善于捕猫的 senior women 对应选项 B 中的 professionals,第五句谈到的就业机会对应该项中的 recruit,因此该项是对第四句和第五句的正确理解,也是题干所问的该组织创造保护区的目的之一。

【排他分析】选项 A 中的 local clans 对应第四段第五句,但是原文完全没有提到 a harmonious surrounding,所以快速排除。选项 C 对应第四段第四句,原文指出该保护区旨在"重新引进几种濒危的哺乳动物",其中包括 25 年前已经从澳洲大陆上消失的动物,说明该保护区的建立不仅仅是为了让这些动物存活下去,而是要让这些动物的种群扩大,因此该项的表述不准确。原文指出该组织建立无猫区是为了"保护哺乳动物",并非选项 D 提到的"保护无猫保护区",因此排除该项。

Para. 5 ①The government wants 2m feral cats culled across Australia by 2020. ②It is funding trials on cat-specific baits, as well as an app allowing humans who venture into the outback to report cat sightings. ③Mr. Hunt insists the baits would work "humanely." ④If they eventually killed even half the cat population, "it would be the most important action for Australian wildlife in 100 years."

参考译文 ①澳大利亚政府希望到 2020 年,该国被捕杀的野猫数量能达到 200 万只。②政府还赞助了专门用于猫的诱饵试验,以及一个应用软件,冒险进入内地的人可以通过该软件报告所看到的野猫的行踪。③亨特坚称利用这种诱饵杀猫的方式会很"人道"。④假如这些猫饵最终能让野猫的数量减少一半,"这将是 100 年内澳大利亚野生动物保护方面最重要的举动"。

原文剖析 本段首句介绍政府提出的"杀猫"目标(到 2020 年捕杀 200 万只)。第二句介绍政府的具体行动,一是赞助猫饵试验,二是赞助可报告野猫行踪的应用软件的开发。最后两句通过引用个人观点,给出对政府解决方案的评价。

设题点睛 本段最后两句为人物观点,可以用来设置正确选项。

生词解析

cull *vt.* 捕杀,宰杀
bait *n.* 饵;诱饵
outback *n.* (尤指澳大利亚的)内地
trial *n.* 试用;试验
venture into 冒险进入
humanely *adv.* 人道地;富人情地

Para. 6 ①The planned feticide has greatly upset some cat people, notably Brigitte Bardot, a French former sex goddess, and Morrissey, a miserable British singer. ②But conservationists say killing cats and fencing enclosures have already saved several species from extinction, including the Gilbert's potoroo in Western Australia and the bridled nail tail wallaby in

参考译文 ①这一杀猫计划令某些爱猫人士十分愤怒,其中最引人注目的是法国前性感女神碧姬·芭铎(Brigitte Bardot)和落魄的英国歌手莫里西(Morrissey)。②然而,环保主义者表示,杀猫和围地的措施已经拯救了若干濒临灭绝的物种,包括西澳大利亚州的吉尔伯特长鼻袋鼠和新南威尔士的尖

New South Wales. ③Mr. Fleming admits an Australia free of feral cats is a long way off: "But the fence strategy can buy time until a silver bullet is found."

尾兔袋鼠。③弗莱明承认,澳大利亚的除猫之路还很漫长,"但是围地策略可以拖延时间,直到找到一劳永逸的新办法。"

原文剖析 本段承接前文内容,给出社会各界对以上方案的不同看法。首句指出爱猫人士反对政府杀猫的计划。第二句转折指出环保人士认为政府杀猫和建立保护区的方案对生态环境有好处(拯救其他物种)。第三句利用个人观点进行总结,综合考虑前两类人的意见之后,围地建立无猫保护区是目前可行的最佳策略(既避免杀猫,又保护了受猫威胁的濒危物种)。

设题点睛 本段最重要的是最后一句,包含观点和转折语意,且起到总结全文的作用,可用来设置考点。

生词解析

feticide n. 堕胎;杀害胎儿
enclosure n. 圈占地,圈用地
bridle vt. 给(马)上马勒
silver bullet 良方,高招

conservationist n. 保护主义者
potoroo n. 长鼻袋鼠(产于澳洲)
a long way off 在远处,离得远

长难句解析

But conservationists say killing cats and fencing enclosures have already saved several species
　　主语　　　谓语　　　　　　　　　　宾语从句
from extinction, including the Gilbert's potoroo in Western Australia and the bridled nail tail
　　　　　　　　　　　　　　　　　　状语
wallaby in New South Wales.

本句为主从复合句。本句主干为 conservationists say…,谓语后为省略 that 的宾语从句,该从句的主语为两个并列的动名词短语,谓语使用了 save… from…(使……免遭……)的结构,including 介词短语作状语,用于举例说明。

4 According to the passage, the planned feticide has _____.

A. aroused anger all over the world
B. hardly fulfilled its ultimate purpose
C. saved the Australian mammals from extinction
D. caused a serious financial damage

根据本文内容,杀猫计划 _____。

A. 引起了全世界的愤怒
B. 还没有实现其最终目标
C. 使澳大利亚哺乳动物免于灭绝
D. 造成了重大的经济损失

【解题思路】B。推理引申题。根据题干关键词(the planned feticide)定位到文章最后一段。该段描述了不同的人对前文所述杀猫方案和圈地方案的不同看法。本段最后一句为总结句和观点句,指出(由于受到爱猫人士的反对)"澳大利亚的除猫之路还很漫长"(an Australia free of feral cats is a long way off),可理解为还没有完成既定目标,与选项 B 的推断一致。

【排他分析】选项 A 对应最后一段首句,该项中的 all over the world 范围太广,原文只提到 some cat people,因此排除。选项 C 对应最后一段第二句,该句指出"杀猫和围

地的措施已经拯救了若干濒临灭绝的物种"(saved several species from extinction),选项 C 所表达的"澳大利亚哺乳动物"范围太大,且不符合常理,因此排除。原文并未提及任何有关经济或金融损失方面的内容,因此可以直接排除选项 D。

5 The author's attitude toward the cat-killing action is _____.

A. confused
B. tolerating
C. contemptuous
D. approving

作者对于杀猫计划的态度是_____。

A. 疑惑的
B. 容忍的
C. 鄙视的
D. 赞同的

【解题思路】D。观点态度题。在原文作者并未给出明确态度的情况下(原文未出现 I/We 作主语的句子),一般利用文章第三方人物的观点进行判断,只要作者没有对其进行反驳,就侧面说明作者支持该观点。本文前几段重点谈论野猫对澳大利亚哺乳动物种群的巨大破坏力,以及政府及非政府组织对此问题的解决方案及评价(用"人道的"描述利用诱饵杀猫的方法,并指出非政府组织采用的圈地策略具有降低野猫的危害和提供就业机会的双重作用)。最后一段借用环保人士的观点指出不能为了保护野猫就以其他哺乳动物的灭绝为代价,反驳了该段首句所述爱猫人士对杀猫策略的反对。综合全文可看出作者应该十分赞成减少澳洲野猫数量的做法,因此选项 D 正确。

【排他分析】其他三项所反映的作者态度在文中缺少支撑细节,因此均可排除。

Text 22

Morning rush-hour and engineering faults are cited as factors, with Network Rail (NR) looking set to miss five-year target. Floods, staff shortages and constant morning rush-hour problems combined to drag down rail punctuality last month.

The two main London-to-Scotland companies—East Coast and Virgin West Coast—ran fewer than four in five trains on time during the period from 9 December 2012 to 5 January 2013, Network Rail said. London Midland, where passengers have experienced repeated staff shortages, only reached a 77.7% trains-on-time figure for the period. But some companies ran almost all of their services on time, with London to Tilbury and Southend company c2c achieving a 98% figure. Overall, a total of 88.2% of trains ran on time in the four-week period compared with 88.8% in the same period over the new year in 2011/12. Virgin's figure was 75.8% and East Coast only reached 77.2%. But nine of the 19 companies achieved at least 90%, with London Overground reaching 96.9% and Merseyrail recording 94.5%.

A spokesperson for Network Rail said: "Severe weather with multiple flooding, landslide and embankment slip events caused severe disruption over a number of days to many train operators and particularly impacted our long-distance customers." Some of the worst of the flooding last month was in the West Country. Yet First Great Western still managed to run 84% of trains on time—albeit down on the 89.5% figure it achieved in the same period a year before. Although the flooding did cause much disruption and London Midland's staff problems contributed to the difficulties, passengers on many lines were also hit by a series of signal faults and broken-down trains at peak times. The latest figures, which come only a few days after passengers saw the price of their season tickets rise by an average 4.2%, do not include cancellations and delays caused by planned engineering work.

In the year from 6 January 2012 to 5 January 2013, train companies ran 91.4% of trains on time. This is below the 92.5% target for the period 2009-14—a five-year target average that NR is set to miss. Announcing to-be-approved 37.5bn plans for the railways earlier this week, NR said its target for 2014-19 would be unchanged.

An Office of Rail Regulation spokesman said: "Some rail passengers have suffered poor performance in recent weeks—far below the high standards they have come to expect in recent years. "The regulator has asked NR to explain the cause of these failings and to provide an update on its progress to improve performance on the key long-distance and London and south-east routes. It is imperative the rail industry learns lessons and improves train punctuality for passengers in the future.

The leader of the RMT transport union, Bob Crow, said: "These figures make a nonsense of the government's McNulty rail review plans, which would axe yet more staff from the railways even though it is clear that punctuality is already being compromised by a shortage of staff. "No matter how the government and the train companies try to dress this up, the fact is that rail travel was more efficient, punctual and cheaper under British Rail and we will continue to press the case for full renationalisation.

(*The Guardian*, 2013.1)

1. It can be concluded from the first two paragraphs that _____.
   A. coastal areas have a harsher climate condition
   B. unpunctuality symbolizes the failure of the five-year target
   C. some of the companies managed to overcome the hardships
   D. morning rush-hour is a more serious problem for Network Rail

2. It is suggested in paragraph 3 that _____.
   A. signal faults are the main reason for the decline of punctuality
   B. natural disaster is not the only culprit behind the rail unpunctuality
   C. long-distance customers suffered most from severe weather conditions
   D. passengers are discontent with the rising price of season tickets

3. The spokesman from the Office of Rail Regulation suggests that _____.
   A. NR should apologize for the decline of its service quality
   B. rail passengers are outrageous for the poor performance they suffered

C. efforts made to improve passengers' satisfaction should be reported by NR

D. passengers' satisfaction should be regarded as the uppermost goal by NR

4. According to the last paragraph, Bob Crow contends that _____.

   A. McNulty rail review plans insist on recruiting more staff

   B. British Rail should not compromise on the shortage of staff

   C. the government calls for a full renationalisation of railway

   D. British Rail is the key to solve the current predicament

5. Which of the following is the best title for the text?

   A. Rail Unpunctuality Chaos: NR under Pressure

   B. The Ever-Brighter Future for the British Rail System

   C. NR's Contribution to Rail Punctuality

   D. British Rail: Privatisation VS Renationalisation

语篇分析与试题精解

Para. 1 ①Morning rush-hour and engineering faults are cited as factors, with Network Rail (NR) looking set to miss five-year target. ②Floods, staff shortages and constant morning rush-hour problems combined to drag down rail punctuality last month.

参考译文 ①早高峰和工程技术方面的故障被认为是英国铁路网公司（NR）无法完成五年计划的原因。②洪水、人员短缺和持续性早高峰问题共同成为上个月列车准点率下滑的原因。

原文剖析 本段首句和第二句都在给出观点：因为各种原因（早高峰、工程问题、自然灾害、人力短缺等），英国的火车晚点情况严重。

设题点睛 本段两句在观点上是重合的，如果设置正确选项，就没有足够的信息用来设置错误选项，所以这种段落一般可用于设置全文主旨题，或者词义理解题，或者结合下一段出题。

生词解析

engineering *n.* 工程技术　　constant *adj.* 经常的

punctuality *n.* 准时

Para. 2 ①The two main London-to-Scotland companies—East Coast and Virgin West Coast—ran fewer than four in five trains on time during the period from 9 December 2012 to 5 January 2013, Network Rail said. ②London Midland, where passengers have experienced repeated staff shortages, only reached a 77.7% trains-on-time figure for the period. ③But some companies ran almost all of their services

参考译文 ①英国铁路网公司表示：2012年12月9日到2013年1月5日，伦敦到苏格兰的两家主要公司，即东海岸和维珍西海岸铁路列车公司，其列车准点率低于80%。②同期，伦敦米德兰铁路公司的列车准点率只达到了77.7%，该公司常出现人员短缺问题。③但是，有些公司的列车准点率几乎达到百分之百，比如伦敦到蒂尔伯里和索

on time, with London to Tilbury and Southend company c2c achieving a 98% figure. ④Overall, a total of 88.2% of trains ran on time in the four-week period compared with 88.8% in the same period over the new year in 2011/12. ⑤Virgin's figure was 75.8% and East Coast only reached 77.2%. ⑥But nine of the 19 companies achieved at least 90%, with London Overground reaching 96.9% and Merseyrail recording 94.5%.

森德列车公司的准点率达到了98%。④总体来说，在四个星期的时间段内，88.2%的列车能准点到达，而2011年年末到2012年年初的四周内，这个数字为88.8%。⑤维珍铁路公司的准点率为75.8%，东海岸铁路公司仅达到了77.2%。⑥但19家公司中，有9家的准点率达到了90%以上，其中，伦敦城铁公司达到了96.9%，默西塞德铁路公司达到了94.5%。

原文剖析 本段由数据贯穿，整体举例证明首段第二句中列车准点率下降的事实真相，分别以英国各个铁路公司的准点率作为描述对象。

设题点睛 本段由各种数据罗列而成，全段都不具备设置考点的条件（没有明确的观点），但很可能会结合首段内容设置考题。从段内的逻辑关系看，本段第三句和最后一句的转折可能用来设置考点。

1 It can be concluded from the first two paragraphs that _____ .

A. coastal areas have a harsher climate condition
B. unpunctuality symbolizes the failure of the five-year target
C. some of the companies managed to overcome the hardships
D. morning rush-hour is a more serious problem for Network Rail

从前两段可以推断出_____。

A. 沿海地区的气候条件更加恶劣
B. 晚点问题标志着五年计划的失败
C. 有一些公司克服了困难
D. 早高峰对于英国铁路网公司而言是一个更为严重的问题

【解题思路】C。推理引申题。根据题干要求定位到前两段。在没有明确定位点的情况下，优先阅读两段中的重点结构。第一段主要谈论了造成铁路列车晚点的若干因素，第二段第三句转折指出还是有一些公司能够基本确保所有列车正点运行，结合这两部分内容，可以推断出这些公司应该是在克服了首段谈到的诸多困难的情况下保证列车准点率的，因此选项C正确。

【排他分析】选项A中的coastal对应第二段首句中的East Coast和Virgin West Coast两大铁路公司，原文指出这两个铁路公司的列车准点率低于百分之八十，虽然从两个公司的名称上判断其行车线路应位于沿海地区，结合首段谈到的"洪水"这一气候问题，可能造成列车晚点的结果，但是原文中并没有明确这一点，也有可能是首段所描述的其他因素导致晚点现象的产生，因此该项属于主观臆断，可排除。选项B中的the five-year target对应首段第一句，原文明确指出是早高峰和工程技术方面的故障导致五年计划难以实现，与该项所指不符，因此排除。选项D所谈到的morning rush-hour虽然在首段两句中反复出现，但是原文并没有对诸多因素的严重程度进行比较，只是列举，因此该项属于过度推断，可以排除。

Para. 3 ①A spokesperson for Network Rail said: "Severe weather with multiple flooding, landslide and embankment slip events caused severe disruption over a number of days to many train operators and particularly impacted our long-distance customers." ②Some of the worst of the flooding last month was in the West Country. ③Yet First Great Western still managed to run 84% of trains on time—albeit down on the 89.5% figure it achieved in the same period a year before. ④Although the flooding did cause much disruption and London Midland's staff problems contributed to the difficulties, passengers on many lines were also hit by a series of signal faults and broken-down trains at peak times. ⑤The latest figures, which come only a few days after passengers saw the price of their season tickets rise by an average 4.2%, do not include cancellations and delays caused by planned engineering work.

参考译文 ①英国铁路网公司的发言人表示:"极端天气加上多次洪水、塌陷和路基滑移事件导致火车运行严重中断多日,尤其对长途乘客的出行产生了影响。"②上个月发生在西南诸郡的几次洪水最为严重。③然而大西部第一铁路公司依然将列车准点率保持在84%,虽然与去年同期的89.5%相比低了一些。④虽然洪水确实造成了很多破坏,并且伦敦米德兰铁路公司的人员短缺问题也确实带来了困难,但是多条线路上的乘客还在高峰时段遇到了信号和车辆故障等情况。⑤最新数据发布几天前,乘客发现季票价格平均上涨了4.2%。该最新数据所统计的准点率还不包括工程计划造成的取消或延误。

原文剖析 本段首句给出英国铁路网公司的官方理由,大意是恶劣的天气及相伴而生的自然灾害造成了晚点现象,呼应首段谈到的一个因素。第二句对其理由进行了支持。但第三句转折指出即便如此仍有铁路运营公司保持了较高的准点率。第四句进一步谈到,自然灾害和人手短缺(客观因素)不是唯一因素,列车的信号和车辆故障等公司的主观管理因素也在影响着乘客体验。第五句进行了补充说明,指出该数据还不包括因工程计划造成的取消和延误情况,暗指列车晚点的情况比统计显示的更为严重。

设题点睛 本段首句是带有观点的长难句,适合设置考点。第四句带有although引导的让步状语,也可设置考点。最后一句虽然是带有否定结构的长难句,但是所表述的观点不如首句明确,用来设置正确选项的概率要低一些。

生词解析

landslide *n.* 塌方,滑坡 embankment *n.* 路堤
disruption *n.* 中断 albeit *conj.* 即使,虽然

2 It is suggested in paragraph 3 that _____.   第三段暗示了_____。

 A. signal faults are the main reason for the decline of punctuality   A. 信号故障是准点率下降的主要原因

 B. natural disaster is not the only culprit behind the rail unpunctuality   B. 自然灾害不是导致火车晚点的唯一元凶

C. long-distance customers suffered most from severe weather conditions

D. passengers are discontent with the rising price of season tickets

C. 长途旅客受到恶劣天气的影响最大

D. 乘客对于季票价格的提高表示不满

【解题思路】B。推理引申题。根据题干要求定位到第三段,题干中没有给出更加明确的定位点,需要重点理解第三段中的考点结构。本段首句为含有观点的长难句,大意是极端天气及随之而来的洪水、滑坡等自然灾害使列车运行中断了数日。这是铁路公司给出的客观理由,该段第四句指出除了这些因素,人员短缺、信号和车辆故障同样也导致了列车晚点现象的产生。最后一句还谈到了工程计划所导致的列车延误或者取消,也属于导致列车晚点的因素之一。选项B合理综合了本段诸多因素,因此是正确答案。

【排他分析】选项A中的signal faults对应本段第四句的内容,原文指出信号和车辆故障也会导致晚点,但这只是造成晚点的诸多因素之一,且该段并未指出哪种因素的作用更大,因此排除。选项C中的long-distance customers对应首句内容,原文中确实指出长途旅客受到铁路运行连日中断的影响更甚,但该项中的suffered一词相比原文所用的impacted而言程度太深,且长途旅客并非直接受到天气情况影响,根本原因还在于铁路运行中断,因此该项与原文意思并不十分一致,故排除。选项D中的season tickets对应本段最后一句的非限制性定语从句中的内容,谈到火车的季票价格上涨了4.2%,暗示票价刚涨上去,但是晚点率依然可观,虽然可以想象旅客应该对此感到不满,但由于原文中并没有明显的语意支持,因此选项D属于过度推断,可以排除。

Para. 4 ① In the year from 6 January 2012 to 5 January 2013, train companies ran 91.4% of trains on time. ② This is below the 92.5% target for the period 2009-14—a five-year target average that NR is set to miss. ③ Announcing to-be-approved £37.5bn plans for the railways earlier this week, NR said its target for 2014-19 would be unchanged.

参考译文 ①2012年1月6日到2013年1月5日,铁路公司的总体准点率达到了91.4%。②这与英国铁路网公司所提出的五年计划目标仍有差距——该公司提出2009至2014年的平均准点率要达到92.5%。③英国铁路网公司这周早些时候宣布该公司即将通过375亿英镑的铁路计划,并且表示其2014至2019年的准点率目标不会改变。

原文剖析 本段首句介绍了英国所有铁路公司2012至2013年的总体准点率(91.4%),为第二句的反驳做铺垫。第二句随即指出已实现的这个准点率低于英国铁路网公司所提出的五年计划的平均目标(92.5%)。第三句谈到英国铁路网公司为此所做的弥补和努力:将启动375亿英镑的铁路计划,并表示将在下个五年实现这一目标。

设题点睛 本段出现了诸多数据。前两句间存在转折语意,明确说明目前实现的准点率与平均目标有差距,由于观点比较单一,不适合设置干扰选项,因此作为考点出现的概率较低。

Para. 5 ① An Office of Rail Regulation spokesman said: "Some rail passengers have suffered poor performance in recent weeks—far

参考译文 ①铁路管理处的一名发言人表示:"近几周内,有些乘客的乘车体验不佳,这和他们这几年

below the high standards they have come to expect in recent years."②The regulator has asked NR to explain the cause of these failings and to provide an update on its progress to improve performance on the key long-distance and London and south-east routes. ③It is imperative the rail industry learns lessons and improves train punctuality for passengers in the future.

期望看到的高标准服务质量有很大差距。"②监管部门已经要求英国铁路网公司对于其服务质量下降的原因给予解释,并要求该公司随时更新其在改善关键长途线路、伦敦和东南线路服务质量方面所取得的进展。③未来铁路行业必须要总结经验、吸取教训,提高准点率。

原文剖析 本段首句为管理部门对目前列车晚点率上升问题的评价,指出这与旅客的期望严重不符。后两句继续谈到管理部门对铁路运营公司的要求:首先给公众合理的解释,其次改善长途线路及伦敦和东南线路的服务质量,并随时公布进展,最终要实现提高准点率的目标。

设题点睛 本段三句话均是政府管理部门对目前铁路晚点现状的评价和要求,均为重要内容,一般会设置考点。

生词解析

failing *n.* 失败;过失　　　　　　　　update *n.* 最新消息;最新进展

route *n.* 路线;航线

3 The spokesman from the Office of Rail Regulation suggests that _____.

A. NR should apologize for the decline of its service quality
B. rail passengers are outrageous for the poor performance they suffered
C. efforts made to improve passengers' satisfaction should be reported by NR
D. passengers' satisfaction should be regarded as the uppermost goal by NR

铁路管理处发言人的意思是_____。

A. 英国铁路网公司应该为其服务质量的下降道歉
B. 铁路乘客对他们所体验到的差劲服务感到愤怒
C. 英国铁路网公司应报告其在改善乘客满意度方面所做的努力
D. 让乘客满意应是英国铁路网公司的最高目标

【解题思路】D。推理引申题。根据题干关键词(spokesman from the Office of Rail Regulation)定位到第五段首句。原文为此人的观点,大意是目前铁路系统出现的晚点现象严重影响了乘客的乘车体验。本段最后一句总结并强调管理机关对铁路公司的要求,即必须吸取教训,提高未来列车的准点率。结合这两句的内容,可看出管理部门认为目前铁路公司的服务没有达到乘客的要求,希望它们为实现这一目标做出努力,与选项D的意思一致,该项中的 uppermost goal 体现第五段最后一句中 It is imperative 的语气。

【排他分析】选项A中的关键词NR在第五段第二句出现,原文只是要求其给出解释,并未要求道歉,因此排除该项。选项B中的 poor performance 对应第五段首句,但原文只是说乘客的乘车体验并没有达到期望值,由此推断乘客应该感到失望,并无法推知乘客会产生愤怒的情绪,因此该项没有原文语意支撑,所以排除。选项C的内容可大致对应第五段第二句中管理部门对NR的要求,但原文是说该公司要实时更新其对长途线路服务质量的提升进度,而非本项所说的要报告其在改善乘客满意度方面所做的努力,该项与原文不符,因此排除。

Para. 6 ①The leader of the RMT transport union, Bob Crow, said: "These figures make a nonsense of the government's McNulty rail review plans, which would axe yet more staff from the railways even though it is clear that punctuality is already being compromised by a shortage of staff." ②No matter how the government and the train companies try to dress this up, the fact is that rail travel was more efficient, punctual and cheaper under British Rail and we will continue to press the case for full renationalisation.

参考译文 ①英国伦敦铁路、海运及运输工会的领导人鲍勃·克罗(Bob Crow)表示:"这些数据让政府的McNulty铁路审查计划毫无意义,该计划还想从铁路行业裁撤更多人员,即便事实证明人员短缺已经大大影响了准点率。"②无论政府和铁路公司如何努力地粉饰太平,事实上,过去英国铁路公司的运营更为有效、更为准时、价格也更便宜。我们会继续推动英国铁路重新国有化。

原文剖析 本段给出工会领导人的观点,此人表示前文谈到的铁路晚点数据让政府的铁路审查计划失去意义,并给出原因:该计划想要进一步裁撤铁路人员,无疑会加剧铁路晚点的现象。此人明显站在了铁路工人一边。第二句给出他对目前铁路晚点情况的评价和建议:铁路系统过去在国有的英国铁路公司的管理下表现得比现在要好,因此建议英国铁路重新国有化。

设题点睛 本段的两个单句都存在比较重要的内容,体现除铁路公司、政府之外的铁路工会的立场和态度,都可设置考点。

生词解析

axe *vt.* 削减 compromise *vt.* 危害
dress up 粉饰,美化 renationalization *n.* 重新收归国有

长难句解析

The leader of the RMT transport union, Bob Crow, said: "These figures make a nonsense of
　　　主语1　　　　　　　　同位语　谓语1　主语2　谓语2　补足语
the government's McNulty rail review plans, which would axe yet more staff from the railways
　　　　宾语　　　　　　　　　　　　　非限制性定语从句
even though it is clear that punctuality is already being compromised by a shortage of staff."
　　　　　　　　　让步状语从句

本句是直接引语,主句为The leader of the RMT transport union said...,引号之中的句子作said的宾语,其中使用了make a nonsense of sth.的结构,可还原为make sth. nonsense,因此nonsense作实际宾语sth.的补足语,which引导的非限制性定语从句修饰McNulty rail review plans,其中还包含一个让步状语从句。

4 According to the last paragraph, Bob Crow contends that _____ .

A. McNulty rail review plans insist on recruiting more staff

通过最后一段可知,鲍勃·克罗声称_____。

A. McNulty铁路审查计划坚持雇用更多员工

B. British Rail should not compromise on the shortage of staff
C. the government calls for a full renationalisation of railway
D. British Rail is the key to solve the current predicament

B. 英国铁路公司不应该就人员短缺问题做出妥协
C. 政府号召铁路重新国有化
D. 英国铁路公司是解决目前困境的关键

【解题思路】D。推理引申题。根据题干中的人名直接定位到最后一段。整段都是此人的观点。在第二句中，此人谈到"事实上，过去英国铁路公司的运营更为有效、更为准时、价格也更便宜"，并号召英国铁路重新国有化，注意在赞美英国铁路公司的管理时使用了过去时 was，可判断英国铁路公司是国有企业，目前已被私有化的铁路公司所取代，才导致了目前的晚点问题。由此可见，选项 D 符合此人的观点。

【排他分析】选项 A 中的 McNulty rail review plans 对应最后一段首句，对该审查的修饰语明确指出其意在裁撤更多铁路员工（which would axe yet more staff），与该项的 recruiting 方向相反，因此排除。选项 B 中的 compromise 和 shortage of staff 对应本段首句，原文是说列车准点率因铁路员工短缺而受到影响，be compromised by 含有"被……连累"的意思，与本项的意思无关，所以排除。选项 C 中的 full renationalisation 对应本段最后一句，根据前半句"无论政府和铁路公司如何努力地粉饰太平"可看出政府和铁路公司的看法与鲍勃·克罗相反，鲍勃·克罗在后半句中表示希望重新实现英国铁路的国有化，则与之观点相反的英国政府不希望铁路重新国有化，因此排除该项。

5. Which of the following is the best title for the text? | 以下哪个选项最适合做本文的标题？

A. Rail Unpunctuality Chaos: NR under Pressure
B. The Ever-Brighter Future for the British Rail System
C. NR's Contribution to Rail Punctuality
D. British Rail: Privatisation VS Renationalisation

A. 铁路晚点导致的混乱：英国铁路网公司压力巨大
B. 英国铁路系统前所未有的光明未来
C. 英国铁路网公司为列车准点做出的贡献
D. 英国铁路：私有化还是再次国有化

【解题思路】A。主旨大意题。文章首段到第三段围绕英国铁路网公司面临因列车准点率低而无法实现五年目标的话题，列举了英国不同列车公司的准点率数据，并分析了造成晚点率高的各种原因。第四段介绍英国铁路网公司对此的举措和反应，第五段谈到政府对英国铁路网公司的要求，最后一段从工会领导人的角度谈论英国铁路国有化才是解决问题的关键。前五段内容都涉及英国铁路网公司，最后一段谈到用国有化公司取代私有化公司的建议。综合分析，选项 A 可概括本文内容，因此是最佳标题。

【排他分析】本文在讨论英国铁路系统面临的问题，与选项 A 谈到的"更光明的未来"矛盾，因此排除。选项 C 与原文谈到的事实相反，文章并没有介绍英国铁路网公司是如何努力保持列车准点率的，相反指出该公司并没有达到其五年计划中有关准点率的目标，且在客户服务上做得也不够，并且相关人士（工会领导人）希望今后由国有的英国铁路公司代替英国铁路网公司,因此排除该项。选项 D 有关重新国有化的内容只在最后一段提到,且全文并没有正面谈及私有化和重新国有化的比较或较量,因此该项属于以偏概全,可以排除。

Text 23

Where does morality come from? Throughout the history of Western civilization, thinkers have usually answered either that it comes from God, or else through the application of reason.

But in *The Bonobo and the Atheist*, primatologist Frans de Waal argues that there's another answer that fits the data better: morality comes from our evolutionary past as a social primate. Like our closest relatives the apes, humans evolved in small, tightly knit, cooperative groups. As a result, again like the apes, we are exquisitely sensitive to one another's moods, needs and intentions.

This well-developed empathy provided the trellis on which morality later flowered. De Waal, who is based at Emory University in Atlanta, Georgia, has been making this case eloquently for many years and over several books, notably in *Good Natured* back in 1997, and in *Primates and Philosophers*, 12 years later.

In his new work, he bolsters the argument by drawing on a lot of new research, carefully footnoted for those who want to dig deeper. De Waal distinguishes two degrees of morality. The first he calls "one-on-one morality," which governs how an individual can expect to be treated, and the second "community concern," a larger, more abstract concept that extends to the harmony of the group as a whole.

Chimps and bonobos certainly have the former—they respect ownership, for example, and expect to be treated according to their place in the hierarchy. But de Waal presents several examples—such as a chimp stepping in to stop a fight between two others—that suggest that they also have a rudimentary form of the latter.

The book's title, incidentally, draws on bonobos because they are more likely than chimps to behave morally, to have concern for each other, to value harmony and so on. This, imagines de Waal, is something morally inclined atheists would want to emulate.

If humans inherited morality from our ancestors, though, what are we to make of religion? Here de Waal moves into territory he has not explored before. Clearly, religion must do something important, since every human culture has it. But instead of religion giving us morality, de Waal turns the tables. Morality, he argues, probably gave us religion as a way of reinforcing the pre-existing community concern.

If he's right, then there may be no absolute code of right and wrong out there to be discovered. Instead, each individual's evolved sense of empathy and concern for the group may help shape the group's consensus on what kind of behavior is appropriate. In short, says de Waal, morality may be something we all have to work out together. It's a persuasive argument, and de Waal's cautious and evidence-based approach is one that many *New Scientist* readers are sure to find congenial.

(*New Scientist*, 2013.5)

1. Frans de Waal holds that morality mainly comes from _____.
   A. our sentiment towards others' needs and intentions
   B. the application of reason
   C. the continuous process of human evolution
   D. our status as a high-level social primate

2. Which of the following is true about morality?
   A. De Waal himself alone promotes the study of morality.
   B. "Community concern" is superior to "one-on-one morality".
   C. "One-on-one morality" leads to the harmony of the whole society.
   D. Well-developed empathy paves the way for the development of morality.

3. What can be learned through de Waal's research?
   A. Hierarchy is a vital factor in cultivating morality.
   B. Hierarchy is more important than ownership.
   C. Primates may sometimes exhibit their concerns for the group.
   D. Chimps are more violent than bonobos.

4. What does de Waal think of religion?
   A. It paves the way for the enhancement of community concern.
   B. It is reinforced by the evolvement of morality.
   C. It helps to form the human society.
   D. It breeds the community concern.

5. It can be learned from the last paragraph that _____.
   A. de Waal's argument is popular among readers in the scientific community
   B. collective effort is required for the formation of morality
   C. a code of right and wrong needs to be found in the future
   D. appropriate behaviors are necessary for the group to achieve consensus

语篇分析与试题精解

Para. 1 ① Where does morality come from? ② Throughout the history of Western civilization, thinkers have usually answered either that it comes from God, or else through the application of reason.

参考译文 ①道德从何而来？②纵观西方文明史，思想家常给出两种回答：道德要么是上帝的馈赠，要么是人类对理性的运用。

原文剖析 本段中的两句构成"设问＋回答"的结构，点出本文要讨论的话题——道德的来源。

设题点睛 从英文文章的一般结构上说,很少会在一开始就直接给出问题的正确答案,因此本段第二句的回答极有可能是错误的(过去的观点皆为错),是要被后文的论述所否定的,因此本段不存在可设置正确选项的内容。

生词解析

morality *n.* 道德;道德准则　　　　　　or else 要不然,否则
reason *n.* 理性;理智

长难句解析

Throughout the history of Western civilization, thinkers have usually answered either that it
　　　　　状语　　　　　　　　　　　　　主语　　　　谓语
comes from God, or else through the application of reason.
　　　　　　　　　宾语从句

本句是主从复合句。本句的主干为 thinkers have answered that...,谓语 answered 后的 that 从句作宾语,该从句还含有一个 either... or else 的结构,表示"要么……要么……"。

Para. 2 ①But in *The Bonobo and the Atheist*, primatologist Frans de Waal argues that there's another answer that fits the data better: morality comes from our evolutionary past as a social primate. ②Like our closest relatives the apes, humans evolved in small, tightly knit, cooperative groups. ③As a result, again like the apes, we are exquisitely sensitive to one another's moods, needs and intentions.

参考译文 ①但是在《倭黑猩猩和无神论者》一书中,灵长类动物学家弗兰斯·德·瓦尔(Frans de Waal)辩称,能够更好地解读数据的答案为:道德来源于人类这一群居型灵长类动物的进化史。②就像我们的近亲——类人猿一样,人类在一个小而紧密合作的群体中进化。③因此,也像类人猿一样,我们对彼此的情绪变化、需求和意图很敏感。

原文剖析 本段首句给出了一个更合理的解释(道德来源于人类的进化),后两句是对首句内容的道理论证,指出群体生活使人类对彼此的情感等要求更敏感,并由此产生了道德。

设题点睛 本段构成了"观点+道理论证"的结构,道理论证部分用于解释原因,因此是重要的考点内容,可用来设置考点。

生词解析

bonobo *n.* 倭黑猩猩　　　　　　　　　　atheist *n.* 无神论者
primatologist *n.* 灵长类动物学家　　　　fit *vt.* 使适合;与……相配;符合
evolutionary *adj.* 进化的　　　　　　　　social *adj.* (动物)群居的
primate *n.* 灵长类动物　　　　　　　　　ape *n.* 类人猿;猿;无尾猿
knit *vt.* 使紧密结合;使严密;使紧凑　　　exquisitely *adv.* 强烈地;异常地;敏锐地

1	Frans de Waal holds that morality mainly comes from _____.	弗兰斯·德·瓦尔认为道德主要来源于_____。
	A. our sentiment towards others' needs and intentions	A. 我们对其他人需求和意图的情感
	B. the application of reason	B. 对理性的运用

227

C. the continuous process of human evolution 　　C. 人类不断进化的过程
D. our status as a high-level social primate 　　D. 人类作为高级群居型灵长类动物的地位

【解题思路】C。事实细节题。根据题干中的人名(Frans de Waal)定位到原文第二段。该段整段都体现此人的观点,第一句指出他认为"道德来源于人类这一群居型灵长类动物的进化史"(morality comes from our evolutionary past as a social primate),选项 C 中的 continuous process of evolution 对应该句中的 our evolutionary past,因此该项正确。

【排他分析】选项 A 中的部分内容在第二段最后一句中有所涉及,但原文只是说"我们对彼此的情绪变化、需求和意图很敏感"(sensitive to one another's moods, needs and intentions),sensitive 表示"对……有细腻感情的",与选项 A 中 sentiment 所表示的"(怜悯、怀旧等)情感"不同,sentiment 所表达的"情感"可能是夸张的或滥施的,尤其与"理智"相对,因此排除该项。选项 B 对应第一段中的内容,是明确被第二段所否定的答案,可以直接排除。选项 D 对应第二段第一句中的 as a social primate,但该项所突出的 status as a high-level 在原文中并未明确体现,且该项不涉及"人类进化"这一关键信息点,因此不是正确答案。

Para. 3 ① This well-developed empathy provided the trellis on which morality later flowered. ② De Waal, who is based at Emory University in Atlanta, Georgia, has been making this case eloquently for many years and over several books, notably in *Good Natured* back in 1997, and in *Primates and Philosophers*, 12 years later.

参考译文 ①这种充分发展的同理心为道德的成长提供了基础。②来自佐治亚州亚特兰大市埃默里大学的德·瓦尔多年来一直从事这项研究,并在许多著作中表达了这一观点,尤其是在其1997年出版的《生来温顺》,以及12年后出版的《灵长类动物与哲学家》这两本书中。

原文剖析 本段首句总结上段观点(即同理心带来了道德),且采用了比喻手法,将道德的成长比喻为"开花"(flowered),将同理心比喻为"花架"(trellis)。第二句具体介绍了德·瓦尔及其研究的背景细节。

设题点睛 本段首句属于观点性内容,相对于第二句背景知识类的细节内容而言,更适合用来设置正确选项。

生词解析

empathy *n.* 同感 　　trellis *n.* 格子棚架
flower *vi.* 开花 　　eloquently *adv.* 善辩地;富于表现力地

长难句解析

This well-developed empathy provided the trellis on which morality later flowered.
　　　　主语　　　　　　　谓语　　　宾语　　　　　定语从句

本句是主从复合句。本句的主干为 This empathy provided the trellis,宾语后是一个介词提前的定语从句,修饰先行词 trellis,可还原为 the trellis which morality later flowered on。

Para. 4 ①In his new work, he bolsters the argument by drawing on a lot of new research, carefully footnoted for those who want to dig deeper. ②De Waal distinguishes two degrees of morality. ③The first he calls "one-on-one morality," which governs how an individual can expect to be treated, and the second "community concern," a larger, more abstract concept that extends to the harmony of the group as a whole.

参考译文 ①在他的新书里,他将新研究的许多结论为己所用,进一步证明了自己的观点,他在书的脚注中详细说明了这些新研究的来源,以便其他人加以探究。②德·瓦尔把道德分为两个级别。③第一个级别被他称为"个人道德",这种道德决定着一个人希望自己被如何对待;第二个是"社会关怀",这是一种能够延伸至整个集体和谐程度的、范围更大且更抽象的概念。

原文剖析 本段承接上段,首句介绍德·瓦尔研究的理论基础。第二句为过渡句,引出第三句德·瓦尔对道德程度的区分:"个人道德"和"社会关怀"。

设题点睛 第三句为带有并列关系的长难句,可以利用并列内容中的任意一点设置题目。

生词解析

bolster *vt.* 支持;加强
footnote *vt.* 给……作脚注
extend to 延伸到,(使)达到

draw on 利用;凭借
distinguish *vt.* 区别,辨别(人或事物)
as a whole 作为一个整体;整个看来

长难句解析

The first he calls "one-on-one morality," which governs how an individual can expect to be
宾语1　主谓　　宾语补足语1　　　　　　　非限制性定语从句
treated, and the second "community concern," a larger, more abstract concept that extends
　　　　　　宾语2　　宾语补足语2　　　　　　　同位语　　　　　　　　定语从句
to the harmony of the group as a whole.

本句是并列复合句。本句的主干为 The first he calls "one-on-one morality" and the second "community concern",第一句的主干使用了倒装语序,可还原为 he calls the first "one-on-one morality",后一句的主干中省略了 he calls,两句的宾语补足语分别由一个非限制性定语从句和同位语修饰,用于补充说明。

2 Which of the following is true about morality?

A. De Waal himself alone promotes the study of morality.
B. "Community concern" is superior to "one-on-one morality".
C. "One-on-one morality" leads to the harmony of the whole society.
D. Well-developed empathy paves the way for the development of morality.

关于道德,以下哪项正确?

A. 德·瓦尔独自一人促进了道德研究的发展。
B. "社会关怀"高于"个人道德"。
C. "个人道德"促成整个社会的和谐。
D. 充分发展的同理心为道德的发展铺平道路。

【解题思路】D。事实细节题。题干中不存在明确的定位提示,只能通过"顺序原则+选项内容"确定大概的定位句。原文第三段首句指出 well-developed empathy provided the trellis on which morality later flowered,表示充分发展的同理心促成日后道德观的形成,原文使用了比喻用法,provided the trellis 与选项 D 中的 paves the way for 属于同义替换,因此该项正确。

【排他分析】第四段首句指出"他将新研究的许多结论为己所用"(by drawing on a lot of new research),由此推断也有其他人曾做过类似研究并得出了相关结论,与选项 A 中的 himself alone 不一致,因此该项错误。第四段第三句中的"个人道德"和"社会关怀"是两个并列的概念,原文并未对两者进行高低比较,因此选项 B 没有原文支撑,可排除。第四段第三句的后半部分指出"社会关怀"的概念可延伸至整个集体的和谐程度,因此选项 C 属于张冠李戴,可排除。

Para. 5 ①Chimps and bonobos certainly have the former—they respect ownership, for example, and expect to be treated according to their place in the hierarchy. ②But de Waal presents several examples—such as a chimp stepping in to stop a fight between two others—that suggest that they also have a rudimentary form of the latter.

参考译文 ①黑猩猩和倭黑猩猩当然具有个人道德,譬如,它们尊重所有权,并期望按照所处的等级地位享受相应的待遇。②但是德·瓦尔给出了几个不同的例子,比如黑猩猩会插手阻止其他两只猩猩的争斗,这表明了它们也具有基本的社会关怀道德感。

原文剖析 本段承接第四段,并再次以灵长类动物为例,指出黑猩猩和倭黑猩猩都具有个人道德和一定程度的社会关怀道德感。

设题点睛 本段属于举例论证,其中第二句为带有转折语意的长难句,可以用来设置正确选项。

生词解析

chimp *n.* 黑猩猩　　　　　　　　　hierarchy *n.* 等级制度
step in 插手干预;介入　　　　　　rudimentary *adj.* 基本的;早期的

长难句解析

But de Waal presents several examples—such as a chimp stepping in to stop a fight between
　　　主语　　谓语　　　宾语　　　　　　　　　　　　插入语
two others—that suggest that they also have a rudimentary form of the latter.
　　　　　　　定语从句　　　　宾语从句

本句是主从复合句。本句的主干为 But de Waal presents several examples that...,破折号中间的部分作插入语,对 examples 的内容进行举例说明,that suggest 定语从句的先行词是 several examples,该定语从句中还包含 that 引导的宾语从句。

Para. 6 ①The book's title, incidentally, draws on bonobos because they are more likely than

参考译文 ①此外,这本书用倭黑猩猩做标题,原因在于倭黑猩猩比黑猩

chimps to behave morally, to have concern for each other, to value harmony and so on. ② This, imagines de Waal, is something morally inclined atheists would want to emulate.

猩更有可能做出有道德感的举动,更懂得关心彼此和重视集体和谐等。②德·瓦尔认为这一具有道德倾向的做法,是无神论者们仿效的对象。

原文剖析 本段首句承接上一段最后的内容,上一段最后指出黑猩猩和倭黑猩猩具有基本的社会关怀道德感,但本书却以倭黑猩猩为题,本句解释这样做是因为倭黑猩猩更有可能表现出道德感。第二句指出这种具有道德倾向的行为是无神论者想要仿效的。

设题点睛 本段首句存在原因分析,第二句为个人观点,都是可设置正确选项的重要内容。

生词解析

incidentally *adv.* 附带地;顺便提一句　　morally *adv.* 道德上;有道德地
inclined *adj.* 倾向于……的　　emulate *vt.* 效法;赶超

长难句解析

This, imagines de Waal, is something morally inclined atheists would want to emulate.
主语　　插入语　　系动词　　表语　　定语从句

本句是主从复合句。本句主干为 This is something morally inclined (that)…,主系表之间插入了一个倒装成分,本句也可还原为 de Waal imagines this is something…。由于修饰 something 的形容词 morally inclined 要后置,因此隔开了定语从句 atheists would want to emulate 与其先行词 something,使这个句子显得有些复杂。

3	What can be learned through de Waal's research?	从德·瓦尔的研究中可以得出以下哪个结论?
	A. Hierarchy is a vital factor in cultivating morality.	A. 等级制度是塑造道德感的重要因素。
	B. Hierarchy is more important than ownership.	B. 等级制度比所有制更重要。
	C. Primates may sometimes exhibit their concerns for the group.	C. 灵长类动物有时会对集体表现出关心。
	D. Chimps are more violent than bonobos.	D. 黑猩猩比倭黑猩猩更凶猛。

【解题思路】C。推理引申题。题干中不存在特别明确的定位线索,因此需要通过"顺序原则+选项内容"返回原文中查找。原文第五段第二句指出 they also have a rudimentary form of the latter,其中的 they 指代黑猩猩和倭黑猩猩,说明这两种动物所代表的灵长类动物具有基本的社会关怀道德感。第六段第一句指出倭黑猩猩相对于黑猩猩更有可能表现出道德感,说明倭黑猩猩在这方面的道德感要更强(因此被选作标题)。选项 C 中的 Primates 指代这两种猩猩,may sometimes exhibit 对应原文的 rudimentary,而 concerns for the group 是对"community concern"的同义替换,因此是正确答案。

【排他分析】选项 A 中的 hierarchy 出现在第五段第一句中,该句指出"(猩猩们)尊重所有权,并期望按照所处的等级地位享受相应的待遇",意在指出猩猩们具有一定程度的个人道德,而"等级地位"与"道德培养"之间的关系并不明确,因此该项属于主观臆断,可排除。同时,该句中与 hierarchy 和 ownership 有关的两个例子属于并列内容,原文并未对两者进行比较,因此排除选项 B。第六段首句对两种猩猩的道德性进行了比较,指出"倭黑猩猩比黑猩猩更有可能做出有道德感的举动,更懂得关心彼此和重视集体和谐等",原文仅针对行为体现的道德感进行比较,并未涉及对两种动物凶残度(violent)的比较,因此选项 D 与本文无关,可排除。

Para. 7 ①If humans inherited morality from our ancestors, though, what are we to make of religion? ②Here de Waal moves into territory he has not explored before. ③Clearly, religion must do something important, since every human culture has it. ④But instead of religion giving us morality, de Waal turns the tables. ⑤Morality, he argues, probably gave us religion as a way of reinforcing the pre-existing community concern.

参考译文 ①如果人类是从我们的祖先那里继承道德的,那么我们应该如何看待宗教?②在这方面,德·瓦尔进入了一个他从未涉足的领域。③宗教固然举足轻重,因为每一个人类文化中都有宗教的身影。④但德·瓦尔转而说道,并非宗教给予我们道德。⑤他认为可能是道德使人类社会产生了宗教,并用宗教强化早已存在于人们心里的社会关怀。

原文剖析 首句提出本段要讨论的另一个相关主题,即宗教对于道德形成的作用。从第二句至本段结束,作者通过德·瓦尔的话运用道理论证的方式给出结论,指出与人们过去的想法不同,道德并非源于宗教,反而是宗教强化了我们早已拥有的社会关怀道德观。

设题点睛 本段首句与后半部分构成了"设问+回答"的结构,最后一句为德·瓦尔对道德来源问题的最终解答,属于重要考点,可以用来设置题目。

生词解析

make of 对……有某种看法;理解   territory n. (行动等的)领域;范围
turn the tables 扭转局势;反败为胜

4 **What does de Waal think of religion?**   **德·瓦尔如何看待宗教?**

A. It paves the way for the enhancement of community concern.
B. It is reinforced by the evolution of morality.
C. It helps to form the human society.
D. It breeds the community concern.

A. 宗教为社会关怀道德感的加强铺平道路。
B. 宗教因道德的演变而得到加强。
C. 宗教有助于构建人类社会。
D. 宗教培育了社会关怀道德感。

【解题思路】A。推理引申题。根据题干关键词(religion)定位至文章第七段。本段最后一句是德·瓦尔对于宗教和道德关系的解释,指出"道德使人类社会产生了宗教,并用宗教强化早已存在于人们心里的社会关怀"(Morality probably gave us religion as a way of reinforcing the pre-existing community concern)。选项 A 既谈到宗教可促进社会关怀道德感的加强,又能体现社会关怀早已存在,并非在宗教之后产生,是对原文的正确理解,因此该项正确。

【排他分析】选项 B 同样对应本段最后一句,但该项是说宗教因道德的进化而得以加强,事实上原文表示宗教因道德而出现,而非"加强",因此排除。第七段主要讨论了道德和宗教产生的先后关系,而非宗教与人类社会产生的先后关系,因此可直接排除选项 C。选项 D 中的 breed 作及物动词时表示"(使)产生,造成,引起",因此本项含有宗教先于社会关怀道德感产生之意,与第七段最后一句的意思直接冲突,因此也可排除。

Para. 8 ①If he's right, then there may be no absolute code of right and wrong out there to be discovered. ②Instead, each individual's evolved sense of empathy and concern for the group may help shape the group's consensus on what kind of behavior is appropriate. ③In short, says de Waal, morality may be something we all have to work out together. ④It's a persuasive argument, and de Waal's cautious and evidence-based approach is one that many *New Scientist* readers are sure to find congenial.

参考译文 ①如果他是对的,那么也许不存在绝对的是非标准。②相反,每一个人对集体的同理心和关怀之心不断演变,有助于集体在什么是恰当行为的问题上达成共识。③总而言之,用德·瓦尔的话来说,道德可能需要我们共同制定。④这种说法比较有说服力,而且德·瓦尔严谨实证的研究方式广受《新科学家》读者的认同。

原文剖析 本段首句和第二句为含有转折语意的"A. Instead, B."的句型结构,出现转折的第二句是更为重要的内容,该句给出一个新的观点,即个人对集体的同理心和关怀之心会促成集体达成对恰当行为方面的共识。第三句和第四句可看作总结,指出道德是由人类共同创造的事物。

设题点睛 本段第二句从逻辑上看属于重要内容,而第三句是德·瓦尔的结论性观点,因此两句都适合用来设置正确选项。

生词解析

code *n.* 规则,准则
work out 制定出,做出
cautious *adj.* 谨慎的

consensus *n.* 共识
persuasive *adj.* 有说服力的
congenial *adj.* 合意的,相宜的,适合的

长难句解析

Instead, each individual's evolved sense of empathy and concern for the group may help shape the group's consensus on what kind of behavior is appropriate.

主语:each individual's evolved sense of empathy and concern for the group
谓语:may help
宾语:shape the group's consensus
后置定语:on what kind of behavior is appropriate

本句为主从复合句。本句主干为 each individual's evolved sense of empathy and concern may help shape the group's consensus,主语较长,individual's 应理解为所有格形式,而非简化了 has 的形式,evolved 是过去分词作形容词,表示"进化了的",谓语 help 后为省略了 to 的不定式,作宾语。最后介词 on 及其之后的宾语从句共同作后置定语对 consensus 的范围和内容进行解释说明。

5 It can be learned from the last paragraph that _____.

A. de Waal's argument is popular among readers in the scientific community
B. collective effort is required for the formation of morality

从最后一段中可看出 _____。

A. 德·瓦尔的说法广受科学界读者的欢迎
B. 道德的形成需要集体的努力

233

C. a code of right and wrong needs to be found in the future
D. appropriate behaviors are necessary for the group to achieve consensus

C. 未来需要找到一种是非标准
D. 恰当的行为对集体达成共识很有必要

【解题思路】B。事实细节题。根据题干要求定位到文章最后一段,在没有更加精确定位点的情况下,优先考查本段的观点句或者有重要逻辑结构的句子。本段第三句借用德·瓦尔的话总结指出"道德可能需要我们共同制定"(morality may be something we all have to work out together),与选项B的内容直接对应,该项中的collective effort与原文中的work out together属于同义替换,因此该项正确。

【排他分析】选项A的内容涉及第八段最后一句,但原文只提到"德·瓦尔严谨实证的研究方式广受《新科学家》读者的认同",该项将此杂志的读者延伸到整个科学界,是对杂志名称的错误理解,可排除。选项C中的code of right and wrong在本段首句中出现,文中明确指出按照德·瓦尔的理论,"那么也许不存在绝对的是非标准",和选项C直接矛盾,因此排除。选项D中的consensus在该段第二句中出现,原文指出"每一个人对集体的同理心和关怀之心不断演变,有助于集体在什么是恰当行为的问题上达成共识",应理解为道德演变促使行为准则的产生,选项D将第二句中的细节张冠李戴,与原句的意思无关,因此排除。

Text 24

Federal regulators should hold Facebook chief executive Mark Zuckerberg "individually liable for the company's repeated violations of Americans' privacy," Democratic Sen. Ron Wyden said Tuesday in a letter to the Federal Trade Commission.

The FTC has been probing Facebook since March 2018 to determine if it violated a 2011 agreement with the government to better protect the private data of its users. Wyden's call for accountability follows a report by the *Post* last week that the FTC is reviewing Zuckerberg's past statements and could seek more oversight of his leadership as part of a settlement to end the federal inquiry.

In his letter, Wyden expressed concern that Zuckerberg, the "public face" of the company, is also its majority shareholder, which "insulates him from accountability to Facebook's board and shareholders." The Democratic senator pointed to documents unearthed as part of a British investigation into Facebook that showed the company struck special data-sharing deals with other companies, potentially without the full knowledge of its users.

Under its 2011 agreement with the FTC, Facebook is required to give users greater notice and control over what happens with their data, and violations could carry steep fines. In its current investigation, agency has sought to seek a fine from Facebook ranging into the billions of dollars, sources previously told the *Post*.

A settlement could also include a requirement that the company's board of directors exercise more oversight of Facebook's privacy practices, according to people familiar with the matter who were not authorized to speak on the record because the talks are confidential under law.

"Given Mr. Zuckerberg's deceptive statements, his personal control over Facebook, and his role in approving key decisions related to the sharing of user data, the FTC can and must hold Mr. Zuckerberg personally responsible for these continued violations," Wyden wrote. "The FTC must also make clear the significant and material penalties that will apply to both Facebook the corporate and Mr. Zuckerberg the individual should any future violations occur."

The FTC did not respond to a request for comment. Facebook declined to comment.

Federal watchdogs considered holding Zuckerberg personally accountable as part of their last investigation into Facebook. The FTC initially sought to put Zuckerberg personally under federal order, which would have exposed him to fines and other penalties for future privacy violations, according to records obtained by the *Post* through the Freedom of Information Act. But agency staff ultimately removed Zuckerberg's name from the final agreement with Facebook in 2011.

(*The Washington Post*, 2019.4)

1. What may contribute to Wyden's call for accountability?
   A. The significance of private data protection.
   B. Mark Zuckerberg's removing of responsibility.
   C. The regulators' reluctance of accepting liability.
   D. FTC's way of ending the investigation of Facebook.

2. The word "insulate" (Para. 3) most probably means _____.
   A. discourage   B. shield
   C. separate   D. persuade

3. The enforcement of 2011 agreement is designed to _____.
   A. ensure the rights for users
   B. strengthen Facebook's abilities
   C. avoid being fined by regulators
   D. make the fines more steep

4. As to holding Zuckerberg personally accountable, Wyden's attitude is _____.
   A. unreasonable   B. resolute
   C. tolerant   D. cautious

5. What is the text mainly discussed?
   A. The loophole in the 2011 agreement should be perfected immediately.
   B. The watchdogs' different attitudes towards Mark Zuckerberg's wrongdoings.
   C. Wyden's letter for calling for accountability should get a positive response.
   D. Mark Zuckerberg should be liable for the company's privacy missteps.

语篇分析与试题精解

Para. 1 ① Federal regulators should hold Facebook chief executive Mark Zuckerberg "individually liable for the company's repeated violations of Americans' privacy," Democratic Sen. Ron Wyden said Tuesday in a letter to the Federal Trade Commission.

参考译文 ①民主党参议员罗恩·怀登周二在致美国联邦贸易委员会的一封信中表示,联邦监管机构应要求脸书(Facebook)的首席执行官马克·扎克伯格"为该公司屡次侵犯美国人隐私承担个人责任"。

原文剖析 本段只有一句话,直截了当地说明了民主党参议员罗恩·怀登的个人观点,即他认为联邦监管机构应要求脸书的首席执行官马克·扎克伯格为该公司屡次侵犯美国人隐私承担个人责任。

设题点睛 本段只有一句话,句子较长,但内容上只是指出了某人对某事的观点,并未指出其观点的前因后果等,因此本段不适合单独设置考题。

生词解析

regulator *n.* 监管者,监管机构
violation *n.* 妨碍,侵害;违反

hold sb. liable for sth. 使某人对……负责

Para. 2 ①The FTC has been probing Facebook since March 2018 to determine if it violated a 2011 agreement with the government to better protect the private data of its users. ② Wyden's call for accountability follows a report by the *Post* last week that the FTC is reviewing Zuckerberg's past statements and could seek more oversight of his leadership as part of a settlement to end the federal inquiry.

参考译文 ①自2018年3月以来,联邦贸易委员会一直在调查脸书,以确定它是否违反了2011年与政府达成的一项协议,该协议旨在更好地保护其用户的私人数据。②怀登的问责要求是在《华盛顿邮报》上周发布了一份报告之后提出的,该报告指出联邦贸易委员会正在探究扎克伯格过去关于隐私的声明,且联邦贸易委员会可能会对他的领导层进行更有力的监督,以此作为结束联邦调查、达成协议的一部分要求。

原文剖析 本段首句指出联邦调查委员会自2018年3月以来对脸书保护用户隐私方面的监管,属于客观论述,不包含任何感情色彩。第二句指出了怀登提出问责要求的时间并暗示了怀登提出问责要求的原因,文章首段指出,怀登认为联邦监管机构应要求脸书的首席执行官马克·扎克伯格为该公司屡次侵犯美国人隐私承担个人责任,而根据第二段第二句的报告内容,联邦贸易委员会的做法与怀登的要求存在偏差。

设题点睛 本段第二句暗含了怀登提出问责要求的原因,且第二句是长难句,可用来设置正确选项。

生词解析

probe *vt.* 调查;探究
oversight *n.* 监督,照管

accountability *n.* 有义务,有责任
settlement *n.* (解决争端的)协议,和解

长难句解析

Wyden's call for accountability follows a report by the *Post* last week that the FTC is reviewing Zuckerberg's past statements and could seek more oversight of his leadership as part of a settlement to end the federal inquiry.

主语：Wyden's call
状语：for accountability
谓语：follows
宾语：a report
状语：by the *Post* last week
同位语从句：that the FTC is ...
宾语补足语：as part of a settlement
目的状语：to end the federal inquiry

本句是主从复合句。主句主干为 Wyden's call follows a report，by 介词短语作状语。其后 that 引导的同位语从句的先行词是 a report，该同位语从句中包含两个并列的谓宾成分。as 介词短语作宾语 more oversight 的补足语，动词不定式 to end the... 为目的状语。

1 What may contribute to Wyden's call for accountability?

A. The significance of private data protection.
B. Mark Zuckerberg's removing of responsibility.
C. The regulators' reluctance of accepting liability.
D. FTC's way of ending the investigation of Facebook.

促使怀登提出问责要求的可能性因素是？

A. 保护私人数据的重要性。
B. 马克·扎克伯格推卸责任的行为。
C. 监管机构不愿承担责任。
D. FTC 结束对脸书的调查的方式。

【解题思路】D。推理引申题。根据题干关键词（Wyden's call for accountability）定位到文章第二段第二句。本题考查促使怀登提出问责要求可能的原因。文章第一段具体说明了怀登的问责要求。第二段第二句指出怀登的问责要求的提出时间是在《华盛顿邮报》上周发布了一份报告之后，且该报告的内容与怀登的问责要求存在偏差。由此可推断，怀登认为联邦贸易委员会结束联邦调查的方式与自身看法不符，所以才会提出问责要求，因此选项 D 正确。

【排他分析】选项 A 保护私人数据的重要性本身没有问题，但是文中并未涉及此内容，因此可排除。文章首段说明马克应该承担个人责任，但并未提及他推卸责任，选项 B 属于过度推理，因此排除。选项 C 中的 liability 将文中的 liable 转换了词性并加上了 regulators 进行干扰，但文中同样未提及监管机构不愿承担责任，因此选项 C 排除。

Para. 3 ①In his letter, Wyden expressed concern that Zuckerberg, the "public face" of the company, is also its majority shareholder, which "insulates him from accountability to Facebook's board and shareholders." ②The Democratic senator pointed to documents unearthed as part of a British investigation into Facebook that showed the company struck special data-sharing deals with other companies, potentially without the full knowledge of its users.

参考译文 ①在信中，怀登表达了他的担忧：扎克伯格不仅代表公司的"公众形象"，也是公司的大股东，这使他"无须对脸书的董事会和各位股东负责。" ②民主党参议员指出，英国对脸书的一项调查中发现的文件表明该公司在其用户不知情的情况下，与其他公司达成了特殊的数据共享协议。

原文剖析 本段首句为观点句,表明怀登担心的态度,接着明确指出怀登所担心的内容,即扎克伯格可能无须对脸书的董事会和各位股东负责,以及担心的原因。本段第二句阐述了一个客观事实,即脸书在其用户不知情的情况下,与其他公司达成了特殊的数据共享协议,暗示脸书违反了2011年与政府达成的协议。

设题点睛 本段首句为观点句,且句子较长,可设置题目;第二句为长难句,且句意有所暗指,可设置题目。

生词解析

insulate *vt.* 使免除;使免受(不良影响)　　　　unearth *vt.* 发现,找到
strike deals 达成(对双方都有利的)协议　　　　knowledge *n.* 知晓;知悉

长难句解析

The Democratic senator pointed to documents unearthed as part of a British investigation
　　　主语　　　　　谓语　　　　宾语　　　　　　　　后置定语
into Facebook that showed the company struck special data-sharing deals with other
　　　　　　　　　　　　　　　　　　定语从句
companies, potentially without the full knowledge of its users.
　　　　　　　　　　　　状语

本句是主从复合句。主句主干为 The Democratic senator pointed to documents that…, unearthed as part of… 作 documents 的后置定语,that 引导的定语从句的先行词是 documents,句中的 strike deals 可看作固定用法,表示"达成(对双方都有利的)协议",potentially without… 作状语修饰整个定语从句。

2 The word "insulate" (Para. 3) most probably means _____.　　单词"insulate"(第三段)最有可能的意思是_____。

A. discourage　　　　　　　　　　　　　　A. 阻止
B. shield　　　　　　　　　　　　　　　　　B. 保护某人或某物
C. separate　　　　　　　　　　　　　　　　C. (使)分开
D. persuade　　　　　　　　　　　　　　　D. 劝说

【解题思路】B。语意理解题。根据题干精确定位到第三段第一句。该词汇位于一个定语从句中,该定语从句表明怀登担心的具体内容。结合第一段,怀登希望马克·扎克伯克承担个人责任,那么他此处的担忧应该与他所希望的相悖,也就是扎克伯格可能不会承担个人责任。再根据第三段首句中扎克伯格不仅代表公司的"公众形象",也是公司的大股东,这些都是对扎克伯格有利的论述,由此更加判定,作者担心这些有利因素使他无须对脸书的董事会和各位股东负责,也就是这些有利因素给扎克伯格提供了保护罩,选项 B 符合此处判断,故为正确答案。

【排他分析】既然该定语从句论述的是对扎克伯格有利的地方,那么该词汇的含义就应该是偏正向的,选项 A 和选项 C 的含义非正向,可直接排除。选项 D 比较简单,可直接代入原文,查看句意,验证语意通顺或符合逻辑与否,验证可知,选项 D 语意不当,故排除。

Para. 4 ①Under its 2011 agreement with the FTC, Facebook is required to give users greater notice and control over what happens with their data, and violations could carry steep fines. ②In its current investigation, agency has sought to seek a fine from Facebook ranging into the billions of dollars, sources previously told the *Post*.

【参考译文】①根据2011年与联邦贸易委员会签订的协议,对于用户数据的使用情况,脸书需要给予用户更多的知情权和控制权,违反规定可能会面临巨额罚款。②在目前的调查中,此前有消息人士向《华盛顿邮报》透露,该机构试图对脸书处以数十亿美元的罚款。

【原文剖析】本段第一句陈述理论情况,即按照协议,对于用户数据的使用情况,脸书需要给予用户更多的知情权和控制权。第二句陈述现实状况,该机构试图对脸书处以数十亿美元的罚款,由此可推知脸书可能违反了规定。

【设题点睛】本段第一句含有观点性内容,可用来设置考点。

【生词解析】
under *prep.* 根据,按照
steep *adj.* 过高的;过分的;不合理的

3 The enforcement of 2011 agreement is designed to _____.

A. ensure the rights for users
B. strengthen Facebook's abilities
C. avoid being fined by regulators
D. make the fines more steep

2011年签订协议的实施旨在_____。

A. 确保用户的权利
B. 加强脸书的能力
C. 避免被监管机构罚款
D. 加大罚款力度

【解题思路】A。推理引申题。根据题干关键词(2011 agreement)和设题顺序定位到文章第四段第一句。本题实际考查2011年签订协议的作用。脸书被要求做的那些事其实是协议的内容,协议指出"对于用户数据的使用情况,脸书需要给予用户更多的知情权和控制权,违反规定可能会面临巨额罚款",给予用户更多的对于自己数据使用情况的知情权和控制权是对用户权利的一种保障,对应选项A的内容,该项提到的"权利"(rights)中包括协议中的内容,因此选项A正确。

【排他分析】由文章可知,该协议的目的在于更好地保障用户的权利,保护私人数据,所以不可能去加强脸书的能力,选项B与文意相反。文中明确指出违反规定可能会面临巨额罚款,选项C与文意相悖,故排除。文中是说违反规定可能会面临巨额罚款,选项D曲解为加大罚款力度,况且一项协议的制定必然不是为了加大罚款力度,因此选项D排除。

Para. 5 ① A settlement could also include a requirement that the company's board of directors exercise more oversight of Facebook's privacy practices, according to people familiar with the matter

【参考译文】①据知情人士透露,和解协议还可能包括要求公司董事会对脸书的隐私政策实践加强监督。这些知情人士没有获得公

who were not authorized to speak on the record because the talks are confidential under law.

原文剖析 本段承接上文指出该协议中还可能包括的内容，即要求公司董事会对脸书的隐私政策实践加强监督。

设题点睛 本段虽然阐述了协议的另外一方面，但主要用于叙述事实，并未体现观点，因此不宜设置考题。

生词解析
authorize *vt.* 授权，批准，认可　　　　on the record 公开发布；正式发言
confidential *adj.* 机密的；保密的；秘密的

长难句解析

A settlement could also include a requirement that the company's board of directors
  主语   谓语   宾语   同位语从句
exercise more oversight of Facebook's privacy practices, according to people familiar
                                                              状语
with the matter who were not authorized to speak on the record because the talks are
                     定语从句   原因状语从句
confidential under law.

本句是主从复合句。本句主干为 A settlement could also include a requirement, that 引导的同位语从句的先行词是 a requirement, according to… 作状语修饰整个主句，其中包含一个由 who 引导的定语从句，其先行词是 people, 还包含一个由 because 引导的原因状语从句，解释说明定语从句的内容。

Para. 6 ① "Given Mr. Zuckerberg's deceptive statements, his personal control over Facebook, and his role in approving key decisions related to the sharing of user data, the FTC can and must hold Mr. Zuckerberg personally responsible for these continued violations," Wyden wrote. ② "The FTC must also make clear the significant and material penalties that will apply to both Facebook the corporate and Mr. Zuckerberg the individual should any future violations occur."

参考译文 ①"鉴于扎克伯格的欺骗性声明，他对脸书的个人控制，以及他在批准与分享用户数据相关的关键决策中所扮演的角色，联邦贸易委员会能够而且必须追究扎克伯格个人对这些持续违规行为的责任。"怀登写道。②"联邦贸易委员会还必须明确适用于脸书公司和扎克伯格个人的重大和实质性的惩罚，以防任何违规行为的发生。"

原文剖析 本段主要论述了怀登所写的信的内容，第一句写了联邦贸易委员会能够而且必须追究扎克伯格个人对这些持续违规行为的责任的几条原因，同时表明了怀登比较坚决的态度。第二句怀登认为联邦贸易委员会还应做出其他努力以防止违规行为的发生。

设题点睛 本段第一句为观点句，可用来设置正确选项。

生词解析

deceptive *adj.* 欺骗性的；误导的　　hold sb. responsible for sth. 认为某人对某事负责
penalty *n.* 罚款，罚金

长难句解析

"Given Mr. Zuckerberg's deceptive statements, his personal control over Facebook,
　　　　　　　　　　　　　　　　状语
and his role in approving key decisions related to the sharing of user data, the FTC
　　　　　　　　　　　　　　　　　　　　　　　　　　　　　　　　　　　　　　　主语
can and must hold Mr. Zuckerberg personally responsible for these continued
　谓语　　　　　　　　宾语　　　　　状语　　　　宾补　　　　　　状语
violations,"…

本句是简单句，但句子较长。本句主干为 the FTC can and must hold Mr. Zuckerberg responsible for…，hold sb. responsible for sth. 可看作固定用法，表示"认为某人对某事负责"，given 介词短语由三个并列的名词短语构成，作整句话的状语。

4	**As to holding Zuckerberg personally accountable, Wyden's attitude is _____.**	关于让扎克伯格承担个人责任这件事，怀登的态度是_____。
	A. unreasonable	A. 不合理的
	B. resolute	B. 坚决的
	C. tolerant	C. 容忍的
	D. cautious	D. 小心的

【解题思路】B。观点态度题。根据题干及顺序原则定位到文章第六段。第六段涉及怀登的态度，第一句明确指出"联邦贸易委员会能够而且必须（can and must）追究扎克伯格个人对这些持续违规行为的责任"，must 意为"必须"，甚至包含着命令的语气，可见怀登对于扎克伯格应该承担个人责任的态度的坚决，因此选项 B 正确。

【排他分析】选项 A 意为"不合理的"，但根据第六段，怀登首先在信里列举了几方面的原因，可见他的态度是有根据可循的，并非无理的，选项 A 错误。由以上分析可知，怀登并没有对此事表示容忍，甚至写信给联邦贸易委员会，因此选项 C 错误。选项 D "小心的"不能通过文章内容证实，属于无中生有，故排除。

Para. 7 ①The FTC did not respond to a request for comment. ②Facebook declined to comment. | **参考译文** ①联邦贸易委员会没有回应置评请求。②脸书拒绝置评。

Para. 8 ①Federal watchdogs considered holding Zuckerberg personally accountable as part of their last investigation into Facebook. ② The FTC initially sought to put Zuckerberg personally under federal order, which would have exposed him to | **参考译文** ①联邦监管机构认为让扎克伯格承担个人责任是他们对脸书进行最终调查的一部分。②根据《华盛顿邮报》通过"信息自由法案"获得的记录，联邦贸易委员会刚

241

fines and other penalties for future privacy violations, according to records obtained by the *Post* through the Freedom of Information Act. ③But agency staff ultimately removed Zuckerberg's name from the final agreement with Facebook in 2011.

开始试图将扎克伯格个人置于联邦政府的命令之下,这本该使他在以后侵犯隐私权时面临罚款和其他处罚。③但是机构人员最终将扎克伯格的名字从2011年与脸书签订的协议中删除了。

原文剖析 第七段和第八段第一句分别说明联邦调查委员会、脸书和联邦监管机构的态度。第八段第二句陈述扎克伯格本该面临处罚的事实,暗示了扎克伯格的确应该承担个人责任,最后一句转折指出扎克伯格不在协议名单中,使得扎克伯格无须承担个人责任。

设题点睛 第七段以及第八段第一句分别表明了不同的态度,无法设置题目。第八段第二句陈述客观事实之后,第三句出现了转折,可用来设置正确答案。

生词解析

decline *vt.* 拒绝,谢绝
initially *adv.* 最初,首先
watchdog *n.* 监察员;监察委员会

长难句解析

The FTC initially sought to put Zuckerberg personally under federal order, which
   主语   谓语   宾语
would have exposed him to fines and other penalties for future privacy violations,
                              定语从句
according to records obtained by the *Post* through the Freedom of Information Act.
                              状语

本句是主从复合句。本句主干为 The FTC initially sought to put Zuckerberg personally under federal order,which 引导的是非限制性定语从句,该从句使用了虚拟语气 would have done,表示对过去事情的假设,意思是"本来会做;本该",according to… 介词短语作状语。

5 What is the text mainly discussed?

A. The loophole in the 2011 agreement should be perfected immediately.
B. The watchdogs' different attitudes towards Mark Zuckerberg's wrongdoings.
C. Wyden's letter for calling for accountability should get a positive response.
D. Mark Zuckerberg should be liable for the company's privacy missteps.

本文主要讨论了什么?

A. 2011年所签协议中的漏洞应该马上被完善。
B. 监管机构对马克·扎克伯格不当行为的不同态度。
C. 怀登呼吁问责的信应该得到积极的回应。
D. 马克·扎克伯格应该为该公司的隐私失策承担责任。

【解题思路】D。主旨大意题。解答本题要求对全文核心内容有所把握。作者在首段借怀登给联邦贸易委员会的一封信引出讨论主题,即马克·扎克伯格应该承担个人责任,接着指出了马克·扎克伯格应该承担个人责任潜在的间接原因和以事实为基础的直接原因,通过最后一段"这本该使他在以后侵犯隐私权时面临罚款和其他处

罚"更加印证了马克·扎克伯格应该承担个人责任,因此选项 D"马克·扎克伯格应该为该公司的隐私失策承担责任"为正确答案。

【排他分析】原文虽然提到了 2011 年所签协议(2011 agreement),但并未提及其存在的漏洞,因此选项 A 错误。文中讨论的是对马克·扎克伯格违反规定、泄露隐私的处罚方式,而不是他的不当行为,选项 B 错误。怀登呼吁问责的信只在文章的部分内容里提到,不能以偏概全成为文章的主旨内容,选项 C 错误。

Text 25

The fact that humans live longer than ever before cuts both ways, because the more time we spend on the planet, the more things can go haywire in our bodies and our minds. It's a particular challenge for neurologists who want to keep our brains healthy. For decades, they have worked to create drugs to prevent, delay or treat cognitive decline in the 5 million older Americans who live with dementia. A miracle pill remains elusive—but researchers are making strides in understanding non-pharmacological strategies that might keep the brain alert and working at close to its younger pace.

So far, they've identified social engagement and learning new things as activities that may slow or stave off cognitive decline and Alzheimer's. Not every kind of intervention works the same, and some previous research about them has been uneven. But in the most rigorous study to date, researchers pitted different types of cognitive training head-to-head and concluded that one strategy in particular—a kind of computerized brain training that helps the mind to process information more quickly—can significantly lower rates of cognitive decline and dementia.

The study, led by Jerri Edwards from the University of South Florida, involved nearly 3,000 healthy older people in a five-week training program. They were assigned randomly to either no intervention or one of three tracks: improving memory skills; boosting reasoning skills; and a computerized program that focused on processing speed. After the five weeks, participants were followed over the course of 10 years.

At the end of the study, only those assigned to the speed-processing training showed improvement. Even though they had only done five weeks of brain training, the effect was dramatic: that group saw a 33% reduction in the amount of dementia or cognitive impairment after 10 years compared with those who received no training. The researchers suspect that training the brain as you would a muscle—to work as efficiently as possible—is what's at play.

The program used in the study was created by a researcher at the University of Alabama and purchased by Posit Science, a company marketing commercial brain-training programs. It developed an updated version, an exercise called the Double Decision that is available as a smartphone app called BrainHQ, which costs $96 for a one-year subscription.

For now, it's the only one of its kind on the market—though if additional research proves promising, others will likely follow.

　　Though the findings will need to be replicated by other researchers, the study's leading author is encouraged. "I think everyone over 50 should start doing it," says Edwards. "There's now evidence that this type of training has multiple benefits, the risk is minimal, and it's not even expensive."

(*Time*, 2016. 8)

1. Neurologists make their efforts to _____.
   A. create a miracle drug to treat dementia
   B. find an alternative way to prevent mental decline
   C. save 5 million older Americans' lives
   D. figure out a non-pharmacological way to completely cure brain diseases
2. According to paragraph 2, what is particularly helpful in dealing with dementia?
   A. A most rigorous study to date.
   B. More social engagement and activities.
   C. A computerized intervention.
   D. An improvement in the speed of information processing.
3. Which of the following is true according to Jerri Edwards's research?
   A. The occurrence of cognitive malfunction could be suppressed by brain training.
   B. Cognitive intervention is not allowed during the experiment.
   C. Time is an essential factor for improving the effect of brain training.
   D. Memory and reasoning skills are necessary for the training.
4. The author mentions BrainHQ to _____.
   A. criticize its high price strategy　　　B. advocate its usefulness
   C. call for others to follow　　　D. show its scarcity in the market
5. It can be learned from the last paragraph that _____.
   A. other researchers have replicated the study to test its validity
   B. elders have expressed concerns about the risk brought by the brain training
   C. people over 50 should start training immediately
   D. the prospect of the research is quite promising

■■语篇分析与试题精解

Para. 1　① The fact that humans live longer than ever before cuts both ways, because the more time we spend on the planet, the more things can go haywire in our bodies and our minds. ② It's a particular challenge for

参考译文　①人类寿命得以延长这个事实有利有弊,因为人类在地球上生存得越久,身体和心理就越容易出问题。②这对神经科的医生而言颇具挑战性,因为他们要确保我们的大脑保

neurologists who want to keep our brains healthy. ③For decades, they have worked to create drugs to prevent, delay or treat cognitive decline in the 5 million older Americans who live with dementia. ④A miracle pill remains elusive—but researchers are making strides in understanding non-pharmacological strategies that might keep the brain alert and working at close to its younger pace.

持健康。③几十年来,针对美国五百万老年痴呆患者,这些医生通过制造新的药物来预防、延缓或治疗其认知减退的症状。④虽然出现特效药的可能性微乎其微,但研究人员在非药物治疗方面却取得了长足进步,这些治疗措施可帮助病人的大脑保持警觉并像较年轻的人的大脑一样以更快的速度运转。

原文剖析 首句较长,给出观点(随着寿命延长,人类身心的问题也可能增加)。第二句承接首句,指出这种事实要求神经科医生找出保持人类大脑健康的办法。第三句是对过去情况的细节描述。第四句是一个长难句,指出目前的研究成果(研究人员在开发非药物方式治疗大脑疾病方面进步很快),该句旨在给出作者观点并引出后文要讨论的话题。

设题点睛 本段第四句采用了"破折＋转折"的结构,且体现了本文的话题和观点,可用来设置题目。

生词解析
cut both ways (行动)有利也有弊
neurologist n. 神经科医师;神经病学家
dementia n. 痴呆
make strides in 在……方面取得进步
go haywire [口语]出毛病;发狂;陷于混乱
cognitive adj. 认知的,认识的
elusive adj. 难以实现的
pharmacological adj. 药理学的

长难句解析

[句1] The fact that humans live longer than ever before cuts both ways, because the more time we spend on the planet, the more things can go haywire in our bodies and our minds.

主语 / 同位语从句 / 谓语 / 宾语 / 原因状语从句

本句是主从复合句。本句主干为 The fact cuts both ways, because...,主语后为 that 引导的同位语从句,对 fact 的内容进行说明。because 引导原因状语从句,其中使用了"the +形容词/副词的比较级,the +形容词/副词的比较级…"的结构,表示"越……就越……"。

[句2] A miracle pill remains elusive—but researchers are making strides in understanding non-pharmacological strategies that might keep the brain alert and working at close to its younger pace.

主语1 / 系动词 / 表语 / 主语2 / 谓语 / 宾语 / 状语 / 定语从句

本句为并列复合句。本句主干为 A miracle pill remains elusive, but researchers are making strides in…,破折号前后为两个完整的句子,后一句中的 in 体现在某一方面取得进步,可看作是修饰谓语的状语,该状语中还包含一个定语从句,其先行词为 non-pharmacological strategies,最后的 working at close to its younger pace 为 working at its younger pace 与 close to 两个短语的杂糅。

1 Neurologists make their efforts to _____.

A. create a miracle drug to treat dementia
B. find an alternative way to prevent mental decline
C. save 5 million older Americans' lives
D. figure out a non-pharmacological way to completely cure brain diseases

神经科的医生努力 _____。

A. 制造治疗痴呆的神奇药物
B. 发现预防智力下降的替代方法
C. 拯救500万美国老人的生命
D. 找出完全治愈大脑疾病的非药物疗法

【解题思路】B。事实细节题。根据题干关键词（Neurologists）和顺序原则定位到文章首段，本题实际考查神经科医生的目标。首段最后一句破折号之后说到 researchers are making strides in understanding non-pharmacological strategies, 这里的 researchers 回指前文谈到的 neurologists, making strides in 相当于题干中的 make their efforts, 因此本句是定位句，该句 in 后的内容体现进步的方面，也就是神经科医生努力的目标，即"非药物疗法"。由于破折号之前提到找到特效药的可能性非常小，因此综合推断"非药物疗法"属于神经科医生努力寻找的替代疗法，因此选项 B 正确。

【排他分析】选项 A 中的 miracle drug 对应最后一句破折号之前的内容，原文虽然提到"出现特效药的可能性微乎其微"，但 but 后的内容才是本句关键，即科学家真正取得进步的是非医药领域，因此排除该项。选项 C 中的 5 million 对应首段第三句的内容，但原文使用的是 prevent, delay or treat（预防、延缓或者治疗）某种疾病，与该项中的 save lives（拯救生命）概念并不一致，因此排除该项。选项 D 中的 non-pharmacological 同样对应首段最后一句破折号后的内容，但原文只是说这种替代治疗方式"可帮助病人的大脑保持警觉并像较年轻的人的大脑一样以更快的速度运转"，并非是"治愈大脑疾病"，且该项中 completely 的意思太过绝对和夸张，因此排除。

Para. 2 ① So far, they've identified social engagement and learning new things as activities that may slow or stave off cognitive decline and Alzheimer's. ② Not every kind of intervention works the same, and some previous research about them has been uneven. ③ But in the most rigorous study to date, researchers pitted different types of cognitive training head-to-head and concluded that one strategy in particular—a kind of computerized brain training that helps the mind to process information more quickly—can significantly lower rates of cognitive decline and dementia.

参考译文 ①到目前为止，研究人员已经找到了可能延缓或预防认知衰退和老年痴呆症的新方法，即社交和学习新事物。②每种干预措施的效果各不相同，而且关于这些干预的研究也并不均衡。③但在一项迄今为止最为严谨的研究中，研究人员将不同类型的认知训练进行对比后发现，一种特殊的计算机辅助型大脑训练可以帮助大脑更迅速地处理信息，因此可显著降低认知衰退和老年痴呆的发病率。

原文剖析 首句顺承上一段最后一句，指出目前科学家已经取得的研究进展。第二句与首句构成语意上的转折关系，暗指并非每一种干预措施都有相似的效果。第三句再次与第二句的内容构成转折关系，指出研究人员已从诸多干预措施中找到了最为有效的方式，即计算机辅助型大脑训练。

设题点睛 本段第三句为长难句,且出现了语意上的转折,用于引出研究结果,属于重点内容,因此可用来设置题目。

生词解析

social engagement 社交,应酬
intervention n. 干预;干涉
rigorous adj. 谨慎的;严密的
head-to-head adv. 面对面地;势均力敌地

stave off 避开;延缓
uneven adj. 不平衡的
pit vt. 使竞争
computerized adj. 计算机化的,电脑化的

长难句解析

But in the most rigorous study to date, researchers pitted different types of cognitive training
　　　状语　　　　　　　　　　　　　主语　　谓语1　　　宾语
head-to-head and concluded that one strategy in particular—a kind of computerized brain
　　　　　　　谓语2　　　宾语从句　　　　　　　　　　插入语
training that helps the mind to process information more quickly—can significantly lower
　　　　　　定语从句　　　　　　　　　　　　　宾语从句
rates of cognitive decline and dementia.

本句是主从复合句。本句主干为 But researchers pitted different types of cognitive training and concluded that...,第二个并列谓语后为 that 引导的宾语从句,该从句中两个破折号之间的部分可看作插入语,对从句的主语 one strategy 进行具体解释,破折号后的部分是该宾语从句的谓语和宾语。

2 According to paragraph 2, what is particularly helpful in dealing with dementia? | 根据第二段的内容,以下哪项在治疗痴呆方面最有帮助?

A. A most rigorous study to date.
B. More social engagement and activities.
C. A computerized intervention.
D. An improvement in the speed of information processing.

A. 一项迄今为止最严谨的研究。
B. 更多社交和活动。
C. 一项由计算机辅助实施的干预疗法。
D. 信息处理速度的提高。

【解题思路】D。推理引申题。根据题干要求定位到第二段,本题考查解决大脑衰退的方法。第二段第三句转折出现"A—B—C"的结构,正常情况下破折号之间的B部分用作插入语,为非重点内容,一般不设置考点,但由于该句中的A、C部分正好对应题干所问,因此需要关注B部分的内容。该句中双破折号之间的部分指出这种有效方式是一种可以帮助大脑更迅速地处理信息(helps the mind to process information more quickly)的计算机辅助型大脑训练,该训练的目的和作用与选项D对应,该项中的 improvement in the speed 是对原文 more quickly 的同义替换,因此正确。

【排他分析】选项A对应本段最后一句中的 the most rigorous study to date,但并未体现研究结果等实质性内容,因此排除。选项B对应本段首句中的 social engagement and learning new things as activities,这两项活动确实有助于延缓大脑衰退,但是第二句随即指出各类干预措施的效果不同,与题干所问的 particularly helpful 不符,因此排除。选项C中的 intervention 表示对某种情况或进程结果的干涉,且该项并未谈及有

关training的内容,没有从根本上解释疗法如何起作用,不够确切和具体,因此排除。

Para. 3 ①The study, led by Jerri Edwards from the University of South Florida, involved nearly 3,000 healthy older people in a five-week training program. ②They were assigned randomly to either no intervention or one of three tracks: improving memory skills; boosting reasoning skills; and a computerized program that focused on processing speed. ③After the five weeks, participants were followed over the course of 10 years.

参考译文 ①这项研究由南佛罗里达大学的杰里·爱德华兹(Jerri Edwards)主持,这个为期五周的训练项目邀请了约3 000名身体健康的老年人参与。②他们要么不接受任何干预,要么被随机编入三组,进行不同的训练:分别是改善记忆训练、强化推理技能训练和侧重信息处理速度的计算机辅助训练。③五周时间结束后,该实验在接下来的十多年里对这些参与者的情况进行了跟踪记录。

原文剖析 本段承接上一段,具体解释该研究的方式和过程,最后一句体现了实验的严谨性和可靠性。

设题点睛 由于本段重在描述实验过程,不涉及结论及原因分析,因此不适合设置考点或选项。

生词解析

be assigned to 被分配到……　　　　track n. 分轨制(或按成绩编组制的)班组

Para. 4 ①At the end of the study, only those assigned to the speed-processing training showed improvement. ②Even though they had only done five weeks of brain training, the effect was dramatic: that group saw a 33% reduction in the amount of dementia or cognitive impairment after 10 years compared with those who received no training. ③The researchers suspect that training the brain as you would a muscle—to work as efficiently as possible—is what's at play.

参考译文 ①研究结束时,只有接受信息处理速度训练的受试者出现了改善的迹象。②尽管他们只接受了短短五周的大脑训练,其效果却令人吃惊:十年之后,将该组和未接受任何训练的受试者对比后发现,前者患老年痴呆或发生认知受损的概率要低33%。③研究人员推测,像训练肌肉一样训练大脑,尽量使大脑有效运转,才是关键所在。

原文剖析 本段是对该实验的发现和结论的描述,用数据详细解释了第二段最后一句所说的"计算机辅助大脑训练可以帮助大脑更迅速地处理信息,因此可显著降低认知衰退和老年痴呆的发病率"的实验结论。最后一句指出要像训练肌肉一样训练大脑,是对该实验结果更进一步的概括总结。

设题点睛 本段第二句较长,且带有"让步+冒号解释"的结构;最后一句是对该实验结论的总结,这两句为重要的考点内容。

生词解析

impairment n. 损伤,损害　　　　be at play 在发挥作用

长难句解析

Even though they had only done five weeks of brain training, the effect was dramatic:
　　　　　让步状语从句　　　　　　　　　　　　　　　　　主语1　系动词　表语
that group saw a 33% reduction in the amount of dementia or cognitive impairment
　主语2　谓语　　宾语　　　　　　　　　后置定语
after 10 years compared with those who received no training.
　　　　状语　　　　　　　　　　定语从句

本句为并列复合句。本句主干为 the effect was dramatic: that group saw a 33% reduction,本句冒号前后为两个完整的句子,冒号后的句子对前一句进行解释,前一句中包含一个让步状语从句。后一句的宾语较长,in the amount of... impairment 作 reduction 的后置定语,句尾出现时间状语和比较状语,比较状语中还包含一个修饰 those 的定语从句。

3 Which of the following is true according to Jerri Edwards's research?

A. The occurrence of cognitive malfunction could be suppressed by brain training.
B. Cognitive intervention is not allowed during the experiment.
C. Time is an essential factor for improving the effect of brain training.
D. Memory and reasoning skills are necessary for the training.

根据杰里·爱德华兹的研究,以下哪项正确?

A. 通过大脑训练可以抑制认知障碍的发生。
B. 实验期间不得进行认知方面的干预。
C. 时间是改善大脑训练效果的重要因素。
D. 记忆和推理技能对于训练而言是必不可少的。

【解题思路】A。事实细节题。根据题干关键词(Jerri Edwards's research)定位到原文第三段和第四段。在各类考试中,考生请务必牢记,文中有关实验的结果和分析才是重要内容。选项 A 和第四段第二句冒号后的实验结果"前者(接受大脑训练的人)患老年痴呆或发生认知受损的概率要低 33%"(that group saw a 33% reduction in the amount of dementia or cognitive impairment)所表达的意思一致,该项中的 occurrence, suppressed 和 malfunction 分别对应原文中的 33%, reduction 和 impairment,因此为正确答案。

【排他分析】原文第三段提到该实验分为无干预组,以及三种不同类型的干预组,和选项 B 的内容直接矛盾,因此排除。选项 C 中有关 time 的信息可能与原文第四段中的实验时间 five weeks(五周)有关,但该时间段只用于强调尽管训练只持续了五周时间,但效果显著,用让步手法突出训练方式的有效性,而非时间,因此排除该项。选项 D 的内容在第三段第二句中出现,原文表示 improving memory skills 和 boosting reasoning skills 是分组训练要达到的不同目的,而不是说 memory 和 reasoning 是达成训练的条件,因此该项本末倒置,也可排除。

Para. 5 ①The program used in the study was created by a researcher at the University of Alabama and purchased by Posit Science, a company marketing commercial brain-training

参考译文 ①该研究所使用的电脑程序是由阿拉巴马大学的一名研究人员开发的,一家名为波赛特科学的专门销售商用大脑训练方案的公司购买了

programs. ②It developed an updated version, an exercise called the Double Decision that is available as a smartphone app called BrainHQ, which costs $96 for a one-year subscription. ③For now, it's the only one of its kind on the market—though if additional research proves promising, others will likely follow.

该软件。②该公司开发的最新版本是一个叫做"双决策"的练习软件，其智能手机应用程序 BrainHQ 已上架，订阅一年需 96 美元。③这是目前市面上唯一一款此类软件，但如果其他研究前景乐观，可能会出现更多类似软件。

原文剖析 本段首句介绍该计算机辅助训练所使用的程序来源，第二句描述此程序的最新手机版本，最后一句出现句内转折，指出这种软件的独特性和未来发展前景。

设题点睛 本段最后一句是带有"破折号＋转折"的长难句，可以用来设置正确选项。

生词解析

market vt. 在市场上出售　　　　　　　　subscription n. 订购；订阅
promising adj. 有前途的

长难句解析

For now, it's the only one of its kind on the market— though　　　if additional
　状语　　　　主系表　　　　后置定语　　　　　让步状语从句　　　条件状语从句
research proves promising, others will likely follow.
　　　　　　　　　　　　　　让步状语从句

本句是主从复合句。本句主干为 it's the only one, though others will likely follow。破折号后为由 though 引导的让步状语从句，由于 though 后接了一个 if 引导的条件状语从句，其结构看上去较为复杂。

4 The author mentions BrainHQ to _____.　　作者提到 BrainHQ 是为了 _____。

A. criticize its high price strategy　　　　　A. 批评其高定价战略
B. advocate its usefulness　　　　　　　　B. 推崇其有效性
C. call for others to follow　　　　　　　　C. 号召其他人效仿
D. show its scarcity in the market　　　　　D. 表明其在市场上的稀缺性

【解题思路】D。例子功能题。根据题干关键词（BrainHQ）定位到第五段第二句，该句引出了名为 BrainHQ 的手机应用程序并介绍其定价等特点，后一句是作者对该程序的进一步评价。第三句主语 it 回指该程序，破折号之前的主句明确指出这是目前市面上唯一一款此类软件（the only one of its kind on the market），only 体现其稀缺性，与选项 D 的 scarcity 对应，因此该项符合原文，为正确答案。

【排他分析】选项 A 有关定价的内容出现在第五段第二句，原文只是介绍该软件一年的使用价格（96 美金），并未就其价格高低进行评价，更谈不上"批评"，因此排除。虽然该手机应用软件的前身是实验中所使用的电脑训练软件，但作者并未说明该手机软件是否一样有效，且最后一句使用了条件句"如果其他研究前景乐观"，说明对该手机软件的有效性尚无其他证明，因此排除选项 B。选项 C 是利用第五段最后一句破折号之后的 others will likely follow 所设置的干扰项，破折号之后的让步状语从句指出如果其他研究证明该类软件有效，其他软件也会出现，作者并非在"号召"，仅在猜测，因此排除该项。

Para. 6 ①Though the findings will need to be replicated by other researchers, the study's leading author is encouraged. ②"I think everyone over 50 should start doing it," says Edwards. ③"There's now evidence that this type of training has multiple benefits, the risk is minimal, and it's not even expensive."

参考译文 ①尽管该结论还有待其他研究者证实,但该研究的第一作者已备受鼓舞。②爱德华兹说:"我认为,五十岁以上的人都应该开始训练。③现在已有证据表明,这种类型的训练有诸多好处,且风险极小,关键是价格也亲民。"

原文剖析 首句使用了让步状语从句,意在突出主句内容,即研究者受到鼓舞,暗指该实验的发现具有积极作用。后两句进一步解释研究者受到鼓舞的理由,总结出这种脑力训练的优势在于物美价廉。

设题点睛 本段用于描述该研究作者对实验结果的乐观评价,可用来设置观点态度类考题。

生词解析

replicate *vt.* 重复;复制   minimal *adj.* 最低的;最小限度的

5 It can be learned from the last paragraph that _____.

A. other researchers have replicated the study to test its validity
B. elders have expressed concerns about the risk brought by the brain training
C. people over 50 should start training immediately
D. the prospect of the research is quite promising

从最后一段可知_____。

A. 其他研究人员已经重复了这项研究以验证其有效性
B. 老年人对大脑训练带来的风险表示担忧
C. 超过50岁的人应立即开始训练
D. 该研究的前景十分乐观

【解题思路】D。观点态度题。根据题干要求定位到文章最后一段。本段主要表达该研究的作者对研究结果的评价。从该段出现的encouraged,everyone over 50,multiple benefits,minimal risk,not expensive等细节可以看出他对此项研究成果的效果及未来应用感到乐观,与选项D中的promising(有前途的)相符,因此该项正确。

【排他分析】选项A对应本段首句中though引导的内容,原文是说"尽管该结论还有待其他研究者证实",will need to be说明目前并未有人重复此项实验,与该项的完成时态不符,因此排除。选项B谈到的the risk出现在最后一句,但是原文指出该训练的风险很小(minimal),与该项矛盾,且原文没有提到老年人在这一方面的看法,因此排除。选项C对应该段第二句内容,原文虽然谈到"五十岁以上的人都应该开始训练",但这只是该研究作者的建议,而非既定事实,因此排除。

Text 26

A rose by any other name might still smell as sweet, but an animal with two scientific monikers can wreak havoc for researchers trying to study it. Since 1895, the International Commission on Zoological Nomenclature (ICZN) has helped ensure animal names are unique and long-lasting, with a panel of volunteer commissioners who maintain naming rules and resolve conflicts when they arise. But the U. K.-based charitable trust that supports all this is slated to run out of money before the year's end—and that could spell trouble. "If the trust ceases to exist it will be very difficult for the commissioners to do their work," says Michael Dixon, chair of the trust's board and director of the Natural History Museum in London. If ICZN disappeared "it would be something akin to anarchy in animal naming."

Knowing the right name for each species is critical for biological research. The ICZN code, which provides guidance for naming new species and resolving conflicts about older ones, is updated periodically. In 2012, for example, after 4 years of debate, ICZN decided to allow species to be named in electronic publications as well as in printed journals. Species-naming records date back centuries, and the concern was that electronic media might not last that long. The commissioners make 30 to 50 judgments a year, some with far-reaching consequences, and the zoological community pays heed.

"Names have to be universal and stable," explains Jonathan Coddington, associate director for science at the Smithsonian Institution National Museum of Natural History in Washington, D. C. There is constant tension, however, between keeping names the same and adjusting them according to new scientific evidence. Consider the popular lab insect, Drosophila melanogaster, which some taxonomists want to assign to a new genus because this fruit fly is but a distant relative to some other Drosophila. The commission will likely have a hand in the ultimate fate of this name.

The nonprofit organization that formed in 1947 to raise funds and administer the ICZN code and the journal—the International Trust for Zoological Nomenclature—has weathered other crises. Net income from its journal is only about $47,000 a year, and the trust's annual expenses now top $155,000. So reserves are about to be exhausted, Dixon says. A few weeks ago, he sent an e-mail plea to directors of natural history museums around the world for emergency relief. In it, he proposed establishing a committee that would come up with a new financial model for the troubled organization. "This is not unlike GenBank," the database of genome sequences that receives government support, Coddington says. "It's the same distributed goods situation, that everyone needs and nobody wants to pay for."

Botanists, phycologists, and mycologists have for 100 years followed an all-volunteer model. Proposed changes to the botanical code are discussed en masse every 6 years at the International Botanical Congress, and disputes are resolved by volunteer subcommittees.

But Dixon says such a model would be tough for zoologists because they don't have an equivalent meeting that's well attended.

Dixon estimates the trust needs $78,000 or more to make it through the year. No single organization may be able to fund it long-term, but a network of 10 or 20 institutions might be able to kick in enough to sustain it, he says.

If support is not forthcoming and ICZN falters, not much would change at first, scientists say. But "communication barriers would start to evolve" over time as names ceased to be systematically assigned and used, says Richard Pyle, a commissioner based at the Bishop Museum in Honolulu. "And that would be tragic."

(*Science*, 2013.2)

1. According to the first paragraph, ICZN is _____.
   A. supported by a powerful trust fund in UK
   B. composed of selfless volunteer commissioners
   C. pivotal in keeping animals' names distinctive
   D. similar to an anarchy in animal naming

2. The example in paragraph 2 is cited to illustrate _____.
   A. that the inheritance of the exact names for species is of paramount importance for research
   B. that electronic media are inferior to printed journals in name recording
   C. that ICZN periodically updates its naming system
   D. that zoological community would be deeply affected by ICZN's updates

3. Which of the following is true according to paragraph 3?
   A. The commission has the predominant role in name adjustment.
   B. Taxonomists always have a conflict with the commission.
   C. New scientific evidence is critical in keeping the old name.
   D. There is a consistent debate on name adjustment.

4. Dixon would most likely agree that _____.
   A. Like the GenBank, ICZN deserves equal financial support
   B. any single organization is not capable of sustaining ICZN
   C. zoologists should follow an all-volunteer model
   D. ICZN has endured a sequence of crises since its establishment

5. According to the author, the consequence of ICZN's disappearance is _____.
   A. understandable   B. unbearable
   C. acceptable   D. controllable

语篇分析与试题精解

Para. 1 ①A rose by any other name might still smell as sweet, but an animal with two scientific

参考译文 ①玫瑰花如果换个名称可能闻起来还是香的,但如果动物有两

monikers can wreak havoc for researchers trying to study it. ② Since 1895, the International Commission on Zoological Nomenclature (ICZN) has helped ensure animal names are unique and long-lasting, with a panel of volunteer commissioners who maintain naming rules and resolve conflicts when they arise. ③ But the U.K.-based charitable trust that supports all this is slated to run out of money before the year's end—and that could spell trouble. ④ "If the trust ceases to exist it will be very difficult for the commissioners to do their work," says Michael Dixon, chair of the trust's board and director of the Natural History Museum in London. ⑤ If ICZN disappeared "it would be something akin to anarchy in animal naming."

个学名则会给其研究者造成很大困扰。②自1895年起,国际动物命名法委员会(ICZN)的志愿者委员们就致力于编写动物命名规则并解决有关动物命名的争议以确保动物命名的唯一性和持久性。③对该委员会工作给予资金支持的慈善信托基金机构总部位于英国。但是,该信托基金机构的资金链将在年底之前出现断裂——这会引发很多问题。④"如果该信托机构不复存在,那么委员们的工作也会难以为继。"该机构董事会主席兼伦敦自然历史博物馆馆长迈克尔·狄克逊(Michael Dixon)说。⑤如果ICZN解散,"那么在动物命名学界将出现一种类似于无政府状态的混乱。"

原文剖析 本段首句利用类比的方式给出观点:动物的名字不像植物的名字,应该只有一个。第二句为长难句,介绍 ICZN 这个组织及其工作和宗旨:编写动物命名规则并解决争议,最终保持动物命名的唯一性和持久性。第三句通过转折指出该组织目前面对的问题:为 ICZN 提供资金支持的英国信托基金机构将出现资金短缺的问题。第四句和第五句利用个人观点对这一问题可能造成的影响进行分析,指出如果资金断链,会使 ICZN 的工作难以为继,从而导致动物学界命名混乱的局面。

设题点睛 本段第二句为长难句,第三句的转折以及最后两句的人物观点都是重要的考点,一般会设置相应的细节题。

生词解析

moniker n. 名字,绰号   wreak havoc 造成严重破坏
zoological adj. 动物学的   nomenclature n. 命名法
slate vt. 预定;注定   spell trouble 带来麻烦
akin to 同类,近似   anarchy n. 无政府状态,混乱

长难句解析

Since 1895, the International Commission on Zoological Nomenclature (ICZN) has
时间状语   主语
helped ensure animal names are unique and long-lasting, with a panel of volunteer
  谓宾   宾语从句   状语
commissioners who maintain naming rules and resolve conflicts when they arise.
                        定语从句   状语从句

本句主干结构为 ICZN has helped ensure…。句中 ensure 的宾语由宾语从句构成;who 引导的定语从句修饰 a panel of volunteer commissioners。

1 According to the first paragraph, ICZN is _____.

A. supported by a powerful trust fund in UK
B. composed of selfless volunteer commissioners
C. pivotal in keeping animals' names distinctive
D. similar to an anarchy in animal naming

根据第一段,ICZN _____。

A. 得到了英国一家强大的信托基金机构的支持
B. 由无私的志愿者委员会组成
C. 在维护动物命名独特性方面有重要作用
D. 在动物命名方面与混乱的无政府状态类似

【解题思路】C。事实细节题。根据题干要求定位到首段有关 ICZN 的内容。第二句介绍 ICZN 的工作内容和最终目标,即通过编写动物命名规则和解决动物命名争议的方式,保证动物名字的唯一性和持久性(unique and long-lasting),这与选项 C 中的保持动物名字的独特性(distinctive)直接对应,且该段最后两句也从该委员会如果不复存在可能导致的后果强调 ICZN 对于保持动物命名标准和秩序的重要性,因此选项 C 是对该组织的合理描述,是正确答案。

【排他分析】选项 A 对应首段第三句关于为 ICZN 提供资金支持的慈善信托基金机构的相关内容,原文明确指出该信托基金将面临资金链断裂的问题,说明其实力并不强大,与该项中的 powerful 矛盾,所以排除。选项 B 对应本段第二句中有关 ICZN 人员构成的内容,原文只提到该组织中的志愿者委员们负责制订命名规则和解决争议,但并不能由此推断该组织的所有工作人员都免费工作,且该项中的 selfless 也并无明确的原文语意支撑,因此排除。选项 D 对应本段最后一句,选项 D 完全是对原文两个细节的随意拼凑,similar to 与该段第五句中的 akin to 同义,但是原文的大意是 ICZN 的解体会让动物命名学界出现混乱的状态,该项与原文意思完全不一致,因此排除。

Para. 2 ①Knowing the right name for each species is critical for biological research. ②The ICZN code, which provides guidance for naming new species and resolving conflicts about older ones, is updated periodically. ③In 2012, for example, after 4 years of debate, ICZN decided to allow species to be named in electronic publications as well as in printed journals. ④Species-naming records date back centuries, and the concern was that electronic media might not last that long. ⑤The commissioners make 30 to 50 judgments a year, some with far-reaching consequences, and the zoological community pays heed.

参考译文 ①明确各个物种的正确名称对于生物学研究至关重要。②ICZN编写的命名规则定期更新,为新发现物种的命名提供指导并解决旧物种命名的争议。③例如,2012 年,在经过了长达 4 年的争论之后,ICZN 最终同意将新物种的命名同时刊发在电子出版物和印刷刊物上。④有关物种命名的记录可以追溯到几百年前,有人担忧电子媒体存在的时间可能不会持续百年之久。⑤委员们一年会进行 30 至 50 次裁定,有些名称的裁定会产生深远的影响,动物学界会对此长期关注。

原文剖析 本段首句提出观点,指出明确物种名称对于生物学研究的重要性,呼应上段末尾 ICZN 的重要性。第二句介绍 ICZN 会定期更新命名规则,以实现为新物种命名提供指导和解决命名争端的作用,回应上段第二句 ICZN 的工作内容。第三句举例指出,ICZN 最终同意将新物种的命名公布在电子出版物上,由此可推断以前只公布在纸质出版物上。第四句谈及人们对 ICZN 这一决定的担忧:电子出版物的存在时间有限。第五句介绍 ICZN 的裁定职能及其深远影响。

设题点睛 本段最重要的结构应该是第三句(例子)及第四句(对例子的解释)的总分结构,可利用该结构设置考题。

生词解析

code n. 准则   periodically adv. 定期地
pay heed 注意

2 The example in paragraph 2 is cited to illustrate _____.

A. that the inheritance of the exact names for species is of paramount importance for research
B. that electronic media are inferior to printed journals in name recording
C. that ICZN periodically updates its naming system
D. that zoological community would be deeply affected by ICZN's updates

第二段中的例子是用来说明_____。

A. 物种确切名称的传承对研究而言至关重要
B. 电子媒体在记录名称方面不如纸质刊物
C. ICZN 定期更新其命名系统
D. 动物学界将深受 ICZN 更新的影响

【解题思路】A。例子功能题。根据题干要求定位到第二段第三句。本题实际考查该例子所支撑的观点。第二段第二句介绍 ICZN 定期更新命名规则的事实,观点性不强。因此应从后文中寻找被支撑的观点。第三句指出 2012 年 ICZN 最终同意将新物种的命名同时公布在电子和印刷出版物上,这也是个事实,观点性不强。第四句中出现了明确的观点,指出有人担心电子出版物的持续性不如纸质出版物,回应第三句所谈到的争论,可理解为有人不同意将新物种命名公布在电子出版物上的理由在于电子出版物的稳定性或持续性不如纸质媒体,侧面体现物种名称的长久性对研究有至关重要的作用,同时回应了该段首句的观点,因此选项 A 是正确答案。

【排他分析】选项 B 对应该段第三句和第四句的内容,原文确实提到了电子媒体和印刷媒体,但是并没有对两者在记录名称方面的能力进行比较,只可从原文中推断出电子媒体在持续性方面不如纸质媒体,因此该项与原文不符,所以排除。选项 C 对应本段第二句,原句指出 ICZN 会定期更新其命名规则,虽然与该项的意思一致,但并非题干所问的例子想要说明的观点,因此排除。选项 D 对应本段最后一句,原文是说动物界会持续关注 ICZN 对于命名的裁定,虽然确实是原文提到的事实,但同样不是题干所问的例子想要说明的观点,因此排除。

Para. 3 ① "Names have to be universal and stable," explains Jonathan Coddington, associate

参考译文 ①"物种的名称必须通用且能保持稳定。"华盛顿特区国

director for science at the Smithsonian Institution National Museum of Natural History in Washington, D.C. ② There is constant tension, however, between keeping names the same and adjusting them according to new scientific evidence. ③ Consider the popular lab insect, Drosophila melanogaster, which some taxonomists want to assign to a new genus because this fruit fly is but a distant relative to some other Drosophila. ④ The commission will likely have a hand in the ultimate fate of this name.

家自然历史博物馆史密森学会副会长乔纳森·科丁顿（Jonathan Coddington）解释道。②然而，在保持名称不变和根据新的科学依据对名称做出调整之间长期存在着争论。③以最为常见的实验室昆虫黑腹果蝇为例，一些分类学家认为这一物种仅是果蝇的远亲，应将其归入一个新种属。④该委员会很可能会参与对这一物种归类的最终裁定。

原文剖析 本段首句给出人物观点，重申了前两段反复强调的观点：动物的命名必须要一致且保持稳定。第二句转折指出在保持命名稳定和根据新的科学依据修改名称之间存在争论。第三句以是否将黑腹果蝇归为新物种的争论为例支撑第二句内容。第四句给出结论：针对该争论，ICZN 将参与裁定，回应上一段末尾对该组织裁定职能的介绍。

设题点睛 第二句（转折＋观点）和第三句（举例支撑）是本段的重要内容，但是由于上一段已经考查了例子功能题，本段很可能利用第二句的转折结构考查细节题。

生词解析

tension *n*. 紧张关系　　　　taxonomist *n*. 分类学者
genus *n*. 类，物种

3	Which of the following is true according to paragraph 3?	根据第三段的内容，以下哪项正确？
	A. The commission has the predominant role in name adjustment.	A. 在名称调整方面，该委员会处于主导地位。
	B. Taxonomists always have a conflict with the commission.	B. 分类学家总与该委员会产生冲突。
	C. New scientific evidence is critical in keeping the old name.	C. 新的科学依据对保持旧称而言十分重要。
	D. There is a consistent debate on name adjustment.	D. 在名称调整方面长期存在争议。

【解题思路】D。事实细节题。根据题干要求定位到第三段，在没有具体定位点的情况下优先理解本段的重点内容。本段第二句含有转折结构，且给出观点，原文表示"在保持名称不变和根据新的科学依据对名称做出调整之间长期存在着争论"，可看出人们争论的焦点在于是否可以根据新证据修改物种名称，而非是否保持物种名称的统一性和持续性（因为该段首句已明确指出保持物种名称通用且稳定是原则），选项 D 是对该争论焦点的正确认识，因此正确。

【排他分析】选项 A 对应本段最后一句，原文提到 ICZN 会参与对前一句谈到的争论的最终裁定，但并没有说名称修改的决定权在 ICZN 手中，原文中 have a hand in 表示"插手，参加"，因此该项意思太过绝对，可以排除。选项 B 中的 taxonomists 在该段

257

第三句的例子中出现，原文指出分类学家认为目前称为黑腹果蝇的昆虫实际与果蝇的亲缘关系较远，要求重新命名，但无法由此推断出分类学家和 ICZN 经常产生冲突，该项属于过度推断，可以排除。选项 C 中的 new scientific evidence 在本段第二句中出现，该句指出争论的一方认为可根据新的科学证据对动物的旧称进行调整，即新的科学依据对修改名称而言很重要，与本项意思相反，因此排除。

Para. 4 ① The nonprofit organization that formed in 1947 to raise funds and administer the ICZN code and the journal—the International Trust for Zoological Nomenclature—has weathered other crises. ② Net income from its journal is only about $47,000 a year, and the trust's annual expenses now top $155,000. ③ So reserves are about to be exhausted, Dixon says. ④ A few weeks ago, he sent an e-mail plea to directors of natural history museums around the world for emergency relief. ⑤ In it, he proposed establishing a committee that would come up with a new financial model for the troubled organization. ⑥ "This is not unlike GenBank," the database of genome sequences that receives government support, Coddington says. ⑦ "It's the same distributed goods situation, that everyone needs and nobody wants to pay for."

参考译文 ①国际动物命名法委员会国际信托（ITZN）成立于1947年，是一个非营利性组织，负责ICZN资金的筹集、命名规则以及期刊的管理。该组织自成立以来经历了种种考验。②每年发行期刊的净收入仅为4.7万美元，而年支出已高达15.5万美元。③因此资金储备即将耗尽，狄克逊说。④几周前，他向世界各地的自然历史博物馆馆长发送了请求紧急支援的电子邮件。⑤在电子邮件中，他建议成立一个委员会，为陷入困境的ICZN建立一个新的财务模式。⑥"这与基因银行没有什么不同。"基因银行就是获得政府支持的基因组序列数据库，科丁顿说道。⑦"这就像分配，所有人都需要，但所有人都不愿意为之付费。"

原文剖析 本段首句对前文提到的为 ICZN 提供资金支持的慈善信托基金机构（ITZN）进行了具体介绍，指出该机构经历了重重危机，可看作观点性内容。第二句和第三句解释 ITZN 资金链即将断裂的原因（入不敷出）。第四句指出 ITZN 负责人为保住 ITZN 所做的努力：请求各地自然历史博物馆伸出援手。第五句和第六句介绍该负责人希望得到的帮助：为 ICZN 建立新的财务模式，并将其与由政府支持的基因组序列数据库的作用相提并论，暗示 ICZN 理应获得更多的资金支持。最后一句用比喻的方式指出目前困境的实质：所有人都想利用，但不想支付报酬。

设题点睛 本段前两句的信息在前文中已经提到，重要的是最后两句对人物观点的直接引用，一般会用其设置事实细节题的选项。

生词解析
weather *vt.* 经受住   plea *n.* 请求
relief *n.* 救济   genome *n.* 基因组

长难句解析
The nonprofit organization　that formed in 1947 to raise funds and administer the ICZN code
　　　　主语　　　　　　　　　　　　　　　　定语从句

and the journal—the International Trust for Zoological Nomenclature—has weathered other crises.

本句主干结构为 the nonprofit organizations has weathered other crises, that 引导的定语从句修饰主语；同位语 the International Trust for Zoological Nomenclature 对 organization 进行具体介绍。

Para. 5 ① Botanists, phycologists, and mycologists have for 100 years followed an all-volunteer model. ② Proposed changes to the botanical code are discussed en masse every 6 years at the International Botanical Congress, and disputes are resolved by volunteer subcommittees. ③ But Dixon says such a model would be tough for zoologists because they don't have an equivalent meeting that's well attended.

参考译文 ①一百年来，植物学家、藻类学家和真菌学家都遵循纯志愿型的工作模式。②国际植物命名规则的修改提案每六年在国际植物学会议上集体讨论通过，相关争议由附属志愿委员会讨论解决。③但是，狄克逊说，这一模式并不适用于动物学家，因为动物学界没有如此广泛参与的同级别会议。

原文剖析 本段首句谈到一种纯志愿型的工作模式，列举的都是植物学领域的学者，phycologists 和 mycologists 的意思可参照与之并列的 botanists 进行推断。第二句继续讨论植物学界的做法：植物命名规则会在每六年举办一次的国际植物学会议上集体讨论通过。第三句对比动物界的做法，转折指出前一句谈到的通过大会解决植物命名问题的方式不适用于动物学界，因为世界上还没有如此大规模的动物学会议。

设题点睛 本段最重要的内容为第三句的人物观点（转折＋原因），可用来设置事实细节题。

生词解析

botanist n. 植物学家　　　phycologist n. 藻类学家
mycologist n. 真菌学家　　en masse 全体地

长难句解析

Proposed changes to the botanical code are discussed en masse every 6 years at the International Botanical Congress, and disputes are resolved by volunteer subcommittees.

本句由 and 连接的两个并列句构成。and 前一句的主干结构为 changes are discussed；后一句的主干结构为 disputes are resolved。

Para. 6 ① Dixon estimates the trust needs $78,000 or more to make it through the year. ② No single organization may be able to fund it

参考译文 ①狄克逊预计该信托基金机构需要7.8万美金或更多才能撑过这一年。②由单个机构为该委员会提

long-term, but a network of 10 or 20 institutions might be able to kick in enough to sustain it, he says.

原文剖析 本段首句回应第一段和第四段的内容,具体说明 ITZN 的资金缺口(78 000 美元或更多)。第二句回应第四段中第六句的建议,重申狄克逊的解决方案:若干机构共同为 ICZN 的运转提供资金。

设题点睛 本段第二句涉及解决方案,属于观点类信息,可用来设置选项。

生词解析

kick in 捐助;加入(股份等)

4. Dixon would most likely agree that _____ .

A. Like the GenBank, ICZN deserves equal financial support
B. any single organization is not capable of sustaining ICZN
C. zoologists should follow an all-volunteer model
D. ICZN has endured a sequence of crises since its establishment

狄克逊最有可能赞同_____。

A. 同基因银行一样,ICZN 也应获得同等的经济支持
B. 任何一个机构都无法独立维持 ICZN 运转
C. 动物学家们应遵循纯志愿型模式
D. 自成立至今,ICZN 已经历了一系列危机

【解题思路】A。事实细节题。根据题干关键词 Dixon 可定位至第四段、第五段和第六段。需要根据选项内容逐个排除。第四段最后两句是对此人观点的直接引用,指出 ICZN 与基因银行(GenBank)一样都需要强有力的资金支持(基因银行由政府出资维持运转)。最后一句用比喻手法谈到目前人们对 ICZN 的态度,指出人们只想享受"配送",但并不想付费,暗示目前的做法并不合理,ICZN 也应根据其付出而获得相应的经济回报,与选项 A 的内容对应,因此该项正确。

【排他分析】选项 B 对应第六段第二句,原文表示没有单一机构可以长期资助 ICZN,但该项没有明确说明支撑的期限是长期还是短期,不够严谨,因此排除。选项 C 对应原文第五段最后一句的转折内容,原文中此人表示在动物学界没有像植物学界一样的大型专门会议,因此无法采用类似的解决命名问题的方式,与该项所谈到的纯志愿者的工作模式无关,因此排除。选项 D 对应原文第四段首句,该句指出经历种种危机的机构是 ITZN,而非本项所说的 ICZN,所以排除。

Para. 7 ① If support is not forthcoming and ICZN falters, not much would change at first, scientists say. ② But "communication barriers would start to evolve" over time as names ceased to be systematically assigned and used, says Richard Pyle, a commissioner based at the Bishop

参考译文 ①科学家们表明,如果资金迟迟不到位,ICZN 就会难以为继,其后果不会马上表现出来。②但一旦物种名称不再系统地得到认定和使用,久而久之,"沟通障碍就会逐步显现",在火奴鲁鲁主教博物馆工作

Museum in Honolulu. ③"And that would be tragic." 的理查德·派尔（Richard Pyle）说道。③"这将会是一场灾难。"

原文剖析 本段开始分析以上问题可能造成的后果。首句指出失去资金支持的ICZN将摇摇欲坠，但其影响可能不会马上显现。第二句通过个人观点，进一步转折指出：但久而久之，一旦ICZN无法发挥作用，动物学界会出现沟通障碍的问题。第三句对第二句的结果进行补充，表示会对动物科学界造成灾难性的影响，回应首段最后一句中谈到的后果"无政府状态式的混乱"。

设题点睛 本段第二句转折引出的内容对首句进行补充，是本段的重要内容。

生词解析

forthcoming *adj.* 即将来临的 bishop *n.* （基督教的）主教

5. According to the author, the consequence of ICZN's disappearance is _____.   在作者看来，ICZN不复存在的后果是_____。

    A. understandable
    B. unbearable
    C. acceptable
    D. controllable

    A. 可理解的
    B. 无法容忍的
    C. 可接受的
    D. 可控的

【解题思路】B。观点态度题。根据顺序原则和题干关键词consequence可定位到文章最后一段。在作者没有明确表达自己观点的情况下，可以寻找没有被作者否定的人物观点来理解作者的态度。最后一段第二句和第三句是理查德·派尔的个人看法，他指出如果ICZN难以为继，其统一动物名称的作用将不复存在，如果动物名称不再统一，长此以往，会给科学家造成沟通上的障碍，第三句将这一后果总结为一场灾难。作者观点应与之呼应，因此选项B是正确答案。

【排他分析】可以迅速判断作者应认同ICZN消失会带来负面后果的观点，选项A和选项C与该感情色彩相反，选项D属于中性词，文中并未出现与之对应的内容，可以很快排除。

Text 27

Like most recovering addicts, Kay Sheppard has a testimony. Hers is this: The Florida mother of two spent years making trips to the store to buy cookies and chips for her family, eating almost every bag and box in the car on the way home. One day, she spied herself eating in the mirror and was horrified. "That was the first time in my 30-some years that I ever thought what I was doing was abnormal, because I had done the same thing year after year after year," she says.

To Sheppard, some people become obese because food has a drug-like power over them. Some scientists think this may be the case with about 15 percent of the population. "I mean, if you had control—if you weren't out of control—wouldn't you go on a diet and lose some weight?" says Sheppard, now a master's-level mental-health counselor.

While scientists have long theorized about an addiction-like quality to certain foods, only recently has the idea been the subject of intense scientific research, scrutinizing what studies call "highly palatable" foods, such as soda, ice cream, french fries and even pepperoni pizza. It's a definition that has to do with how much the foods appeal to our appetite—and how hard they are to resist.

That may help explain why it's difficult to keep from eating badly once it becomes a habit. In some experiments, the brain-imaging scans of an obese person resemble the brain scans of an addict. One of the most notable studies in this vein came in the early 2000s, when Nora Volkow and her team at Brookhaven National Laboratory placed 10 obese volunteers into a PET scanner to study the reward mechanisms in their brains. (Volkow later became head of the National Institute on Drug Abuse.) They found that the brains of these obese people looked different from those of people of normal weight; specifically, the obese people lacked certain receptors to dopamine, one of the brain chemicals associated with reward and drug abuse. Two channels for dopamine signaling in the brain occur through receptors known as D1 and D2. If you lack D2 receptors, as Volkow found in her subjects, you will not be able to inhibit the strong urges that are then sent into the areas of the brain involved in action, she says, leading to overeating. She says the deficit in D2 could also encourage overeating by making people less sensitive to the pleasure of eating itself, needing greater quantities of food to feel the reward.

But the biology that separates an almond from an Almond Joy goes far beyond dopamine. One of the key hormones involved in appetite, called ghrelin, is also involved with the reward system in the brain that drives us to eat, says Jeffrey Zigman of the University of Texas Southwestern Medical Center at Dallas. In fact, so much wiring in the brain appears to drive us toward high-calorie eating that some scientists suspect food is perhaps the reason drug addiction exists in the first place.

That programming is probably there to make sure our ancestors took advantage of times when they could load up on calories. But along came hyper-refined substances like cocaine and alcohol that could hijack the system and take it to a new intensity. And maybe, if the research is correct, that's possible with other highly processed substances like high-fructose corn syrup and 1,000-calorie cheeseburgers.

(*Newsweek*, 2016.1)

1. Kay Sheppard's testimony is mentioned to _____.
   A. stress the importance of repetition
   B. criticize her irresponsibility toward her family
   C. introduce the topic of what makes people obese
   D. explain how Sheppard feel about her eating habit
2. To Sheppard, what is essential to lose weight?
   A. Self-control ability.　　　　　　　　B. Drug-like addiction.

  C. Higher education degree.   D. Mental maturity.
3. The word "palatable"(Para. 3) is the closest in meaning to _____.
  A. resistible   B. fatty   C. multiple   D. addictive
4. Which of the following is true according to paragraph 4?
  A. Brain-imaging scans are important in separating the obese from the addict.
  B. The functions of D1 resemble those of D2.
  C. D2 receptor can reduce people's satisfaction with food.
  D. Dopamine receptor can be a vital factor in curing obesity.
5. It can be learned from the last two paragraphs that _____.
  A. food consuming can lead to drug addiction
  B. our ancestors are capable of consuming more calories
  C. high-calorie cheeseburger is as harmful to human health as cocaine
  D. drug-addiction may be provoked by certain physiological mechanism

语篇分析与试题精解

Para. 1 ①Like most recovering addicts, Kay Sheppard has a testimony. ②Hers is this: The Florida mother of two spent years making trips to the store to buy cookies and chips for her family, eating almost every bag and box in the car on the way home. ③One day, she spied herself eating in the mirror and was horrified. ④"That was the first time in my 30-some years that I ever thought what I was doing was abnormal, because I had done the same thing year after year after year," she says.

参考译文 ①与众多参加康复治疗的成瘾者一样，凯·谢泼德(Kay Sheppard)也有一段自白。②她的描述是这样的：这位两个孩子的母亲来自佛罗里达州。几年来，她一直到商店为家人采购饼干和薯片，但每次在回家的路上她都会把采购的食品全部吃光。③有一天，她从后视镜里看到自己吃东西时的样子，被自己吓到了。④"30多年来，我第一次意识到我的行为是反常的，因为我年复一年地做着同一件事。"她说。

原文剖析 本段整体描述一个事例。首句表明主人公身份：正在治疗中的成瘾者。后三句是对事例的具体描述：她的上瘾症状表现为会在回家的路上忍不住将刚买的食物全部吃光。预示本文与食物成瘾有关。

设题点睛 针对本段出题，一般不会从事例本身出发设置细节题，更有可能考查这段话在文章中的意义或功能所在，即考查篇章结构或例子功能题的概率更大。

生词解析
testimony *n.* 证言；声明   spy *vt.* 看见，发现
abnormal *adj.* 反常的

Para. 2 ① To Sheppard, some people become obese because food has a drug-like

参考译文 ①在谢泼德看来，有些人之所以变得肥胖，是因为食物对于他们来说

power over them. ②Some scientists think this may be the case with about 15 percent of the population. ③"I mean, if you had control—if you weren't out of control—wouldn't you go on a diet and lose some weight?" says Sheppard, now a master's-level mental-health counselor.

有着毒品一样让人上瘾的效用。②一些科学家认为，可能有15%的人都面临着这一问题。③"我的意思是，如果你能控制自己——或者说不会失控的话——难道不会节食减肥吗？"谢泼德说。如今，她是拥有硕士学位的心理健康顾问。

原文剖析 本段首句为人物观点：食物有令人上瘾的魔力。第二句承接首句，指出有很多人都面临着这一问题。第三句为带有人物观点的长难句，指出需要依靠自我控制来实现控制饮食的目标，暗示食物有时令人难以自控。

设题点睛 本段首句是对前一段内容的总结，是重要的观点性内容，可用来设置考点。剩余两句话中，第三句为含有人物观点的长难句，也可能被用来设置事实信息题进行考查。

生词解析

obese *adj.* 肥胖的   counselor *n.* 顾问

长难句解析

"I mean, if you had control—if you weren't out of control—wouldn't you go on a diet and
 宾语从句   条件状语从句   插入语   宾语从句
lose some weight?" says Sheppard, now a master's-level mental-health counselor.
                    谓语   主语   同位语

本句为直接引语，主句是 says Sheppard，引号中的内容作 says 的宾语从句，该从句中还包含一个条件状语从句，破折号之间的内容作插入语，补充说明条件状语的内容，句末的名词性短语作主语的同位语，说明其身份。

1 Kay Sheppard's testimony is mentioned to _____.	提到凯·谢泼德的自白是为了_____。
A. stress the importance of repetition	A. 强调重复的重要性
B. criticize her irresponsibility toward her family	B. 指责她对家庭不负责任
C. introduce the topic of what makes people obese	C. 引出人为什么会肥胖的话题
D. explain how Sheppard feel about her eating habit	D. 解释谢泼德对自己饮食习惯的感受

【解题思路】C。例子功能题。根据题干关键词 Kay Sheppard 和 testimony 定位到文章首段，本题询问以此人的经历为例是为了说明什么问题。解决这类题目时，一定要明白事例存在的意义是对主题进行说明或支持。当例子在首段中出现时，往往是为下文进行铺垫，因此解答本题需要从后文中寻找答案。第二段首句指出在谢泼德看来，一些人肥胖的原因在于抵御不了食物的诱惑并因此上瘾，将食物与毒品进行类比（some people become obese because food has a drug-like power over them），与首段的描述大致相同（年复一年在回家的路上将采购的食品全部吃光），由此可见举例的目的是为了解释一些人发胖的原因，与选项 C 一致。

【排他分析】选项 A 中的 repetition 对应首段最后一句中的 year after year，只是一个细节，且原文并未体现其重要性，与主题"食物"与"上瘾"均无关，因此排除。首段虽然谈到谢泼德每次都会在回家的路上将刚采购的食物吃光,但并不能从中推断出她缺乏对家庭的责任感,因此选项 B 属于过度推断,可以排除。选项 D 中的 feel 对应首段第三句中的 horrified(惊吓)一词,该词用于体现主人公突然意识到自己行为的反常性,也属于事实细节,不能代表本文想表达的观点,因此排除。

2 To Sheppard, what is essential to lose weight?
对于谢泼德而言,减肥最重要的是什么?

  A. Self-control ability.
  B. Drug-like addiction.
  C. Higher education degree.
  D. Mental maturity.

  A. 个人的自制力。
  B. 像毒品一样让人上瘾的效果。
  C. 高等教育学历。
  D. 心智的成熟。

【解题思路】A。事实细节题。根据题干关键词 Sheppard 和 lose weight 定位到第二段第二句。原文中此人用反问句表示如果人们有一定的自控能力就可以通过节食的方式减肥,had control 与 weren't out of control 与选项 A 呼应,因此该项正确。

【排他分析】选项 B 对应第二段首句中的 drug-like,原文是说食物对某些人而言就像是毒品一样容易令人上瘾,这会让人增肥而不是减肥,因此本项南辕北辙,可以排除。选项 C 对应第二段最后一句中的 a master's-level,原文只是介绍谢泼德目前的学历,与减肥毫无关系,因此排除。选项 D 可能对应本段最后一句中的 mental-health,但该项中的 maturity 在文中从未提及,因此排除。

Para. 3 ① While scientists have long theorized about an addiction-like quality to certain foods, only recently has the idea been the subject of intense scientific research, scrutinizing what studies call "highly palatable" foods, such as soda, ice cream, french fries and even pepperoni pizza. ② It's a definition that has to do with how much the foods appeal to our appetite—and how hard they are to resist.

参考译文 ①尽管科学界早就为某些食物具有毒品一般令人上瘾的效应提出了理论,但直到最近这一想法才成为科学家们集中研究的主题。科学家们详细研究被称作"特别美味"的食物,如汽水、冰淇淋、法式炸薯条甚至意大利香肠比萨。②这一定义与这些食物引起人们食欲的程度以及抵挡这些食物的难度有关。

原文剖析 本段首句承接上段首句,指出食物令人上瘾这一现象目前已经成为科学家们集中研究的主题,并提出了"特别美味"的食物的概念。第二句对这一概念做了进一步解释,给出了食物引起食欲的程度和抵挡食物的难度两个指标。

设题点睛 本段首句给出概念,第二句对该概念进行解释,可看作总分结构,第二句的解释性内容为重要考点,可用来设置语意理解题。

生词解析
scrutinize *vt.* 细察
pepperoni *n.* 意大利香肠
palatable *adj.* 美味的,可口的
appeal to 有吸引力,引起……好感

长难句解析
While scientists have long theorized about an addiction-like quality to certain foods,
    让步状语从句

only recently　has　the idea　been　the subject of intense scientific research,
时间状语　助动词　主语　系动词　表语　后置定语
scrutinizing what studies call "highly palatable" foods, such as soda, ice cream, french fries
状语　插入语
and even pepperoni pizza.

本句是主从复合句,本句主干为 While…, has the idea been the subject,句首为让步状语从句,主句中时间状语提前因此采用了部分倒装的语序,主句为主系表结构,现在分词 scrutinizing 及其宾语从句作状语,体现主句的结果,such as 作插入语,进行举例说明。

3 The word "palatable" (Para. 3) is closest in meaning to _____.

A. resistible
B. fatty
C. multiple
D. addictive

"palatable"（第三段）一词的意思最接近于_____。

A. 可抵抗的
B. 富含脂肪的
C. 多样的
D. 使人上瘾的

【解题思路】D。语意理解题。根据题干要求定位至第三段第一句"highly palatable" foods,该词用于修饰食物,短语之后用 such as 引出例子,则其后的汽水、冰淇淋、薯条和比萨都属于"highly palatable" foods,根据常识可知这些都是很受欢迎的食物。第二句是对引号中内容的具体解释,指出这个词与引起人们食欲的程度以及抵挡这些食物的难度有关(how much the foods appeal to our appetite—and how hard they are to resist)。根据例子和第二句的解释可看出修饰这些食物的形容词 palatable 应表示"极其美味的,难以拒绝的"意思。只有选项 D 与这一意思类似。

【排他分析】选项 A 的意思与正确项相反,如果食物是"可抵抗的",那么就不存在上瘾的问题,科学家也就不必研究了,因此排除。选项 B 表示"富含脂肪的",例子中汽水并非含有脂肪的食物,因此该项与原文不符,可以排除。原文虽然列举了若干例子,但是通过本段第二句对其的解释可以确定 palatable 与"多样的"并无语意联系,所以选项 C 排除。

Para. 4 ①That may help explain why it's difficult to keep from eating badly once it becomes a habit. ②In some experiments, the brain-imaging scans of an obese person resemble the brain scans of an addict. ③One of the most notable studies in this vein came in the early 2000s, when Nora Volkow and her team at Brookhaven National Laboratory placed 10 obese volunteers into a PET scanner to study the reward mechanisms in their brains. ④(Volkow later became head of the National

参考译文 ①这或许有助于解释,为什么一旦大吃特吃成为习惯,就很难控制自己不这么做了。②在有些实验中,肥胖者的脑成像扫描结果与吸毒者的扫描结果相似度较高。③这一领域最为著名的研究项目之一是在21世纪初进行的。当时,诺拉·沃尔考（Nora Volkow）及其研究小组成员在布鲁克黑文国家实验室对10名肥胖志愿者进行正电子放射断层造影术（PET）扫描,以研究其大脑中的奖励

Institute on Drug Abuse.) ⑤They found that the brains of these obese people looked different from those of people of normal weight; specifically, the obese people lacked certain receptors to dopamine, one of the brain chemicals associated with reward and drug abuse. ⑥Two channels for dopamine signaling in the brain occur through receptors known as D1 and D2. ⑦If you lack D2 receptors, as Volkow found in her subjects, you will not be able to inhibit the strong urges that are then sent into the areas of the brain involved in action, she says, leading to overeating. ⑧She says the deficit in D2 could also encourage overeating by making people less sensitive to the pleasure of eating itself, needing greater quantities of food to feel the reward.

机制。④(后来沃尔考担任了国家药物滥用研究所所长。)⑤他们发现,肥胖者的大脑与正常体重者的不同。肥胖者的大脑中尤其缺乏一些多巴胺受体。多巴胺是一种与奖励及药物滥用有关的脑内化学物质。⑥多巴胺向大脑发出信号要通过两条受体通道,这两条通道通过被称作 D1 和 D2 的受体实现。⑦如果你缺少 D2 受体,正如沃尔考在受试者身上发现的那样,那么你就无法抑制传递到大脑中负责行动区域的强烈冲动。她说,这会导致暴饮暴食。⑧她还表示,D2 受体的缺乏还会降低人们对吃东西本身所产生的愉悦感的敏感程度,这样人们要吃更多的食物才能产生这种感觉,最终导致过度饱食。

原文剖析 本段首句 That 回指上段最后谈到的"highly palatable" foods 的概念,指出这也许就是人们很难控制自己的原因(食物太美味,形成了习惯)。第二句谈到肥胖人士和吸毒者的脑成像扫描相似度很高,说明暴饮暴食和吸毒在某一方面性质相同,都是对某事物上瘾的表现。第三句和第四句引出某个最著名的实验。第五句到本段结束描述了这一实验的结果:肥胖者和正常人的大脑不同,肥胖者的大脑缺乏多巴胺的 D2 受体(该受体有两个功能:抑制冲动和增加人们对食物所带来的愉悦感的敏感程度),由于缺乏这一受体,肥胖者只能通过消耗大量食物来获得满足感。

设题点睛 本段后半部分谈到实验结果且解释了原因,属于重要内容,一般会用来设置细节题。

生词解析

badly *adv.* 极度,非常　　　　　　in this vein 在这方面
receptor *n.* 受体;接收器　　　　　dopamine *n.* 多巴胺
signal *vt.* 用信号传递(信息)

长难句解析

If you lack D2 receptors, as Volkow found in her subjects, you will not be able
　　条件状语从句　　　　　非限制性定语从句　　　　主语　　谓语
to inhibit the strong urges that are then sent into the areas of the brain involved in action,
　　　宾语　　　　　　　　　　　定语从句
she says, leading to overeating.
插入语　　结果状语

本句为主从复合句。本句主干为 if..., you will not be able to...,句首为 if 引导的条件状语从句,as 引导的非限制性定语从句中 as 充当 found 的宾语,对 if 从句进行修饰。主句中还

4 **Which of the following is true according to paragraph 4?**　　根据第四段内容,以下哪项正确?

A. Brain-imaging scans are important in separating the obese from the addict.
B. The functions of D1 resemble those of D2.
C. D2 receptor can reduce people's satisfaction with food.
D. Dopamine receptor can be a vital factor in curing obesity.

A. 在区分肥胖者和吸毒者时,脑成像扫描非常重要。
B. D1 受体的功能与 D2 相似。
C. D2 受体可以降低人们对食物的满意度。
D. 多巴胺受体是治愈肥胖症的关键因素。

【解题思路】D。事实细节题。根据题干要求定位到第四段。在没有明确定位点的情况下,优先阅读重要的考点结构。本段从第五句开始具体介绍实验结果,并解释原因,是重要内容。第五句指出肥胖人士尤其缺乏某种多巴胺受体。第七句指出肥胖的受试者缺乏名为 D2 的多巴胺受体,造成的后果是无法抑制对食物的冲动,因此导致暴饮暴食。第八句进一步补充 D2 受体的另一个作用,即帮助人们增强对吃东西所产生的满足感的敏感程度,缺乏这种受体会使人们吃更多的食物。从这三句可看出缺乏多巴胺的 D2 受体可导致肥胖,则该因素对于治疗肥胖症而言也至关重要,因此选项 D 是正确答案。

【排他分析】选项 A 中的 brain-imaging scans 对应第四段第二句和第三句,原文指出通过脑成像扫描发现肥胖者和吸毒者的大脑相似度很高,与该项所说的 separating 意思相反,因此排除。选项 B 对应该段第六句,该句提到多巴胺的 D1 和 D2 受体,后文主要谈及 D2 受体的功能,无法从中推知 D1 受体的功能是否与其相似,因此排除该项。选项 C 对应本段最后一句,原文的意思是 D2 受体的缺乏会降低人们对于饮食产生的愉悦敏感度,反过来说,D2 受体具有增强该愉悦敏感度的功能,与该项中的 reduce 直接相反,因此排除。

Para. 5 ①But the biology that separates an almond from an Almond Joy goes far beyond dopamine. ②One of the key hormones involved in appetite, called ghrelin, is also involved with the reward system in the brain that drives us to eat, says Jeffrey Zigman of the University of Texas Southwestern Medical Center at Dallas. ③In fact, so much wiring in the brain appears to drive us toward high-calorie eating that some scientists suspect food is perhaps the reason drug addiction exists in the first place.

参考译文 ①而有一种能区分杏仁和喜乐杏仁巧克力糖的生物体的作用则远远超过了多巴胺。②胃饥饿素是掌管食欲的关键激素之一,它还与大脑中刺激我们吃东西的奖励机制有关,达拉斯德克萨斯大学西南医疗中心的杰弗里·吉格曼(Jeffrey Zigman)说。③事实上,大脑似乎在努力让我们食用高热量食物,一些科学家甚至怀疑食物可能是药物成瘾的最初原因。

原文剖析 本段前两句介绍了人体中另外一种比多巴胺更重要的刺激饮食的激素:胃饥饿素,并解释其作用(掌管食欲、与大脑奖励机制有关)。第三句给出观点:人类大脑的生物构成似乎在促使人类倾向于食用高热量的食物,并指出这与药物成瘾的关系(是药物成瘾的最初原因)。

设题点睛 本段前两句的信息量较多,可以针对这两句中的任意一句设置细节题,也可结合最后一段出题。

生词解析

almond *n.* 杏仁　　　　　　　　　hormone *n.* 激素,荷尔蒙
ghrelin *n.* 胃饥饿素　　　　　　　wiring *n.* 线网

长难句解析

In fact, so much wiring in the brain appears to drive us toward high-calorie eating
　　　　　主语　　　　　　　　　系动词　　　　　　　表语
that some scientists suspect food is perhaps the reason drug addiction exists in the first place.
　　　　　　　　　　　　结果状语从句

本句为主从复合句。本句主干为 so much wiring appears to… that…,采用了"so+形容词+不可数名词+(that)+从句"的结构,that 引出结果状语从句。

Para. 6 ①That programming is probably there to make sure our ancestors took advantage of times when they could load up on calories. ②But along came hyper-refined substances like cocaine and alcohol that could hijack the system and take it to a new intensity. ③And maybe, if the research is correct, that's possible with other highly processed substances like high-fructose corn syrup and 1,000-calorie cheeseburgers.

参考译文 ①这一机能的存在很可能是为了确保我们的祖先充分利用可以摄取热量的机会。②但随后出现了高提纯物质,如可卡因和酒精。这类物质能挟持这一机能并使其作用上升到一个新高度。③如果这项研究是正确的,那么其他精加工类物质,如高果糖玉米糖浆或卡路里高达1 000的芝士汉堡,很可能和高提纯物质所产生的效果一样。

原文剖析 本段首句中的 That programming 回指上段最后一句提到的大脑似乎努力让人们食用高热量食物的机能,本句对这一机能出现的原因进行分析(保证祖先在有机会时尽可能多地摄入能量)。第二句转折指出目前出现的新情况:高提纯物质的出现挟制了这一机能,并增强了这一机能的效果(暗指这一机能会使人们对如可卡因和酒精在内的高提纯物质上瘾)。第三句回应文章有关食物上瘾的主题,顺接前一句谈到的研究结果,指出如果事实如此,则富含卡路里的精加工食物也和高提纯物质一样可挟持人类大脑的这一机能,使人们对食物上瘾。

设题点睛 本段第二句转折,第三句用于解释,都是重要的考点结构,可用来设置考题。

生词解析

load up on 大量储存;大量摄入　　　　　　hijack *vt.* 劫持
high-fructose 高果糖

5 It can be learned from the last two paragraphs that _____.

A. food consuming can lead to drug addiction
B. our ancestors are capable of consuming more calories
C. high-calorie cheeseburger is as harmful to human health as cocaine
D. drug-addiction may be provoked by certain physiological mechanism

从最后两段中可知_____。

A. 食物消耗可能导致药物成瘾
B. 我们的祖先有能力消耗更多热量
C. 对人体健康而言,高热量的芝士汉堡与可卡因一样有害
D. 药物上瘾可能由某种生理机能触发

【解题思路】**D**。推理引申题。根据题干要求定位到文章最后两段,在没有精确定位点的情况下,优先阅读考点结构。倒数第二段最后一句为观点句,谈到科学家猜测食物也许是人们会对药物上瘾的初始原因(food is perhaps the reason drug addiction exists in the first place),暗示食物与药物成瘾出现有先后关系。最后一段首句介绍了人类的一种特定的生理机能,该机能可确保远古人类能充分利用多吃的机会尽量补充能量,第二句指出如今出现的高提纯物质(毒品或酒精)可利用该机能,将其鼓励人类尽量多吃的功能发挥到了新的极致,因此导致人类上瘾。选项 D 是对这一推断的正确总结,为正确答案。

【排他分析】选项 A 对应第五段最后一句,原文是说吃东西与药物上瘾可能有因果关系(结合最后一段,其实表述人脑中刺激人们吃东西的奖励机制被高提纯物质控制,产生上瘾的副作用),并非像该项表述的关系这么简单,因此排除。选项 B 对应第六段首句,原文并没有将远古人类与现在的人类进行对比,该项属于无中生有,所以排除。选项 C 对应第六段最后一句,原文只是猜测如果该理论正确,那么这一理论也可用于解释干奶酪汉堡使人上瘾的现象,此外根据常理也可推断出,可卡因和汉堡的危害不可相提并论,两者不存在可比性,因此排除。

Text 28

Virtual reality and artificial intelligence are not the only technologies to get excited about. It is 25 years since Sony released a commercial version of the rechargeable lithium-ion battery, which now sits snugly in countless smartphones, laptops and other devices. In an era of robots and drones, artificial intelligence and virtual reality, the lithium-ion battery lacks futuristic glamour. Its deficiencies are quotidian and clear: witness the scrum of people around charging stations at airports. Yet few areas of technology promise as great an impact in as short a time.

Increasingly, lithium-ion batteries are vaulting out of pockets into power tools, vehicles, homes and even power stations. Carmakers in America, China and Japan are rushing to secure supplies of lithium to prepare for a more electric future. Such is the scramble, that the metal, used in small quantities in each battery cell, today is one of the world's only hot commodities. The price of lithium carbonate imported to China more than doubled in the last two months of 2015.

Until now, the limits on the use of batteries have been storage capacity, cost and recharging times. But large-scale production is overcoming these hurdles. The head-turner at this week's Detroit motor show was not a car but a battery—that of the 2017 Chevrolet Bolt, which General Motors' boss, Mary Barra, said had "cracked the code" of combining long range with an affordable price. Tesla, an electric-carmaker, is promising to start mass production of lithium-ion batteries this year in a giant "giga factory" in Nevada. BYD, a Chinese rival, is hot on its heels. In ten months last year Chinese firms sold more electric vehicles than Tesla has since 2008.

Electric cars are not the only source of demand. Batteries are also playing an increasingly important role in providing cleaner power on and off electricity grids. In South Africa, Australia, Germany and America, Tesla this year will start selling a $3,000 Powerwall for homeowners to store the solar energy from their roofs. Utilities are going even further. They are installing millions of lithium-ion battery cells into power plants to regulate supply at times of peak demand, and when it fluctuates because of intermittent wind and solar energy. California has ordered its electricity firms to offer 1.3 gigawatts (GW) of non-hydroelectric storage capacity within five years. That compares with total American power generation of more than 1,000GW, but is still more than double the 0.5GW of batteries plugged into grids around the world today. In 2016 a solar plant equipped with batteries will be installed in Hawaii, promising power after sunset at prices cheaper than diesel.

There is still a long way to go. As yet lithium-ion batteries do not have the capacity to store grid-scale power for more than a few hours. Costs are still too high; and the recent price spike in lithium will encourage researchers beavering away on other types of battery. Yet the more cells that are made, the more understanding and performance improve. Rising demand and higher prices will eventually also generate more lithium supply. Increasingly, lithium is becoming to batteries what silicon is to semiconductors—prevalent, even among worthy alternatives. In one form or another, the lithium-ion battery is the technology of our time.

(*The Economist*, 2016.1)

1. According to the first paragraph, what is the flaw of lithium-ion battery?
   A. It lacks the sustainability for nowadays electronic devices.
   B. It hinders the development of virtual reality.
   C. It brings the futuristic glamour to Sony.
   D. Robots have a higher demand for lithium-ion battery.
2. What contributes to the rising price of lithium?
   A. China's large amount of lithium carbonate import.
   B. A fierce competition for lithium in the electronic industry.

C. Lithium's ability to increase the temperature of the commodities.

D. The scramble for hot battery cells among carmakers.

3. It is suggested in paragraph 3 that _____.

   A. General Motors is in the leading position in lithium-ion battery research

   B. Tesla is the key factor in expanding the production of lithium-ion battery

   C. BYD has the largest demand for lithium-ion battery all over the world

   D. Barriers exited in lithium-ion battery application can be solved through mass production

4. The author mentions Tesla in paragraph 4 to _____.

   A. stress electric cars' high demand of lithium-ion battery

   B. illustrate lithium-ion battery's pivotal role in eco-power supply

   C. highlight the impact of intermittent wind and solar energy on battery

   D. emphasize the importance of non-hydroelectric storage battery

5. What is the author's attitude toward the future of lithium-ion battery?

   A. Ambiguous.　　B. Supportive.　　C. Understanding.　　D. Tolerating.

语篇分析与试题精解

Para. 1 ① Virtual reality and artificial intelligence are not the only technologies to get excited about. ② It is 25 years since Sony released a commercial version of the rechargeable lithium-ion battery, which now sits snugly in countless smartphones, laptops and other devices. ③ In an era of robots and drones, artificial intelligence and virtual reality, the lithium-ion battery lacks futuristic glamour. ④ Its deficiencies are quotidian and clear: witness the scrum of people around charging stations at airports. ⑤ Yet few areas of technology promise as great an impact in as short a time.

参考译文 ①虚拟现实和人工智能并非是唯一让人兴奋的技术。②索尼公司在25年前发布的商用可充电锂离子电池如今成了无数智能手机、笔记本电脑和其他电子设备的标配。③在当今这个以机器人和无人机、人工智能和虚拟现实为代表的时代,锂离子电池似乎缺少了些未来主义的光环。④它的不足显而易见:机场的充电站附近总是人头攒动。⑤然而,能够像锂离子电池这样能在如此短的时间内产生如此大影响的技术并不多。

原文剖析 本段前两句构成"否定+解释"的结构,引出文章讨论的主题(锂离子电池)。第三句和第四句同样构成"否定+解释"的结构,指出锂离子电池目前存在的缺陷:容量不足且充电资源有限。最后一句转折指出作者对锂离子电池技术的极高评价:属于少数能在短时间内发挥巨大影响力的科学技术。

设题点睛 本段出现两组"否定+解释"的结构,属于原因解释类信息,可用来设置细节题或因果题。

生词解析

lithium-ion n. 锂离子
drone n. (无线电遥控的)无人驾驶飞机
quotidian adj. 寻常的;司空见惯的
snugly adv. 舒适地;隐蔽地;贴身地;紧密地
futuristic adj. 未来主义的;未来派的
scrum n. 拥挤的人群;并列争球

长难句解析

Yet few areas of technology promise as great an impact in as short a time.
　　主语　　　后置定语　　　谓语　　　　　　　状语

本句是个简单句。本句主干为 few areas promise…，最后的状语部分体现了方式，该部分采用了双重"as + *adj.* + a/an + *n.* + as"的结构，该结构的用法在于如果第一个 as 后的形容词作定语修饰名词，则应该将该名词及有关修饰语全部放在第一个 as 之后。该双重 as… as 结构可还原为 as great an impact as this area of technology（第一个 as… as 结构）in as short a time as this area of technology（第二个 as… as 结构）。

1 According to the first paragraph, what is the flaw of lithium-ion battery?

根据第一段的内容，以下哪项为锂离子电池的缺陷？

A. It lacks the sustainability for nowadays electronic devices.
B. It hinders the development of virtual reality.
C. It brings the futuristic glamour to Sony.
D. Robots have a higher demand for lithium-ion battery.

A. 对如今的电子设备而言，此类电池的续航能力较差。
B. 此类电池阻碍了虚拟现实的发展。
C. 此类电池为索尼公司带来了具有未来主义的光环。
D. 机器人对锂离子电池有更高的要求。

【解题思路】**A**。推理引申题。根据题干要求定位至第一段。有关锂离子电池缺点的句子为本段第四句（该句出现 deficiencies），该句冒号之后指出"机场的充电站附近总是人头攒动"（witness the scrum of people around charging stations at airports），其中的 scrum 一词有"争抢"的意思，因此本句暗示往往能在机场中看到人们为了给电子设备的锂离子电池充电而争抢电源的现象，可由此推断出现这种现象的原因在于人们所使用的锂离子电池续航能力不足，需要频繁充电，因此选项 A 正确。

【排他分析】首段第一句和第三句中都出现了 virtual reality（虚拟现实），但并没有谈到"虚拟现实"和"锂离子电池"之间有什么关系，因此选项 B 属于无中生有，可排除。选项 C 将第三句中的 futuristic glamour 和第二句中的 Sony 随意拼凑，干扰作用不强，可直接排除。选项 D 中的 robots 在该段第三句中与 drones, artificial intelligence 和 virtual reality 并列，而原文列举这四类科技的作用在于要将锂离子电池的前景和它们做比较，原文并没有谈到这四类技术对锂离子电池的"要求"如何，该项内容属于无中生有，故排除。

Para. 2 ① Increasingly, lithium-ion batteries are vaulting out of pockets into power tools, vehicles, homes and even power stations. ②Carmakers in America, China and Japan are rushing to secure supplies of lithium to prepare for a more electric future. ③ Such is the scramble, that the metal, used in small quantities

参考译文 ①锂离子电池不再只见于较小的私人电子用品之中，如今已经逐渐适用于大型电动工具、车辆、家庭甚至发电站。②美国、中国和日本的汽车制造商正在加紧对锂的储备，以便为未来的电子化世界做好准备。③这种少量存在于每块电池中的金属，

in each battery cell, today is one of the world's only hot commodities. ④ The price of lithium carbonate imported to China more than doubled in the last two months of 2015.

目前已经成为当今世界上最抢手的商品之一。④ 2015年的最后两个月，中国进口的碳酸锂价格增长了不止一倍。

原文剖析 本段前两句介绍了当前锂离子电池科技的发展（适用范围更广）以及各国对锂电池发展的态度（积极准备）。第三句给出作者观点（锂金属是最抢手的资源）。第四句通过列举碳酸锂价格的飙升，印证第三句的观点。

设题点睛 第三句是对前两句的总结，第四句是对第三句的举例论证，因此第三句为本段重点内容，可用来设置题目。

生词解析

vault *vi.* 跳跃；腾跃   rush to 急着做某事
scramble *n.* 争夺，抢夺   lithium carbonate 碳酸锂

长难句解析

Such   is   the scramble, that the metal, used in small quantities in each battery cell,
表语 系动词   主语   同位语从句   后置定语
today is one of the world's only hot commodities.
             同位语从句

本句为主从复合句。本句的主干为 Such is the scramble that…, 本句采用了 such is sth. that 的句型结构，such 提前，因此句子用了倒装形式，such 实际上在句中作表语。that 从句作 such 的同位语，具体说明 such 指代的内容，本句型结构可理解为"某事就是如此"。

2	What contributes to the rising price of lithium?	锂价格上涨的推动因素是什么？
	A. China's large amount of lithium carbonate import.	A. 中国对碳酸锂的大量进口。
	B. A fierce competition for lithium in the electronic industry.	B. 电子产业领域对金属锂的激烈竞争。
	C. Lithium's ability to increase the temperature of the commodities.	C. 金属锂增加商品温度的能力。
	D. The scramble for hot battery cells among carmakers.	D. 汽车制造企业对热门电池的争夺。

【解题思路】B。推理引申题。根据题干关键词（rising price）定位到第二段最后一句。本题考查锂价格飙升的原因。该段第二句指出多国的汽车制造商为了应对未来电动化的趋势（electric future）而加紧储备锂，第三句进一步指出锂成为最热门的商品之一（one of the world's only hot commodities），由此可看出此类金属价格上升的原因在于强劲的市场需求，正是因为供不应求，才导致原材料价格上涨。选项 B 中的 fierce competition 可以对应第三句中的 scramble，因此是正确答案。

【排他分析】选项 A 的内容对应第二段最后一句，但该句的作用是通过事实印证前一句所说的金属锂的热销，即用中国所进口的碳酸锂价格的上涨印证锂金属抢手，这是表现而非原因，因此排除。选项 C 是对第二段第三句中 hot commodities 的误解，hot 修饰

"商品"时表示"紧缺的,销路好的",而与商品的温度无关,因此排除。选项 D 的错误原因和选项 A 类似,第二段第二句确实提到汽车制造商正在加紧对锂的储备,是为了说明锂离子电池对于未来世界的电动化发展很重要,且汽车制造商只是锂离子电池的使用者之一,并不能因此推断它们对锂的竞争导致该资源的价格上涨,因此排除。

Para. 3 ①Until now, the limits on the use of batteries have been storage capacity, cost and recharging times. ② But large-scale production is overcoming these hurdles. ③The head-turner at this week's Detroit motor show was not a car but a battery—that of the 2017 Chevrolet Bolt, which General Motors' boss, Mary Barra, said had "cracked the code" of combining long range with an affordable price. ④ Tesla, an electric-carmaker, is promising to start mass production of lithium-ion batteries this year in a giant "giga factory" in Nevada. ⑤ BYD, a Chinese rival, is hot on its heels. ⑥In ten months last year Chinese firms sold more electric vehicles than Tesla has since 2008.

参考译文 ①到目前为止,电池应用的局限性在于其存储容量、成本和充电时间。②然而,大规模生产正在突破这些障碍。③本周,在底特律车展上,最吸引眼球的并不是汽车,而是一块电池,也就是雪佛兰 2017 年推出的新款电动车博尔特所使用的电池,通用汽车公司的老板玛丽·巴拉(Mary Barra)说,"(该电池)破解了难题",能够增加续航里程,且价格实惠。④电动汽车制造商特斯拉,有望今年在内华达州的一个超级工厂里大规模生产锂离子电池。⑤该制造商的中国竞争对手——比亚迪——也紧随其后。⑥仅在去年的十个月内,中国企业卖出的电动汽车数量比特斯拉自 2008 年以来的汽车销售总数还要多。

原文剖析 本段前两句的语意形成转折,指出通过大规模生产的方式可以克服当前电池存在的三种问题。第三句到第六句,分别以通用汽车、特斯拉和比亚迪三家电动汽车生产厂商为例,说明当前制造商正在采用大规模扩大产能的方式克服电池续航局限。

设题点睛 第二句带有转折语意,且是后文举例说明的对象,因此是重要的观点句,可用来设置正确选项。

生词解析

overcome vt. 克服
head-turner n. 吸引人目光的事物
giga n. 千兆;十亿
on one's heels 跟随……;紧跟……

hurdle n. 困难
crack vt. 解决;揭开(秘密等)
rival n. 对手;竞争者

长难句解析

The head-turner at this week's Detroit motor show was not   a car but a battery—that of
　　主语　　　　　　后置定语　　　　　　　　　系动词　　表语1　　表语2
the 2017 Chevrolet Bolt, which General Motors' boss, Mary Barra, said had "cracked the
　　同位语　　　　　　　　　　　非限制性定语从句
code" of combining long range with an affordable price.

本句是主从复合句。本句的主干为 The head-turner was not a car but a battery…,主句部分使用了 not... but... 的结构,but 作连词,表示"而,相反",连接两个并列成分。破折号后为 battery 的同位语,该同位语还受到 which 引导的非限制性定语从句的修饰。

3 It is suggested in paragraph 3 that _____.

A. General Motors is in the leading position in lithium-ion battery research
B. Tesla is the key factor in expanding the production of lithium-ion battery
C. BYD has the largest demand for lithium-ion battery all over the world
D. Barriers exited in lithium-ion battery application can be solved through mass production

第三段暗示_____。

A. 通用汽车在锂离子电池研究方面首屈一指
B. 特斯拉是扩大锂离子电池产量的关键因素
C. 比亚迪是全世界对锂离子电池需求最大的厂商
D. 在锂离子电池应用方面存在的问题可通过大规模生产得到解决

【解题思路】D。事实细节题。根据题干要求定位到文章第三段，当题干中没有给出明确定位点的情况下，所考查的往往是段落中的观点性内容。本段观点性内容出现在第二句，联系第一句内容后可看出第二句意在指出大规模生产可以解决电池在存储容量、成本和充电时间方面存在的障碍（large-scale production is overcoming these hurdles），锂离子电池也是电池的一种，因此选项 D 正确。该项中的 mass production 和 solved 分别对应原文中的 large-scale production 和 overcoming。

【排他分析】选项 A 中的 General Motors 出现在第三段第三句，原文指出通用汽车公司的老板表示雪佛兰新款电动车所用的电池破解了难题，应看作对自家产品的"自卖自夸"，并不代表通用汽车确实在该领域处于领先地位，因此排除该项。选项 B 中的 Tesla 出现在本段第四句，原文只是提到特斯拉将大规模生产锂离子电池，并没有指出该企业是扩大产量的关键所在，因此排除该项。选项 C 中的 BYD 对应本段最后两句，原文完全没有提到比亚迪与锂离子电池需求量之间的关系，可以直接排除。

Para. 4 ①Electric cars are not the only source of demand. ②Batteries are also playing an increasingly important role in providing cleaner power on and off electricity grids. ③In South Africa, Australia, Germany and America, Tesla this year will start selling a ＄3,000 Powerwall for homeowners to store the solar energy from their roofs. ④Utilities are going even further. ⑤They are installing millions of lithium-ion battery cells into power plants to regulate supply at times of peak demand, and when it fluctuates because of intermittent wind and solar energy. ⑥California has ordered its electricity firms to offer 1.3 gigawatts（GW）of non-hydroelectric

参考译文 ①电动汽车并不是锂离子电池唯一的需求方。②电池能提供更洁净的能源，因此在电网和非电网中越来越重要。③今年，特斯拉将在南非、澳大利亚、德国和美国发售价格为3 000 美元的能量墙，消费者能用其在自家屋顶储存太阳能。④供电机构更是走在了前面。⑤它们正给发电厂安装数百万个锂离子电池，目的是在用电高峰期，或者当可利用的风能和太阳能处于间歇性波动期时，调控电力供应。⑥加利福尼亚州已经要求其电力公司的非水电存储量在五年内达到1.3 千兆瓦。⑦这一存储容量相

storage capacity within five years. ⑦ That compares with total American power generation of more than 1,000GW, but is still more than double the 0.5GW of batteries plugged into grids around the world today. ⑧In 2016 a solar plant equipped with batteries will be installed in Hawaii, promising power after sunset at prices cheaper than diesel.

对于美国的总发电量(超过1 000千兆瓦)而言不算太大,但还是比目前全球范围内接入电网的电池容量(0.5千兆瓦)要多出一倍多。⑧2016年,夏威夷将要建立一座配备电池的太阳能发电厂,有望在日落之后以低于柴油发电的价格供电。

原文剖析　本段前两句总结指出锂离子电池除了可用于电动汽车之外还可用于电网,并给出原因(锂电池是清洁能源)。从第三句到第八句,分别用特斯拉、供电机构、加利福尼亚州和夏威夷为例,论证锂离子电池在电网方面的发展。

设题点睛　本段和上段的结构类似,都采用总分方式进行举例论证,因此其中的观点句或总结性内容适合设置正确选项。

生词解析

grid n. 系统网络,高压输电网
fluctuate vi. 波动,涨落,起伏
gigawatt n. 千兆瓦,十亿瓦
plug into 接入;接通

utility n. 公用事业;公用事业公司
intermittent adj. 间歇的;断断续续的
hydroelectric adj. 水力发电的
diesel n. 柴油

长难句解析

They are installing millions of lithium-ion battery cells into power plants to regulate supply
　主语　　谓语　　　　　　宾语　　　　　　　　　　　状语　　　　　目的状语
at times of peak demand, and when it fluctuates because of intermittent wind and solar energy.
　　　　时间状语　　　　　　　　　　　　　　　原因状语

本句是主从复合句。本句主干为 They are installing battery cells to…,不定式引出目的状语,该目的状语中还包含一个 at times of 和 when 引出的时间状语,以及介词词组 because of 引出的原因状语。

4 The author mentions Tesla in paragraph 4 to _____.

A. stress electric cars' high demand of lithium-ion battery
B. illustrate lithium-ion battery's pivotal role in eco-power supply
C. highlight the impact of intermittent wind and solar energy on battery
D. emphasize the importance of non-hydroelectric storage capacity

作者在第四段提到特斯拉是为了_____。

A. 强调电动汽车对锂离子电池的高需求
B. 说明锂离子电池在生态能源供应方面的关键作用
C. 突出间歇性风能和太阳能对电池的影响
D. 强调非水电存储容量的重要性

【解题思路】B。例子功能题。根据题干要求定位到文章第四段,本题考查作者以特斯拉为例的目的。该段第三句提到了特斯拉,谈到"特斯拉将在南非、澳大利亚、德国和

277

美国发售价格为3 000美元的能量墙",与前一句并无转折连词连接,因此可看作对前文内容的顺承,回应了第二句给出的观点"电池……在电网和非电网中越来越重要","能量墙"将太阳能转化为电能储存在电池中,可看作是电池在"非电网"中的应用。第二句指出电池的性质是清洁能源(cleaner power),第三句谈到此类电池是利用solar energy充电,说明"能量墙"是一种清洁环保的供电方式,与选项B中的eco-power supply所指一致,因此该项正确。

【排他分析】本段首句明确将电池的应用范围从电动汽车转向了能源,所以可以直接排除选项A。选项C和选项D分别对应该段第五句和第六句的内容,这两句与第三句提到的特斯拉形成并列的关系,都作为例子说明第二句的观点,三个例子之间并不用于互相证明,可排除。

Para. 5 ①There is still a long way to go. ②As yet lithium-ion batteries do not have the capacity to store grid-scale power for more than a few hours. ③Costs are still too high; and the recent price spike in lithium will encourage researchers beavering away on other types of battery. ④Yet the more cells that are made, the more understanding and performance improve. ⑤Rising demand and higher prices will eventually also generate more lithium supply. ⑥Increasingly, lithium is becoming to batteries what silicon is to semiconductors—prevalent, even among worthy alternatives. ⑦In one form or another, the lithium-ion battery is the technology of our time.

参考译文 ①然而未来的路还很长。②到目前为止,锂离子电池还没有储存电网规模电量的能力,其电量使用时间不超过几个小时。③此外,成本依然很高;最近锂价的上涨会导致研究人员努力研究其他类型的电池。④但是,生产的电池越多,对电池的了解就会越深,电池的性能也会越好。⑤需求增多,导致价格上涨,但价格上涨最终也会促使锂的供应量增多。⑥慢慢地,未来锂之于电池会如同硅之于半导体,即便有其他类似的替代品出现,锂在电池中的应用仍具有普遍性。⑦无论以何种形式存在,锂离子电池都是可以代表我们这个时代的科技。

原文剖析 本段前三句让步指出锂离子电池目前的发展还面临很多限制因素。第四句和第五句转折指出只要生产(回应第三段)和需求(回应第二段)增加,以上问题就可以逐步得到解决。第六句和第七句对全文的观点进行总结,认为锂离子电池应被视为现代科技的代表。

设题点睛 本段最后两句给出作者观点,且第六句是带有破折号的长难句,适合设置观点态度题。第四句和第五句的观点回应前文,因此再次考查的概率相对偏低。

生词解析
as yet 迄今为止
beaver away 努力工作,辛勤劳动
semiconductor n. 半导体

spike n. 猛增,急升
silicon n. 硅;硅元素
prevalent adj. 流行的;普遍的

长难句解析
Increasingly, lithium is becoming to batteries what silicon is to semiconductors—prevalent,
状语1　　　　　　　表示比较意义的句型　　　　　　表语

even among worthy alternatives.

本句是简单句。本句的主干是一个具有同级比较意义的句型,其结构为:A is to B what C is to D,表示两种相似关系的对比,具有比喻的修辞效果,常译为"A 之于 B 犹如 C 之于 D"。破折号之后的 prevalent 是形容词,可看作省略了主语和系动词的句子,可还原为 lithium is prevalent。

5 What is the author's attitude toward the future of lithium-ion battery?   作者对锂离子电池的未来持什么态度?

A. Ambiguous.   A. 模糊的。
B. Supportive.   B. 支持的。
C. Understanding.   C. 理解的。
D. Tolerating.   D. 容忍的。

【解题思路】B。观点态度题。本题考查作者对本文主题——锂离子电池的未来的看法,也可看作观点总结题。根据顺序原则可定位到文章最后一段。该段第四句转折之后的内容为作者的观点,其中第六句指出"未来锂之于电池会如同硅之于半导体"(lithium is becoming to batteries what silicon is to semiconductors),is becoming 表明是对未来趋势的判断。根据常识可知硅对于计算机产业十分重要,作者将两者相提并论是为了表明锂离子电池的重要性,并且最后一句总结指出"锂离子电池都是可以代表我们这个时代的科技"(the technology of our time),再次证明作者对于锂离子电池科技的高度评价和乐观展望,因此选项 B 正确。

【排他分析】虽然本文在许多地方采取了欲扬先抑的写法,但本文明显体现出了作者对锂离子电池的较高评价,因此可排除含有消极意义的选项 D。从最后一段的总结部分也可看出作者的态度是鲜明的,而非模棱两可或表示理解的,因此排除选项 A 和选项 C。

Text 29

The recent crashes of two Boeing 737 Max 8 airliners provide a reminder of the difficult choices the world faces as it moves even faster toward "intelligent" transportation systems. Though the exact causes of the air crashes are still to be determined, the inability to make a successful shift from automated control to pilot control seems to be a common factor. That should be a useful lesson for almost all forms of transport being built to reduce the high costs of tragedies caused by human error.

Whether in the air, on highways and railways, or on the water, the transportation industry is undergoing a revolutionary transition in the use of artificial intelligence. Fully autonomous vehicles are already being tested on roads. A year ago, a pedestrian in Tempe, Arizona, was killed by a self-driving Uber car undergoing such a test. Despite the questions that the tragedy raised, Tesla founder Elon Musk said recently he was certain his "autopilot" cars would soon be able to fully operate hands-free.

Such confidence is up against widespread fear. More than 70 percent of American drivers would be afraid to ride in a self-driving vehicle, according to an AAA poll. Despite those sentiments, the truth is that technology is constantly making travel safer and bringing down the death toll of decades past. The Canadian Pacific Railway says it will soon become the first rail line to use electromagnetic sensors to detect tiny cracks in rail car wheels that can lead to fractures and derailments. Partial automation is already in newer automobiles, often equipped with features such as lane-change warnings and controls that keep a certain distance from a vehicle ahead. Half of the cars sold in the United States today are equipped with automatic emergency braking that requires no foot on the pedal. Such equipment is expected to be on virtually every new car by 2022.

In general, air travel is safer than ever because of constant innovation and better pilot training. But the consequences of any lapses in safety are so profound that eternal vigilance is requisite. It's likely that the cause of the two recent crashes will lead quickly to corrective measures.

Today's most innovative transport relies heavily on automation during crucial moments. Problems arise when operators take too long to regain control after a system fails. Long stretches of inactivity can produce what is called "passive fatigue," which may lengthen their response times. Ironically, as planes and road vehicles become more automated, pilots and drivers will have less and less "practice" controlling their machines.

The next leap in such technologies will be to leave humans out of the equation altogether and avoid the tricky handoffs in the human-machine interface. Despite the recent troubling setbacks, "leave the driving to us" will probably be the motto of the machines that convey us in the future.

(*The Christian Science Monitor*, 2019.3)

1. The recent air crashes are seen as _____.
   A. a symbol of worldwide disaster
   B. a warning of safety of automated vehicles
   C. a lesson for the existing transportation industry
   D. an example of immature automated control
2. Which of the following is TRUE according to paragraph 3?
   A. Automatic driving is already safe enough.
   B. The U.S. has advanced technology in cars.
   C. Worries about self-driving vehicles are reasonable.
   D. Some people's panic may be more than what is due.
3. The word "lapse" (Para. 4) most probably means _____.
   A. slip   B. move
   C. sense   D. comment

4. We may learn from paragraph 5 that pilots and drivers _____.
   A. should practise controlling regularly
   B. have a relatively long response times
   C. will probably be replaced by automation
   D. may be confronted with unemployment

5. The author's attitude toward automatic drive may be _____.
   A. optimistic   B. ambiguous
   C. indifferent   D. neutral

语篇分析与试题精解

Para. 1 ①The recent crashes of two Boeing 737 Max 8 airliners provide a reminder of the difficult choices the world faces as it moves even faster toward "intelligent" transportation systems. ②Though the exact causes of the air crashes are still to be determined, the inability to make a successful shift from automated control to pilot control seems to be a common factor. ③That should be a useful lesson for almost all forms of transport being built to reduce the high costs of tragedies caused by human error.

参考译文 ① 近期的两起波音737 Max 8大型客机空难事件提醒我们,世界在更快速地迈向"智能"运输系统时面临着艰难抉择。② 虽然这两起空难的确切起因尚有待确定,但无法成功地从自动控制转换为飞行员控制似乎是一个共同因素。③ 对于几乎所有正在建设的运输形式而言,这都应是个有益的教训,以减少人为错误导致的悲剧的高成本。

原文剖析 本段由波音飞机空难事件引出讨论话题——自动化交通工具的安全性。第一句由波音飞机空难事件初步引出讨论话题:"智能"运输系统发展面临着艰难抉择(difficult choices)。第二句进一步说明话题,通过分析波音客机失事原因,指出"抉择"内容:"机控和人控间的转换",并指出二者转换会影响运输安全。第三句就波音客机事件做出评论,指出人机转换对整个运输行业的发展都有重要意义。

设题点睛 本段首句和第三句均为观点句,可用来设置正确选项。

生词解析

crash n. 碰撞;相撞   airliner n. 大型客机;班机
reminder n. 引起回忆的事物   inability n. 无能;不能
transport n. 交通运输系统

长难句解析

That should be a useful lesson for almost all forms of transport being built to reduce
主语 谓语   宾语   状语1   后置定语1

the high costs of tragedies caused by human error.
        状语2   后置定语2

本句是一个包含两个复杂状语的简单句。句子主干为主谓宾结构,主语为that,指代前一句话的内容,谓语部分为should be,宾语为a useful lesson。for almost... built 为状语1,说

281

明宾语所对应的对象，being built 为 transport 的后置定语；to reduce… error 为状语2，表示目的，caused by human error 为 tragedies 的后置定语。

1 The recent air crashes are seen as _____.

A. a symbol of worldwide disaster
B. a warning of safety of automated vehicles
C. a lesson for the existing transportation industry
D. an example of immature automated control

最近的空难被视为_____。

A. 一个世界性灾难的象征
B. 自动驾驶安全性的一个警示
C. 现有运输业的一个教训
D. 一个不成熟的自动控制的例子

【解题思路】B。事实细节题。根据题干关键词（recent air crashes）可定位到第一段。首句指出，近期的两起波音 737 Max 8 大型客机空难事件提醒我们，世界在更快速地迈向"智能"运输系统时面临着艰难抉择。"intelligent" transportation systems 就是自动化驾驶，"difficult choices"就是安全方面的问题，选项 B 中的 warning 与第一句中的 reminder 为同义替换；safety of automated vehicles 就是文中的迈向"智能"运输系统时面临着艰难抉择，因此选项 B 正确。

【排他分析】选项 A 文中未提及，属于无中生有，且表意过于夸大，可排除。文章提到，对于几乎所有正在建设的运输形式而言，这都应是个有益的教训，文中说的是 being built，而选项 C 为 existing，故排除。文章指出两次空难的一个共同原因是无法成功地从自动控制转换为飞行员控制，而不是不成熟的自动控制，选项 D 排除。

Para. 2 ①Whether in the air, on highways and railways, or on the water, the transportation industry is undergoing a revolutionary transition in the use of artificial intelligence. ②Fully autonomous vehicles are already being tested on roads. ③A year ago, a pedestrian in Tempe, Arizona, was killed by a self-driving Uber car undergoing such a test. ④Despite the questions that the tragedy raised, Tesla founder Elon Musk said recently he was certain his "autopilot" cars would soon be able to fully operate hands-free.

参考译文 ①无论是空运、公路运输还是铁路运输，或者是水路运输，交通业在人工智能的运用方面正经历着一次革命性转变。②全自动汽车已投入公路测试。③一年前，亚利桑那州坦佩市的一位行人因被一辆正在接受公路测试的自动驾驶优步车撞击而丧生。④虽然这起悲剧引发了一些问题，但是特斯拉创始人埃隆·马斯克近期表示，他确信他的"自动驾驶仪"汽车很快便能完全实现自动操作。

原文剖析 本段进一步阐释话题，指出处理好人工智能的安全问题对于运输业的发展很关键。第一句指出，人工智能对于各种运输方式的发展都是关键的一环。第二句至第四句例证第一句。第二句介绍发展动态；第三句引用具体事例，指出自动驾驶具有安全隐患。第四句转折，引用业界权威人士话语说明自动化驾驶有望提高安全性能，摆脱对人工的依赖。

设题点睛 本段首句为观点句，可用于设置正确选项；第三句引用具体事例，可设置例子功能题;最后一句为转折句,包含权威人士的观点态度,可设置题目。

生词解析

highway *n.* (尤指城市间的)公路　　　　railway *n.* 铁路
undergo *vt.* 经历,经受(变化、不愉快的事等)　　autonomous *adj.* 自主的;有自主权的
pedestrian *n.* 行人　　　　　　　　　autopilot *n.* (飞机的)自动驾驶仪
hands-free *adj.* 解放双手的,免提的

长难句解析

Despite the questions that the tragedy raised, Tesla founder Elon Musk said recently
　　状语　　　　　　　定语从句　　　　　　　　主语　　　　　　谓语　时间状语
he was certain his "autopilot" cars would soon be able to fully operate hands-free.
　　　　　　　　　　　　　宾语从句

本句是主从复合句。本句主干为 Tesla founder Elon Musk said…,despite the questions 为介词短语作让步状语,其后 that 引导的是定语从句,先行词为 questions。主句的宾语为省略了引导词 that 的宾语从句。

Para. 3 ① Such confidence is up against widespread fear. ② More than 70 percent of American drivers would be afraid to ride in a self-driving vehicle, according to an AAA poll. ③Despite those sentiments, the truth is that technology is constantly making travel safer and bringing down the death toll of decades past. ④The Canadian Pacific Railway says it will soon become the first rail line to use electromagnetic sensors to detect tiny cracks in rail car wheels that can lead to fractures and derailments. ⑤Partial automation is already in newer automobiles, often equipped with features such as lane-change warnings and controls that keep a certain distance from a vehicle ahead. ⑥Half of the cars sold in the United States today are equipped with automatic emergency braking that requires no foot on the pedal. ⑦Such equipment is expected to be on virtually every new car by 2022.

参考译文 ①对自动驾驶汽车的信心也面临着普遍的担忧。②根据美国汽车协会的一项民意调查,超过百分之七十的美国司机不敢乘坐自动驾驶汽车。③虽然存在这些担忧,但事实是技术发展不断使出行变得更安全,并降低了过去几十年的死亡总数。④加拿大太平洋铁路表明,其将很快成为第一条使用电磁感应器检测轨道车辆车轮上微小裂缝的铁路线,这些微小裂缝可能会导致车轮断裂和脱轨。⑤新型汽车已实现了部分自动化,通常配备变道警告装置和与前方车辆保持一定距离的控制装置。⑥美国现在售出的汽车中,有半数配备自动紧急制动装置,不需要将脚放在踏板上。⑦预计到2022年,几乎所有的新汽车都会配备这种自动制动装置。

原文剖析 本段举例说明自动化可以提高驾驶的安全性。第一句至第二句让步,指出自动化驾驶的安全性被广泛怀疑。第三句转折,明言技术发展赋予了自动化驾驶更高的安全性。第四句至第七句例证第三句。第四句指出自动化能够排查细微故障从而减少意外事故的发生。第五句至第七句以变道警告、车距控制、自动制动为例,说明得益于技术发展,自动化已经并会继续提高驾驶的安全性。

设题点睛 本段多处涉及观点态度，可设置正确选项或设置推理判断题。

生词解析

up against sth. / sb. 面临某事/某人
sentiment n. (基于情感的)看法；情绪
toll n. (死亡、事故或灾难的)总数
fracture n. 折断；破裂
lane-change 变换车道
poll n. 民意调查
bring down sth. / bring sth. down 减少；降低
electromagnetic adj. 电磁的
derailment n. (火车的)出轨，脱轨
virtually adv. 几乎；差不多

长难句解析

The Canadian Pacific Railway says it will soon become the first rail line to use
   主语   谓语   宾语从句
electromagnetic sensors to detect tiny cracks in rail car wheels that can lead to
  后置定语   目的状语   地点状语   定语从句
fractures and derailments.

本句是主从复合句。本句主干为 The Canadian Pacific Railway says… ，谓语 says 后面为省略了引导词 that 的宾语从句。to use… 为不定式作 the first rail line 的后置定语，to detect… 为不定式作目的状语，in rail car wheels 作地点状语，其后 that 引导的是定语从句，其先行词为 tiny cracks。

2 Which of the following is TRUE according to paragraph 3?   根据第三段，以下哪项是正确的？

A. Automatic driving is already safe enough.   A. 自动驾驶已足够安全。
B. The U.S. has advanced technology in cars.   B. 美国在汽车行业拥有超前的技术。
C. Worries about self-driving vehicles are reasonable.   C. 对自动驾驶汽车的担心是合理的。
D. Some people's panic may be more than what is due.   D. 有些人的恐慌可能超过了应有的程度。

【解题思路】D。推理判断题。根据题干直接定位到第三段。第一、二句让步，指出自动化驾驶的安全性被广泛怀疑。第三句转折，指出技术发展赋予了自动化驾驶更高的安全性。第四句指出自动化能够排查细微故障从而减少意外事故的发生，可见人们对于自动化驾驶的担忧或恐慌过度了，选项 D 属于合理推断，故为正确答案。

【排他分析】文中提到，技术发展赋予了自动化驾驶更高的安全性，自动化能够排查细微故障从而减少意外事故的发生，自动化已经并会继续提高驾驶的安全性，并不能推出自动驾驶已经足够安全，选项 A 属于过度推理，因此排除。第六句提到，美国现在售出的汽车中，有半数配备自动紧急制动装置，不需要将脚放在踏板上，并未提及超前的技术等，选项 B 无中生有，因此排除。文中只提到超过百分之七十的美国司机不敢乘坐自动驾驶汽车，但并未说明其中的原因，所以合不合理不得而知，选项 C 排除。

Para. 4 ①In general, air travel is safer than ever because of constant innovation and better pilot training. ②But the consequences of any **lapses** in safety are so profound that eternal **vigilance** is **requisite**. ③It's likely that the cause of the two recent crashes will lead quickly to **corrective** measures.

参考译文 ①总体而言，由于不断的创新和更优质的飞行员训练，航空旅行比从前更加安全。②但是任何安全疏忽带来的结果都非常严重，因此需要时刻保持警惕。③这两次空难的起因很可能会迅速带来纠偏措施。

原文剖析 本段为过渡段，承上启下，首先指出总体上技术进步和飞行员训练优化使航空旅行更安全，然后指出安全问题时刻不能放松。第一句指出，总体上技术进步和飞行员培训优化使航空旅行更安全。第二句转折，强调安全问题时刻不能马虎。第三句联系首段空难事件，表示这两次事故会促进纠偏措施，暗示航空旅行会变得更安全，照应本段第一句。

设题点睛 本段第二句but转折句为观点句，且含有生词，可设置语意理解题。

生词解析

lapse n. (尤指)疏忽；小错　　　　vigilance n. 警惕；警戒
requisite adj. 必需的；必备的　　　corrective adj. 改正的；纠正的

3 The word "lapse" (Para. 4) most probably means _____.

A. slip
B. move
C. sense
D. comment

单词"lapse"（第四段）最有可能的意思是_____。

A. 差错
B. 行动
C. 感觉
D. 评论

【解题思路】**A**。语意理解题。根据题干关键词定位到第四段。单词所在句及上一句指出，总体而言，由于不断的创新和更优质的飞行员训练，航空旅行比从前更加安全。但是任何安全_____的结果都非常严重，因此需要时刻保持警惕。根据单词所在句的句意，结果非常严重肯定就不是好事，所以该单词的意思为贬义，而且是负面的，观察各选项，只有选项A符合此处判断，因此选项A为正确答案。

【排他分析】根据以上分析可知，其余三个选项均与原文语境不符，且代入后语意不当，故均排除。

Para. 5 ①Today's most innovative transport relies heavily on automation during **crucial** moments. ②Problems arise when **operators** take too long to regain control after a system fails. ③Long **stretches** of **inactivity** can produce what is called "passive **fatigue**," which may lengthen their response times. ④Ironically, as planes and road vehicles become more **automated**, pilots and

参考译文 ①当今最具创新性的运输系统在关键时刻很大程度上依赖自动化。②系统故障后，如果操作员需要很长时间才能恢复控制，就会出现问题。③长时间不工作会导致"被动疲劳"，这会延长操作员的反应时间。④具有讽刺意味的是，随着飞机和公路交通工具更加自动

drivers will have less and less "practice" controlling their machines.

化，飞行员和司机"练习"控制他们机器的机会将越来越少。

原文剖析 本段承接上文，通过介绍自动化在关键时刻对交通工具的安全运行具有重要作用并优于人工，说明自动化是解决驾驶安全问题的一条可靠路径。第一句承接上文，初步回答第四段第二句提出的安全问题，指出自动化能更好地满足安全驾驶对时效性的要求。第二句至第三句解释第一句，通过介绍人工在关键时刻反应过慢会误事，反衬出自动化能够更好地为安全驾驶服务。第四句评论，指出自动化的发展会减少人工操作机会，联系第二句和第三句，可以得出"自动化的发展使人工反应变慢"，暗示在自动化发展的大趋势下，人工驾驶或将被淘汰。

设题点睛 本段有两处加了引号，可针对其引申含义设置正确选项，且最后一句包含观点态度，可设置正确选项。

生词解析
crucial *adj.* 至关重要的；关键性的
stretch *n.* （连续的）一段时间
fatigue *n.* 疲劳；疲惫
operator *n.* 操作人员
inactivity *n.* 不做任何事；不工作
automate *vi.* 使自动化

4 We may learn from paragraph 5 that pilots and drivers _____.

A. should practise controlling regularly
B. have a relatively long response times
C. will probably be replaced by automation
D. may be confronted with unemployment

我们可以从第五段中了解到飞行员和驾驶员_____。

A. 应定期进行控制练习
B. 有一个相对较长的反应时间
C. 可能将会被自动化取代
D. 可能面临失业

【解题思路】C。推理引申题。根据题干要求定位到第五段。第二句和第三句通过介绍人在关键时刻反应过慢会误事，反衬出自动化能够更好地为安全驾驶服务。第四句评论，指出自动化的发展会减少人工操作机会，联系第二句和第三句，可以得出"自动化的发展使人工反应变慢"，暗示在自动化发展的大趋势下，人工驾驶或将被淘汰，也就是可能会被自动化取代，因此选项 C 为正确答案。

【排他分析】选项 A 利用最后一句的 practise controlling 作干扰，但从原文中 practise 加引号可知，practise 在这里并非为字面意思，选项 A 排除。文中第二句说，系统故障后，如果操作员需要很长时间才能恢复控制，就会出现问题。而不是操作员有一个相对较长的反应时间，选项 B 排除。或将被淘汰并不一定就会失业，选项 D 推理过度，因此排除。

Para. 6 ①The next leap in such technologies will be to leave humans out of the equation altogether and avoid the tricky handoffs in the human-machine interface. ②Despite the recent troubling setbacks, "leave the driving to us" will probably be the motto of the machines that convey us in the future.

参考译文 ①自动驾驶技术的下一次飞跃将会把人类完全排除在综合考虑之外，避免人机操作之间棘手的切换。②虽然近期的挫折令人担心，但是"把驾驶交给我们"可能是机器将来传递给我们的箴言。

原文剖析 本段得出结论:自动化的发展方向是全面取代人工,表达作者对自动化的肯定和期待。第一句承接上文,并照应第一段,指出解决人机切换问题的途径为"机器完全取代人工"。第二句表达作者对完全自动化的认可和期待。

设题点睛 本段包含作者的观点态度,可设置观点态度题。

生词解析

leap *n.* 飞跃,跳跃;骤变;激增
altogether *adv.* (用以强调)完全,全部
handoff *n.* 传球;给球
setback *n.* 挫折;阻碍
convey *vt.* 传达;传递

equation *n.* (多种因素的)平衡
tricky *adj.* 难办的;棘手的
interface *n.* (人机)界面
motto *n.* 箴言;座右铭

5 The author's attitude toward automatic drive may be _____.

A. optimistic
B. ambiguous
C. indifferent
D. neutral

作者对自动驾驶的态度可能是_____。

A. 乐观的
B. 模棱两可的
C. 漠不关心的
D. 中立的

【解题思路】A。观点态度题。根据顺序原则定位到最后一段。第一句承接上文指出解决人机切换问题的途径为"机器完全取代人工",第二句暗含的转折之意表达作者对完全自动化的认可和期待,由此可知作者的态度是积极乐观的,因此选项 A 为正确答案。

【排他分析】选项 C 可首先排除,因为如果作者对此主题漠不关心,就不会写这篇文章对此展开论述。第二句话中包含的转折含义,以及将"leave the driving to us"说成是自动化的箴言,可见作者的态度并非模棱两可或中立的,选项 B 和选项 D 排除。

Text 30

Taking a call on a mobile phone seems to boost activity in parts of brain closest to the device, but there's no evidence of detriment. Radio waves from mobile phones appear to boost activity in parts of the brain that are closest to the devices' antennas, according to U.S. government scientists. Researchers found that a 50-minute call led to a localized increase in brain activity of 7%, but they said there was no evidence to suggest the rise was harmful.

To rule out the variation in brain activity that would be expected when someone listens to a call normally, changes in activity were monitored while the phone was taking a call but has no sound. The team, led by Nora Volkow, director of the National Institute on Drug Abuse in Maryland, found that brain activity rose in line with the strength of the electromagnetic field to which the particular brain region was exposed. Mobile phones use radio waves to send and receive calls and these produce small electromagnetic fields that can be absorbed by the head and brain. "Although we cannot determine the clinical significance, our results give evidence that the human brain is sensitive to the effects of radio-frequency electromagnetic fields from acute cellphone exposures," Dr. Volkow said. The study appears in the *Journal of the American Medical Association.*

The dramatic rise in mobile phone use around the world has prompted concerns about possible harmful effects, including brain tumors. Last year, the much-delayed Interphone report found no hard evidence that mobile phones increase the risk of cancer, but the issue remains unresolved.

In the new study, 47 volunteers were given two brain scans, each on different days. The scans, which used a technique called positron emission tomography (PET), were designed to monitor changes in the way the brain metabolized glucose, the fuel it needs to function. Before being scanned, the volunteers had a mobile phone positioned against each ear. In one scan, both phones were switched off. But in the other scan, the phone on the right ear was switched on, muted, and set to receive a lengthy recorded message. The volunteers were not told which scan was which. When they compared scans taken in these two different scenarios, Volkow's team discovered a pattern of increased brain activity in the right orbit-frontal cortex and the lower parts of the right superior temporal gyrus.

In these areas of the brain, glucose metabolism rose from 33.3 to 35.7 micromoles of glucose per 100g each minute. Brain activity can rise a lot more than this when a person simply looks at images on a screen. In 2006, Andrei Vlassenko at Washington University School of Medicine reported that viewing images could boost brain activity by between 6% and 51%. Volkow said these rises were caused by thinking about images, while mobile phones appeared to boost activity "artificially." She said it was ambiguous how mobile phone radiation might affect brain metabolism and added that more studies were needed to investigate whether the effects could be harmful to health. Since completing the study she has started using an earpiece with her mobile phone, a move she described as "conservative, not paranoid." However, if increases in brain activity caused by mobile phone use are found to be harmless, Volkow said, the phenomenon could be exploited to stimulate patients who have under-active brain areas.

(*The Guardian*, 2011.2)

1. The word "detriment" (Para. 1) is the closest in meaning to _____.
   A. benefit   B. risk   C. intensity   D. endurance
2. According to paragraph 2, Dr. Volkow holds that _____.
   A. the effects of electromagnetic fields rise in line with the volume of cell phones
   B. the discovery of electromagnetic fields can affect the clinical research
   C. animals other than human beings can receive the small electromagnetic fields
   D. brain activity is susceptible to the impact of electromagnetic fields

288

3. Which of the following is true according to paragraph 4?
   A. PET is essential to the detection of electromagnetic fields.
   B. Glucose helps maintain the functioning of the brain.
   C. Specific regions of the brain are more sensitive to radio waves.
   D. Muted phones exert a bigger influence on the subjects.
4. It can be inferred from the last paragraph that _____.
   A. brain metabolism can be damaged by mobile phone radiation
   B. electromagnetic fields may be used to treat some brain-related diseases
   C. brain activity could be artificially increased by looking at images
   D. using earpiece can ease the harm caused by electromagnetic fields
5. Which of the following is mainly discussed by the text?
   A. Future medical application of electromagnetic fields.
   B. A looming threat caused by mobile phone use.
   C. A modification to the long-standing distortion over cell phone use.
   D. A progress enabled by the use of PET.

语篇分析与试题精解

Para. 1 ① Taking a call on a mobile phone seems to boost activity in parts of brain closest to the device, but there's no evidence of detriment. ② Radio waves from mobile phones appear to boost activity in parts of the brain that are closest to the devices' antennas, according to U.S. government scientists. ③ Researchers found that a 50-minute call led to a localized increase in brain activity of 7%, but they said there was no evidence to suggest the rise was harmful.

参考译文 ①用手机接电话似乎会促进离手机最近的大脑部位的活动,但并没有证据证明这对大脑有害。②美国政府的科学家说,手机的无线电波似乎能够促进大脑靠近移动设备天线部分的活动。③研究人员发现,50分钟的通话使得大脑的局部活动增加7%,同时他们也表示还没有证据表明活动增加是有害的。

原文剖析 本段中三句话的意思基本一致,都在表明使用手机会刺激大脑部分区域的活动,但是没有证据证明这种大脑活动的增强会带来坏处。

设题点睛 首段整体谈到了一个观点,可用来设置题目。

生词解析
boost vt. 促进,增加   detriment n. 损害
antennas n. 天线   localized adj. 局部的

1	The word "detriment" (Para. 1) is closest in meaning to _____.	"detriment"(第一段)一词与下列哪个选项的意思最为接近?
	A. benefit	A. 益处
	B. risk	B. 风险

289

C. intensity
D. endurance

C. 强度
D. 耐力

【解题思路】B。语意理解题。根据题干要求定位于首段第一句。本句存在句内转折结构,转折前的内容表示使用手机通话会对大脑局部的活动产生促进作用,but 转折后的部分表示"但没有证据证明……"。最后一句同样存在转折结构,前半部分中的 increase in brain activity of 7% 呼应了首句前半部分的 boost activity in parts of brain,转折后出现的 no evidence 也可对应首句中的 no evidence,因此最后一句的后半部分应对应首句后半部分内容,则 detriment 与 harmful 的意思类似,故选项 B 是正确答案。

【排他分析】如果没有发现本段最后一句与首句的对应关系,最正常的做法是把选项代入原文进行翻译。将其他三项代入后,首句后半部分分别表示"没有证据证明对大脑有利""没有证据证明强度有多大"和"没有证据证明耐力有多强",虽然都说得通,但与全文的语意没有呼应,因此都可排除。

Para. 2 ① To rule out the variation in brain activity that would be expected when someone listens to a call normally, changes in activity were monitored while the phone was taking a call but has no sound. ② The team, led by Nora Volkow, director of the National Institute on Drug Abuse in Maryland, found that brain activity rose in line with the strength of the electromagnetic field to which the particular brain region was exposed. ③ Mobile phones use radio waves to send and receive calls and these produce small electromagnetic fields that can be absorbed by the head and brain. ④ "Although we cannot determine the clinical significance, our results give evidence that the human brain is sensitive to the effects of radio-frequency electromagnetic fields from acute cellphone exposures," Dr. Volkow said. ⑤ The study appears in the *Journal of the American Medical Association*.

参考译文 ①为排除人们在正常接听手机时促进大脑活动变化的因素,实验过程中控制了一些变量:在实验者接电话时手机中并无声音。②美国马里兰州国家药物滥用研究所主任诺拉·沃尔考(Nora Volkow)博士及其团队发现,大脑活动的增加与大脑特定区域所接触的电磁场强度是一致的。③手机利用无线电波打电话和接电话,而这些无线电波产生了小型的、能够被头部和大脑吸收的电磁场。④沃尔考博士说:"尽管我们无法确认这一发现对临床医学的影响,但我们的实验结果初步证明人类大脑对无线电频率所产生的电磁场的效应十分敏感,这种效应由突然接触手机产生。"⑤该研究结果发表在了《美国医学会杂志》上。

原文剖析 本段介绍得出上段结论的实验。本段首句指出实验控制了可造成人类大脑活动的声音因素,即让实验者接手机电话,但手机中并无声音,体现实验的严谨性。后三句是对实验结果的解读,与首段观点类似,但进行了细化和阐释,给出了新观点:人脑活动强度与手机发出的电磁场强度呈正比,且大脑可以吸收手机无线电波形成的小型电磁场。第四句总结指出人脑对手机电磁场效应很敏感这一实验结论。

设题点睛 本段最重要的内容应该是有关人物观点和实验发现的部分,是对首段观点的进一步证明和阐述,信息量较大,可以用来设置事实细节题。

生词解析

rule out 排除
electromagnetic *adj.* 电磁的
in line with 与……一致
clinical *adj.* 临床的

长难句解析

Although we cannot determine the clinical significance, our results give evidence
　　　　　让步状语从句　　　　　　　　　　　　　　　主语　谓语　宾语
that the human brain is sensitive to the effects of radio-frequency electromagnetic fields
　　　　　　　　　　　　　　　同位语从句
from acute cellphone exposures.

本句主干结构为 our results give evidence that…；句中同位语从句的主干为 human brain is sensitive to…，解释说明 evidence。

2 According to paragraph 2, Dr. Volkow holds that _____.

A. the effects of electromagnetic fields rise in line with the volume of cell phones
B. the discovery of electromagnetic fields can affect the clinical research
C. animals other than human beings can receive the small electromagnetic fields
D. brain activity is susceptible to the impact of electromagnetic fields

根据第二段的内容，沃尔考博士认为_____。

A. 电磁场效应随着手机音量的增大而增强
B. 有关电磁场的发现会影响临床研究
C. 除人类外的动物可以接收小型电磁场
D. 大脑活动易受电磁场的影响

【解题思路】D。事实细节题。根据题干要求定位到第二段，本题考查人物观点，可继续定位至本段第二句和第四句。其中，第四句谈到实验证明人类大脑对无线电频率电磁场所产生的效应很敏感（is sensitive to the effects of radio-frequency electromagnetic fields），与选项 D 的内容一致，该项中的 is susceptible to 是对原文 is sensitive to 的同义替换，因此是正确答案。

【排他分析】选项 A 中的 in line with 出现在本段第二句中，但原文表示大脑活动的增强与大脑特定区域所接触的电磁场的强度一致，但电磁场强度和手机音量的关系在文中并未体现，本项是对原文细节的随意拼凑，可以排除。选项 B 中的 clinical research 对应该段第四句让步状语中的内容，原文表示目前还不能确定手机电磁场对大脑活动有影响这一发现对临床医学的意义，与该项的意思不一致，因此排除。选项 C 中的 receive the small electromagnetic fields 对应本段第三句，原文提到人类大脑可以吸收小型电磁场，但并没有提到其他动物的大脑是否也有此特点，因此该项属于主观臆断，可排除。

Para. 3 ①The dramatic rise in mobile phone use around the world has prompted concerns about possible harmful effects, including brain tumors. ② Last year, the much-delayed

参考译文 ①手机在全球范围内的大量使用使得人们开始担心手机是否会对人体带来伤害，比如说是否会引发脑瘤。②去年，几经拖延的对讲机报告发

Interphone report found no hard evidence that mobile phones increase the risk of cancer, but the issue remains unresolved.

原文剖析 本段回应上段谈到的研究发现,指出人们因此而产生的担忧:使用手机是否会导致脑瘤。第二句给出解答:尽管没有证据证明两者之间确实有关系,但也没有证据证明两者间没有关系,此问题悬而未决。

设题点睛 本段基本不存在明确的观点信息,虽然第二句中出现转折连词,但是并未引出明确观点,因此不适合设置考点。

生词解析
prompt *vt.* 引起 tumor *n.* 肿瘤
unresolved *adj.* 未解决的

现,并没有切实的证据能够证明手机会增加使用者罹患癌症的可能性,但是这一问题始终没有得到最终的解答。

Para. 4 ①In the new study, 47 volunteers were given two brain scans, each on different days. ②The scans, which used a technique called positron emission tomography (PET), were designed to monitor changes in the way the brain metabolized glucose, the fuel it needs to function. ③Before being scanned, the volunteers had a mobile phone positioned against each ear. ④In one scan, both phones were switched off. ⑤But in the other scan, the phone on the right ear was switched on, muted, and set to receive a lengthy recorded message. ⑥The volunteers were not told which scan was which. ⑦When they compared scans taken in these two different scenarios, Volkow's team discovered a pattern of increased brain activity in the right orbit-frontal cortex and the lower parts of the right superior temporal gyrus.

参考译文 ①在一项新研究中,47位志愿者被安排进行了两次大脑扫描,每次扫描的日期不同。②大脑扫描采用正电子放射断层造影术(PET),用来监测大脑对葡萄糖代谢方式的变化(葡萄糖是大脑活动的燃料)。③在扫描之前,志愿者两耳旁都放有一个手机。④在一次扫描中,两个手机都处于关机状态;⑤但在另一次扫描中,右耳边的手机处于开机但静音的状态,并被设定为接收一段时间较长的录音信息。⑥志愿者并未被告知两次扫描中手机的具体状态。⑦当对两次扫描结果做比对的时候,沃尔考博士的团队发现右侧额叶眼眶面皮质和右上颞叶脑回下部区域出现了大脑活动增加的情况。

原文剖析 本段描述了一个新的研究过程以及实验结果。首句概括介绍实验对象和实验方式。第二句指出实验用的技术及其功能(监测大脑对葡萄糖的代谢方式)。第三句到第六句是对实验过程的描述(两次扫描,两种设置不同)。第七句给出实验的结果:通过比较两次大脑的扫描结果后发现,大脑活动有增加的现象。

设题点睛 本段有关新研究的实验过程及其实验结果都比较明确,可用来设置细节题。

生词解析
positron *n.* 正电子 tomography *n.* x线断层摄影术
metabolize *vt.* 新陈代谢 glucose *n.* 葡萄糖
muted *adj.* 无声音的 scenario *n.* 情景
orbit *n.* 眼眶 cortex *n.* 皮质
temporal *adj.* 颞的,太阳穴的 gyrus *n.* 脑回

3 Which of the following is true according to paragraph 4?

A. PET is essential to the detection of electro-magnetic fields.
B. Glucose helps maintain the functioning of the brain.
C. Specific regions of the brain are more sensitive to radio waves.
D. Muted phones exert a bigger influence on the subjects.

根据第四段的内容,以下哪项正确?

A. PET 对于探测电磁场而言十分重要。
B. 葡萄糖有助于维持大脑功能。
C. 大脑某些区域对无线电波更加敏感。
D. 静音的手机会对实验者产生更大影响。

【解题思路】B。事实细节题。根据题干要求定位到第四段,因为题干中没有更加明确的定位点,所以本题需要根据选项内容阅读相关句子。本段第二句的同位语部分对大脑中葡萄糖的功能进行说明,指出葡萄糖是大脑运转的燃料(the fuel it needs to function),与选项 B 的内容对应,因此该项正确。

【排他分析】选项 A 中的 PET 对应本段第二句,原文谈到 PET 用于探测大脑对葡萄糖代谢方式的变化,并没有谈到 PET 和电磁场的关系,所以排除。选项 C 中的 specific regions of the brain 对应本段最后一句中的 right orbit-frontal cortex 和 lower parts of the right superior temporal gyrus,考生不必知道这两个部分的具体所指,只要明白是大脑中的特定区域即可,虽然原文表明这两个大脑区域的活动在实验中出现了变化(增强),但根据第一段对实验结论的描述,应该是所有靠近手机的大脑区域都可能受到影响,并没有哪个区域更容易受影响的说法,因此排除该项。选项 D 中的 muted 对应本段第五句,为何将手机调至静音的理由在第二段中已经提到(排除其他变量带来的干扰),由此看出,没有静音的手机才会对实验者产生更大的影响(除无线电波外,还有声音对大脑的影响),与该项的意思相反,所以排除。

Para. 5 ①In these areas of the brain, glucose metabolism rose from 33.3 to 35.7 micromoles of glucose per 100g each minute. ②Brain activity can rise a lot more than this when a person simply looks at images on a screen. ③In 2006, Andrei Vlassenko at Washington University School of Medicine reported that viewing images could boost brain activity by between 6% and 51%. ④Volkow said these rises were caused by thinking about images, while mobile phones appeared to boost activity "artificially." ⑤She said it was ambiguous how mobile phone radiation might affect brain metabolism and added that more studies were needed to investigate whether the effects could be harmful to health. ⑥Since completing the study she

参考译文 ①在这些大脑区域中,葡萄糖代谢从每分钟每百克33.3微摩尔上升到35.7微摩尔。②当人们仅仅看着屏幕上的一幅图像时,大脑活动的增强就会远大于此。③2006年,华盛顿大学医药学院的安德烈·沃拉森科(Andrei Vlassenko)就报告称,观看图像会使大脑活动增加6%至51%。④沃尔考博士表示,这种增强是人们思考图像造成的,而手机似乎是"人工地"增强了大脑活动。⑤她表示,手机辐射如何影响大脑代谢尚不可知,还需要更多的研究来进一步验证该效应是否对人体健康有害。

has started using an earpiece with her mobile phone, a move she described as "conservative, not paranoid." ⑦ However, if increases in brain activity caused by mobile phone use are found to be harmless, Volkow said, the phenomenon could be exploited to stimulate patients who have under-active brain areas.

⑥完成该项实验后,她开始使用耳机接听电话。她表示,这"不是疑神疑鬼,而是保险起见"。⑦然而,沃尔考博士表示,如果能够确认使用手机引起的大脑活动增强不会损害健康,那这种现象就可以用来治疗大脑某些区域不活跃的病人。

原文剖析 本段首句承接上一段的实验结果,继续描述大脑对葡萄糖代谢方式的变化(出现上升趋势)。随即第二句和第三句给出一个新的观点:人在看图时大脑活动的强度变化更大。第四句区别这两种大脑活动的不同性质,指出人在看图时会进行思考,是有意识的行为,自然会导致大脑活动的增强,但手机对大脑活动造成的影响并不是人通过思考来实现的,是一种无意识的客观作用。第五句和第六句指出并不知道手机对大脑活动的客观影响是有益还是有害,但最好防患于未然。最后一句转折指出如果手机的这种效果被证明无害,就可以用于临床治疗。

设题点睛 本段第二句和第三句给出新观点,最后一句出现转折语意,这两个部分可用来设置正确选项。

生词解析

micromole n. 微摩尔
ambiguous adj. 模糊不清的
paranoid adj. 多疑的
artificially adv. 人工地
conservative adj. 保守的
exploit vt.（尤指为利益而）利用

长难句解析

However, if increases in brain activity caused by mobile phone use are found to be harmless,
连词　　　　　　条件状语从句

Volkow said, the phenomenon could be exploited to stimulate patients who have
插入语　　　　主语　　　　　谓语　　　　　　目的状语　　　　定语从句

under-active brain areas.

本句主干结构为 the phenomenon could be exploited to stimulate patients who…; who 引导的定语从句修饰先行词 patients;条件状语从句中过去分词结构 caused by mobile phone use 作 activity 的后置定语,该从句的主干结构为 if increases are found to be harmless。

4 It can be inferred from the last paragraph that _____ .

A. brain metabolism can be damaged by mobile phone radiation
B. electromagnetic fields may be used to treat some brain-related diseases
C. brain activity could be artificially increased by looking at images
D. using earpiece can ease the harm caused by electromagnetic fields

从最后一段中可以推断出_____。

A. 手机辐射会破坏大脑代谢
B. 电磁场也许可以用来治疗某些大脑疾病
C. 可以通过看一些图片来人为地增强大脑活动
D. 使用耳机可以减轻电磁场带来的伤害

【解题思路】B。推理引申题。根据题干要求定位到最后一段,题干中没有更明确的定位点,所以需要通读整段,而正确选项往往出现在段落中相对重要的结构里。本段第二句和第三句提出新观点,最后一句是转折句,属于特殊结构,可看作重要内容。其中,最后一句谈到如果能够确认使用手机引起的大脑活动的增强不会损害健康,那么这一效果可用于治疗大脑某些区域不活跃的病人(be exploited to stimulate patients who have under-active brain areas),与选项 B 的意思一致,该项体现电磁场具有能增强大脑活动的作用,选项 B 中的 treat some brain-related diseases 同义替换了原文中的 stimulate patients who have under-active brain areas。并且根据原文内容,需要在确定手机对脑部无害的前提下这样操作,因此选项 B 使用了 may 来体现可能性。

【排他分析】选项 A 对应本段第一句,原文用数据指出大脑接触手机区域的葡萄糖代谢增加了(rose from 33.3 to 35.7),选项 A 与此意相反,因此排除。选项 C 对应本段第三句和第四句,这两句中确实出现了 looking at images, artificially 等词,但是两句所指并不一致,第三句谈到人们是通过思考图片进而促进脑部活动增强的,第四句谈到手机对人脑活动的促进作用可看作"人工地"(即不是由本人发起的),选项 C 将这两句的内容进行了杂糅,与任何一句的观点均不一致,因此排除。选项 D 中的 earpiece 对应本段倒数第二句,原文谈到该研究的负责人完成实验后开始使用耳机接听手机电话,她表示这是一种保险的方法,但使用手机是否伤害大脑并无定论,因此该项属于过度推断,可排除。

5 Which of the following is mainly discussed by the text?   本文主要讨论了以下哪项内容?

A. Future medical application of electromagnetic fields.   A. 电磁场在未来医药方面的应用。
B. A looming threat caused by mobile phone use.   B. 使用手机造成的潜在威胁。
C. A modification to the long-standing distortion over cell phone use.   C. 纠正长期以来人们对使用手机的误解。
D. A progress enabled by the use of PET.   D. 使用 PET 促成的进步。

【解题思路】C。主旨大意题。需要纵观全文寻找答案。前两段通过实验结果论述一个观点:手机通话时所产生的电磁场确实会增强大脑活动,但是没有证据证明这种增强有害。第三段提出人们的担忧:大量使用手机会不会造成大脑疾病。第四段和第五段再次用另一个实验结果回应前文谈到的担忧:通过对大脑中葡萄糖代谢方式的检测发现手机的电磁场确实有促进大脑活动的作用,但仍没有明确的证据证明使用手机对大脑有害。综合所有段落的大意,选项 C 与全文的内容最为吻合,因此是正确答案。

【排他分析】选项 A 只针对文章的最后一句,原文谈到在证明手机电磁场效应对大脑无害的前提下,确实可用其治疗大脑不活跃的病人,但是这只是一个细节,且并非现实,无法概括全文,所以排除。选项 B 中的 threat 可呼应第三段谈到的人们对使用手机是否会危害大脑健康的担忧,而原文多次重申并无确切证据证明手机的电磁场对大脑有害,因此该项是原文一再要澄清的误解,可以排除。选项 D 中的 PET 只是本文所谈到的某一实验所使用的工具,属于典型的细节信息,与全文主旨观点无关,因此排除。

第四章 题源报刊精选文章模拟自测

CHAPTER FOUR

Text 1

Leaving the European Union would save every Dutch household €9,800 ($13,400) a year by 2035, claims Capital Economics, a London consultancy, in a report commissioned by Geert Wilders' far-right PVV party. Mr. Wilders calls this "the best news in years", painting a picture of a country freed from the choke hold of Brussels, mass migration and high taxes, and enjoying more trade, more jobs and a booming economy.

The report lists the benefits of departure, or "Nexit": lower business costs because of less regulation; no more net payments to the EU; a doubling of the share of trade with emerging markets; faster economic recovery. The only cost is the transition from the euro to a new guilder, and this is "modest and manageable." The report concludes that Dutch GDP would be 10%-13% higher by 2035.

This finds a receptive audience among those Dutch who are looking for scapegoats. Unemployment has doubled since 2008 and the economy is flat. A recent poll finds a majority of Dutch voters in favour of leaving the EU if that would lead to more jobs and growth. The PVV is leading in opinion polls before the European elections in May.

Yet there are problems with the Capital Economics report. The idea that the economy would miraculously recover if freed from the European Central Bank's policies ignores the structural failings that hold it back. The assumption that having the guilder would allow a much looser monetary policy is, at best, questionable. And it defies political reality to imagine that the post-Nexit Netherlands would enjoy virtually cost-free access to the EU's single market, which takes 75% of Dutch exports. Norway and Switzerland both pay for the privilege and have to comply with most EU laws and regulations; the latest Swiss vote for quotas on EU migration threatens the entire relationship.

Despite its flaws, the report fires a welcome starting-gun for a debate about what is good and bad about the EU. Some 66% of the Dutch feel their "No" vote in the 2005 referendum on the EU constitution was largely ignored. If regulation costs as much as the report claims, and if the ECB's monetary policy is too restrictive, both should be changed. Defenders of the EU also need to stress its less tangible benefits, such as peace, shared interests and the boost to the fight against cross-border crime.

Like many Europeans, the Dutch ask why jobs are scarce, why they cannot sell their houses and why life is so expensive. Mr. Wilders has a simple answer. Those who disagree must work to convince voters that Nexit would be a disaster.

(*The Economist*, 2014.7)

1. According to Wilders, the Netherlands' departure from the European Union would _____.

    A. increase the taxes for the Dutch
    B. retrench the cost of the PVV party

C. bring economic benefits for Dutch households

D. seize the control of Brussels from the EU

2. It is indicated in paragraph 2 that _____.

   A. the impact of currency shift is mild for the Dutch

   B. EU's trading market is recovered

   C. EU's GDP will suffer a considerable loss by 2035

   D. the cutoff of regulations results in the decline of net payment

3. Switzerland is cited as an example to show _____.

   A. the threat caused by EU migration

   B. the privileges offered by EU laws and regulations

   C. the structural flaws concealed within the European Central Bank

   D. the merits generated by the EU's trading market

4. According to paragraph 5, which of the following statements is true?

   A. EU largely deprived the voting right of its citizens.

   B. EU indirectly improved the living-standard for its citizens.

   C. Cross-border crime was the major problem of EU.

   D. The monetary policy of the Dutch government curbs the income of its residents.

5. What is the subject of the text?

   A. Challenge to a current political system.

   B. Analysis of the gains and losses of Nexit.

   C. Criticism from the report commissioned by the PVV party.

   D. Satire on the extravagant lifestyle of the Dutch.

Text 2

In 2007, the Supreme Court defined greenhouse gasses as air pollutants under the 1970 Clean Air Act and required the Environmental Protection Agency to develop rules to reduce the generation of these pollutants. This week, President Barack Obama issued the regulations for reducing greenhouse gas emissions from America's power plants. The regulations would require a 32 percent cut in powerplant carbon dioxide emissions by 2030 from 2005 levels. States are required to submit plans on how they would achieve reductions and begin implementation of these plans in 2018. If a state refuses to submit a plan, EPA will save them the trouble and submit one for them.

Before the Obama administration Clean Power Plan was even released, the "job killing" regulation rhetoric was flying and the campaign against the rule was well underway. This is unfortunate because, the rule could well be a way for states to push their utilities to upgrade their energy efficiency programs and make it possible for their electrical grid to accommodate decentralized generation of renewable energy. Greater energy efficiency and greater use of renewable energy could lower the energy bills paid by America's households.

The transition to a renewable energy economy is necessary to reduce the impact of climate change, but it is also needed to reduce the environmental and economic impact of massive increases in fossil fuel extraction from the earth. With over 2 billion people in the rapidly growing economies of India and China bidding on the same fossil fuels that we need here in America, the price of those fuels can only go up in the long run.

In contrast, renewable energy uses the sun as its basic fuel. That fuel is free and the cost of the technology that transforms it to energy and stores it for our use has been coming down rapidly. Just as the price of computer memory has come down dramatically over the past several decades, so too will the cost of renewable energy technology as its use increases and its technology advances. Battery technology is developing rapidly and nanotechnology may soon reduce the size and price of solar cells.

We may not know the specific shape that new energy technology will take, but we do know that regulatory requirements will encourage businesses to invest in the development and use of renewable energy and energy efficiency technologies. Even before the rules come into effect, smart businesses are anticipating the changes and making investment decisions based on the new rules. When regulations are carefully developed and intelligently enforced they can create jobs and foster new businesses. For example, automobiles are safer, more efficient and less polluting today than they were before they were regulated; and someone has to be hired to make those seatbelts and airbags. Our energy system is badly outdated. It is vulnerable to disruption and needs greater resiliency. Too much of the power we generate is lost during transmission.

A modern energy system could reduce energy costs while mitigating climate change. However, while the Clean Power Plan will create the demand for new energy technologies, the federal government would be wise to invest in the basic and applied science of renewable energy to ensure that the supply of new technology is adequate to meet the demand. Our scientific community is eager to help.

(*U. S. News and World Report*, 2015.8)

1. Paragraph 1 shows that EPA _____.
   A. has been manipulated by the Supreme Court
   B. is required to reduce greenhouse gas emissions
   C. is supervising the implementation of the state-plans
   D. has the authority to enact the plans for the states
2. In the author's opinion, the campaign will _____.
   A. undermine the current employment rate
   B. go against the Obama administration
   C. hinder the improvement to the energy facilities
   D. cut the energy cost paid by the American households
3. It can be inferred from paragraph 3 and 4 that _____.
   A. computer memory is the catalyst for the price rise of the renewable energy
   B. cost is a crucial impetus to boost the development of renewable energy

C. nanotechnology is essential for the development of renewable energy

D. environmental degradation has been eased by the use of clean energy

4. Automobiles are cited in paragraph 5 as an example of _____.

A. foresighted responders to the new regulations

B. users saving the power lost during transmission

C. the losing party because of the new rules

D. initiators improving the safety standard to suit the new rules

5. The author suggests in the last paragraph that _____.

A. scientific community is independent of the federal government

B. Clean Power Plan impedes the progress of the new energy technology

C. the federal government is eager to reduce the energy expenditure

D. the federal government should concentrate on the development of renewable energy

Text 3

In the final days of the Great Federal Debt Showdown of 2013, there was much high-minded talk in Washington of Congress bringing a "clean CR," or continuing resolution, to a vote. The concept of a bill that was free of any muddying riders, kickbacks or pork was portrayed by some legislators as essential to any potential debt deal's passage.

But as so often is the case in D. C., the measure passed Wednesday night to fund the federal government through January 15 and authorize it to pay its debts until February 7 has been tainted by the greedy officials. Though it comes nowhere near the pig roast that major legislation like the U. S. Farm Bill often becomes, it's got bacon bits sprinkled throughout, and one big chunk of fat near the middle that has observers on both sides of the aisle reaching for their Lipitor. Here are three choice cuts.

"**Kentucky Kickback**"

The 35-page bill starts out innocuously, detailing how the federal government will grind back to life, back-pay government workers and start flowing once again to key agencies. But then comes goodies like the "Kentucky Kickback." Many far-right voters say they believe the $2.2 billion increase to an existing appropriation was what it took to win the support of Senator Minority Leader Mitch McConnell (R-Kentucky). The funds will go toward a dam and locks river project in McConnell's home state that has been under way for years, and though it has come under fire as a kickback, Senator Lamar Alexander (R-Tennessee) told BuzzFeed that he and Senator Dianne Feinstein (D-California) were responsible for its inclusion in the final version of the bill.

"According to the Army Corps of Engineers, 160 million taxpayer dollars will be wasted because of canceled contracts if this language is not included. Sen. Feinstein and I, as chairman and ranking member of the Energy and Water Appropriations Subcommittee, requested this provision. It has already been approved this year by the House and Senate,"

Alexander said. And a Democratic Senate aide told CNN that McConnell didn't advocate for it to be in the bill. Still, a "Senate insider" told BuzzFeed that, "there's legitimate arguments for this. But there's legitimate arguments for things like this across the country. That's the problem."

Death Benefit

Deep in the final text of the debt deal measure is a section outlining a $174,000 payment to be made to Bonnie Englebardt Lautenberg, the widow of Senator Frank Lautenberg (D-New Jersey), who died at the age of 89 on June 3. Worth the equivalent of a year of a senator's salary, the death benefit is a long-standing tradition in Congress, but its place in the debt deal does have raised controversy, as Lautenberg was one of the wealthiest members of the Senate when he died. News that the death benefit will be disbursed came just before the Tuesday special election that decided Lautenberg's Senate replacement, Democratic Newark Mayor Cory Booker.

Flood Recovery

Though the new funds are going to a good cause, Congress did include $350 million more for the Department of Transportation to use on flood rebuilding in Colorado than the $100 million that was already available under the Disaster Relief Appropriations Act. Large swaths of the Centennial State were torn apart by catastrophic floods in September that killed at least eight people, left six missing and caused an estimated $1 billion in damage. The language, pushed by Senator Mark Udall (D-Colorado) provided funding that had languished in the House, and due to its benevolent aim made its way into the budget.

(*Newsweek*, 2013.10)

1. The metaphor used in the second sentence of paragraph 2 is meant to _____.
   A. illustrate the legitimacy of the major legislation in the U.S.
   B. satirize the corrupt practice inside the government
   C. highlight the huge profit of the U.S. Farm Bill
   D. criticize the officials' reliance on Lipitor

2. Many far-right voters hold that _____.
   A. the additional appropriation was for partisan backup
   B. the existing appropriation was distributed evenly
   C. the funds were mainly spent on improving water services
   D. most part of the bill is innocuous

3. The death benefit for Bonnie Englebardt Lautenberg is controversial because _____.
   A. the Congress's long-standing tradition would hurt the public benefit
   B. the payment is too high to be accepted by other senators
   C. it could stimulate the public objection against the debt deal
   D. the senator's wealthiness makes the death payment a corruption

4. The Congress accepted Senator Mark Udall's proposal because _____.
   A. the previous appropriation on flood rebuilding is insufficient for Colorado

B. the flood has caused a devastating damage in Colorado

C. the funds are proposed in the name of humanitarianism

D. there is no objection from the House

5. Which of the following is the best title for the text?

A. Federal Debt Is on the Cliff   B. Rivalry Between the Congress and the House

C. U.S. Congress Is on the Alert   D. Federal Debt Is Under Siege

Text 4

In that mythical era when children were seen and not heard, and did as they were told without argument, everyone knew that regular bedtimes were important. "Dream on!" most modern parents might reply. But research by Yvonne Kelly of University College, London, shows that the ancient wisdom is right—half the time. Daughters, it seems, do benefit from regular bedtimes. Sons do not.

Dr. Kelly knew of many studies that had looked at the connection between sleep habits and cognitive ability in adults and adolescents. All showed that inconsistent sleeping schedules went hand in hand with poor academic performance. Surprisingly, however, little such research had been done on children. She and a team of colleagues therefore examined the bedtimes and cognitive abilities of 11,178 children born in Britain between September 2000 and January 2002, who are enrolled in a multidisciplinary research project called the Millennium Cohort Study.

The bedtime information they used was collected during four visits interviewers made to the homes of those participating in the study. These happened when the children were nine months, three years, five years and seven years of age. Besides asking whether the children had set bedtimes on weekdays and if they always, usually, sometimes or never made them, interviewers collected information about family routines, economic circumstances and other matters—including whether children were read to before they went to sleep and whether they had a television in their bedroom. The children in question were also asked, at the ages of three, five and seven, to take standardised reading, mathematical and spatial-awareness tests, from which their IQs could be estimated.

Dr. Kelly's report, just published in the *Journal of Epidemiology and Community Health*, shows that by the time children had reached the age of seven, not having had a regular bedtime did seem to affect their cognition, even when other pertinent variables such as bedtime reading, bedroom televisions and parents' socioeconomic status were controlled for. But that was true only if they were female. On the IQ scale, whose mean value is 100 points, girls who had had regular bedtimes scored between eight and nine points more than those who did not.

Boys were not completely unaffected. Irregular bedtimes left their IQs about six points below those of their contemporaries at the age of three. But the distinction vanished by the time they were seven.

This difference between the sexes is baffling. Dr. Kelly did not expect it and has no explanation to offer for it. As scientists are wont to say, but this time with good reason, more research is necessary.

Meanwhile, in the going-to-bed wars most households with young children suffer, the sons of the house have acquired extra ammunition. Mind you, those with the nous to read and understand Dr. Kelly's results are probably not suffering from their sleep regimes anyway.

(*The Economist*, 2013.7)

1. What does the author mean by saying "Dream on!" (Para. 1)?
   A. Children always have dreams during their sleep.
   B. Conventional wisdom is not fit for modern families.
   C. Children do not follow their parents' order nowadays.
   D. Regular bedtimes are not as important as they are believed.
2. The experiment conducted by Dr. Kelly and her partners is meant to _____.
   A. testify a long-standing belief   B. challenge the ancient wisdom
   C. justify a wide-spread phenomenon   D. undermine a current theory
3. What can be learned from the result of the experiment?
   A. Cognitive development of children is decided by their bedtimes.
   B. Boys aged above seven years old are not strongly affected by irregular bedtimes.
   C. Parents' financial condition will not influence daughters' IQ scores.
   D. Regular bedtimes may exert a bigger impact on girls than on boys.
4. It can be inferred from the last two paragraphs that _____.
   A. the gender difference shown in the IQ test can not be explained by Dr. Kelly
   B. more research is required to improve the teenagers' sleep quality
   C. parents should not worry too much about their boys' sleep pattern
   D. boys are always at war with their parents
5. Which of the following is mainly discussed by the text?
   A. Pertinent variables in deciding children's intelligence.
   B. Significance of regular bedtimes for girls.
   C. Divergent cognitive abilities between two sexes.
   D. The conflict between modern and traditional wisdom.

Text 5

Elderly people who did 10 sessions of brain training had half as many crashes on the road as untrained counterparts—even though the training didn't directly relate to driving itself. "There are no other cognitive training programs, or 'brain games', that have been demonstrated by published, peer-reviewed studies to enhance driving performance," says Jerri Edwards of the University of South Florida in Tampa, a co-leader of the study.

The results contradict a study of 11,000 people earlier this year, carried out by Adrian Owen at the University of Cambridge and colleagues, which found that brain training didn't help improve cognitive skills outside the game itself. "Overall, people need to know that not all brain training is equal," says Edwards. "Some programs work and some don't."

With an average age of 73, the 908 participants in the latest study were assigned to one of three different computer training programs or to no training at all. One program focused on improving reaction speed, another on reasoning skills and the third on memory. Each course lasted for 10 sessions, and then the participants were tracked for six years to see how many times they had road crashes for which they were personally responsible. It turned out that the reaction speed and reasoning skills programs helped reduce accidents by 50 percent, but the memory training made no difference. Of the participants with no training, 18 percent had at least one crash, just slightly ahead of the 16 percent of memory course participants who had accidents. By contrast, only 10 percent of the speed-training group had crashes, and 12 percent of those on the reasoning course.

Over the 10 sessions, the courses cranked up the skills of the participants by presenting them with progressively tougher tasks. In the reaction-speed program, for example, participants had to fulfill tests such as identifying targets flashing up on a computer screen with quicker speed. The reasoning course challenged participants to recognize patterns to solve problems. "On the road, the brain needs to process a lot of visual information quickly," says Steven Aldrich, chief executive of Posit Science, the company in San Francisco, California, that developed the programs. "So the visual speed-of-processing training directly improves brain functions involved in driving safely, making them faster and more accurate."

In the light of the findings, Edwards recommends that the elderly try cognitive training programs—but only ones that have been validated by research. Also, she says they should maintain physical exercise, as this helps to keep the brain fit too. "Research shows that over long periods of time, participation in cognitively stimulating activities may stave off dementia," says Edwards. "However, engagement in effective and challenging brain exercises targeting specific cognitive abilities may be required to immediately improve cognitive and everyday function of older adults," she says.

Aldrich says that participating in the courses had other beneficial spin-offs. Trained brains were 38 percent less likely to develop depression up to a year afterwards, and less likely than controls to develop health problems when checked two and five years after training. Also, 68 percent of those who took the reaction-speed course retained their increased reaction times at a two-year follow up. Torkel Klingberg, who develops cognitive training programs at the Karolinska Institute in Stockholm, Sweden, says the study shows that training in basic cognitive abilities can improve everyday performance too. "Both the reasoning training and the speed-of-reaction training would improve attention skills, which are important in driving," he says.

(*New Scientist*, 2010.11)

1. According to the first two paragraphs, Edwards holds that _____.
   A. driving performance could not be strengthened outside the game
   B. cognitive training is critical in improving driving skills
   C. part of the brain's cognitive ability could be enhanced by training
   D. senior citizens could benefit from certain brain training
2. Which of the following is true according to paragraph 3?
   A. Memory ability is not as important to the elders as reasoning.
   B. The control group performed worst in the study.
   C. Researchers can get an accurate result at the end of the training.
   D. The finding is only valid for the elderly.
3. Safe driving mainly depends on _____.
   A. driver's reaction speed
   B. driver's reasoning ability
   C. driver's speed of processing visual information
   D. driver's memory ability
4. According to paragraph 5, Edwards believes that _____.
   A. elder people can enhance their mental ability quickly
   B. cognitive training can stimulate dementia
   C. his research has validated some brain training programs
   D. physical exercise can immediately improve cognitive ability
5. It is suggested in the last paragraph that _____.
   A. depression could be cured by the training
   B. the result of the experiment is in accordance with the prediction
   C. increased reaction speed would diminish after the experiment
   D. people with degraded cognitive performance will find it hard to concentrate

Text 6

Nobody wants to spend hours picking through a steady stream of garbage; this is why many recycling operations rely on automated systems to separate plastic containers, glass bottles, aluminum cans and mixed paper. But these systems have an imperfect track record, so human workers must stand by to nab what the machines fail to catch. Waste Management, a trash-hauling corporate titan with 100 recycling facilities in North America, employs about 3,000 human sorters—but it has difficulty finding workers willing to show up every day, and many quit within hours. This is one reason the company has begun testing new types of robots that could eventually join humans in the sorting lines.

The United States generates massive volumes of waste. An optical sorter developed by Quebec-based manufacturer Machinex separates recyclables at up to 3,000 objects per minute. This type of technology relies on magnets to pull out some metals, eddy currents to catch others that are nonmagnetic, and near-infrared light to help optical sorters detect different grades of plastic. But their accuracy is <u>compromised</u> by the high rate of contamination inherent to U.S. recycling systems.

Unlike most industrialized countries, the U.S. has overwhelmingly embraced a convenient single-stream recycling approach that lets people toss plastics, glass, metals and paper into one collection bin. This convenience leads to high recycling rates and relatively efficient collection. But it also worsens contamination: U.S. industry estimates suggest 20 to 25 percent of submitted items are unrecyclable trash. The problem stems partly from consumer confusion about what items qualify, along with "wish recycling": taking a chance that chucking something in a designated bin will give it a new life.

Instead of struggling to find humans to constantly oversee the process, some companies are testing AI-driven robots equipped with grippers or suction cups to pick out recyclable objects. They use cameras and other sensors, coupled with machine-learning software, to recognize visual patterns associated with specific items. In order to replace people, however, such bots will eventually have to outperform us—human quality-control workers pick out about 30 to 40 items per minute. "If this [robot] can pick two times or three times as many objects as human workers, then we could start looking at the economics and seeing if we can justify a purchase," Bell says.

Robots that can demonstrate superhuman sorting speeds without too many mistakes may prove good enough to join the recycling lines. But beyond new technologies, companies such as Waste Management and Rumpke still emphasize the need to educate customers about what they can recycle and how they should do it. It is a long-term struggle to change humanity's wasteful lifestyles—and everyone acknowledges that AI and robots cannot solve the recycling crisis without humans doing their part.

(*The Scientific American*, 2019.5)

1. According to paragraph 1, we know that _____.
   A. automatic recovery systems do not require humans
   B. nobody is willing to be a garbage sorter in America
   C. Waste Management resorts to new tech to address its problem
   D. there are many kinds of electronic devices for garbage classification
2. The word "compromised" (Para. 2) most probably means _____.
   A. endangered   B. offsetted   C. overlooked   D. enhanced
3. The single-stream recycling approach aggravates pollution partly due to _____.
   A. there are lots of garbage that can't be recycled
   B. people's uncertainty about recyclable categories
   C. some wastes are valuable enough to be reused
   D. consumer's lack of knowledge about waste composition
4. AI-driven robots can be adopted if _____.
   A. they can carry out the work on their own
   B. they are more efficient than people
   C. the sorting process is simple and efficient
   D. the price is affordable for governments

5. What is essential to address the recycling crisis according to the author?
   A. A faster sorting speed.
   B. Garbage classification education.
   C. Developing more smart robots.
   D. The man-machine cooperation.

Text 7

For too long, lawmakers have marveled at Facebook's explosive growth and overlooked their responsibility to ensure that Americans are protected and markets are competitive. Any day now, the Federal Trade Commission1 is expected to impose a $5 billion fine on the company, but that is not enough. We are a nation with a tradition of reining in monopolies, no matter how well intentioned the leaders of these companies may be. It is time to break up Facebook.

Since the 1970s, courts have become increasingly hesitant to break up companies or block mergers unless consumers are paying inflated prices that would be lower in a competitive market. But a narrow reliance on whether or not consumers have experienced price gouging fails to take into account the full cost of market domination. It doesn't recognize that we also want markets to be competitive to encourage innovation and to hold power in check.

Some economists are skeptical that breaking up Facebook would spur that much competition, because Facebook, they say, is a "natural" monopoly. Natural monopolies have emerged in areas like water systems and the electrical grid, where the price of entering the business is very high—because you have to lay pipes or electrical lines—but it gets cheaper and cheaper to add each additional customer. In other words, the monopoly arises naturally from the circumstances of the business, rather than a company's illegal maneuvering. In addition, defenders of natural monopolies often make the case that they benefit consumers because they are able to provide services more cheaply than anyone else.

Facebook is indeed more valuable when there are more people on it: There are more connections for a user to make and more content to be shared. But the cost of entering the social network business is not that high. And unlike with pipes and electricity, there is no good argument that the country benefits from having only one dominant social networking company.

The cost of breaking up Facebook would be next to zero for the government, and lots of people stand to gain economically. A ban on short-term acquisitions would ensure that competitors, and the investors who take a bet on them, would have the space to flourish. Digital advertisers1 would suddenly have multiple companies vying for their dollars.

But the biggest winners would be the American people. Imagine a competitive market in which they could choose among one network that offered higher privacy standards, another that cost a fee to join but had little advertising and another that would allow users to customize and tweak their feeds as they saw fit. No one knows exactly what Facebook's competitors would offer to differentiate themselves. That's exactly the point.

1. We may infer from paragraph 1 that _____.
   A. Facebook impaired Americans and the markets
   B. Facebook's intentions are actually applaudable
   C. America has many monopoly companies traditionally
   D. FTC will fine Facebook more than $5 billion
2. The word "gouging" (Para. 2) most probably means _____.
   A. restraint   B. overage
   C. regulation   D. overcharge
3. Compared with a "natural" monopoly, Facebook _____.
   A. became stronger based on normal competition
   B. failed to benefit the nation from its monopoly
   C. provided its consumers with cheaper services
   D. attracted consumers through unlawful means
4. American people would be the biggest winners because breaking up Facebook _____.
   A. is conducive to protecting users' privacy
   B. will generate a more competitive market
   C. will encourage competition and innovation
   D. is forced to give them lots of compensation
5. Which of the following would be best title for this text?
   A. Benefits of breaking up Facebook.
   B. It's time to break up Facebook.
   C. The true colors of Facebook.
   D. Reasons for breaking up Facebook.

Text 8

The Trump administration made a change to America's safety-net in January 2018. The new rule lets states experiment with forcing recipients of Medicaid to work, volunteer or study in exchange for their government-funded health insurance. So far, only one state—Arkansas—has imposed extensive work requirements on Medicaid. Fourteen other states have applied to follow its example. They should look at what has happened in Arkansas and think again.

The theory behind tying cash benefits to work requirements is sound. Asking people to do something in exchange for a payment can build political support for welfare programmes. Without the requirements, beneficiaries are easily dismissed as beggers. Moreover, encouraging people back into work is the best anti-poverty scheme.

Even so, tying health care to work is a mistake, for two reasons. The first is practical. Safety-net programmes work best when they are simple, well-understood and governed by rules that are easy to administer. The Arkansas experiment fails this test. To be eligible for Medicaid, you must earn less than $17,000 a year and must prove that you are working, studying or taking care of young children or infirm relatives for at least 80 hours a month. Many people who earn so little have unpredictable patterns of work. One month they will put in enough hours to meet the criteria for eligibility, the next they will not.

Worse, Arkansas made it unnecessarily hard for people to register their work effort. In a state with one of the lowest rates of internet usage, Medicaid recipients had to log their working hours on a website that shut down between 9pm and 7am. As a result, 18,000 of the approximately 80,000 people who were asked to report their schedules lost their coverage.

Supposing these problems can be overcome, tying access to health care to work is still wrong, because it is based on a misconception about incentives. When the Trump administration announced the new policy, it observed that "higher earnings are positively correlated with longer lifespan." That is true, but the White House has the causation backwards: People do not work in order to be healthy; they can work because they are healthy already.

Medicaid does have a problem with work incentives, but it is not the one the White House has identified. When Obamacare became law, the intention was that low-income Americans would either be eligible for Medicaid or for government subsidies to help them buy their own, private insurance policies. In fact 14 states decided not to implement part of the law. That left about 2m Americans in a state of uncertainty, earning too much to qualify for Medicaid but too little to be eligible for Obamacare subsidies. In these 14 states, people whose earnings are close to the cut-off for Medicaid eligibility can lose their health insurance if they work a few more hours. This is a huge disincentive to extra work. If states want to fix the real problem with Medicaid, that is where to look.

(*The Economist*, 2019.2)

1. According to paragraph 1, Trump's new rule _____.
    A. enables states to compel work requirements for Medicaid
    B. grants receivers more funds for health care
    C. has brought certain benefits for many states
    D. sets a good example for other countries worldwide

2. Working in exchange for benefits would _____.
    A. drive people out of poverty
    B. ease work-force shortage
    C. earn support for programmers politically
    D. enable more beggers to become beneficiaries

3. The malfunction of the Arkansas experiment can be partly attributed to _____.
    A. its complicated registration process

B. its unpredictable and simple planning

C. its poor internet service

D. its recipient's unstable income

4. The Trump administration believes that longer lifespan _____.

    A. is not a stimulus for keeping working

    B. benefits from outputs from work

    C. is not the motive to stay in job

    D. is the basis of higher medical subsidies

5. The real problem with Medicaid lies in the fact that _____.

    A. it prevents recipients from working more to maintain eligible

    B. its work incentives problems are hard to identify for White House

    C. it has brought about many uncertainties for numerous Americans

    D. its recipients haven't decided to choose Medicaid or government subsidies

Text 9

The recently published government No Health Without Mental Health implementation framework promises to give psychological conditions "parity of esteem" with physical ones. Since its publication, figures show that mental health spending is in fact falling further behind physical health for the first time in 10 years, as demand is rising.

This disjunction between rhetoric and reality has made it so hard for mental health service user-led charity, the National Survivor User Network (NSUN), to fully commit to the framework we helped to shape. NSUN connects nearly 2,000 groups and people in England with experience of mental health distress to encourage service user involvement and influence in commissioning and policy. As part of that work we have gained places on influential forums, not least in contributing to the implementation framework. Charity staff and trustees thought long and hard before deciding to put our name to this document. We had to weigh up whether remaining a critical friend inside or campaigning outside is better for our members and the wider community.

Earlier this year we claimed that many government policies were not only failing to advance the strategy but were actually undermining its aims. For example, the Department for Education's decision to remove well-being and community cohesion from the school inspection regime is in direct contradiction to the strategy's call for more early intervention and education. Freed from these requirements, many schools are shutting counselling services and nine out of 10 academies are serving their pupils junk food, damaging mental and physical health with expensive consequences.

While we have criticized when appropriate, NSUN has also sought to work constructively with government in efforts to improve the situation where we find allies. Standing up to government policies we believe damage mental health while seeking to increase the positive influence of service users in government is a difficult line to tread. In the end we decided that the Department of Health had given us a fair say, had incorporated many amendments suggested by us and our members—for example, we managed to change much of the document's tone so that it no longer subjectively branded all mental health conditions an "illness" and disempowered service users as "victims" and "sufferers" suggesting they have no control over their lives—and that we would be doing more harm than good to distance ourselves.

In practical terms, our suggestions to emphasize the value of involving service users in the commissioning of their own services to an agreed standard, and enabling self-help, peer support, personalized budgets, training and education have all been taken up and will form part of the implementation instructions to medical and social care professionals, local authorities, commissioners, providers and employers, among others.

In essence we have been able to stress that mental health service users recover best when they are given control over their own lives and treated as having assets and potential rather than as problems to be medicated and managed. Apart from it being morally right to give people control over their own lives, we found this approach can produce significant savings as people gain in confidence, skills and recovery when they are given control and resources.

(*The Guardian*, 2012.8)

1. No Health Without Mental Health intends to _____
   A. restore the self-esteem for people suffering physical problems
   B. prevent a reduction in the spending on mental health
   C. promote the implementation of the government policy
   D. even the financial spending on physical and mental health
2. Which of the following is true according to paragraph 2?
   A. NSUN may be not able to fulfill the commitment immediately.
   B. The disjunction between promise and reality can be erased.
   C. Outside campaigning is appealing to a wider range of members.
   D. Influential forums offer the solution for NSUN.
3. According to paragraph 3, the decision made by the Department for Education may _____.
   A. help reduce the junk food outside of schools
   B. improve the accuracy of the counselling service
   C. advocate more early intervention
   D. damage the mental and physical health of schoolchildren
4. The example cited in paragraph 4 shows _____.
   A. the compromises made by the government
   B. the policies created for NSUN

C. the positive changes found among the victims

D. the criticism against the government

5. It is suggested in the last paragraph that _____.

A. personal assets and potential have a significant impact on recovery

B. people are more interested in gaining skills rather than assets

C. individual autonomy is vital for the treatment of mental problems

D. morality should not be ignored during the treatment of mental distress

Text 10

Building houses and offices out of toxic waste sounds like a pretty eccentric idea. Yet it may become commonplace if Ana Andrés of the University of Cantabria in Spain has her way. For Dr. Andrés and her colleagues suggest, in *Industrial & Engineering Chemistry Research*, that the humble brick need not be made of pure clay. Instead, up to 30% of its weight could be slag—the toxic gunk left over when steel is made.

Waelz slag, to give its technical name, is composed mainly of silica but is also undesirably rich in poisonous metals like lead and zinc. Getting rid of it safely is thus a problem. Getting rid of it usefully might sound like a miracle. But that is what Dr. Andrés proposes. A series of experiments she has conducted over the past three years suggests this is not only possible but will make bricks cheaper and more environmentally friendly.

Her research started after she read of previous work which had shown that many ceramics suffer no loss of integrity when the clay used to make them is mixed with other materials, and that the molecular structure of some ceramics acts to trap atoms of toxic heavy metals. She wondered whether these things might be true of brick clay and Waelz slag, and she began experimenting. The answer, she found, was that they are. Bricks show no loss of useful mechanical properties even when 20%-30% of their content is slag. Nor do they leak.

To check that, Dr. Andrés and her team ground their bricks into powder and soaked them in water, shook them in special machines for days at a time, and even tried to dissolve them in nitric acid. The pollutants stayed resolutely put. Moreover, adding slag to the clay reduced by a third the amount of carbon dioxide each brick released during its manufacture, because wood pulp is added to clay before it is fired, and less clay means less pulp is needed. The cost, too, fell, because slag is free, whereas clay costs money.

There is, of course, the problem of customers. Whether people will be willing to live and work in structures that double as waste dumps is moot. But for those who want to make an eco-point, what better way could there be than, literally, to build their green credentials?

(*The Economist*, 2011.6)

1. Ana Andrés holds that Waelz slag is _____ .
   A. commonplace in nowadays construction business
   B. a replacement of the toxic gunk
   C. inexpensive comparing to lead or zinc
   D. vital in producing eco-friendly bricks
2. According to paragraph 3, the molecular structure of some ceramics could _____ .
   A. keep the brick clay from leaking
   B. capture atoms inside the poisonous metals
   C. prevent the slag loss of up to 20% -30%
   D. stabilize the ceramics to keep their integrity
3. Which of the following could be inferred according to paragraph 4?
   A. Nitric acid is used to dissolve the pollutants inside the bricks.
   B. Brick clay is mainly made of wood pulp.
   C. Wood pulp will create carbon dioxide during the manufacture of bricks.
   D. The use of wood pulp reduces the cost of bricks.
4. What is the author's attitude toward the use of toxic waste?
   A. Skeptical.   B. Indifferent.   C. Impartial.   D. Supportive.
5. Which of the following would be the best title for the passage?
   A. The Bright Prospect of a Green Building Material
   B. Slag, Brick Clay and the Green Credential
   C. Evolution of the Modern Building Technology
   D. Customer's Positive Attitude Toward Slag

Text 11

Not long after being snapped up by News Corporation in 2005, MySpace became a much emptier space when many teenagers who had used the social network to share music and photos of themselves in various states of undress decided it was no longer the cool place to be online. A recent blog post has sparked a debate about whether Facebook, which has 1.2 billion users, is suffering a similar exodus.

The fuss matters because investors have been very bullish about Facebook's prospects. Its share price more than doubled in 2013, ending the year above $54. This partly reflects the market's insatiable appetite for social-media stocks, but it is also a sign of investors' conviction that Facebook's users will not tire of it. Hence the interest in an article on The Conversation, a website showcasing academic research. Published by Daniel Miller, a professor at University College London, it said young people were "turning away in their droves" from Facebook and that the social network "is not just on the slide, it is basically dead and buried." Teenagers now prefer to hang out on new photo-sharing and messaging services such as SnapChat (reportedly attacked by hackers this week), WhatsApp and

Instagram, where mums and dads don't lurk.

Mr. Miller said he concluded that Facebook was losing its attraction to teenagers after interviewing 16- to 18-year-olds in Britain as part of a European Union-funded study of social networks. But critics were quick to point out that his sample just 40 students was tiny and that it was therefore rash to extrapolate from it. In a subsequent blog post, the academic defended his work, saying he had based his observations on a broader set of discussions. He also revealed that his original post had been crafted by a journalist and said he would be more careful about allowing his work to be "sexed up" in future.

So Facebook is not facing a MySpace moment. However, it should not be complacent. Like many other big networks, it has been vacuuming up older customers. And its growing reputation as a sort of parental NSA (National Security Agency) may explain why some youngsters are more wary of it. In October 2013 David Ebersman, Facebook's chief financial officer, admitted that daily visits by younger teenagers had decreased.

But there is no mass defection under way. Instead, teenagers are using different social networks for different things, says Lee Rainie of the Pew Research Centre's Internet and American Life Project. They post less intimate stuff to Facebook and more risque material to networks not yet gatecrashed by their parents. Mr. Miller's research has also highlighted this habit.

The danger for Facebook is that one of these newer places starts to attract parents. That is why the firm swallowed Instagram in 2012 and recently tried to snap up SnapChat. The teenagers on Facebook may not be rebelling, but keep an eye on them.

(*The Economist*, 2014.1)

1. The word "exodus" (Para. 1) most probably means _____.
   A. purchase   B. disgust   C. distrust   D. departure
2. According to paragraph 2, Facebook's investors believe that _____.
   A. Facebook's share price will continue to surge
   B. Facebook will be replaced by other social media
   C. young people are fascinated by Facebook
   D. parents should stay away from Facebook
3. In paragraph 3, Miller suggests that _____.
   A. Facebook is no longer the priority option for teenagers
   B. his observation was made inaccurate by a journalist
   C. sex difference should be included in his report
   D. it is necessary to expand the range of samples
4. Younger teenagers visit Facebook less frequently because _____.
   A. parents can supervise their kids through Facebook
   B. they disapprove Facebook's complacence
   C. Facebook imitates many other big networks
   D. they are cautious about NSA's investigations

5. According to the text, the author suggests that _____.
   A. teenagers should post less risque materials on Facebook
   B. social networks other than Facebook should be provided to users
   C. Facebook should keep parents away
   D. Facebook should be alert to the changing composition of its users

Text 12

Helmut Schmidt became chancellor of West Germany in the spring of 1974, shortly after Harold Wilson was re-elected as prime minister in the UK. The two men took office at the worst possible time. Sharply rising oil prices had put an end to the postwar economic boom. Business costs were rising rapidly, profits were under pressure, jobs were being shed.

Yet West Germany and Britain had contrasting fortunes in the years that followed. In the UK, inflation hit a postwar peak of almost 27%, the pound came under savage attack on the foreign exchanges and the International Monetary Fund was called in. West Germany emerged with its reputation as Europe's economic powerhouse not merely unscathed but enhanced because the country showed it could cope even when the going got tough.

Schmidt was not chancellor during the years of the so-called Wirtschaftswunder—the economic miracle—that had transformed a country wrecked by the Second World War. In a sense, previous chancellors such as Konrad Adenauer, Ludwig Erhard and Schmidt's immediate predecessor, Willy Brandt, had it much easier. They enjoyed the benefits of pent-up demand, the Marshall plan, debt relief and an undervalued currency during the 25 years in which West Germany was transformed from a country where the population was starving into the third biggest economy in the world. Schmidt's task was harder. The postwar Bretton Woods fixed exchange rate system had broken down, leaving currencies to find their own level. The mark had been rising fast in the years before Schmidt became chancellor, making life a lot harder for West German manufacturers.

His job was made both more difficult and easier by West Germany's system of economic governance that put enormous power in the hands of the country's central bank, the fiercely independent Bundesbank, which had responsibility for controlling inflation through the setting of interest rates and restrictions on the supply of money. It was tougher because the Bundesbank could violate any attempts by the West German government to boost demand and jobs by running bigger budget deficits—the policy pursued by Wilson in Britain. The reason it also made his life easier was that the anti-inflation Bundesbank bias forced West Germany into alternative ways of making its exports more competitive. The chancellor used his influence with the trade unions to persuade West German workers to take cuts in their wages and living standards so that exports became cheaper.

West Germany, like every other developed western nation, suffered from lower growth, higher inflation and higher unemployment than had been the norm in the postwar "golden age"; but in relative terms Schmidt was able to boast of a better record than any of his contemporaries, Wilson and James Callaghan in Britain, Jimmy Carter in the US and Valéry Giscard D'Estaing in France.

This was a period that shaped West German thinking and the European project in three big ways. Firstly, it reinforced the West German bias against inflation and deficit spending. Under pressure from the Americans, Schmidt agreed to a global reflationary package in 1978, but the experiment ran into a second wave of oil price increases and was speedily abandoned in West Germany. Secondly, it persuaded Schmidt that steps had to be taken to prevent European currencies from gyrating against each other. He was instrumental in the creation of the European exchange rate mechanism that proved to be the forerunner of the single currency. This development chimed with Schmidt's passionate belief in closer European ties. Finally, it convinced the next generation of German policymakers, including Angela Merkel, that the way to solve economic problems was through sacrifice and hard work rather than devaluation, cheap credit or higher budget deficits.

(*The Guardian*, 2015.11)

1. Which of the following statements is true according to the first two paragraphs?
    A. The re-elected Harold Wilson caused the economic depression in UK.
    B. UK's inflation rate was brought down by the International Monetary Fund.
    C. Germany survived and thrived through the worst economic times.
    D. Harold Wilson's re-election led to Schmidt's political success.
2. According to paragraph 3, Schmidt's administration was made harder by _____.
    A. the breakdown of a post-war monetary order
    B. the impact of the Second World War
    C. the mismanagement of his predecessors
    D. the continuous expansion of German population
3. It can be learned from paragraph 4 that Bundesbank can _____.
    A. independently formulate the German financial policies
    B. overturn some policies made by the German government
    C. work out alternative methods to improve the Germany's export
    D. influence the policies made by Wilson in Britain
4. According to paragraph 6, the success of German economy could be attributed to _____.
    A. the second wave of oil price escalation
    B. the establishment of the European exchange rate system
    C. the repression of inflation and deficit spending
    D. a consistent emphasis on diligence and devotion
5. The author's attitude towards Schmidt is one of _____.
    A. disapproval   B. appreciation   C. tolerance   D. indifference

Text 13

It's an unwritten rule of the workplace that we drop other roles when we walk through the door. The modern workplace may be so relaxed that we don't have to wear a suit any more, but we're not mums, dads, bikers, comedians or poets or whatever we do in our spare time. It's quite possible to forget your hobbies, but not those ever-present responsibilities and implications of parenthood, and despite all the policy advances in recent years, the traditions and culture of work haven't really changed. In that respect, we're still pretty much stuck in the 1950s, where women become mums and men focus on their career.

If any of the current and planned legislation on parental leave is going to have the desired effect—supporting families under strain and helping more people stay in work—then what's needed is more recognition and awareness that parents are different. Something with visibility that can be less easily bypassed and played down than a discretionary policy. Parent passports would be a step forward.

As voluntary documents made accessible to human resources departments and line managers, the passports could hold relevant information provided by employees who have, or are expecting, children. The passports would be gender-specific to make fathers visible and to avoid assumptions that the term "parenthood" applies only to women. The passport could allow, for example, the provision of reciprocal cover arrangements in the event of regular childcare needs or emergencies. No need to constantly explain your personal situation to different managers or renegotiate practices, it's all there on the table.

The idea is backed up by our research with Working Families into the problems faced by fathers at work. While work-family policies are intended to be gender neutral, many are still (perhaps inadvertently) developed and written to be used in conjunction with ideas of motherhood, based on the prevailing cultural assumptions that women will relegate themselves to the status of dependent second income earners or non-earners.

British fathers, especially those white-collar middle class men who you would expect to be best placed to take advantage of flexible working, are reported to show greater degrees of inflexible presenteeism and work longer hours than their peers. Paternal presenteeism is even worse as these fathers tend to work more intensely at this point than any other in their careers. And despite all the evidence, mothers are still often unfairly associated with unreliability, unpredictability, irrationality and poor health; while men are assumed by employers to be healthy, rational, reliable and highly committed.

In our conversations with working fathers we found they are well aware of the company policies and offerings, but feel it's a mistake to use them. Having an unsupportive manager was a near insurmountable obstacle to requesting a more flexible working life. They don't want to rock the boat, just in case. If they do make requests for flexibility then senior managers are very capable of either finding ways to block the change happening in practice, or agreeing in principle and resisting the practice.

Parent passports would start to redress this "invisibility" among working fathers and help genuine work-life balance to be introduced. Everyone seems to agree on the usefulness of flexibility to modern living, but letting go of those last strings of attachment to presenteeism, the remnants of old-school attitudes to what's done, is proving very difficult. This kind of scheme could well be divisive. Parents who jump up waving their passport whenever times get tough are never going to be popular. But the fact is that no one is winning in the current, ossified set of arrangements. Stressed parents make poor workers. Stressed parent bosses, in particular, can make the worst managers. Only by making parent roles visible and part of an ongoing conversation about how people work best will we ever get closer to a practical, maybe even enjoyable, compromise.

(*The Guardian*, 2013.1)

1. It can be learned from the first two paragraphs that _____.
   A. parents deserve more understanding in the workplace
   B. role playing is fashionable in modern workplace
   C. discretionary policy can be easily ignored by parents
   D. parents used to concentrate more on household affairs
2. According to paragraph 3, parent passports _____.
   A. are especially assigned to male employees
   B. verify the employees' parenthood
   C. demonstrate the employees' responsibilities in child-rearing
   D. replace the excuses for urgent reciprocal cover arrangements
3. The example of British fathers in paragraph 5 is cited to show _____.
   A. the inhumane aspect of paternal presenteeism
   B. the prejudice against women in child-rearing
   C. the harsh situation confronted by male employees
   D. the shortcomings of working mothers in workplace
4. The statement "They don't want to rock the boat, just in case" (Para. 6) implies that _____.
   A. it is dangerous to rock the boat against the will of the senior managers
   B. company policies and offerings are obstacles for male employees to get promotion
   C. male employees often bend to their unsupportive supervisors
   D. male employees need to sacrifice their personal hobbies for flexibility in workplace
5. According to the last paragraph, the author believes that _____.
   A. presenteeism will still have a dominant position
   B. parent passports may ease the burden of the parents
   C. visible workers will obtain maximum working efficiency
   D. workers should keep the parent passports to themselves

Text 14

When a company takes on the task of providing financial services to people overlooked by large banks, that would seem to be a good thing: Such customers need bank accounts, debit cards, and credit just like everyone else. In 2013, nearly 10 million American households didn't have any interaction with a bank, and nearly 25 million households had bank accounts but used alternative financing options (such as prepaid debit cards, alternative credit cards, or payday loans) to make ends meet.

One would hope that financial offers geared toward the under-banked—who often have low credit scores, histories of financial instability, and limited education—would include modest interest rates, easily decipherable language, and enough oversight to ensure that already-struggling families don't get taken advantage of. But that is often not the case. (For examples, payday lenders frequently charge astronomically high interest rates for those who are unable to quickly pay off their debts, and prepaid-card companies often include additional fees that owners of standard debit cards don't have to deal with, such as charges for simply loading money onto their cards.)

These practices can leave people, who are already struggling to get their finances in order, in even worse shape than they were when they signed up for a new product. The problem isn't that companies targeting the under-banked exist at all, but that many exploit a lack of financial knowledge and alternative options to extract excess money from their customers.

Credit-card issuers that target those with poor credit scores are another group with questionable practices, according to a recent report from the Consumer Financial Protection Bureau. In its research, the CFPB found that the costs of cards issued by these companies are significantly higher than the costs of cards issued by more traditional competitors. These specialized lenders are much more likely to approve not just subprime individuals, but the deepest subprime individuals—those with credit scores that fall below 600.

Why isn't a higher approval rate for those with very bad credit a good thing? Isn't that more inclusive? Not always. Some credit-card companies' business models depend on charging their customers high fees—people who are unlikely to be able to afford them. These increased fees are for things that are inescapable, such as monthly account maintenance. (Major credit-card companies, on the other hand, are making most of their money from collecting late payments and interest, not recurring fees.) Customers of these subprime companies don't need to do anything unusual to rack up fees—that's just a part of signing up.

But perhaps worse than the high costs of the cards is the way that these companies recruit customers. They target them by mailing pre-approved offers that contain intentionally opaque, high-level financial language and agreements that are, on average,

70 percent longer than card agreements from other lenders, according to the CFPB.

"Despite offering longer and more complex credit-card terms than mass market issuers, they send those mailings disproportionately to consumers with lower levels of formal education," the CFPB report found. "Specifically, agreements for credit-card products marketed primarily by subprime specialist issuers are particularly difficult to read." According to the report, making sense of these statements would typically require at least two years of college or post-high-school education. Less than half of the people targeted by these lenders have any college education, and the number of such households sent direct mail by these lenders doubled between 2012 and 2014.

(*The Atlantic*, 2016.1)

1. The examples cited in the parentheses (Para. 2) show that _____.
   A. payday loans are no better products than prepaid debit cards
   B. Large banks in America often ignore the already-struggling families
   C. financial companies should provide high-quality services to poor families
   D. indigent American households are exploited by financial companies
2. According to paragraph 3, the under-banked may be subjected to _____.
   A. a lack of updates on economic information
   B. a greater personal financial loss
   C. the sign-up of a new financial product
   D. the exploitation of alternative choices
3. The author suggests the credit cards for the subprime individuals _____.
   A. should be issued under CFPB's supervision
   B. should be issued by large banks rather than financial companies
   C. should be issued on the basis of their credit scores
   D. should be restricted to reduce the financial risks on the poor
4. According to paragraph 6, the author believes the subprime companies' pre-approved agreements are _____.
   A. useful because of their professional content
   B. compelling because of their format
   C. misleading because of their vague instruction
   D. objective because of their high-level financial language
5. Which of the following can be inferred from the last paragraph?
   A. Poorly-educated consumers are welcomed by the financial companies.
   B. Complex credit-card terms are needed for the lenders' safety.
   C. Credit cards could be issued only to people with college education.
   D. There might be a boom of financial companies between 2012 and 2014.

Text 15

Thirteen summers ago, when a pair of shows called *Survivor* and *Big Brother* debuted on CBS, there were uneasy cries that reality TV was going to coarsen our civilization. Contestants were encouraged to lie and backstab one another! People were eating actual rats! Won't someone think of the children? You can debate how well, by 2013, reality TV has fulfilled its potential as a hell-bound handbasket. But I do know this: when the regular TV season ended in May and the summer-premiere season started, it was an exciting time at home, because it meant *Master Chef* was coming back, and my wife and I could watch it together with the kids. Pioneer families had the evening taffy pull; we watch people caramelizing sugar on Fox.

Reality TV is a big, diverse medium, of course. Some of it is raunchy, some obnoxious (like the despicable let's-fire-someone fest *Does Someone Have to Go?* also on Fox), and some very, very good. In other words, it's not unlike scripted TV. But an unexpected thing has happened over the past generation: reality TV has become the new version, and perhaps the last bastion, of prime-time family viewing.

It's not just *Master Chef* for us: excepting old reruns, nearly every TV series my kids and I watch together is a reality show. We handicap *The Voice* contestants' odds every week. *The Amazing Race* has given us a new perspective on navigating through airports on vacations. *Shark Tank* (on which people pitch for funding for their fledgling companies) captivates the kids and has shown me—one of the least entrepreneurial-minded people I know—what a fascinating process conceiving and valuing a business is. *Chopped*, *Market Warriors*, *Top Chef*—if it involves cooking something or selling something or cooking something to sell it, we'll watch it.

Before you call Child Protective Services on me, let me explain. People sometimes assume that because I'm a TV critic, I'm permissive about what my kids (who are 8 and 11) watch. It's really the opposite, maybe because I'm professionally exposed to what's out there. And plenty of their classmates' parents have found safe harbor in reality's Kardashian-and-Snooki-free sectors. About a decade ago, the decency-policing PTC (Parents Television Council) condemned reality shows that "revel in participants' eagerness to publicly parade their lack of moral integrity." Today, its recommended-viewing lists include *Cupcake Wars* and *Undercover Boss*.

When people complain that there are fewer good shows than there used to be for families to watch together, it's often assumed this means that TV has become more vulgar or adult. Which is true in some ways, but really the overall trend is that TV has become more specific. Everyone has a demographically targeted TV, toddlers and adults alike. We actually live in a pretty great era for kids' TV, and prime time is rich with sophisticated dramas like *Mad Men* that could exist only at a time of greater creative license.

But most adults have limited tolerance for kids' programs (show me the American parent not traumatized by the phrase Swiper, no swiping!), and it will be years before I show my kids more than the title sequence for *Game of Thrones* (Which they love.).

(*Time*, 2013.6)

1. According to the first two paragraphs, the author thinks reality shows are _____.
   A. ambiguous   B. contemptuous   C. beneficial   D. critical
2. The reality shows listed in paragraph 3 are meant to _____.
   A. demonstrate reality shows' usefulness in gaining life experience
   B. advocate reality shows' role in teaching business knowledge
   C. prove reality shows' significance for family time
   D. reflect the richness of reality shows' contents
3. It is suggested in paragraph 4 that PTC _____.
   A. has changed its previous view on reality shows
   B. believes in the adverse effect brought by reality shows
   C. has a laissez-faire attitude towards reality shows today
   D. recommends reality shows that are without morally repugnant celebrities
4. It can be inferred from the last paragraph that _____.
   A. TV programs have become more vulgar for adult viewers
   B. current TV programs are filled with creative ideas
   C. children are particularly suitable for a demographically targeted TV
   D. children are allowed to watch a restricted range of TV programs
5. What is mainly discussed in the text?
   A. Reality shows' role in creating family time.
   B. PTC's recommendations for TV viewers.
   C. More abundant contents for reality shows.
   D. A fierce debate about reality shows.

■■参考答案

Text 1 CADBB	Text 2 DCBAD	Text 3 BADCD	Text 4 CADCB
Text 5 DBCAD	Text 6 CABBD	Text 7 ADBCB	Text 8 ABCAC
Text 9 DADAC	Text 10 DBCDA	Text 11 DCAAD	Text 12 CABDB
Text 13 ACCCB	Text 14 DBDCA	Text 15 CCADA	